Before You Talk to Your Child About Sex . . .

Learn why young people are feeling such an intense desire to be sexually active. **Why Wait?** will tell you
- How the media distorts their views on love and sex
- What youth desire most in a relationship
- Why your child needs love and limits within the family
- When to begin sharing the reasons to wait
- How to build lasting bridges of communication

Discover What Your Child Is Thinking and Feeling

Teens want to wait. In a recent study on adolescent sexuality teenagers were asked if they had ever engaged in sexual activity when they did not really want to. 47% of the boys and 67% of the girls said they had, with 24% saying they often felt pressured into sexual contact because they did not know how to say no. One teen wrote, "I was looking for reasons not to have premarital sex, and I didn't receive any."

Use *Why Wait?* to Start Discussions About Sex

When you read **Why Wait?** think about which portions you'd like to share with your child. The majority of this book is written to you — the parent, pastor or youth worker — but frequently Josh and Dick turn their attention to young people and address them directly. These sections will be especially helpful to you as you seek to
- Confidently share about sex
- Mold your child's basis for his/her moral convictions
- Provide a compelling, positive and practical response to the adolescent sexuality crisis

JOSH McDOWELL
DICK DAY

WHY WAIT?

What You Need to Know About the Teen Sexuality Crisis

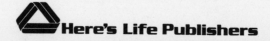
Here's Life Publishers

Published by
Here's Life Publishers, Inc.
P. O. Box 1576
San Bernardino, CA 92402

HLP Product No. 951723
© 1987, Josh McDowell and Dick Day
All rights reserved.
Printed in the United States of America.

Library of Congress Cataloging-in-Publication Data

McDowell, Josh.
    Why wait?

    1. Sexual ethics. 2. Youth — Sexual behavior.
3. Parenting. I. Day, Dick. II. Title.
HQ32.M386   1987   649′.125   1987   87-194
ISBN 0-89840-174-7 (pbk.)

FOR MORE INFORMATION, WRITE:

L.I.F.E. — P.O. Box A399, Sydney South 2000, Australia
Campus Crusade for Christ of Canada — Box 300, Vancouver, B.C., V6C 2X3, Canada
Campus Crusade for Christ — Pearl Assurance House, 4 Temple Row, Birmingham, B2 5HG, England
Campus Crusade for Christ — P.O. Box 240, Colombo Court Post Office, Singapore 9117
Lay Institute for Evangelism — P.O. Box 8786, Auckland 3, New Zealand
Great Commission Movement of Nigeria — P.O. Box 500, Jos, Plateau State Nigeria, West Africa
Campus Crusade for Christ International — Arrowhead Springs, San Bernardino, CA 92414, U.S.A.

FIRST PRINTING, JULY 1987
SECOND PRINTING, AUGUST 1987
THIRD PRINTING, AUGUST 1987
FOURTH PRINTING, SEPTEMBER 1987
FIFTH PRINTING, JANUARY 1988
SIXTH PRINTING, MAY 1988

CONTENTS

EXPLANATION OF REFERENCE NOTES AND BIBLIOGRAPHY

The section titled "Bibliography" at the end of the book combines the bibliography and the sources referred to within the text of the book. After each quote in the text, you will find a number or a set of numbers. Some of these numbers will be divided by a diagonal (example: 80/432). The number at the left of the diagonal refers to the source of the quote, which is listed by that number in the bibliography, and the number at the right refers to the page or pages where the quote is located in the source. Where there is no diagonal, the number simply refers to the source.

ACKNOWLEDGMENTS

Why Wait? was possible only because of the efforts of so many people:

Matt Judge, Carroll Nyquist and Pam Richardson, who contributed greatly toward getting the manuscript into written form.

Dave and Neta Jackson, who composed the two sections, "Forgiveness" and "Open Mouth, Closed Ears," from some of my other work.

Marcus Maranto, Jim Pourchot and Steve Gillespie, who spent nights and days researching the facts.

Paul Frala and Mike Romberger, who helped extensively in the library to insure proper documentation.

Duane Zook, who personally encouraged the authors, and who worked unsparingly to coordinate the material from the "Write Your Heart Out" essay contest.

Les Stobbe, of Here's Life Publishers, who gave direction to the project, and who helped organize the vast amount of material.

Virginia Hearn, who improved the manuscript through her freelance editing expertise.

Jean Bryant, of Here's Life Publishers, who did yeoman's work in the final editing and organization of the 900-page manuscript and guided it by the hand through the production process.

Terri Childs, who labored long hours to enter it all into the computer.

Barb Sherrill, of Here's Life Publishers, who so diligently entered all the revisions and corrections.

Dick Day
has given a great deal of input
to this book,
and he definitely deserves the rank of co-author
as indicated on the front cover.
However, for the sake of simplicity in communication,
both authors have chosen the "I" to be
Josh McDowell.

PART 1

THE CRISIS

1

WHY *WHY WAIT?*

Premarital sex gave me fear as a gift . . . and shame to wear as a garment. It stole my peace of mind and robbed me of hope in a bright future. Sex smashed my concentration in class to smithereens. My desire for church activities was ground to a pulp. It made crumbs of the trust I had known in Christ . . . and in men and women. Sex gave me a jagged tear in my heart that even now, seven years later, is still healing.

———————— ♥ ————————

Those words represent the hearts of thousands of teens who have written our ministry to express similar heart-breaking experiences. The effects of premarital sex can be devastating. Look with me into the lives of several young people who intimately share the emotional pain they have suffered from engaging in premarital sex.

————————————————

Having premarital sex was the most horrifying experience of my life. It wasn't at all the emotionally satisfying or the casually-taken experience the world perceives it to be. I felt as if my insides were being exposed and my heart left unattended.

♡ ♡ ♡

It's not a pretty picture. It's not a TV soap opera either. The reality of pregnancy outside of marriage is scary and lonely. To have premarital sex was my choice one hot June night, forcing many decisions I thought I would never have to make. Those decisions radically changed my life.

♡ ♡ ♡

It took losing my virginity at a very young age, losing my self-respect and possibly my fertility, helping to ruin another person's marriage and family life, acquiring a non-curable virus, not getting the fulfillment that sex should provide in marriage, and living with the guilt that Satan always tries to make me feel . . . for me to realize how detrimental sex before marriage can really be.

———————— ♥ ————————

As Dick and I have worked with young people over the years, we have seen an increasing amount of sexual promiscuity. The effects *are* detrimental. We are experiencing today what I call an "adolescent sexuality crisis." Thousands of hurting teens are crying out.

———————————————————————

Dear Mr. McDowell,
Can you help me? I'm thirteen and I've just ruined my life. I thought Mike really loved me, but last night we had sex for the first time and this morning he told my girl friend that he didn't want to see me any more. I thought giving Mike what he wanted would make him happy and he'd love me more. What if I'm pregnant? What am I going to do? I feel so alone and confused . . . I can't talk to my parents, so could you please write me back and help me. I don't know how I can go on.

———————— ♥ ————————

So many young people are asking for help. Over the last three or four years, high school and college students have been asking remarkably personal and penetrating questions that reflect painful struggles with their sexuality.

———————————————————————

I love him. He said he loved me too. But after we did it, he called me all sorts of names and left me. The reason I'm writing is, I don't understand this. We went together for months and I thought we had something special . . . I really need help. I have this feeling that no one cares about me, and no matter what I do I am not able to make any man happy. If it's not too much trouble *could you write me back and tell me what to do?* I'd appreciate it.

♡ ♡ ♡

The reason I'm writing this is I'm alone and confused. My boyfriend kept pursuing me for sex . . . I had sex with him thinking that I owed it to him . . . Later when I learned I was pregnant he blew up, said to get an abortion, and that it was all my fault. So, to save my parents heartache and to keep Matt, I had an abortion. Now Matt has left me . . . How can God love me after all I have done? Could you please write back? I'm just so confused. Can God really love and forgive me?

♡ ♡ ♡

It's so hard sometimes — like last week, when I was over at Bill's, and his roommate Tom started talking to me again. He knows Bill and I haven't slept together, and he's basically told me I'm too Victorian. But what really hurt was his accusation that *there's something wrong with anyone who doesn't want to have sex before marriage.* I didn't know what to say.

———————— ♥ ————————

Over and over again I hear young people expressing their confusion about premarital sex.

"I was looking for reasons not to have premarital sex, and I didn't receive any answers," confesses Michael at the University of Wisconsin.

"I don't trust my boyfriend," writes a coed, "and he doesn't respect me. I knew it wasn't 'right' but I never knew why."

A fifteen-year-old girl tells of her first sexual experience:

When I met my boyfriend at the beginning of my sophomore year, we began having sex as soon as we started kissing. I didn't really want to at all — I don't even think he did — but we couldn't think of any reason why we shouldn't do it. 95/284

After interviewing thousands of young people, I am convinced that many teens and young singles are sexually active, not because they really want to be, but because they don't have any deep personal reasons for waiting until they are married. The latest research confirms that conclusion. In a study of sexual habits teenagers were asked: "Have you ever engaged in sexual activities with dates when you didn't really want to?" Forty-seven percent of the boys and 65 percent of the girls, fourteen to sixteen years old, answered yes.137 In another study of 1,006 teenage girls, 24 percent said they have often felt pressured into sexual contact because they don't know how to say no. 108

Teens struggle with how and why to say NO:

I had been told all my life that sex before marriage was wrong, but no one ever told me why. In the twelfth grade I found myself dating one boy for a long period of time. We spent a lot of time alone, and as a result our relationship became more physical. I felt guilty, bitter, frustrated and dirty. Because of those feelings, I would say to him, "We need to stop having sex, or at least slow down." Well, we tried to slow down, but that didn't work. Instead of getting closer, we grew farther apart. After two years of dating I finally said, "No more sex," and he said, "Good-bye." Since then, whenever I dated another person for a length of time, sex became a part of the relationship. Tears always came because I knew I had blown it again.

♡ ♡ ♡

I had already achieved the impossible. I was almost eighteen and I was still a virgin. I had just never wanted to "do it". . .I was very much in love, or thought I was, with a dashing college man, and from time to time he would mention that he had never dated a girl who said no as many times as I had. After a while, my resolve weakened, and since I had no reason to say no, *I decided that I would do it to show how much I loved him. I didn't really want to,* but in my own mind I couldn't rationalize not having sex. *I gave in to pressure* because saying yes was easier than saying no and trying to explain why not.

♡ ♡ ♡

I'm a junior in high school and captain of the football team. I have a girlfriend whom I like very much. Her name is Gwen. We have been going together for about seven months. Lately I've been getting a lot of pressure to have sex, but I don't think Gwen is ready. My buddies say something must be wrong with me not to have had sex with her yet. I sometimes feel like telling them to shut up, but what good would that do? When I really think about it, the guys are right. *I should start putting a little more pressure on Gwen to have sex with me.*

♡ ♡ ♡

I feel like sex is OK as long as you don't get pregnant, but if you get pregnant, then you should get married to the guy. I disagree with the statement that a person should wait until marriage to engage in sex. My question is, Why? I know God will show me, but I have a real hard time getting it all straight. Sometimes when I get to the point where I want sex, I run to this certain guy. Most of the time it's not his fault, but mine, that we have sex. I really love this guy and I pray that I marry him, but I want it to be OK in God's eyes. Why isn't it?

———————— ♥ ————————

One young man after hearing me speak at the University of Wisconsin told me:

What you said really hit me. If I could have just one wish in life, it would be for me to be twelve years old again and hear this same lecture. I have made some wrong decisions in dating and now I'm feeling pain from my choices.

The National Sunday School Association's Youth Survey asked 3,000 teenagers what kind of help they would like to receive from their churches. Counseling for sexual problems ranked first among twenty-one items. One out of three asked for help in this area. In a similar survey by the Lutheran Church, instruction on Christian views of sex, courtship and marriage ranked first among forty items. 29/83

Committed Christian young people are struggling to find answers that make sense about sex. Ralph, a college student who is an active witness for Jesus Christ on his campus, told me that once while sharing his faith he was asked, "Do I have to stop having sex with my girlfriend in order to become a Christian?"

This question precipitated a long discussion about commitment and the lordship of Christ. "It also left me pondering a question I wrestled with for months: Why wait?"

For the first time, Ralph felt uneasy about his understanding of God's prohibitions on premarital sex. The student — to whom he'd witnessed — told Ralph how much he loved his girlfriend; she was taking birth-control pills, and they both felt that engaging in sex added a deeper level of meaning to their already firm relationship. "We gave him answers from God's Word, yet in the recesses of my own heart I joined him in asking, Why not?"

In his dorm room, after what had proved to be a frustrating witnessing experience, Ralph began to question God even more.

"I had to find an answer," he said. "I argued with God that prohibitions against premarital sex in light of advanced birth control methods, etc., did seem to be a bit archaic. Perhaps the apostle Paul's admonitions against fornication needed revising."

Finally, Ralph realized that God is neither archaic nor blind to twentieth-century ways. "I concluded that I just had to be patient and wait for His answer . . . *even though I could not understand the reasons.*"

Without solid reasons for saying no, young people are very vulnerable. Sexual pressures on them are at an all-time high. As one young woman told her father, "When I see how casually sex is treated by my classmates, when they make it all sound so natural and inevitable, there are times when *I wonder what I'm waiting for.*"

Young students today face sexual decisions that older generations never had to contend with. For many of them, those decisions are made with little thought about consequences. According to one fourteen-year-old high school student, "All they think is that they really want this guy to like them, and so they're going to do it." The results are frequently heartbreaking.

One teenager wrote about the heartache she felt when her lips said yes as her heart was saying no:

She was extremely young, but she didn't feel young. It seemed like such a mature jump . . . from the immature age of twelve to the much more exciting, official-teenager age of thirteen. She really loved being and "acting" older. She thought everything was great!

She was an honor student and was also very involved in extracurricular activities. She loved to do things and share deep dark secrets with her best friend. She had a good family and her parents taught her well the *difference between right and wrong*. She was sensible and had a good head on her shoulders . . . so it seemed.

He was older than she and extremely popular. He was very talented and was always the center of attention. She was overwhelmed with joy when he started to pay special attention to her. She was so pleased when he picked her as a girlfriend, rather than any of the other girls who would have died for the chance.

One day he told her, "I love you." But she had nothing to say in return. She did not love him, yet adored the popularity he gained for her. She was blinded by the new attention she received from that newly discovered "popularity." Everyone said "Hi" to her. Everyone wanted to know her.

He asked her if he could express his love to her. She said she wasn't ready. He said, "I love you." She did not reply.

Later he told her something had happened. He said he showed his "love" to someone else. She said it was all right. He said, "I love you." She was naive. She looked down and said nothing.

She had never had so many friends before. So many people wanted to talk with her. In fact, she noticed that boys were paying a lot more attention to her. But, she stayed with him . . . because he loved her.

Then he told her it had happened again. He showed "love" to someone else, yet he did not really love that someone else. He even told her who the girl was. She looked away. She felt threatened. But he told her, "I love you." She looked down and quietly replied the same. He told her to show her love for him. She didn't want to, but she didn't want to lose him to someone else. So she "showed her love."

She was violated. She was innocent no longer. She broke up with him. He asked her to take him back. He told her, "I love you." But she rejected him.

A few days later, he was "in love" with someone else. She was impure and unwholesome. She was used. She was drowned with shame. She was swallowed up by guilt. She was very alone.

She is afraid to love ever again. She is afraid to ever be loved again. She knows she can never change the past. She has stained her life . . . a stain that will never come out.

She was extremely young. She finally realized how young.

——————————— ♥ ———————————

That girl no longer needs answers to the question, "Why wait?" She found them the hard way. What she does need is an understanding of God's cleansing forgiveness and grace. Her autobiographical account breaks my heart, but the story is far from unique. I know firsthand countless similar stories.

Our young people desperately need to know more than just the "difference between right and wrong." They need to know and understand *the reasons.*

> True sexual freedom provides the option of saying no to these consequences. It says, "We are human beings with procreative powers capable of mature love and rational choice. Our free will provides us with self-control and self-respect." 244/T-5

Young people clearly need and want more information, especially on the "why" of sexual relationships rather than the "how". They need those reasons now. One of my major concerns is the *urgency* behind these cries for help. How many more beautiful lives will be damaged if we fail to provide our young people with "Why Wait?" answers — soon?

As parents, pastors and teachers we need to equip ourselves to address adequately the delicate yet difficult issue of waiting until marriage for sex. We need to provide our young people with down-to-earth answers that make sense spiritually, socially, psychologically and physically.

The so-called sexual revolution has created a dangerous moral precipice from which many are falling to destruction. We must do more than put an ambulance at the bottom of the cliff or a fence around the top. We must keep our young people off the cliff. To do that requires a moral tidal wave that will destroy the very foundations of the sexual revolution.

But to know what to do and how to do it, we must first understand the times in which we live. Let's take a look at some startling statistics that convey the depth of the problem.

Facts About Teenage Sex

- By age twenty, 81 percent of today's unmarried males and 67 percent of today's unmarried females have had sexual intercourse. 103

- The number of never-married teenage girls having intercourse increased by two-thirds in the decade of the '70s. 149/1538

- One study showed that 50 percent of today's sexually active nineteen-year-old males had their first sexual experience between the ages of eleven and thirteen. 45/73

- Eighty-seven percent of sexually active teens say they had sex before age seventeen.

- Most research shows that the average age for first having sex is fifteen for girls and fourteen for boys.

- Of the teens who say they have had intercourse, 49 percent say they have sex less than once a week; 20 percent say they tried it only once. 51/C7

- The New York polling firm Audits and Survey research study showed that 57 percent of high school students and 79 percent of college students had lost their virginity. 238/112

- Teens who engage in sex from once a month to once a week: high school — 33 percent; college — 52 percent. 238/112

- More than half the teens (54 percent) first had intercourse at their own or their partner's house. 45/72

- Twenty percent of thirteen-year-old boys have touched a girl's breast; 54 percent of fourteen-year-old boys have engaged in breast play, but only 31 percent of the girls. 45/57

- For some teens, oral sex comes before intercourse; 41 percent of seventeen-year-old girls say they have performed fellatio.

- A research study of 5,000 students at thirty-two educational institutions showed that 25.5 percent of coeds have been raped or sexually attacked since the age of fourteen. 305/162-70

- A Kent State University study showed that 57% of the coeds that had been raped there were raped by their dates. 305/162-70

The average age at which a youngster in this nation experiences sexual intercourse for the first time has changed significantly:

- In the late 1940s, Alfred Kinsey reported that 3 percent of the nation's females and 40 percent of the males had bid farewell to their virginity by age sixteen.

- Statistics reveal that 29 percent of the 397 middle schoolers (ages eleven through thirteen) and 54 percent of the 800 high schoolers (ages fourteen through eighteen) surveyed in Culver City, California, say they are sexually active.

- Among the middle school boys who admit to sexual activity, the average age at loss of virginity was 11.1; for the sexually active girls, 11.7.

- According to the sexually active high school boys, the average age at which they lost their virginity was 13.2; average age for the girls, 14.6.

- The above is probably *not* the average for most teens.

Facts About Teenage Pregnancy

- Over the last twenty years the percentage of illegitimate births to women nineteen years of age or under has increased from 15 percent to 51 percent. 134/5

- This year more than 1,100,000 teenage girls will become pregnant. 12/507

- Three out of every four pregnancies will be unintentional. 224/56-60

- Of those pregnancies, about 400,000 will end in abortion, a 100 percent increase since 1972. Another 137,000 will end in miscarriage. Of the 490,000 births, 270,000 will be to unwed teens, a three-fold increase since 1960. 249/E4

- Sixty percent of these girls will be pregnant again in two years.

- One research study showed that only 17 percent of the teen pregnancies are conceived following marriage. Ten percent of the pregnancies are conceived premaritally *but* are legitimated by marriage. 224/56-60.

- Teen pregnancy rates are at or near an all-time high. A 25-percent decline in birth rates between 1970 and 1984 is due to a *doubling* of the abortion rate during that period. More than 400,000 teenage girls now have abortions each year. 175

- Teens who feel abortion is the best solution to a pregnancy: high school — 56 percent; college — 50 percent. 238/115

- Each year, 30,000 of the girls who become pregnant are under fourteen years of age. 12/507

- Eighty percent of these pregnant girls will drop out of school.

- Of the teenage girls who give birth out of wedlock, 96 percent of these girls will keep their babies.

- Seventy percent of unwed teen mothers will go on welfare.

- Of teens who marry because of pregnancy, 60 percent will be divorced in five years.

- If present trends continue, 40 percent of today's fourteen-year-old girls will be pregnant before age twenty. 35/78

- Since the popular push for contraceptives for teens, teenage sexual activity and teenage pregnancy have increased almost FOUR HUNDRED PERCENT.

- A teenage-relationship survey reveals that "religion-conscious girls are 86 percent more likely to say it's important to be a virgin at marriage than nonreligion-conscious girls. However, religion-conscious girls are only 14 percent more likely to be virgins than non-religion-conscious girls." 108/66-67

Facts About Teenage Health

- With adolescent sexual activity more prevalent than at any other time in American history, sex and its consequences have become a major health problem for teenage girls. A Baltimore medical clinic with 18,000 patients under eighteen reported recently that "51 percent of all hospitalizations were related to sexual activity — abortions, births and sexually transmitted diseases." 119/E4

- We are currently seeing an unprecedented outbreak of sexually transmitted diseases among American teenagers. The statistics are staggering. The gonorrhea rate among teen girls has increased 400 percent since 1965 and is the highest of any age group. Overall the teen rate for all sexually transmitted diseases is second only to that of twenty- to twenty-four-year-olds. 119/E4

Do those statistics alarm you as they do me? No wonder the problem of teen pregnancy is considered epidemic and has been called by some "the most important issue of the remaining years of the twentieth century."

Our church young people are not immune; many of them are included in these statistics. When it comes to premarital sex, their church going seems to have limited deterrent value.

Something has happened to the moral fiber of our nation. At every turn, today's society is telling our young people, "If it feels good, do it" — "Life comes around only once; live it to the fullest, *now!*"

How do we adequately refute this "get-it-now" approach? If sex is truly satisfying, and it can be, why should adolescents wait to enjoy it? Why shouldn't the young in heart and body explore this fascinating dimension of their humanness when they feel the "urge to merge"? After all, no one else seems to be waiting.

Are we really surprised to discover that 78 percent of all young people ages eighteen to twenty-nine believe there is nothing wrong with having sex before marriage as long as both people are emotionally ready? An overwhelming permissive attitude toward premarital sex prevails throughout our society. As a consequence, young people are paying the price for the recent sexual revolution which promised "joy, liberation and good health" but in fact "delivered misery, disease, and even death." 136/156

The "Why Wait?" question needs to be answered. We cannot afford simply to tell our young people no and try to deal with sex in the negative.

I have found that most adolescents have not learned the biblical basis for waiting until marriage to experience the joys of sex. They do not know the "whys" of their moral beliefs. Consequently, when they face the tremendous temptations to give in to the physical, they lack the necessary foundational basis for their convictions.

A generation without moral convictions is a generation crumbling under the pressures of a secular world view.

Recently I ran into an old friend who shared an interesting story. She had begun teaching eighth-grade girls in her local church. "Several weeks ago, I had seven of them over to the house for a slumber party. Just before everyone went to bed I asked them, 'How many of you plan on being a virgin when you get married?' Not one of them said yes. Finally one girl spoke up and asked, 'How many of us *are* virgins?' They *all* were. That night I went to bed in a turmoil, wondering what to do."

The next morning my friend asked the girls to watch a video of one of our movies, "The Secret of Loving." After watching and discussing the program with the girls, she again asked, "How many of you *now* intend to wait until marriage for sex?" This time all seven said they did.

Before leaving, one of them came back to her and said, "Mrs. Duke, no one before ever gave us any reasons for waiting."

The above vignettes and statistics illustrate why Dick and I feel we *need* to address this issue. Young people are looking for answers. They want to know why they should wait and how they can say no.

A 1984 study shows that in the last ten years, guilt and remorse resulting from sexual involvement have *doubled* among teenagers. In a recent study done in the Atlanta school system, students were asked what they wanted most in a sex-education program. The overwhelming majority answered, "How to say no to physical involvement." For the first time in my memory, teenagers are seeking solid reasons for waiting.

In response we have taken a number of creative steps to address the issue of waiting until marriage for sex. We gathered together twenty-three men and women, representing over 150,000 U.S. churches, to discuss with us the seriousness of the problem and to identify some causes of and solutions to the crisis. Next we conducted a research study among evangelical youth to determine the extent of the problem within the church. As has been said, these youth are not immune from sexual promiscuity. The amount of sexual involvement among Christian youth has taken a devastating toll on discipleship, evangelism and missionary recruitment.

In addition, we sponsored a national essay contest for young people. We asked them to describe their struggles, pressures, hurts and victories. We received more than 7,000 pages of personal stories. They wrote intimately on reasons youth are involved physically, the ways to say no to sex and what they wished their parents knew about their sexuality.

Throughout this book, we replay their transparently shared stories. This is a rare opportunity for adults to see through the eyes of today's young people. We hope you will gain insight and understanding of your teen's life, as well as learn effective ways to communicate positive reasons for waiting until marriage for sex.

We also recommend the book, *Teens Speak Out,* comprised primarily of hundreds of responses from teens themselves and revealing what they think and feel. The purpose of *Teens Speak Out* is to inform parents and youth workers about the problems and pressures teens are facing so the adults will know better how to help their teens.

2

WHERE YOUTH ARE

"They understood the times in order to know what to do" (1 Chronicles 12:32, author's paraphrase).

―――――――――― ♥ ――――――――――

The Culture in Which Youth Live

We cannot help young people unless we understand the times in which we live and the effects these times are having on them. Significant issues in our culture tremendously affect the attitudes and behavior of young people. We want to tell you *where* we think young people are today, *what* kind of a world they live in, and *why* they're there and what they're feeling.

Where Our Young People Are

"Me-ism"

Most people would agree that we are living in a "me-ism" culture, a culture preoccupied with self. The U. S. Army has changed its advertising slogan from "You can make a difference" to "Be all that *you* can be." Other successful advertising slogans proclaim "*You* deserve a break today," and "Who says *you* can't have it all?" It is clear that the advancement and pleasing of self make up the number-one priority in our world. A recent survey revealed that teens consider "enjoyment" more important than "helping people" or "pleasing one's parents." 57

Although everyone agrees that self-centeredness is rampant, people *disagree* on the reasons for this preoccupation with self. Many educators, psychologists, pastors and evangelists place the blame on *narcissism,* the love of self. They indict our culture for being in love with itself.

Self-love is not the only cause of our culture's preoccupation with self. Today's young people, because of the breakup of the home, are faced with emotional and social problems with which they are unable to cope. Many teens are preoccupied with themselves not so much because of self-love, but because of a basic need for self-preservation. Their problems limit their freedom to love others. They simply cannot take their eyes off their own problems. They are unable to concern themselves with the needs of others because of the magnitude of their own problems. The cause of their self-centeredness is often painful self-hurt, not just self-love.

Youth today are crying out for identity: Who am I? Why am I here? Where am I going? Yet most young people do not believe that there are answers to life's most important questions. Life for them has little meaning or purpose. A majority of our young people do not feel significant. Can you imagine waking up in the morning and feeling that what you're going to do today doesn't matter?

Trying to Cope

A sixteen-year-old explained why he had turned to drugs. "Well, if I can't feel significant, at least I can feel good." That is how many teenagers attempt to deal with their problems. They turn to drugs, alcohol and sex as ways to "feel good." But those are only temporary avenues of escape, not long-term solutions.

Youth don't need our condemnation. They need our forgiveness and love. This is why, wherever I go today, one of my most important talks for young people is on self-image. "In God's eyes, you are special!" I tell them.

Suicide

One indicator of the emotional hurts of our young people is the suicide rate. For the last twenty years the death rate from suicide has declined in every age bracket except from ages fifteen to twenty-four. Teen suicide has tripled since 1950, making it the number two killer, second only to accidents, of Americans aged fifteen to nineteen. 114/76 Over the last three years the suicide rate has gone up 89 percent for young people ages twenty to twenty-four. Among persons of college age, suicide is the second leading cause of death (Weddige and Steinhilber). Some 1,700 youths in this age group take their lives every year. The suicide rate for youths under fifteen has also increased, tripling since 1960.

The results of the most extensive study ever done on teenage suicide have just been released. In two decades the rate of teen suicide attempts has gone from ten out of 1,000 to eight out of 100. 54/C5

So many teens are committing suicide today that a representative of the U.S. Centers for Disease Control in Atlanta said, "If people in society were dying from a disease at the same rate that teenagers are dying from suicide, it would be considered a major epidemic."

Today we are facing an AIDS epidemic. Last year 4,963 people in the United States died of AIDS. In the same period 5,500 teens committed suicide. This year more than 7,000 teens are expected to commit suicide.

Why is that, you ask? I think there are many reasons.

A study published by the Dallas *Morning News* listed "feeling all alone" as the number one reason for teen suicide. Problems with parents was also cited as a major factor. 51/C7 In study after study, the home lives of suicidal children have been characterized as "disruptive or chaotic." 114/47 One study singled out 458 youths from troubled home situations. Of them, 57 percent said they sometimes consider suicide. In a study of youth with low self-esteem, 62 percent had contemplated suicide.

Thus, suicide and suicidal feelings seem to be tied closely to low self-esteem and to family problems. 114/47

Do these young people really want to die? I don't think so. Certainly I have never met a teenager who really wanted to die. A young woman whose parents had gone through a devastating divorce attempted suicide. But later she said, "I didn't want to die. I just wanted the pain to stop!"

I am convinced that the reason teen suicide has reached epidemic proportions in our country is the number of youth suffering from deep self-hurt.

What Kind of World Our Young People Are Living In

A Transient Society

What are some of the causes of the pain that young people feel? One factor is the transient nature of American life. We live in a mobile society. This year thirty-five million Americans will move.

People relocate for a variety of reasons — some of the reasons are: to find better jobs, more favorable weather, or cheaper rent; or because they are transferred by their employers. The moving may be from coast to coast or merely from one housing development to another. But the results are the same. Very few people today "put down roots."

An Isolated Society

In some areas — as in California, for example — homeowners are isolated from their neighbors by block wall fences. But in those parts of the country without fences, the isolation is just as real. Today, particularly in new communities, most people are not acquainted with their next door neighbors. As each family faces the various crises of life they are often alone. Their neighbors never know their joys or sorrows.

A friend of mine told me he learned from a newspaper that the sixteen-year-old son of a family living across the street had been killed in a car accident. Prior to reading the tragic news story he had not even known the name of the family, nor that they had a teenage son.

Think about the last funeral you went to. If more than a handful of people attended, it was an exceptional funeral. I know of situations where the funeral director has recruited pallbearers from among the mourners because the family couldn't suggest enough names. Thousands of people are buried (or cremated) with no memorial service at all.

Many weddings today are poorly attended for similar reasons. I know one family who could not think of anyone from their church whom they knew well enough to invite to their daughter's wedding. There is no doubt that most of us live isolated lives in this mobile society.

When I was a boy in Michigan everyone in our neighborhood knew everyone else for miles around. Of course, our entire county had fewer residents than the high-density housing developments of today. Not only did people know each other, but they also had lived in that same area for years, and many of us were related. Within the radius of a few miles we had uncles, aunts, cousins and grandparents. When any crisis arose, we supported each other.

Meaningful relationships take time to develop. So many young people today have never lived in any one place long enough to develop the solid relationships that can help carry them through their stressful adolescent years. They do not have the traditional support systems to fall back on that so many of us who are now adults have had.

An Uncertain Society

A majority of today's young people view the future of society with apprehension and so have lost hope in their own future. Research shows that 68 percent of younger teens do not believe that this world even has a future, and 32 percent believe they will be directly affected by nuclear annihilation.

Instead of optimistically seeing the future as a time of opportunity, many young people view it bleakly, as a time of fear. And their fears have changed drastically in recent years. Two years ago the *New York Times* reported on a study done by Nadine Brozan in which she found that the five greatest fears of a primary school child twenty years ago were loud noises, dark rooms, high places, dangerous animals and strangers. Today the average primary child's greatest fears are losing a parent through divorce, and being a victim of burglary, mugging, rape or cancer. 18/B5

What makes these negative views about the future so significant is the fact that for most of us, 90 percent of our life motivations are based on the future: future job, future family, future home, future vacation, future retirement, future reward, and so on. We are motivated by our hopes for the future. When you have lost hope in the future you have lost one of the greatest motivations for life in the present — especially for living a pure and righteous life.

A sixteen-year-old in Oakland, California, said, "I feel like I'm preparing for nothing." Another teen said, "I think I'm going to grow up, and there won't be anything to live for." With the dulling of their hopes for the future most young people are influenced easily to make their decisions on the basis of short-term pleasure rather than long-term consequences.

Why should a teenager who believes he or she lives in a "doomsday world" follow that Christian advice to wait until marriage for sex? They have been taught that with one push of a button the world can be blown apart. Tomorrow they may be gone, so "Why not?"

WHY Our Young People Are Where They Are

Students at certain universities are not renowned for their benevolence to visiting speakers, especially those with conservative and/or Christian views. As I waited my turn to speak at the outdoor Free Speech Platform of one of those schools, I felt butterflies of nervousness in my stomach. *What I say had better be right on,* I realized, *or it will be shoved right back down my throat.* If the students are not interested in the topic, or how the speaker develops it, they simply ignore him or her.

Two Deep Fears

As I stepped up to speak, the crowd was noisy and not particularly hospitable. There was no public address system so I had to rely on old-fashioned lung power to be heard. I had only seconds in which to get their attention. The butterflies were still there as I began. "Almost every one of you has two fears. First, the fear you'll never be loved, and second, the fear you'll never be able to love." Everyone became very quiet. No one was looking around. I wasn't surprised.

Psychologists believe that "love famine" is one reason many young girls become pregnant. Lisa, who is sixteen and pregnant, would agree:

> My mother kept asking, "Why . . . Why?" 'Cause I wanted to be loved, that's why. Is that so terrible? I wanted someone to tell me that I'm pretty . . . that they cared about me.

Learning to love is not something that happens automatically. We don't just grow up, reach puberty and find that all of a sudden we know how to love. I'm not talking about sex. I'm talking about caring, transparency, vulnerability and intimacy.

Love Is Learned

We learn to love by seeing love modeled. Love is not primarily a feeling. Love is first and foremost action. Paul makes that clear in the thirteenth chapter of 1 Corinthians. Saying "I love you" has no meaning if it is not supported by action.

We can't teach love. Love is not a lecture class; it's a lab course. We learn to give and receive love by experiencing it. Love is learned by responding to its expression.

God intended for us to learn to love by seeing both parents first love each other and then love us. We learn through role models; through seeing our parents' love for each other, and then through their love for us.

A person can't learn to love God automatically either. It isn't that somebody comes along, shares the gospel with you, and then instantly you know how to love God. No. God's ideal is that you learn how to love *Him* by seeing your father love your mother, and then seeing your parents both love you.

When the home breaks down, and parental models cease

to function, the result is a generation of children who grow up without knowing how to give or receive love. For these children, to develop close, intimate relationships may be impossible.

After listening to one of my talks in England, a sixteen-year-old wrote me: "I wish someone would just love me. I want someone to show me they care. I just wanted you to know that. I want love but I don't know how to accept it or give it." Despite a desperate need for love, young people are afraid they will never find it.

The Effect of Divorce

A readers' survey of *Children and Teens Today* asked, "What do you see as the major stresses/problems facing today's teenagers?" The response of 72.4 percent was: "Problems arising from parental divorce/remarriage." 49/1-2

Evidence of the emotional consequences of divorce on young people is everywhere. One of the great fears of many young children and teenagers is the loss of a parent through divorce — and with good reason: One out of two marriages today ends in divorce.

One day a few years ago, when my son Sean was six years old, he wasn't quite himself when he came home from school. I asked what was wrong.

"Aw, nothing, Dad."

Sean and I have pretty good communication so I said, "Come on, share with me what you're feeling."

He hesitated, and then asked, "Daddy, are you going to leave Mommy?"

I knew that question would come up someday. "What makes you ask that?"

Three of his friends' dads had just divorced their mothers, Sean told me, and he was afraid I might do the same.

I sat down with Sean, looked him in the eye and said, "I want you to know one thing. I love your mother very much. I'm committed to her, and I'll never leave her. Period."

That little six-year-old breathed a sigh of relief, smiled at me and said, "Thanks, Dad." He didn't need reinforcement of my love for him; he needed the security that comes from knowing that his mother and I love each other and are committed to a permanent relationship. Like all young people today, Sean needs to be part of a lasting relationship.

Our friends Dick and Charlotte had a similar experience. Their son Jonathan at age ten asked, "You and Mom wouldn't get a divorce, would you?" They both reassured him that though they may have differences from time to time, they are committed to each other, and to working out any differences. Jonathan too had been impacted by the divorce of the parents of some of his friends and wanted verbal reassurance.

Before Olivia Newton John's recent marriage she was asked why she hadn't married sooner. She answered that she had been devastated by the divorce of her parents when she was ten years old. Then she said something so typical of young people today, "If you've never seen a relationship that lasts forever, you tend not to believe it's possible." 250/113

Losing a Parent

Psychiatrist Jean-Francois Saucier of the University of Montreal says that divorce has a more severe effect on a child's outlook than the death of a parent. "People think divorce is better than death . . . because a child can still be with both parents . . . When a child loses a parent [through death], there is a period of mourning, [but] then he can recuperate." 251/D1

There are several reasons it is easier for most children to lose a parent through death than divorce.

First, when you lose a parent through death, you don't feel personally responsible. When youngsters lose parents through divorce they often feel it is their fault, even though in the majority of cases they had nothing to do with it. Almost every child of divorce goes through life carrying that heavy load of guilt.

A boy of ten said to me in all seriousness, "If I had kept my room clean, my dad wouldn't have left my mother." I asked him what he meant. He said his dad used to complain (as I think most dads do) about his room always being messy. Then one day his dad and mother separated, and he thinks it was his fault. I'm afraid that this boy will go through high school, college and into a career believing he was personally responsible for the breakup of his parents' marriage. What an awful, awesome burden to carry.

I counseled a twenty-three-year-old woman, whose parents were divorced when she was sixteen. She said, "If I had been a better cook, my father would never have divorced my mother." As a teenager, because her mother worked outside the home, it was Debbie's responsibility to keep the house clean and prepare the evening meals. Her father often complained about her cooking. Then one night this man, whom she loved and admired more than anyone on the face of the earth, packed his bags and left. Seven years later, Debbie remains convinced — no matter what anyone tells her — that "my father divorced my mother because I was a lousy cook." Her cooking had nothing to do with the divorce of her parents, but regardless of how many counselors she may see (she's now with her fifth psychologist), Debbie probably will go through life blaming herself.

After I had spoken at a conference, another woman came to me and asked for help. She told me that two weeks earlier her husband had served divorce papers on her. That afternoon as she was driving to the conference with her fourteen-year-old son, he said to her, "Mom, I'm sorry. I'm sorry. Forgive me!" Then he began crying. When she asked what he was sorry about, he answered, "I'm sorry for making Dad divorce you." The woman told her son he had nothing to do with the divorce, but he kept insisting. "Yes, I did." When she asked why he thought it was his fault, he answered, "Well, if I hadn't loved soccer so much he would never have left you."

I see it all the time. Young people feel responsible for their parent's divorce.

The second reason it is easier to lose a parent through death than through divorce is the lack of finality. When you lose a parent through death there is a finality to it. After a period of painful mourning you go on with your life. But, unlike death, divorce does not bring that sense of finality. Divorce isn't over in the lives of kids when the papers are signed. There is no mourning period after which one picks up the pieces, goes on with life and begins the healing process. The reality of divorce returns every holiday, every summer vacation and (for many youngsters) every weekend. The pain goes on and on. Christmas here. New Year's there. Presidents' Day here. Easter there. Memorial Day here. Summer vacation there. Labor Day here. Thanksgiving there. There's no end to it.

I hear so many divorced fathers and mothers say, "You know, it was my children who really handled the divorce well." These parents are trying to take comfort from what they see as the strength of their children. That may be the way it seems from the outside. Teens often can do that — fool us about what's happening on the inside — but you know they've got to be hurting.

For years social scientists have been able to provide us with the statistics of divorce, but they couldn't quantify its emotional impact on children. Now we know that "teens from divorced families are less optimistic and have more psychological problems than those whose parents stay together." Girls from divorced families believe their future prospects to be much lower than girls from traditional families. 251/D1 We already have talked about the consequences for young people, brought about by a loss of hope in the future. Divorce is a major cause of the dulling of those future hopes.

3

MEDIA LIES

Picture this scenario:

Boy meets girl. Boy and girl find each other attractive and want to know each other better, so they set aside an evening. Do they talk and discuss? No. They spend ten dollars to sit side by side in a movie theater and stare at the screen.

On the screen: Boy meets girl. Boy and girl find each other attractive and want to know each other better, so they set aside an evening. Do they talk and discuss? No. They remove their clothes and have sex to the sound of violins. The movie has a happy ending.

After the movie, real-life boy and girl still want to get to know each other. On top of that, their hormones are roaring. They have just been surrounded by a movie that said, "Sex is a great way to get to know someone." Their minds reel with flashes of skin, beautiful music and happy endings. They look deeply into each other's eyes and have sex in the car.

Boy thinks girl is easy. Boy dumps girl. Girl wonders what went wrong.

Does that sound possible? Far fetched? Familiar? Read part of a letter I received from a girl in West Virginia:

I accepted Jesus as Savior when I was nine. I have been going to church all my life and still do. At age seventeen I began dating a boy who had graduated and gotten work with a factory in town. I thought he was *cool*. Well, one night we went to see the movie *10*. One the way home we took a detour and had intercourse in the back seat of his mother's car. After five months of dating, he broke up with me. I was crushed.

A Junior Achievement report reveals that media (TV, radio, movies) ranks third, behind peers and parents, in influencing the values and behavior of teens. This represents a dramatic shift since 1960 when media ranked eighth behind such factors as teachers, relatives and religious leaders. 253/4

What does the media tell our young people? Well, in the area of sexuality the media mostly tells them lies.

Maybe you don't agree. Perhaps you think I'm exaggerating to make a point. After all, we all watch television. Is it really communicating "lies"? Let me show you what I mean.

A research study estimates that the average person views approximately 9,230 sex acts, or implied sex acts, a year on television. 43/1-2 and 254/171 Of that sexual activity, 81 percent is outside the commitment of marriage. This means that if the average young person, watching ten years of television from age eight to eighteen, watched 93,000 scenes of suggested sexual intercourse, 72,900 of those scenes would have been pre- or extramarital. What kind of impression does that make on young people — especially when the participants are the "beautiful people" of shows like *Dynasty, Dallas,* and *Knots Landing?*

The *Journal of Communication* reports that "television portrays six times more extramarital sex than sex between spouses. Ninety-four percent of the sexual encounters on soap operas are between people not married to each other." 269/n.p.

But you may say, "We admit that's a lot of sex for any one person to see . . . and showing excessive examples of sexual activity on television is undoubtedly a bad influence on our young people, but in a society as sexually permissive as ours, where's the lie?"

No One Pays

You can answer that question for yourself by doing a little calculating. First, tell me how many years you have watched television. Then calculate the number of sex scenes you have seen. (Remember that ten years of viewing adult shows would net you approximately 92,000 scenes of sexual activity. If you are twenty years of age or older, you have probably observed at least 92,000 scenes of sexual activity on television.) Now try to remember if you have ever seen anybody on television contract a sexually transmitted disease. What's your answer?

I often ask that question of the audiences to whom I speak. Even in crowds as large as 5,000 I have hardly ever had a *yes* answer.

So, where's the *lie?* Let me remind you of some well documented facts: Every day 33,000 Americans become infected with a sexually transmitted disease (STD). 33/53-57 This year the total will be approximately twelve million persons. That's *reality.*

It's clear that the American media has not been telling it like it is. From a medium that self-righteously expresses its concern for "the public's right to know," what we have been getting in this area is *definitely a lie.*

The best thing that could happen on TV for young people in our country would be for J. R. to get VD. I'm sure that Larry Hagman wouldn't let anyone write that into the script, but such a development would be reality.

NO ONE ON TELEVISION PAYS THE PRICE OF ILLICIT SEX. YOU ONLY DO THAT IN REAL LIFE.

The current alarm regarding the spread of AIDS, however, has triggered some healthy signs of change. You still do not see anyone in the media acquiring an STD from promiscuity, but there appears to be a trend toward recognizing that possibility. Jack Curry said in *USA Today* that we are entering the "dawning of the age of responsible sex." He added, "AIDS-think has made mattress hopping and the single mingle risky business." 112/D1 The trend seems to be toward portraying more monogamous relationships and expression of regard for safety, both for oneself and for the other person.

While these trends could bring some positive changes, we must be aware of the subtle ways in which they also will promote promiscuity and premarital sex. The expected changes will not bring a godly morality, with its fulfilling expression of genuine love, into being. Rather, they will make the changing mores appear respectable.

Pregnancy

Last season on the soap, "Another World," high school senior Thomasina Harding became pregnant. However, her boyfriend quickly married her, got a college scholarship, became the star of the football team, and got a good job. "The new baby is beautiful, hardly ever cries, and everybody is deliriously happy. It's hard to imagine a less realistic depiction of the experience of adolescent pregnancy." 256/7

"In the old days of television, unmarried couples who 'did it' suffered tragically. If a girl had sex out of wedlock, she got pregnant or got hit by a truck or both. And because it was so unreal, it was kind of a joke. It didn't scare kids into not having sex . . . But TV changed a lot . . . 'The Love Boat' was a good example. On that show, people did it like minks. And no tragedy followed. And no guilt. Sex was as casual as breakfast. But in doing away with guilt, TV also did away with responsibility." 257/6-8

And not everything we see on television is make believe. Teens see Jerry Hall on television talking about having Mick Jagger's second out-of-wedlock child and saying what a wonderful life she has. A procession of unmarried stars, including Farrah Fawcett and Jessica Lange, have joined Hall in proclaiming on television the "joys" of extramarital pregnancy.

When was the last time you saw anybody on television say no to sex? Think about it. You can see why a sixteen-year-old girl who had just lost her virginity wrote me to say, "Mr. McDowell, *I couldn't compete with television.*"

"Teens . . . lack the life experience that would allow them to view the stories more realistically . . . Even news stories on television or in newspapers have an effect. When kids read that teens are more sexually active than ever, they aren't appalled. Rather, they wonder what's wrong with them." 256/18

What are the results? "Bombarded by thousands of messages promoting sex but omitting a few crucial facts of life, a million teens get pregnant each year." 257/7 By and large, the secular broadcast media does little to reinforce moral values or demonstrate the consequences of irresponsible moral behavior.

Advertising

We are often told that television doesn't affect behavior very much. The tobacco industry, at a time of public pressure to remove tobacco ads from TV declared that media commercials don't effect a change in a person's lifestyle, and that media ads would not cause a person to take up smoking. That's about the craziest thing I've ever heard. Why does the tobacco industry spend hundreds of millions on commercials? They're not stupid. If there is no relationship between TV commercials and viewers' behavior, then why have *American businesses spent three billion dollars on advertising each year — for prime time television alone?* "Billions more are spent on daytime television, radio, magazines, newspapers, billboards and innumerable other media. According to *TV Guide*, in 1981 the number of network commercials run each week was 4079, more than double the figure of 1967." 62/84 In 1983, more than $16 billion were spent on television advertising and more than $5 billion on radio advertising. 268/62-63

The media bombards us daily with messages about sex. Sex

is a primary ingredient in most advertising. It is used to sell everything from automobiles to deodorants. Our radios, television sets, movie screens, record players, books, magazines, and newspapers loudly proclaim that "sex is normal, available and certainly not restricted to adults, much less married couples." 255/V3

On daytime and nighttime soaps, glamorous stars pass from one sex partner to another like musical chairs. Advertising spots suggest that our sex life will improve if we wear designer jeans, drive sporty cars, put on certain colognes, use the right toothpaste gel. The radio blares out songs like "Tonight's the Night" and MTV vividly illustrates lewd and suggestive lyrics.

Surgeon General Koop reports on a study funded by his office:

> In Michigan, in four cities that studied junior high and high school girls, it was found that the girls watch an average of two and a half to three hours of soap operas per day, and that there is one episode of sexual intercourse per hour on those films — almost always between unmarried people. But more surprising to us was that the movies these youngsters wanted to see most were R-rated movies, and we found that 66 to 77 percent of the girls in these four cities had seen the six top R-rated films that year. The fascinating thing to me is that not one of these girls was ever challenged at the box office although all of them were under age, and the movies contained eight instances of sexual intercourse among unmarried people per film. Two of those films had even more than that. One had fourteen. That one was so popular with young people that it has now been made into a television series.
>
> I think the media have downgraded morality in this country to the point where kids think if they do what they see, they are behaving according to the norm of society. 208

Misrepresented Values

For years now we have allowed the media to misrepresent casual sex and free love. Young people have been shown that the cure for everything is to jump into bed. It doesn't matter if it's morning, afternoon or evening; or on television, in popular music, in movies and videos; sex is proclaimed as a cure-all. It's a cure for emptiness and loneliness. It's a cure for lack of significance. All lies. Sex is not a cure-all. There's no such thing as casual sex. There's no such thing as free love.

For the most part we have *allowed* our young people to determine who they are as sexual beings on the basis of these lies propagated by the mass media. This deception is crucial — because our sexuality affects everything we say, hear, think and do. Sexuality is at the core of our human existence. And we have *allowed* our young people, who are growing up right now, to base their sexuality on lies.

A survey of 500,000 fourth graders regarding drugs and alcohol revealed that four years ago the strongest influence in getting them to try drugs and alcohol was peer pressure, but in 1987 TV most prompted their use. 306/D1

Enticing erotic TV ads and scenes communicate to our teens "be active." The focus is on immediate sexual gratification. Yet the concerned parent says "wait" and promotes celibacy as the standard for teens. Our teens are getting mixed signals about sexual behavior — no wonder there is so much confusion.

The media not only distorts sexual realities but it also cultivates feelings of inadequacy among teen viewers. A tremendous emphasis on the value of a person is based on the physical. First, the media communicates that the value of a person is primarily his or her physical attractiveness. We are bombarded with a constant parade of beautiful women, which gives teenage girls a very unrealistic standard by which to judge their own attractiveness. I hope that most of us realize that the media's beauty standard is not a normal one. What's more, it's constantly changing. For a time, large breasts were the standard. Sometimes the emphasis has been on a woman's legs. A few years ago Farrah-Fawcett-styled hair was the desirable. Then tight fashion jeans were the "in thing," with emphasis on the buttocks. It's ridiculous.

Think what that does to the average young person. Many a young woman has a totally distorted sense of self-worth. If by comparison to the latest standards of physical beauty she is not attractive, she sees herself as without worth or value, which results in tremendous feelings of inadequacy.

The young male is also affected. He develops totally unrealistic ideas about a woman's true beauty. Why do most men place physical attractiveness above all other considerations when they seek relationships with the opposite sex? Because of the media, of course. All the male heroes on TV have "beautiful women."

Powerful Influences

What gives the media such power over young people is the amount of time they spend listening and watching it. The average preschooler spends more time watching television than a university student spends in the classroom earning a bachelor's degree. One study reveals that preschool children watch twenty hours of television a week and grade school children twenty-two hours. "Sleeping is the only activity that commands more of their time. By the age of eighteen, they will have spent more time in front of the TV set than anywhere else, including school." 46/39 Another study estimates that by graduation the average high school student has spent 22,000 hours watching TV, which is twice the amount of time spent in twelve years of school.

From grades seven and twelve, kids listen to an average of 10,500 hours of rock music. The total amount of time spent in school over a period of twelve years is just 500 hours more than the time spent listening to rock music. 118/46

Consequently, young people spend less time interacting with real adults. "Teenagers are inordinately influenced by the media. They have less interaction with real adults than ever before, so their friends and the 'models' presented in the media have an even greater impact." 256/17-18

So either the media or the listening and viewing habits of young people must change if their attitudes about sex are going to change.

While we have been permissively silent, the media of our culture has been telling our children that you find intimacy through the physical, that intimacy comes from jumping into bed and getting it on, and that there is such a thing as casual sex or free love. Because of that, most of our young people have developed their concept of sexuality based upon this fiction from TV without realizing the price tag that comes with free love and casual sex. If they are unable to revise their attitudes, They eventually will pay a high price.

A young lady tells of that price:

> What the movies and the soap operas don't tell us about is the devastation and the broken hearts that occur due to affairs and premarital sex. I do not make light of the consequences of wrong . . . sexual involvement. Without a doubt, the hardest and most painful thing I've gone through . . . more than major surgery, tests for cancer, a broken family, and numerous job rejections . . . is getting over a sexual relationship with a married man.

Sad to say, most young people, even from church families, have not learned about their sexuality in church. Even a greater tragedy, most did not learn about their sexuality at home. They have learned it from television, movies and music. Those are three great influences on teens.

Changes Needed

Before placing all the blame on the media, however, I think we should also examine what, if anything, we have done to counteract the situation. Many Christian parents share in the blame because of their permissiveness. Often television is seen as a harmless "electronic babysitter." How much guidance have you given your children about what television programs and movies to watch? What about the music they listen to? Have you ever written to your local television stations when they broadcast something you did not approve of? In most cases I think we have lost the battle without even putting up a fight. For years, too many of us have been silent about the dangerous effects of watching and listening.

We have also permitted the media to lie to us in many other ways. How often do we see lost jobs, crippling car accidents, or broken families in wine or beer commercials? How many cigarette ads in our magazines and newspapers show people dying of lung cancer? Can we really expect the media to be more truthful when it comes to showing the disastrous effects of extramarital sex?

But if the media were to change and become more honest, would that have any positive effect? Roger Simon thinks it would. "Attitudes about sex . . . won't change without changes on TV . . . Take a look at what has happened to cigarette smoking on TV. You used to see it on shows all the time. At dramatic moments, romantic moments, fun moments, the hero would light up a cigarette. But think hard about TV today. When was the last time you saw someone light a cigarette? It happens, but not often. And this, more than anything else, has changed the way young people look at smoking. It simply does not have the allure it once did. And that's largely because people on TV don't do it anymore." 257/8

Social commentator Benjamin Stein points out that "positive images would be more effective — [TV] shows that promote good family life, responsibility and moral choices. If those images were supported by adults in their conversations with teenagers, then things might begin to change." 110/14

4

"FREE SEX"

So-called "free love," sex that is free of commitment or obligation, has a high price tag — physically, emotionally, psychologically and spiritually. There is no such thing as *free* love or *free* sex.

Somebody Always Pays

Someone always pays for promiscuity — and it is not always the primary participants who pay the most.

This year there will be 1.2 million pregnant teenagers. Do you know that it costs federal and state governments an average of $100,000 in medical and welfare costs for every single teen who has a child?

WASHINGTON [AP] - Teenage child-bearing cost the nation $16.6 billion last year and the 385,000 babies who were the firstborn to adolescents in 1985 will receive $5 billion in welfare benefits over the next 20 years, according to a study just released . . . The study estimated that the government spent $16.5 billion last year in welfare costs to support the families started by teenage mothers. This estimate includes payments for AFDC, Medicaid and food stamps as well as the costs of administering these programs.

"This figure represents minimal public costs in that it does not include other services such as housing, special education, child protection services, foster care, day care and other social services," the report's summary said. 261/sec.1, p. 3 In the next twenty years the American taxpayer will pay in excess of $100 billion for the net results of teenage pregnancies. 110/99 *That's not free sex.* That's expensive sex. And we're paying for it.

The January 10, 1986, issue of the *Journal of the Medical Association* reported: "It is estimated that the first 10,000 cases of AIDS in the United States cost $1.6 million hospital days, $1.4 million in expenditures, 8,387 years of work lost, and $4.8 million because of premature death . . . New York City alone picks up $45 million a year in unpaid hospital bills of AIDS patients." 6/213

Infants often pay the price for so-called "free" sex. For example, one of the most serious epidemics in American history was the polio epidemic of the '50s. But in the last twelve months alone, more babies were born with birth defects caused by sexually transmitted disease than the total number of children who suffered from the crippling effects of that post World War II polio epidemic, which lasted about ten years. 20/73

I recently read a report just released by the U.S. Centers for Disease Control. It too was heartbreaking; tears ran down my face as I read it. The report told about the rising number of pregnant women who will require birth by Caesarean section because of sexually transmitted diseases (STDs). If their babies were delivered normally they would be born blind.

In our society even unborn human beings frequently pay for their parents' "free" sex by dying as the result of abortion. I don't know about you, but that makes my heart ache. It must also break God's heart to see His innocent creatures, born or unborn, paying the price for their parents' wrongdoing. When we ignore God's loving, protective commandments, someone always pays the price. No sexual encounter is free if others have to pay for it.

Sexually Transmitted Diseases

The rapid and widespread growth of sexually transmitted diseases, with all their terrible suffering, is another of the prices we pay for promiscuity. If everyone practiced monogamy, STDs would soon be nonexistent.

Twenty years ago there were two basic sexually transmitted diseases. Today there are twenty-seven. Approximately every nine months a new one is discovered. Every day 33,000 Americans will contract an STD. That's twelve million this year. 33/53

A newcomer to the list of sexually transmitted diseases is the dreaded AIDS. Almost every day there are more articles and

TV reports about the enormity of this disease. It is estimated that in the next three years hundreds of thousands of babies will be born with the deadly AIDS virus. The cost of treating the average AIDS victim during the two years it generally takes for the disease to run its fatal course currently averages about $147,000. For many businesses, one or two AIDS cases could trigger a ruinous hike in health insurance premiums. By 1991 it will cost us an estimated $19 billion a year, just for AIDS. If we combine that with the costs of other STDs we can expect soon to be paying at least $30 billion a year for "free" sex.

Except within the commitment of a monogamous marriage relationship there is always a price to be paid for engaging in sex. The only way a person can be certain that he or she has no risk of contracting a sexually transmitted disease is to be in a monogamous relationship with someone who also has been monogamous. Otherwise, medical authorities say, you must now have to consider not only your current sex partner, but also all of your partner's other sexual involvements during the past ten years. It is possible for a person to be a carrier of some STD, like AIDS, for ten years without knowing it.

Psychological Costs

In addition to the financial costs of casual, promiscuous sex, there are the psychological costs. What about the teenage mother? Her prospects are often dismal. Her chances of finishing school, obtaining a good job, or being happily married are minimal.

What about the physical and psychological costs of being born to a teenage mother? Infant mortality. Low birth weight. Mental retardation. Physical disabilities. Further, the chances of such children being physically abused, or becoming drug-addicted, are much greater than if they were born to older women. The reason is not so much their age, but rather their health care. Teen mothers do not take care of themselves as well as older women.

In addition, there is a mental and emotional price to promiscuity. Your mind and emotions are affected whenever you engage in sexual activity. The mind has the capability to play "reruns" of past sexual experiences, often forcing you to compare a current sexual partner with a previous one. That can occur even when you finally have married and begun a genuine committed relationship. These "ghosts of relationships past" can be devastating to future intimacy in marriage.

Apart from Jesus Christ, only the most callous individuals can overcome the guilt feelings that result when their sexual activities have been little more than indulgence of their selfishness.

All of us, Christian or not, are created in the image of God. As such, it is unnatural for us to harm the dignity of another human being without experiencing remorse. Most of us cannot "use" or abuse another person for self gratification without feeling some guilt.

Spiritual Costs

Spiritually, too, there is a price for promiscuity. If, as a Christian, you participate in casual sex, you are violating God's principles and commandments. How damaging that is to any disciple of Jesus Christ. You can't witness effectively. You can't experience God's blessing. Christians who engage in pre- or extramarital sex pay a high price in *fruitlessness*.

Casual sex? Free sex? No. Promiscuity affects our total person — body, mind, soul and spirit.

"A Private Act"

In the area of sexuality, we believe that intolerant attitudes, often cultivated by orthodox religions and Puritanical cultures, unduly repress sexual conduct. The right to birth control, abortion and divorce should be recognized. While we do not approve of exploitive, denigrating forms of sexual expression, neither do we wish to prohibit, by law or social sanction, sexual behavior between consenting adults. 62/64

Those words from the Humanist Manifesto II, express a current sexual attitude much in vogue: Sex is a *private act* between two individuals behind closed doors and therefore it is none of our business. We shouldn't tell other people how they should behave. We are told, for example, that the government has no right to enact or enforce laws that affect anyone's private sexual conduct. Schools should not teach principles to guide sexual behavior.

Even many Christians will say, "I guess that's right. Whatever someone wants to do in private is their business and not mine. After all, they'll suffer the consequences, not me. Right?"

Wrong!

Still Costly

If sex is merely a private act behind closed doors, why does the government annually pay large sums of money for abortions?

If sex is a private act behind closed doors, why has the Surgeon General advocated the use of public funds for sex education in all our schools beginning at the third grade?

If sex is a private act behind closed doors, why is the U.S. government spending so much money on AIDS research? Why does the U.S. Centers for Disease Control spend so much of its time, at taxpayer expense, on sexually transmitted diseases?

Ironically, many groups that pressure for public funding of abortions, and for public care for victims of STD, also defend their absolute right to have unlimited sexual freedom *behind closed doors.* Their position is a gross philosophical contradiction.

Sex is *not* a private act! Not when persons practice casual sex behind closed doors and then come out from behind those doors and demand that the government spend billions of dollars on AIDS research. Not when teenagers become pregnant behind closed doors and then pass the costs of those children onto taxpayers.

Almost every state in the union has set up task forces to combat the spread of AIDS among heterosexuals. A great fear today in the hearts of promiscuous heterosexuals is that of receiving a phone call from an AIDS task force worker: "Hello, are you alone? . . . Your name has been given to us. Can we talk?" Imagine getting a call like that.

No Guarantees

Further, an honest answer from a sex partner about sexually transmitted disease is no guarantee that a person is safe. Even while dormant in one person, an STD can be transmitted to another. Dr. Edward Wiesmeier, director of the UCLA Student Health Center, warns students that "one chance encounter can infect a person with as many as five different diseases." 33/56

Dr. Lawrence Laycob says that "when you're casual about sex, chances are the person you're casual with has been casual with someone else. So there's a third, fourth, or twenty-fifth party out there that you have no knowledge of." 33/56

The Only Way

A recent bulletin from the U.S. Centers for Disease Control declares that the only certain way to avoid sexually transmitted disease is for a monogamous man to enter into a monogamous relationship with a monogamous woman. There is no other positive way.

Surgeon General Koop soberly stated that "it is a very frightening thing. Today if you have sexual intercourse with a woman, you are not only having sexual intercourse with her but with every person that woman might have had intercourse with for the last ten years and all of the people they had intercourse with." 208

Because of the sexual practices of others, we who are parents are faced with the necessity of explaining to our children that when they get married they cannot have peace of mind on their wedding night (or afterward) unless they know the *detailed sexual history of their mates.* It won't be easy telling that to my three daughters and my son. But I've got to tell them.

God said long ago that illicit sex, though a private act between two individuals, still has potentially widespread and horrendous physical, social, political, economical, emotional, and moral implications. If you study history you find that it was not primarily religious groups like the Puritans who originated legislation to regulate the sexual activities of a given culture. It was often secular governments who had enough common sense to realize that sex is not merely a private act, but rather an act with appalling public consequences and costs.

Think of the implications within a marriage if the husband has an extramarital affair. What if he repents and goes back to his wife? She could become frigid because of legitimate fear: "If I have sex with my husband now, it's as if I'm having sex with that woman he had sex with — plus everyone she's had sex with for the last seven to eight years." When we break God's loving commandments the price is awesome.

No, sex is not a private act when:
— unwanted children pay the price;
— the public pays the price;
— it results in deadly public epidemics.

A young married man, who isn't a Christian, urged me, "Please keep on telling people what you're telling them about sex." When I asked him why, he said, "Because of people like me. I've had a real loose lifestyle with a lot of free love and plenty of casual relationships. When herpes came onto the scene, it didn't really change my lifestyle, even though I knew you can never get rid of it. Fortunately, I never got it.

"Now a whole new strain of herpes has hit nationwide," he continued. "You won't hear much about it. It's asymptomatic. You don't even know you have it. You don't have blisters, but you can still pass it on. The one way you know for sure you have it is if you have a child born with a birth defect. But that didn't change my lifestyle either.

"Then AIDS came on the scene. That got my attention. It's fatal. So, I decided, OK, that's it. I'm going to change my lifestyle, fall in love, settle down and have children." Which is exactly what he did.

Then his wife gave him herpes.

This kind of thing is happening everywhere. After a meeting with a group of high school students in Orlando, Florida, I was approached by a big, husky, handsome young man. Tears were streaming down his cheeks as he told me he'd spent his entire life striving for his father's love. "I'd done everything I could to get my father to put his arms around me, to hug me, to tell me 'I love you.' He never did. So, about six months ago I finally joined the Marines."

"But I got so lonely in the Marines that when I met this girl I went to bed with her. I'm a Christian. I know Christ personally, and it's the only time in my life I've done something like that. She gave me herpes." Then the tears really began to flow. "Josh," he asked, "will anyone ever love me?"

The situation is so heartbreaking when you think of what God intended for us in the area of sex, and of how human beings have misused and desecrated one of His most beautiful gifts.

Only in the context of a marriage commitment — "for better or for worse, in sickness and in health, as long as we both shall live" — can sex between two individuals even come close to being considered a private act.

5

FOUR SIGNIFICANT FACTORS

Puberty

Puberty is that time of life when a young person's body undergoes changes in preparation for sexual activity and biological reproduction. Basically two kinds of changes occur in this maturation process: some are primary, or internal; others are secondary, or external. The basic primary changes involve the reproductive organs themselves; the changing of secondary sexual characteristics involve external physical appearance. Before the age of puberty there is a good bit of similarity between the physical appearance of males and females. But with the onset of sexual maturity certain distinctions become obvious.

Differences

A young man's voice begins to deepen. His shoulders become broader, his chest bigger, his legs longer. Hair begins to grow on his face, chest and legs. With a young woman her bust begins to develop. Her hips begin to round out and her legs become shapely. The timetable for these changes varies from person to person. Some develop quickly; others develop very slowly. Girls tend to experience such changes approximately two years earlier than boys.

These changes have considerable effect on the sense of identity of each young person. Generally the young male who develops quickly becomes a more secure individual, largely because our society places a great deal of importance upon the physical stature of the male. On the other hand, the female who develops early may feel very insecure; she is the first one among her peers to be experiencing these things, and she doesn't quite know how to handle it.

The young man who is late in developing his secondary sexual characteristics is often looked down upon by parents and peers as immature and unmanly. The young woman who develops slowly may feel awkward and undesirable. Because of their physical appearance, these slow developing young people often find themselves left out of the teen dating scene.

These days, because our general health is better, young people are maturing sexually at an earlier age. This means that children today face a much longer interval between sexual maturity and marriage than our grandparents did.

In the 1870s the average girl first menstruated when she was sixteen or seventeen. In the 1980s she is more likely to menstruate at twelve or thirteen.

In 1870 the average age of puberty was 16.5. Today the average age is about 12.5.

In 1870 the average marriage age was 18. Today the average age is 22.8.

In 1870 the average interval between puberty and marriage was about two years. Today the average interval is at least ten years.

These changes have taken place gradually, over a period of more than one hundred years. "Few experts believe that this gradual change in early [sexual] maturation is the reason for the trend toward early sexual activity, which developed much more recently and with relative suddenness. They suspect that more complex factors are at work, and that one of them is the changing role of the family in teenagers' lives." 38/58-60

When such factors as earlier sexual maturation and later marriage are combined with media sexual pressure and a breakdown of the American family — which leaves teens desperately searching for close relationships — it is not surprising that teens today are so vulnerable to the influences of their sexual hormones. Yet even though twelve- and thirteen-year-olds may be physiologically mature enough to function sexually and to bear children, they are not emotionally mature enough to function wisely as sexual beings or as parents.

Lack of Emotional Maturity

One recent study shows that girls who first have intercourse at age fifteen or younger are almost twice as likely to become pregnant within the first six months of sexual activity than are those who wait until they're eighteen or nineteen. This may be related to both their ignorance about methods of birth control and to their level of overall maturity. "They simply don't understand — or rather, don't believe — the cause-and-effect relationship [between sex and pregnancy]. They think it will never happen to them." 38/58-60

Today's teens are considered to be the most "educated" generation ever, when it comes to quantitative knowledge. This is largely the result of an information explosion, which has seen more facts amassed during the last several decades than were previously gathered since the beginning of recorded history. Young people, however, have never before been so intellectually mature — and so emotionally immature.

That general emotional immaturity is rooted in the breakdown of the family, especially in its nurturing functions. Emotional maturity cannot be taught in school. It can be learned only in the context of loving, supportive relationships with adults who are themselves emotionally mature. Often this is no longer the case in the American family. Many parents, who may be immature themselves, have little time to pay attention to their children's needs — and those parents frequently look to their children for love and support.

Statistics now indicate that about half of all teenagers from fifteen to nineteen are sexually active. Many begin sexual experimentation even earlier. Their bodies are mature; their minds may be mature; but their emotions are not. They are totally unprepared to handle the pressures of their sexual hormones.

Two Cultures

When I was a teenager many voices told me that premarital sex was wrong. If my parents said anything about it, they would say, "It's sin; don't do it!" If my pastor said anything about it, he would say, "It's sin; don't do it!" If I turned on the radio or television, I would hear, "Don't do it!" At school I would be told, "Don't do it!" Most of my peers would say, "Don't do it!" If you grew up in a Christian home a generation or so ago, you know what I mean. At home, at church, in school — just about everywhere you went — your society reinforced what you had been taught about sex.

But that's no longer true. Young people growing up today

may hear their pastor say, "It's sin; don't do it!" if he says anything at all. They may hear their Christian parents say, if they say anything at all, "It's sin; don't do it!" BUT they turn on television, and *everybody's doing it!* They turn on their music and hear, "Let's do it!" They go to school and hear, "We're setting up clinics for you, to make sex safe." They talk to their friends and hear, "We're doing it, and it's great!"

A Time of Transition

We live in an unusual period in Western civilization. We're going through a transition between two cultures. Most of us who are parents today grew up at a time when Judeo-Christian values and morals were strongly promoted, especially in the area of sex. We lived in a culture that derived its sexual mores from the Old (Judeo) and New (Christian) Testaments.

Our young people for the most part are growing up in a post-Judeo-Christian culture. The sexual mores of this culture are derived from secular humanism which teaches, (at best) that you follow "situational ethics." That is, one's subjective interpretation of the circumstances dictates what is right or wrong. Or (at worst) it teaches: "There is no right or wrong!"

Here's the problem. We now have those two cultures within the same household. Twenty years ago that was not true. Then we had only one culture; parents were living in the same culture as the teens. Today in one household we have parents who are still living in a Judeo-Christian culture; in the same household we have young people who are living in the post-Judeo-Christian culture. And there's little or no communication between the two. In most cases, parents treat their young people as if they are living in the same culture. It's not a generation gap, it's a cultural gap.

In a culture where Judeo-Christian values have been almost totally forsaken, those pastors and parents who tell their children that premarital sex is sin and that they should wait for marriage are seen by teens as either "spoil-sport villains" or "out-and-out fools."

As Christian pastors and parents, we are in the minority. A recent poll indicated that 75 percent of Canadian adults believe premarital sex to be acceptable. 104/53 Because that Judeo-Christian framework no longer prevails in the world beyond our homes, we can no longer guide our young people in the area of sex by simply saying, "It's sinful; don't do it!" or, "It's wrong; don't do it!" We can't do that anymore and expect it to work.

Communication Needs

Before you accuse me of "watering down my message," listen to my reasons. Differences always exist between generations which make intercommunication difficult. But today, when teens actually live in two cultures at the same time, communication may be close to impossible — particularly if parents are unaware that two cultures exist.

How can we adults ever understand how different things are for young people today from what they were when we grew up? At home and at church their environment may be similar, but at school, with their friends, and when they watch and listen to media, it's a totally different world. Different languages are spoken. Words even have different meanings. No one is more vulnerable than Christian teenagers who live on the "cutting edge" between the parallel cultures.

What can Christian leaders do? On the one hand, we need to help Christian parents. The family that holds to Judeo-Christian values needs all the help it can get to strengthen the faith and morality of its children. During this difficult and risky time, struggling parents desperately need the church's support.

The church should provide not only wholesome activities but clear teaching to counterbalance the totally un-Christian emphases our young people are exposed to every day. We need to do more for our church young people than "socialize" them. Our purpose in church should be more than just giving them some place to go on Sunday or Friday nights. I agree with Tony Campolo that we must give teens something worth living and dying for.

What can we do as parents? I think we can bridge this cultural gap by giving our children a lot more of our time and attention.

Inattentive Parents

I held a one week youth conference at the largest (and one of the wealthiest) evangelical churches in our country. I had counseling appointments with forty-two junior and senior high school students. Their number one question was "Josh, what can I do about my dad?" When I asked what they meant, they made statements like "He never has time for me." "He never takes me anywhere." "He never talks to me." "He never does anything with me."

I asked all forty-two of them, "Can you talk with your father?" Only one said yes.

I also asked all the girls, "If you got pregnant, could you go right to your father and share this with him?" Most of them didn't feel they could. That's heartbreaking, isn't it? If there ever is a time when a young woman ought to be able to go to her father and talk to him, it is in a situation like that.

I often am asked to give one single reason why youth are where they are today. Of course I always reply that there are innumerable reasons for teen pregnancy, suicide and the other symptoms of the "self-hurt" that afflicts young people today. However, if I had to narrow the reasons down to just one, it would be this: *inattentive parents.*

Parental inattentiveness creates a "love famine" that affects both parents and children. It also creates a vicious self-perpetuating cycle in which parents who are starved for love raise children who are even hungrier for love. The results are devastating.

Fathers

A study was made of 1,337 medical doctors who graduated from Johns Hopkins between 1948 and 1964. The purpose of the study was to find out if there were any common causal factors for hypertension, coronary heart disease, malignant tumors, mental illness and suicide. Only one common factor was found, and it was this: lack of closeness to parents. 262/48-54 If you do not have a close relationship with your parents, you have a much higher probability of being susceptible to those things listed. Why? All of those conditions are related to stress. And young persons who have a close relationship with their parents, especially with their fathers, can handle stress much better than those who don't.

A study of thirty-nine teenage girls who were suffering from the eating disorder anorexia nervosa showed that thirty-six of them lacked close relationships with their fathers. 263/D5

Johns Hopkins University researchers found that "young, white, teenage girls living in fatherless families . . . were 60 percent more likely to have had intercourse than those living in two-parent homes." 38/60

Perhaps some of you fathers are feeling that I'm being unfair. "I thought you said the problem was inattentive *parents.* You seem to be focusing only on fathers. What about inattentive *mothers?"*

Of course there are inattentive mothers and they undoubtedly have a damaging effect on their children. But I think that we men must shoulder much of the blame for our teens being where they are. Most of us are very busy. We are gone from home a lot because of our jobs. When we come home tired, it is easy to neglect our children. What we men need to realize is how important it is to our children that we have a close, loving relationship with them. Sure, mothers are important, but they can't do the job of loving our children alone.

One reason divorce is so damaging to young people, is that it generally removes fathers from day-to-day contact with their children. Today men spend much less time in the home than they did in past generations, either because of heavy workloads, or because of divorce.

Mothers

Ninety percent of the children of divorce live with their mothers. By the time a child today is eighteen, the odds are that he or she will have spent some part of life living with the mother alone. Single and divorced women now head almost one-fifth of all American homes. 264 In almost every case, divorce means a fatherless home. One-half of the children with divorced parents *do not* see their fathers regularly. This situation is not expected to improve.

By 1990 the number of children living with single mothers is expected to increase by 57 percent. Three out of five children born today will live with a single parent by age eighteen.

Also, the role of the mother has changed in ways that make it much more difficult for her to be attentive to her children. When my friends Charlotte and Dick got married, more than 70 percent of all American families had full-time stay-at-home mothers. Today almost 90 percent of families are two-income families, with both husband and wife working outside the home. The full-time mother and stay-at-home housewife are now virtually nonexistent. More than half of the children in this country are being raised by working women who struggle with two full-time jobs, as wage earners and as mothers.

It is little wonder that more than half of the teens in a recent adolescent-parent study "spend less than thirty minutes a day with their fathers; and 44 percent spend less than thirty minutes with their mothers." Now that's not time spent in meaningful dialogue. That's simply the amount of time in which they share the same "space." Most parents spend more time every day watching TV news. Even more alarming, "one-fourth of the ninth graders in this study spend less than five minutes (in an average day) alone with father to talk, play, or just be together." 107/79

Peers

Also, parents today spend more time with other adults than with their children. According to University of Chicago sociologist

James S. Coleman, "Parents are much more involved, socially, with people their own age than they used to be. The result has been a tendency to leave their children alone, to let them be as free as possible as soon as they seem old enough. And that, of course, can leave some children lonely." To fill the vacuum, Coleman believes that some teenagers turn with even greater intensity than they otherwise would to their peers. "Adolescents have a special need for close and intimate relationships with one or more other persons, and that need is being filled by families much less than it used to be." 38/60

Peer pressure obviously has strong influence on young people, but peer pressure is far less influential in the lives of teens who have a close relationship with their parents.

What happens when parents pay little or no attention to their children? What happens when adult role models are gone or absent from the home? Our Judeo-Christian values are not communicated effectively, if at all. Children and young people are left starved for love.

An essay written by a young woman in her twenties illustrates the critical importance of parental love and attention:

> When I was fourteen, I dated an eighteen-year-old boy. After a month or so of dating he told me that he loved me and had to have me. He said if I loved him I would have sex with him. And if I wouldn't, he would have to break up with me. What did I think at fourteen years of age? I knew sex was wrong before marriage, yet I so desired to have a man love me.
>
> I was so insecure about my father's love; I always felt like I had to earn it. The better I was at home with my chores, the more my father loved me. The more A's on my report card, the more my father loved me.
>
> So here's my boyfriend, whom I really liked and thought I loved, telling me he loved me. Well, I needed that love. And if the conditions to keep that love were to have sex with him, I felt I had no choice. I didn't want to lose my virginity, but I also didn't want to lose the man who loved me. So I finally gave in.
>
> After two years I broke up with my boyfriend, and soon had another and went through the same cycle with him, and then another, and another. Was I more secure? No. I was a puppet in the hands of any man who said "I love you." I wanted so desperately to find someone who would love me unconditionally. Isn't that ironic, the main thing I searched for, unconditional love, was being offered to me conditionally? "If you love me you'll have sex with me."
>
> At the age of twenty-one I found that unconditional love . . .

This young woman found Jesus Christ, who accepted her just as she was. She ended her essay with an entry from her personal diary. In it we see the inner self of a beautiful human being who has suffered immeasurably in her search for her father's love:

> I felt lonely tonight, and I thought about the many times in my life that I have felt lonely . . . intense loneliness, as though I were here in life all alone. And I realized that what I was lonely for was a daddy, to be able to call him up when I hurt, have him listen to me, hear him say he understands. But I never had that with my dad, so I'm lonely without that link to my past.
>
> Yet tonight God spoke to me in that still, quiet way and said He was there for me. As my tears poured, I said, "Will You be my daddy? Will You be there to talk to . . . just to talk to? And will You listen? Yes, I know You will. And the most wonderful thing about You as my daddy is that I can be with You all the time."
>
> Then I thought about the girl who this very night will lose her virginity because she is searching for her daddy's love. And I want to be able to stop her somehow and tell her that she'll never find it in another man.
>
> How my heart is wrenched when I think of this girl . . . when I think of myself, so many years ago. My life has been a search for my daddy's love. *And in Jesus, I am found and I am loved. Forever.* August 11, 1985

The Need for Love

Several years ago Marvin Gaye, forty-four-year-old rock artist — a man who made and lost millions, whose recordings were number two in sales with Motown Records — was shot and killed by his father. The courts declared it a justifiable homicide. Gaye never felt that his father appreciated his accomplishments. He had said often to his friend Curtis Shaw, "I wish I had my father's love." 265/D1-2

Many young people are uncertain of their parents' love. When several thousand high school students were asked what single question they would like their parents to answer, 50 percent answered that they wanted to know *if their parents loved them.* 61/43 I personally know many parents who definitely love their children, but whose actions don't always show it.

Here again I think that fathers often are the worst offenders. One reason is that men have real problems with showing their emotions. Some men even hide any tender feelings they might have by pretending to be cynical about love. They are uncomfortable with any serious discussion of love. And those who can't talk about love usually have difficulty expressing it. I really believe that lots of hugs between fathers and teen daughters could do more to stop the teen pregnancy epidemic than any other single factor.

Where teenage pregnancy is concerned, the only foolproof

solution is prevention. This begins with parents spending time with their children long before hormones, peers and the media begin pressuring them about sex.

A teenager writes:

> When I was eight years old I first had sex with a boy of fifteen. I did it because I lack love and attention from my parents. I need love, and my parents never show me any. Nothing really changed at home, and at fifteen I became pregnant. My boyfriend blamed me and left. I had nowhere to turn, I was trapped, so I had an abortion. Now I'm afraid to date anyone, and I cry myself to sleep every night. 63/5

Parents, your children (whatever their age) are hungry for your love and attention. Give it to them. Spend time with them. Love them — with words and with actions.

6

WHAT TEENS REALLY WANT

A Happy Home Life

Do you know what today's lower-age teens (13-15 years) really want? Their number-one desire is for a happy home life. Not success in college; not success in business or career. Interestingly, teen boys today want this even more than teen girls. 258

More emphasis on closer family ties is desired by 86 percent of teens, with only slightly greater emphasis on this value noted among young women (90 percent) than among young men (82 percent). Is it surprising then that 75 percent of the surveyed teenagers felt that it is too easy to get a divorce in this country? Of teens from divorced homes, 74 percent said that their parents didn't try hard enough. A research institute study showed that out of a list of twenty-four values, the two most important to young adolescents in grades five through nine are "To have a happy family life" and "to get a good job when I am older."

When divorcing parents ask their children, "Do you want us to continue our painful relationship for your sake?" the answer is almost universally "Yes, we do!" Young people today want to be part of a loving, lasting relationship.

Lasting Relationships

One of the greatest securities of a child comes from the love of the parents for each other. When Sean asked if I was going to leave his mother, he wasn't looking for reinforcement of my love for him. He wanted the security of knowing that I was committed to and would stay in love with his mother.

Young people today are longing for relationships that will last. They are crying out for role-models of men and women who have it together — in love, marriage, sex and family. They are desperately looking for relationships that work. One of the greatest things parents can do for their children is to love one another and let their children know it.

However, although young people today may want lasting relationships, they are seldom successful in finding them. It is one thing to desire something and another thing to know how to get it. Without the right role models, children not only don't learn how to have positive relationships, but also they actually learn how to have negative relationships. Jesus said that a student is not greater than his teacher, but is like his teacher (Luke 6:40). In other words, "Like begets like."

Affection

According to a *Seventeen* magazine survey, most girls opt for affection over sex. "Nearly two-thirds feel strongly that affection is much more important than sex in a relationship and another 29 percent agree somewhat. In fact only 1.1 percent assert that sex is more important." 67/107

"And most teenagers (67 percent) feel that sexual intercourse is less important than dating and friendship. They like to spend time with someone who is easy to be with and in whom they can confide." 259/B5

After my last speaking tour in England, a student wrote me a letter in which she said, "I just want someone to love me (not physically)." Then she made a statement which I think communicates where most young people are today, not just in our western culture, but around the world. "I want someone who cares. I want to love and I want to be loved, *but I don't know how to do either.*"

James Toussieng observes that the "high divorce rates result in many single-parent homes and a lack of supervision. Young people are left alone with rising sexual impulses. *They are starved for affection, and they turn to each other and they don't know better than to have sex.*" 43/1-2

"We are all running around needing to get hugged . . . the

dilemma for some . . . is that 'if I want to be touched, if I want to be held, I have to have sex.' " 26/1-2 Robert Olson, health educator with the Department of Public Health, has said that "many pregnant teens say wanting 'a man to hold me' was their motivation rather than having sexual relations with someone." 26/1-2

In an article on teenage virginity, Eric Zorn of the *Denver Post* observed, "Kids want closeness and acceptance, and they've been skipping over the emotional and the intellectual to try sex. I tell them they should develop friendships and other ways of closeness first because sex will be a whole lot better if they wait until then." 23/28

Intimacy

"Mr. McDowell, in the last five nights I've gone to bed with five different men." The young university woman had called me long-distance. "Tonight," she said, "I got out of bed and asked myself, is that all there is?"

Then she began crying. When she regained her composure enough to speak, she said, "Please tell me there's something more."

I said, "There certainly is. It's called intimacy."

What is intimacy? A fifteen-year-old girl once described intimacy as "a place where it's safe to be real."

A recent survey of 300 women ages eighteen to sixty found that women of all ages want men with whom they can be close. "They want intimacy, which is more than just love and sex," according to psychologist Lois Leiderman Davidz of Columbia University. 252/D1

Shere Hite discovered that "most women interviewed enjoyed hugging, kissing, cuddling, closeness and conversation as much as intercourse. Overall, intimacy was more important than orgasm." 110/30-31

Several years ago I took part in a three-hour television debate with Anson Mount, co-author of the so-called "playboy philosophy." About the only area in which Anson and I agreed was my contention that "in the last twenty or so years we have not gone through a sexual revolution, but rather a revolution in our search for intimacy." Most young people today do not want sex nearly as much as they want intimacy, a close and caring relationship.

Regarding teenage sexual involvement, Surgeon General Koop observes that teens "are not so much seeking a sexual experience as they are to establish intimacy with somebody who respects them as an individual. I think one of the sad things that has happened in our culture is that with two working parents, and youngsters starting off as latch-key kids and then growing up into adolescence and being very much on their own, they lack the intimacy that they used to have with their parents and so they seek it someplace else. They mistake it for sex so when they are given the opportunity, they say this is what I have been looking for." 208

In a research study where teenagers were asked to select from a list of twenty items the six most important to them, their first choice (67 percent) was a *close, intimate relationship* with someone of the opposite sex. In most cases sex was the last item selected.

False Intimacy

Our main problem today is not sexual. It's relational. We have embarked on a false quest for intimacy, because we haven't understood what real intimacy is all about. We have allowed our culture to dictate to us that the only way you can find intimacy is through the physical. I am personally convinced that most young people use sex as a means of achieving intimacy. They don't want sex as much as they want closeness with another human being. The tragedy is that people are jumping from one bed to another in their search for intimacy. At best they find a sense of caring for the short duration of an orgasm. Then they are left feeling worse than they felt before. "Another letdown . . . but I'll just have to try again."

Today we see people getting involved in sexual activity, often promiscuous sexual activity, for the simple reason that they don't understand what true intimacy is. Sexual experience becomes a substitute for intimacy. We use phrases like "making love" and "being intimate" in talking about sexual intercourse. Yet most sexual involvements, outside the loving commitment of marriage, express very little genuine love or closeness.

Not only do many people misunderstand what real intimacy is, but they are afraid of it. Existential psychologist Rollo May has said, "There is so much use of the body as a substitute for psychological intimacy. It's much easier to jump into bed with somebody than it is to share your fears, your anxieties, your hopes . . . all that goes on in your psychological life. Because the body is used as kind of a buffer, the intimacy gets short circuited and never becomes real intimacy." 303/56

Why do people fear intimacy? Because intimacy inevitably brings vulnerability. Emotional sharing requires self-disclosure, and for many of us the idea of opening up our innermost selves is a scary prospect. Many young people repeatedly share their bodies because they are afraid to share themselves. They participate in countless "one-night stands" because they are afraid to be vulnerable.

Real Intimacy

Real intimacy is the result of letting another person see who you are. But if you don't feel good about yourself and your identity, you will keep yourself hidden and never achieve intimacy. Only a person with a relatively good sense of security and identity can fully enter into the experience of intimacy.

We can never enjoy the full potential richness of a meaningful relationship — for which we were created — without becoming intimate with at least one other person. Again, I am speaking primarily about psychological and spiritual intimacy — which is the result of being open and transparent. It is more a matter of communication and sharing than of any kind of grand passion. When two people confide in each other about their innermost dreams, hopes and thoughts, they are "being intimate." True intimacy involves being able to remove all the masks and disguises we hide behind, without fear of rejection, and be known and loved for ourselves.

Listen to this personal account of one young person's search for intimacy:

> I used to search for intimacy through latching on to a "special someone," because I felt that as long as I had *his* love and approval everything would be OK. Yet, there was usually a high price tag . . . the giving of my body. The penalty I paid was that of feeling cheap, used and guilty. I began to wonder if there would ever be someone who would love and accept me without demanding that I . . . do something to earn that love.
>
> Then, I learned of the unconditional love that God has for me and made a decision to ask Jesus Christ to come into my life . . . and teach me what true love is all about. I can say with certainty that He has made a difference! Instead of feeling cheap, used and guilty, I now know that I am valuable, forgiven . . . and have a new life that began the moment I asked Christ into my life. Because I have experienced an intimate love relationship with God first, I am now able to develop lasting, meaningful relationships with those around me. I also know that when I do marry and can enjoy sex in its proper context, my sex life won't be mediocre, but will be excellent because that's what God desires for those who choose Him: excellence in all areas of their lives!

For young people, or anyone, the first step to real intimacy is a life-changing relationship with Jesus Christ.

PART 2

REASONS YOUTH HAVE PREMARITAL SEX

INTRODUCTION

It has been said that the typical high school student "faces more sexual temptation on his way to school each morning than his grandfather did on Saturday night when he was out looking for it!" 244/18

Times have changed significantly since today's parents were growing up. Not only has sex become blatant, but it is encouraged in almost every segment of society.

What surprised this book's authors, and I'm sure will startle you, are the multitude of reasons people enter into premarital sex. The reasons listed and explained in this section initially came from entries in an essay contest called "Write Your Heart Out." One question teens wrote about was, Why do people in your age group become sexually involved? We chose the reasons to be included here based on (1) the number of young people writing on each one and (2) further research to determine the validity of each reason given.

The reasons for premarital sex portrayed in this book have been broken down into various categories for a number of reasons. It helps us understand that not all people are sexually active for the same reason; it helps us differentiate between motives that appear similar on the surface but may have diverse origins; it helps us deal with each cause individually instead of giving general answers; and, for the purposes of this book, it gives us a reference volume we can turn to when we encounter a specific problem.

People, however, don't fit into precise categories. Separating the reasons for premarital sex lets us identify individual problems — but each sexually active teen may have two or three reasons he (or she) has allowed this to be a part of life. It complicates matters, of course, but we live complicated lives.

To muddy the waters further, a teenager may have no clear idea why he is sexually active. Many of the reasons for premarital sex listed here have come from people who took time to analyze both themselves and their culture, something not all teens (let alone adults) have done.

Some of the most revealing reasons came from people in their twenties who were looking back. They have the advantage of time in their analyses. They are better able to look objectively at a tumultuous period in their lives, to see how and why they acted as they did and to see the results of those actions.

As you read this section we trust you will (1) be moved by the tremendous pressures society puts on our teens to be sexually active, and (2) realize that the pressures and causes of teenage sexual activity are both profound and extensive. Today's teenagers desperately need our help and love. Many of the pressures for their premarital sexual involvement seem so right to them, when in reality the consequences are devastating. "There is a way that seems right to a man but in the end it leads to death" (Proverbs 14:12, NIV). What is intriguing is not that the way leads to death, but rather that it "seems so right."

To make an intelligent decision about involvement in premarital sex, teens need to be aware of the specific pressures on them to be sexually active as well as all the risks inherent in that involvement.

7

PHYSICAL REASONS

1. You Always Want More

The law of diminishing returns tells us that when something ceases to accomplish what we want it to accomplish, we search for more. In the case of sex, it means that something which previously brought pleasure (for example, kissing) will eventually lose its glamor. More physical activity will be needed to reach the same level of pleasure.

In their own words:

Another reason for premarital sex is that "nothing else is left." Alan and Susie went on their first date. They were both shy. As the night went on, they felt more comfortable and they held hands. At the end of the date, Alan gave Susie a short goodnight kiss. The next date, one kiss was not enough. Alan kissed Susie continuously for several minutes. Eventually, that was no longer satisfying.

French kissing entered the scene, then bodily caressing and then heavy petting. Before Alan and Susie knew what had happened, they had gone too far because there was nothing left to satisfy their desires. Their lives were ruined and there was no turning back.

♡ ♡ ♡

The progression of a physical relationship is as follows: holding hands, hugging, kissing, French kissing, petting and finally inter-course. It is like drugs and alcohol; you need a little more each time to get a bigger high.

♡ ♡ ♡

That satisfied him that night, but with each date his requests became more convincing. After all, we did love each other. Within two months I gave in, because I had justified the whole thing. Over the next six months, sex became the center of our relationship. Like a cancer, it just took over. At that same time, some new things entered our relationship, things like anger, impatience, jealousy and selfishness. We just couldn't talk any more. We grew very bored with each other and I desperately wanted a change, so I broke up with him.

♡ ♡ ♡

Could another cause be that feelings and relationships move and change so quickly that kids don't know where they're headed until it's too late? Are they, in effect, wading out into such deep water that they drown? That happened to a girl I know; she became involved before she realized what was happening.

♡ ♡ ♡

We were in love. The commitment made. Ring bought. Date set. Gown ordered. Attendants fitted. Reception planned. Invitations addressed. Showers given. Apartment rented.

That was the first mistake, renting the apartment before the wedding. It was no longer my parents' basement or his car. The apartment was ours. We combined hand-me-downs from each side of the family with special pieces of our own. It was now our future home together and mine to care for in the meantime.

The privacy was more than we could handle. Hand-holding turned into embraces. Kisses found their way down the neck. No longer could we just sit in the same room; we had to be next to each other, embraced in each others arms. Hands began to wander up and down the back. Hugs involved the entire body. His excite-ment was obvious and my pleasure verbal.

I don't know what I felt or what I was thinking. I guess our being married shortly was the easiest rationalization. After all, marriage is a commitment, not a ceremony. Or maybe because, clinically, virginity has to do with the actual culminated sex act. Since that never happened, all the other acts of foreplay seemed harmless. But whatever the reason, night after night we engaged in physical foreplay, but not the emotional "lovemaking" needed for a strong marriage.

Then something happened. I don't know quite when, just that it did. The arguments started. We'd yell for a while and then kiss and "make out," but that solved nothing. We saw each other in a different light. When he saw my fears and insecurities, he tried to cover them with authority and knowledge.

Soon, in tears, the ring came off. The wedding plans waned. Then finally the announcement, first to my parents, then to close friends. The news spread by itself. Gifts were returned. Invitations destroyed. Plans and reservations cancelled. The gown prepared for storage. The rings returned. The commitment shattered.

Have I hurt any future relationship by experiencing with one man what will never be the same with any other? Maybe if we would have prayed more, maybe if we hadn't been so afraid, maybe if we would have loved each other more than we loved ourselves, maybe if we could have said no to our desires, maybe if the apartment hadn't been rented . . .

♡ ♡ ♡

Some people have sex because they have a weak body and mind. They don't have the willpower to say no. Once they start kissing and petting, they can't stop themselves.

♡ ♡ ♡

1 Corinthians 7:9 sheds yet another light on premarital sex: "If they do not have self-control, let them marry, for it is better to marry than to burn" (NASB). This Scripture indicates to me that premarital sex is not so much an exercise of personal freedom as a lack of self-control.

♡ ♡ ♡

I felt the same pressure to have sex when I was dating Mike. My folks stressed good morals and values all my life. I knew right from wrong, so it wasn't too difficult to do what was right. At least until I had gone out with Mike for two years.

Mike and I had really gotten to know one another well by then and realized we were in love. I remember one night, though, when he started "using his hands." I was really embarrassed, but I enjoyed it too.

After that date, things kept progressing. One night Mike told me he wanted to show how much he loved me by making love to me. I couldn't believe it! I remember just sitting on the couch, silent for a couple of minutes. I was shocked; I wouldn't even consider it. I realized that what he wanted to do was definitely morally wrong. I told him I just couldn't give in like that and disappoint my parents.

———————— ♥ ————————

The law of diminishing returns confronts a teenager with a basic question: How far is too far? You have gone too far the moment you cannot righteously satisfy the arousal.

In other words, when you create in someone a desire you cannot righteously fulfill, you have gone too far. If a man creates within a woman who is not his wife a desire for sex, he has defrauded her. He has violated her person. Not being her husband, he cannot satisfy those desires within God's righteousness.

When the diminished returns of kissing and hugging fail to bring physical satisfaction, a person may try to set the other person up, as in the situations above. A girl meeting resistance from her boyfriend may try to arouse him to the point where he stops resisting. She may achieve her momentary goal, but she has taken advantage of him, and she will not settle for less than the new plateau the next time.

1 Thessalonians 4:3-6 tells us,

It is God's will that you should be holy; that you should avoid sexual immorality; that each of you should learn to control his own body in a way that is holy and honorable, not in passionate lust like the heathen, who do not know God; and that in this matter no one should wrong his brother or take advantage of him. (NIV)

To build mutual trust into a relationship, both sides must be honest. If, for example, a girl finds holding hands to be physically exciting, she should tell her boyfriend truthfully that she does not want to do that. If both are truly interested in maintaining God's standards, and if they truly care for each other, he will respect her wishes and will not intentionally try to arouse her by holding her hand. If he does, he is manipulating her, and trust in the relationship is damaged.

Along the same lines, it is important to remember that we each come from a different home environment and are at different levels of emotional maturity. If one family hugs a great deal, the children of that family may hug others without a second thought. But people from families with limited physical contact may find a hug to be stimulating.

The law of diminishing returns must be broken from the start. If a hug brings you pleasure and so you hug more and more, be assured you will eventually want more. (This even applies to the abundance of hugging found in some churches. Much of it is done for the feeling of the physical contact, not for any other reason. If you ever wonder about your own motives, remember this: When in doubt, do without.) If holding hands gets your motor running, don't hold hands. You are voluntarily starting up the ladder of increasing physical contact, a ladder that is leaning against a blank wall. Because you will not find the satisfaction you are looking for apart from marriage, fanning the flames doesn't make sense.

2. Early Dating

Early dating may lead to early sex, according to research done by Brent C. Miller of Utah State University and Terrence D. Olsen of Brigham Young University. Among 2,400 teens the findings were:

The younger a girl begins to date, the more likely she is to have sex before graduating from high school. It is also true of girls and boys who go steady in the ninth grade. Of girls who begin dating at twelve, 91 percent had sex before graduation — compared to 56 percent who dated at thirteen, 53 percent who dated at fourteen, 40 percent who dated at fifteen, and 20 percent who dated at sixteen. Of boys with a ninth-grade steady, 70 percent said that they'd had sex compared to 60 percent of girls. Of boys who dated occasionally as freshmen, 52 percent had sex compared to 35 percent of girls.

Also, more teens of "not very" or "very" strict parents had sex than those with "moderately" strict parents. We can see the effect of early dating as well as of autocratic parents who are not relating to their children, only controlling them. 201/D1

The accompanying chart will help you visualize the impact of early dating in the life of a teen.

Age of Dating	% Who Have Sex Before Graduation
12 years	91%
13 years	56%
14 years	53%
15 years	40%
16 years	20%

3. It's the Natural Thing to Do

In their own words:

To my friends, premarital sex seemed a very natural thing to do, even more so than remaining celibate.

♡ ♡ ♡

The main force driving people my age to premarital sex is the view of society that sex is only natural. In this kind of atmosphere, people don't see the need to hold out until they are married.

———————— ♥ ————————

Sex was not intended to be mere physical interaction, but rather an expression of permanently committed love. We are not animals who respond without thinking to primal urges. We are rational beings, created in the image of God, having the dignity, worth and importance He gave us. We are not bound to the call of nature.

Love is not just a feeling. Love is primarily an act of the will, a choice to make the welfare and happiness of another individual more important than our own. And since sex is an act of love, not a primal response, our most important sex organ is not found below the belt; it is the *mind.* It is here we make decisions.

The brain takes in information, sifts through it, accepts some elements, rejects others and arrives at conclusions. It is in the brain, not in some primitive instinct, that the choice is made to pursue sex or not to pursue sex. Therefore, to claim that sex is only natural is to deny our ability to make choices.

Sex is not so much a drive as a desire, since it is conditional. We can say no. We are not at the mercy of our sexual urges.

When we fill our minds with ungodly thoughts about sex, our decisions are going to reflect those thoughts. The phrase used by computer programmers, "Garbage in, garbage out," is tossed around a lot, but it is especially true in the area of sex. When we give in to the societal mindset that sex is merely an act of nature, and saturate our thoughts with fantasies of instant sexual gratification, we encourage the desire for sex to extreme degrees. We become addicted to our thoughts.

If sex without marriage is natural, then so is AIDS. So is emotional insecurity. So is a shattered self-image. So is divorce caused by infidelity. So are manipulation and psychological abuse. So are using and debasing other persons for personal gratification. These things walk hand in hand with premarital and extramarital sex and must be measured by the same standard. If they are not natural, then sex without marriage (and the ramifications of marriage) is really unnatural and wrong, and the biblical standard is right.

Since we have minds, we can decide for ourselves which is natural. All we have to do is weigh the evidence.

4. It Feels Good

In their own words:

To most kids sex is really nothing, so they go ahead and have it just because they like it.

♡ ♡ ♡

Another argument that no Christian young person should get caught up in is one I bought into without any excuse, that of situational ethics. A recent popular song has the enchanting words, "It can't be wrong when it feels so right." I fell for that argument even though I knew better. If right and wrong are based on our feelings, it would be right to strike out at or even murder another person in a fit of rage — for such behavior would be consistent with the emotion. Emotions are a beautiful gift given us by our Maker, but they are never meant to determine our judgments and set the boundaries of our values. We are given the Word of God to set the standard and to form our convictions as Christians (2 Timothy 3:16). It's a dangerous thing to let your emotions make your decisions in a romantic setting, because they will guide you astray. Wait, and see if the feeling will last. Then it will be right and blessed by the one who gave us the gift of sexual expression.

♡ ♡ ♡

No one can deny the fact that sex is enjoyable whether it is premarital or not. God designed the human body to enjoy sex; if it were not fun, people would not do it. I used to know a guy who had sex many times and saw nothing wrong with it. One day I asked him what he did that weekend, and he said he had a girl over for the weekend. I asked if his mom knew, and he said no, she was out of town. I then asked if he saw anything wrong with what he did. He said, "No, if it feels good, do it."

♡ ♡ ♡

Where I live, many of my girl friends and guy friends are involved in sex because they just want to do it. When I ask them why, they usually say it makes them feel good, although some say they do it because their friends are doing it.

───────── ♥ ─────────

Many teens today are saying, "I want what is real and relevant, and I want it right now." Let's face it, if sex weren't enjoyable before marriage, it wouldn't be after — your body doesn't know if you're married or not. Sex isn't something magical so that at some point in the future, when you get married, sky rockets will start.

A study on *Sex and the American Teenager* showed that when asked "what effect their first intercourse had on the relationship encompassing it, only 12 percent of boys and 15 percent of girls said the relationship had become worse as a result, whereas 44 percent of the boys and a whooping 63 percent of the girls said it had become better." 45/81

The same study indicated that when asked "How much do you enjoy intercourse? 53 percent of the boys and 45 percent of the girls answered, 'A great deal.' " 45/85

To understand how "feeling good" can override values one may hold about sex and prompt one to premarital sexual activity, we need to look at our search for pleasure in a larger context.

We live in a fallen world which causes us to go through life with a great deal of pain. Rather than sit and suffer, we try to alleviate that pain. The Bible points out repeatedly that we always have two choices in dealing with problems: the wrong way and the right way; the world's way and God's way; the irrational way and the rational way; the illegitimate way and the legitimate way. Ephesians 5:18 verifies that we have two choices by instructing us: "Do not get drunk with wine . . . but be filled with the Spirit" (NASB).

God in His great commandment says we should love Him and love our neighbors as we love ourselves. But note that only two of those are commanded: love of God and love of neighbor. God doesn't have to tell us to love ourselves, because we do that anyway. Even people who feel they don't like themselves still love themselves. We know that's true because at any given moment they are looking out for their own best interests, their own safety, their own security, their own happiness.

Man in his fallen state does not love God. Some of us will respond to God's love in the course of our lives, but it is a struggle to maintain a loving relationship with Him because we are so busy loving ourselves. The same holds true for our love for our neighbor.

In this endless love for ourselves we seek out pleasure to deaden the pain of life. Again, this self-love is manifested either rationally according to truth or irrationally, according to non-truth.

Because we are a part of a fallen world, we automatically love ourselves irrationally. We don't see ourselves as God sees us. Without God's infallible standard by which to measure ourselves, we make up our own definitions of self-love. We settle for a subjective rather than absolute standard of love.

In our quest to meet the basic needs of life, we can either turn to God or turn from Him. Those are the choices.

One of our God-given desires is the need for intimacy. Genesis 2 tells how man was created to be intimate with other human beings, not just with God. We feel pain when that desire for intimacy is not met.

Our love for ourselves tells us to alleviate the emotional pain caused by lack of intimacy. When we seek to do that, we either follow God's truth, which is rational and absolute, or we turn from God's truth to something irrational, subjective and fleeting.

Instead of going to the Holy Spirit, we often go to our five senses. This irrational attempt to ease emotional pain with physical feelings is like breaking your arm, and then taking pain killers instead of going to the hospital. The pills do block out the pain for a while, but when they wear off, your arm is still broken. You used the wrong treatment.

Just as pills deaden real physical pain, sensory feelings can deaden emotional pain. For many people, sex is the drug that momentarily delivers them from emotional emptiness. It feels good.

Our culture calls for a vending-machine approach to alleviating emotional pain. We need acceptance, but we feel the pain of rejection so we become angry and violent. A husband throws his wife against the wall because, at that moment, it feels good to him.

We need personal fulfillment and satisfaction, but we come up empty so we drown ourselves in materialism and drugs. He buys another sportcoat he'll never wear. She scores another week's worth of cocaine and snorts another line because it feels good right then.

We can neither find nor offer the intimacy we desperately seek, so we turn to a whirlwind of sexual activity. The letdown, the deepening pain, the fear, the uncertainty, will all come later, but for now it feels good.

"It feels good" could be tacked onto most of the headlines in the newspaper:

> Half of All Athletes on Drugs — It Feels Good
> Arsonist Sets Hotel Ablaze — It Felt Good
> Protesters Clash With Police — It Felt Good
> Student Date-Rapes Coed — It Felt Good

The things you desire at the moment may seem good and pleasurable, but the consequences are just the opposite.

What if:

1. You are very angry with your dad and your feelings say, "Punch him out"?

2. You are depressed over a situation and your feelings say, "Go ahead, end it all"?

3. You are sexually aroused and your feelings say, "Go for it"?

The above examples are momentary emotions. They will pass in time. They *cannot tell you if they are right or wrong* or if the action suggested is the best thing for you. Rational thinking must take over and foresee results of taking such action.

If you:

1. Punch your dad, you will be punished.

2. End it all, you will be dead.

3. Go for it, you face many consequences that your feelings

could never dream of.

So, our momentary feelings cannot be trusted to give us the whole picture.

Ernest Hemingway said, "What is moral is what you feel good after, and what is immoral is what you feel bad after." 302/317-318 The question is, How long after? An hour? A day? A week? A year? Is it *moral* at the feelings of the orgasm and *immoral* when you learn you have herpes? Also, one partner's pleasure can be another's misery. Is it moral for a guy as he walks away feeling like a "man," and immoral for the girl who discovers she's pregnant and decides to abort? Is it moral for a man who feels so good and macho after raping a girl? What about the girl? "If it feels good, do it," means that you fulfill your passions immediately, and usually at the expense of another person's welfare or happiness.

Turning from God's solutions leaves us with only our own. Why do we do it? Because it feels good. It's an answer, for the moment, even if it isn't the right one.

Proverbs 20:17 states a timeless truth: "Food gained by fraud tastes sweet to a man, but he ends up with a mouth full of gravel" (NIV).

5. It Provides a Thrill

In their own words:

Teenagers are bored. Technology has provided them with so much passive entertainment — television, video games, etc. — that the ordinary, God-given, wholesome things in life have no meaning. LIFE is boring! No thrills, no challenges . . . so . . . create your own thrills!

♡ ♡ ♡

Sex is a cheap thrill. Having sex is one date that costs very little money and can be done almost anywhere. Life is empty anyway, so "go for it!"

———————— ♥ ————————

The problem with a thrill is that you have to come down. Boredom doesn't stay away after sex. It keeps coming back.

There are thrills and then there are *thrills!* Compare the following thrills:

A. He picks her up in his mom's car, they drive out to a secluded spot, and have sex. They think the spot is secluded, but they freeze up whenever they see headlights. A quick thrill, then it's done. Later, they go home, she to her house, he to his house. He's pretty sure she was on the pill or something, but he's not really at ease. He hopes she won't start calling him all the time now. She is home, trying to prove to herself she can have casual sex and not let it bother her. But it does. She feels lonely and uncertain about the relationship. She hopes he hasn't had sex with any sleazy girls lately. She wonders if she should call him.

B. They have the house all to themselves. It is *their* house. He helps his wife finish the dishes as they try to keep the smiles off their faces. In a room lit by a single candle, they rediscover the thrill that seems to get better every time. When it's over, they enjoy just being close. When they wake up, they will still be together. Nothing to hide, nothing to fear, nothing to change. And it will stay like this for the rest of their lives.

Which of these is the real thrill? Which of these is worth looking forward to? Which of these is a thrill that *lasts?*

Sex is a thrill, no doubt about it. But the true pleasure of sex cannot be enjoyed unless each can be completely open with the other. There must be complete trust, complete commitment, complete acceptance. Such attitudes are possible only in marriage. It is worth waiting for.

Mature persons don't just seek out what will make them feel good for an instant, but rather ask, "Is there a value to this?" before undertaking something. It doesn't mean that he or she has to be a stick-in-the-mud, but only that they don't make foolish choices. The two of them don't settle for a cheap imitation when they know the real thing is waiting ahead.

6. It Releases Tension

In their own words:

One of the reasons [for having sex] most overlooked is that of pressure. Not the pressure of friends, either. I'm talking about the pressure of having to get good grades, make a certain athletic team, go out with a certain girl, plan a career after high school. The list goes on and on. The problem is that some teens find themselves not performing up to everyone else's standards and this reflects on them — they feel like they're not capable of doing a certain thing. As this vicious cycle progresses, the one thing a teen can do is have sex, whether it be to release tension or to have a sense of doing something right or succeeding at something.

———————— ♥ ————————

Teenagers live under many kinds of stress, and parents usually are unaware of how intense that stress may be.

Dr. Urie Bronfenbrenner, a child psychologist at Cornell University, shows the effects of family stress upon children:

> What threatens the well-being of children and young people the most is that the external havoc can become internal, first for parents and then for their children. And that is exactly the sequence in which the psychological havoc of families under stress usually moves.
>
> Recent studies indicate that conditions at work constitute one of the major sources of stress for American families. Stress at work carries over to the home, where it affects first the relationship of parents to each other. Marital conflict then disturbs the parent/child relationship. Indeed, as long as tensions at work do not impair the relationship between the parents, the children are not likely to be affected. In other words, the influence of parental employment on children is indirect, operating through its effect on the parents.
>
> That this influence is indirect does not make it any less potent, however. Once the parent/child relationship is seriously disturbed, children begin to feel insecure — and a door to the world of alienation has been opened. That door can open to children at any age, from preschool to high school and beyond.
>
> My reference to the world of school is not accidental, for it is in that world that the next step toward alienation is likely to be taken. Children who feel rootless or caught in conflict at home find it difficult to pay attention in school. Once they begin to miss out on learning, they feel lost in the classroom, and they begin to seek acceptance elsewhere . . . they often find acceptance in a group of peers with similar histories who, having no welcoming place to go and nothing challenging to do, look for excitement on the streets. 80/432

When emotional and mental pressures begin to mount, sex can provide an immediate sense of satisfaction. It involves the body, mind and emotions, and gives a short-term release of tension.

The pressure teenagers are under is real, and the feeling of release that sex provides is also real. It does not resolve stressful situations, of course, but it does supply a temporary escape.

Desire to escape stress through sex is a sign of immaturity, just as is a person's drinking heavily when under stress. A mature person has a healthy sense of self-worth. A mature person shows self-control. A mature person can make decisions that will not necessarily alleviate the stressful situations, but will help him or her deal with stress without having to run away from it.

A mature person has a solid set of values that he can rely on, even when the pressure is intense.

One reason we feel so much stress is we make ourselves responsible for things beyond our control. We want to accomplish certain things in life, but situations don't always work the way we want them — so we feel tension.

We can understand this better and reduce the tension we feel more effectively once we understand the difference between goals and desires.

For example, I want to have a good marriage and be a good husband. Therefore, my *goal* is to be a good husband. No one has any control over that except me. If I am a bad husband, I have no one to blame but myself. My *desire* is to have a good marriage. Since my wife is also involved, she has the ability to prevent that desire from being fulfilled. I do not control her.

If my goal were to have a good marriage and my wife prevented it, I would feel anger and tension, because I was trying to accomplish something over which I did not have complete control.

Each person is responsible only for himself or herself — no more. No one owns the rights to the thoughts or actions of another. A person may be responsible *to* another person, but we are not responsible *for* that person — and we cannot assume ownership of something that isn't ours.

A sexually active teenager may blame the situation on stress, but only he is responsible for his actions. He cannot control the future, or his relationships (remember, there are two persons involved), or the flow of traffic on the way to school — but he can control himself.

I once saw a bumper sticker that said, "Stop Continental Drift." It made its point. We take tasks upon ourselves that are out of our control, and then feel stressed when the situation overwhelms us. Such stress can then cause us to act irrationally and out of accordance with God's will.

When teenagers are better able to deal with stress, they won't feel the need to resort to sex as a release. When they quit trying to stop continental drift, and instead focus on the quality of their own character, they can establish and strengthen their personal set of values and gain control of their lives.

7. It's a Way to Have a Child

Most teenagers, for whatever reason they are sexually active, want desperately to avoid pregnancy. Still, there are some girls who feel so bad about themselves and so unloved that they try intentionally to have a child, someone they can love and who will love them back.

Here again the issue of maturity arises. A girl wanting a baby to fill her need for someone to love and to demand love from is far too immature to be a proper mother. She expects a child to solve her self-image problem, which puts unrealistic expectations on the baby even before it is born.

Most teenage sex is done for certain expected results. One person hopes it will make him popular, another hopes it will help her keep her boyfriend, another thinks it will make him an adult, another thinks it will make her feel good about herself. Still others (although very few) hope that a baby will result who will be the great solution they have been waiting for. In each case, the problem lies in an improper view of oneself. In each case, a baby only compounds the problem.

Some girls want to get pregnant as a means of getting a boy to marry them. One girl told me that when her boyfriend broke up with her she found another guy who had similar physical features, had sex with him and became pregnant. She then used it as leverage to get her former boyfriend to marry her. It was all for naught, because she had a miscarriage. But it reveals the extent to which some teens will go in order to save a relationship.

8

ENVIRONMENTAL REASONS

1. Lack of Moral Standards

In the Schools

In their own words:

Sex education is taught in detail without any standards. When the book says an orgasm feels great, it makes a person want to go and see how great it really feels. When you know a little, you are confident — but you actually know just enough to be dangerous. People are told they could solve the pregnancy problem if they would teach more and at a younger age . . . brilliant!

———————— ♥ ————————

A high school freshman told me the following story: "The school nurse was giving a sex education class and was telling us all the different ways to keep from getting pregnant. She finished by saying, 'The only method that is 100 percent guaranteed is not to have sex, but, of course, that isn't very practical.' "

This is what teenagers are up against at school, the institution that influences them for more hours and with more repetition than any other. With parents working and everyone keeping different schedules, not even the family has as much influence.

When sex education talks only about what the body can do, without teaching the dignity and value of the individual, no context is given in which sex is right or wrong. It is simply available. The kids may have learned some basics of anatomy, but, more than that, they have had their curiosity aroused.

It is easy to say, "Sex education must begin in the home," yet it can be quite difficult for parents to overcome their own embarrassment and uncertainty with their kids. That's why the church needs to offer biblically based sex education as an aid to families. Again, it is easier to say what should be done than to do it. But when individuals who are able to teach reach out to their congregations, kids can learn about the values that accompany sex. They will understand the proper use of sex in God's design along with the biological facts before they even hear what the schools have to say.

It is understandably difficult for public schools in a pluralistic society to take a stand on moral issues, because for every person they placate, they may offend two others. This is why sex education must begin in families and churches.

Society doesn't suffer when biblical standards are followed. That goes for teenagers too.

In Society

The majority of teens desperately want guidelines and restrictions. Ask a teenager if he wants rules and he will probably laugh at you. Deep inside, however, teens want someone in authority to say, "No further." Yet, for many, no one does. Consequently, they become their own god.

———————— ♥ ————————

Teenagers without guidelines are adrift in a world they neither made nor chose. Caught in a crush of teenage gods, each making his or her own decision independent of others, they find themselves in chaos.

Two forces are at work against young people in their daily attempts to make sense out of their world. The first is the increasingly relativistic nature of our society: *Everything* is said to be relative. There are no absolutes, no universal truths.

But without a standard of right and wrong, how is one to decide? Cultural relativism has taken away our framework for making decisions. Our culture says, "Do what you think is right and what you think will bring you pleasure."

A youth pastor observed that his "best teachers in school were the toughest. They laid down the law and expected a great deal from us. As a youth pastor I was lovingly tough on my kids. I expected a lot out of them and set down guidelines. They grumbled some, but after I'd follow through a few times they felt a security in my leadership. They actually want restrictions, because it shows them that someone really cares. When I left the group to travel, almost all of their letters thanked me for caring so much for them. They knew that I had their best interest in mind."

In the Home

The second force working against most teenagers is the breakdown of the family. Without role models to show how values are determined and acted upon, our teenagers' sturdiest fortress against the world's chaos is gone. They are swept along in the mudslide of their culture. A synergy takes place as culture erodes the family, and the broken family erodes the culture.

Without guidelines, without restrictions, we all wander in a maze. In one sense, all of us say "I don't want to be held back." But when we get little or no direction, especially with the multitude of decisions to be made in contemporary society, we have no map by which to choose direction. Without guidelines, teenagers have no reason to say no to anything. Yet rather than making them free, their lack of values make them indecisive.

Indecisiveness is powerlessness. The more decisions we have to make, the more we need a framework by which to make them. But instead of looking to the biblical values known to be true for thousands of years, we have abandoned the framework we desperately need. Our inability to make decisions is evident in our culture.

Without the biblical point of reference, we feel confused and empty, which leaves us powerless. That in turn leads to insecurity and the need to hold on to something or someone; that is, it drives us to search for intimacy with another person.

But intimacy requires giving of one's self, and in a culture that is self-centered, we quickly give up hoping to find lasting intimacy. Instead, we settle for temporary physical closeness. Without guidelines, teenagers don't recognize right and wrong. They know only that they have found a closeness that makes them feel good for the moment. They have submitted to society's relativism.

When teens do have guidelines, it helps them in three major ways:

1. *They have an "out."* Caught in a tough situation, the teenager with restrictions always has an out: "Sorry, my parents won't let me"; or "I can't; my parents say no." When a young person has been kept from undesirable situations, his character can

develop with fewer unwanted influences.

2. *They can exercise decisiveness.* When teenagers are told, "You can do whatever you want within these parameters," their field of options is narrowed and they are better able to make decisions, to know *why* they have made them, and to stand by them.

3. *They can demonstrate self-control.* When young people follow guidelines, they learn to obey, and when they learn to obey they learn self-control. It has been said wisely that if you don't have enough will power to submit to someone else, you'll never have the will power to submit to yourself.

Self-control and decisiveness are two important elements of maturity. These two powerful tools will help teenagers deal with sexual temptations that surround them.

2. Lack of Information About Sex

In their own words:

Teenagers are ignorant about what they are doing. All they know is that they were made with certain body parts, so they might as well find out what they're used for. Sort of like test-driving a car just to see how well it performs.

♡ ♡ ♡

Lack of accurate information about sex, although less of a problem than in our parents' adolescence, is still quite common, and young people often don't realize how far they are going. Before they know it, they have an unexpected pregnancy on their hands. It must be pointed out that some parents are much to blame since they have not informed their children on the topic of sex, either because they are too embarrassed to discuss it, are irresponsible, or are ignorant themselves.

———————— ♥ ————————

Sex education begins at home, whether parents are aware of it or not. When sex is honestly discussed, the home becomes a source of both objective facts and moral understanding. When sex is a taboo subject, kids discern that it is something mysterious and forbidden, and therefore something probably worth exploring. As one researcher notes, "Parents are a child's earliest models of sexuality and authority; they communicate with their children about sex and sexual values indirectly and nonverbally." 142/122

A study on teenage sex-related values and behaviors was done by sociologist Brent Miller at Utah State University and reported in *The Family's Role in Adolescent Sexual Behavior.*

Miller discovered that the more openly parents discussed their
sex-related values and beliefs with teens, the less their children
displayed either negative sexual attitudes or promiscuous sexual
behavior. He also shows that teens who learned the sexual facts
from parents were significantly less likely to be sexually active
than those who first heard about sex from their friends. 142/73-130

So the process of educating children about sex in an intelligent and open manner must begin at home. This is especially
important among Christians. The church also must be involved
in the education of its young members. Teenagers are going to
find out one way or another how their bodies work, and when
parents and the church deny kids the information they so vitally
need, they set their young people up for trouble. As one 1977
survey shows, "Girls who did not receive early education about
menstruation and sexual activity from their family were more
likely to become pregnant during their adolescence." 127

Teenagers need to know that the changes in their bodies
and the changing emotions that accompany them are normal.
They need to know that their increased sexual awareness is also
normal.

But the parents' most vital role is in explaining what sex is
and in what *context* it belongs. A health class at school may
teach some basic anatomy, but it won't teach students the sanctity
of sex or God's plan for sex in their lives.

This must be started at a very young age and continued as
the child grows up. Sex education in the home is an eighteen
year course of love and insight.

If you wait for the "big talk" it probably will come too late;
by the time you get around to it, your child probably already
knows more than you do (or at least he or she will think so).

It is one thing for someone to say, "Teach your kids about
sex," and quite another to find parents eager to do so. But we
must respond to the needs of our children. Secular educators
and family planning organizations are more than happy to fill
the void that many Christian parents are leaving, and our kids
are paying the price for learning sex without morality.

The New York polling firm Audits and Surveys discovered
many interesting facts about conflicting views of parents and
young people.

1. Frequency with which today's parents say they talk to their
   own kids about sex: every two months — 49 percent; never — 6
   percent.
2. Frequency with which today's high school teens say their
   parents actually talk to them about sex: every two months — 23
   percent; never — 22 percent.
3. Parents who believe they get honest answers when talking to

their teens about sex — 81 percent; those who believe they get somewhat honest answers — 9 percent.

4. Teens who say they are totally honest when talking to parents about sex: high school — 22 percent; college — 27 percent.

5. The pollsters discovered that parents believed they were getting straight answers when they asked sexual questions. The teens said they almost never tell the whole truth. What some parents regard as bracing sex talk, their children see as "deluded pap." 238/110-121

What many parents don't realize is how much their teens (and pre-teens) *want* to discuss sex with them. A 1983 study among churched families by Search Institute found that:

> Sexuality is a dimension of life adolescents wish they could discuss with their parents. When asked to indicate the one "to whom they most likely would turn for help or advice when having questions about sex," their overwhelming preference was parents. Though the percentage that prefers parents drops sharply following the seventh grade, there are still more ninth-graders who prefer their parents to personal friends or other adults for help or advice.
>
> The study showed these adolescents preferred to go to their parents with their problems over peers except under one condition. They preferred to discuss academic stress, relationship strains, sexuality pressure, and every other issue with their parents as long as the problem was not accompanied with feelings of *guilt.* 107/57

Kids don't want to discuss something they feel guilty about, because they don't want to let their parents down. Nor do they want their parents to add to their guilt. They want their parents to be happy with them, yet the actions that led to the guilt may have resulted in part from a lack of instruction from Mom and Dad.

But the objective here is not to find someone to blame. The objective is to bring about understanding, and thereby, change.

It's a change that must overcome the traditional inhibitions most of us in the older generation have about discussing sex. As *Family Life and Sexual Learning of Children* reports:

> Most parents did not learn about sexuality from their parents and thus lack role models to help them in approaching their own children; they often perceive themselves to be uninformed about sexuality and may be confused about the sexual values they wish to communicate to their children.
>
> A survey of 1400 parents of children aged 3-11 found that less than 15 percent of mothers and 8 percent of fathers had ever talked to their children about premarital sex or sexual intercourse. 193/238

Another researcher found the following:

In one 1978 study, 80 percent of mothers with daughters aged 11-14 had talked about menstruation; however, only 4 percent had explained in any detail the relationship between menstruation and pregnancy. 33/56

Kids really want to find the answers they need — at home. What often turns them off is that parents jump to conclusions or over-lecture instead of really listening to what their teens are trying to say.

If we parents show an interest in our children when they're young, they will show an interest in us later. Good communication with teenagers and younger children requires a lot of time and thought, but it is the start of a lifelong family relationship. The right time to start is now.

For more information on communicating with your teen, see "Open Mouth, Closed Ears?" beginning on page 388 of this book.

3. A Broken Home

In their own words:

An overwhelming number of teenagers come from broken homes. Teenagers' attitudes were developed mostly when they were children. Sometimes, regrettably, children grow up to be like their parents. Broken homes can cause instability and the inability to make wise decisions.

♡ ♡ ♡

Mary is a seventeen-year-old adolescent who has two younger brothers and a married sister. Her parents have been divorced for almost a year. Mary and her brothers have been living with their mother who works outside the home all day. Mary has a perfect boyfriend, which is the dream of every girl. His name is Erick. He is a senior and a very popular, gorgeous-looking football player. He has been Mary's only source of comfort for months now. Therefore, he feels entitled to ask Mary to have sex. Mary's loneliness enhances her fear of rejection, so she consents.

———————— ♥ ————————

When God said, "Let us make man in our image," He didn't just make a male. He made a female also. Although each individual is hand-crafted by God, the complete image of God is shown in the relationship of a man and a woman. When that relationship is broken, the image of God in the home is shattered.

God the Father is the model for earthly fathers. Earthly fathers are to point their families to God the Father. This is the design, yet it has all but disappeared from American society in the last two decades. We are seeing many results of this in our kids, one of the results being early sexual involvement.

A broken home is a major influence in teenage sexual involvement. For instance, only one teenager in five (20 percent) whose parents are separated or divorced report that their parents' attitudes about sex affect them positively. Almost twice that number (40 percent) of teenagers whose parents are still married report such positive influence. 14/78

Another study shows that "teenagers whose parents are divorced or separated are much more likely to have had intercourse than those whose parents are married or widowed. On the extremes, the gap is almost a two-to-one margin." 45/77

A 1971 study by demographers John F. Kanter and Melvin Zelnik of Johns Hopkins University found that "young, white, teenage girls living in fatherless families were 60 percent more likely to have had intercourse than those living in two-parent families, the girls who said they confided in their parents were 'substantially less likely' to have had intercourse than those with little parental communication — an effect that did not hold true once the girls were over the age of sixteen or so." 38/60

Broken homes can lead to premarital sex in at least four ways. One is the lack of value structure that results from such a family. Children are taught to say "I'm sorry," to put things back where they got them, to be polite, to be nice to their little sisters. Yet Mom and Dad are unforgiving, unaccepting and mean to each other. Without adult role models, the concepts of right and wrong disappear.

A broken home also can lead to premarital sex due to the fact that the influence and pressure from peers becomes stronger than that in the home. The closeness and sharing that should take place in the family is sought elsewhere.

In addition, a lack of security in the home may motivate a teenager to look for intimacy in irrational ways. Physical closeness will not provide true intimacy, but it gives a temporary and sensory substitute for security.

A fourth reason is the effect of divorce on the child's self-image. Children of divorced parents not only feel rejected by the parents, but they also usually hold themselves accountable for the divorce, as though their actions caused it. The feelings of rejection and guilt may cause a teenager to seek a boost in his or her self-image through sex. Sex allows that teen to feel important and attractive to *someone*.

Once again, if teenagers don't find love modeled at home, they will go elsewhere to get it — no matter what the cost.

4. Lack of Understanding of Love

In their own words:

Too often sex and love are confused. Granted, they should go together in the right context, but they are not synonymous. They are two separate concepts. *Sex* should be an act performed by two people committed to loving each other for life; *love,* in varying degrees, can be felt by anyone.

♡ ♡ ♡

Teens misunderstand what real love is. Today's teenagers think love is an act instead of a commitment. Ninety percent of all guys and eighty percent of all girls will lose their virginity by age twenty. They have no example of real love in their lives, and many have been taught sex education without morals from grade school on.

───────── ♥ ─────────

Each person has an innate desire for love, a desire given by God. But love is something that must be learned. It can't be written out as a definition and have an impact. It must be acted out by role models. When people see a model of love, they learn how to respond to love and act in love. This is why the Scriptures say, "We love because He first loved us."

The Bible, for the most part, doesn't define love. Rather, it shows us love in action, as in the deeds of Christ, the explanation of active love given in 1 Corinthians 13 and Matthew 25, and God's boundless love for a stubborn and rebellious Israel, and so on.

Since love is learned from role models, the family is the most important influence on how a child perceives love (followed by peers and society in general). When parents are to an appreciable degree acting out the imagery of God, displaying to a perceptible extent the attributes of Christian love, children will grow up learning that love.

Children in such homes grow up learning to be accepted and appreciated, which leads them to a feeling of security and significance. These children, in turn, will respond to that love in obedience to the parents' authority, and will begin internalizing the principles taught by the parents.

This is why the destruction of the family is so devastating. Children grow up learning from their parents that love means "Get what you can from the other person, and when that person doesn't perform properly, get out of the relationship." Such is the feeling of "love" that many kids today are confusing with sex.

Children can grow up desiring to love their parents, but still not feel secure in the relationship. Often in order to get the love of their parents, they fall into the "flight syndrome." That is, they put themselves on a performance basis for their parents' love, and when they do something they think won't be pleasing, they cover it up. They run from honesty. They are afraid that their shortcoming will lead to rejection.

This can happen when well-meaning children try to please Mom and Dad, but it has a stifling effect. Open communication is blocked when the children think that honesty will lead to parental disappointment. They may cease trying new things for fear of failure. They may stop taking risks to stretch their horizons.

These kids then enter their teenage years equating love and performance. When they say, "If you love me, you'll have sex with me," they are only keeping in line with their own distorted definition of performance/love.

The biblical picture of love is one of giving without expecting anything in return, accepting another person without conditions, and experiencing a security in the relationship that is not dependent on performance. This is a far cry from the shallow and self-centered type on the market today. And it is in the home where this love must be modeled.

5. Peer Pressure

"Everyone Is Doing It"

In their own words:

Why wait? It's the number-one teen question. My parents are always telling me what to do and what not to do. I hate their nagging. Besides, everyone has done it. Nobody's a virgin.

♡ ♡ ♡

Not only is there direct pressure, but there is also indirect pressure to have sex. After learning the truth that she is the only one who is still a virgin, the "last remaining" girl gives in to worrying and feeling abandoned. She feels awkward and wonders if she should have "done it," too.

———————— ♥ ————————

A study of 1,000 teenagers shows that 76 percent would go far enough sexually to feel experienced and not feel left out. 108/Appendix II, p. 58 Here we have one of the greatest pressures on young people: the pressure not to be left out of the sex derby. *Teenagers get the idea that "everyone else is doing it" and they don't want to be different. They feel that if they just conform to what all the others are doing, they'll be in the norm and won't be a loner.*

The following story was entered in the "Write Your Heart Out" essay contest. It clearly depicts the everyone-is-doing-it sexual pressure.

> He stood alongside the busy highway, walked a few paces, then turned to face the oncoming traffic. With his arm extended, the young man thumbed the sky, hoping a traveler would stop to offer him a ride. Somebody did. A green Volkswagen bug came to a halt. The young man, we shall call him Joe, slid into the front passenger's seat and greeted my fiancé, Herb Coates. Herb was eagerly heading to Indianapolis, Indiana, to join my family and me. The long-awaited hour, our wedding, was just a few days away from being history. After exchanging this and other general information, Joe's conversation with my future husband took an interesting twist. It sounded something like this:
>
> "So, you're on your way to getting hitched. Is your lady 'good'?"
>
> "Good? Oh, she's the best!" Herb replied.
>
> Not completely sure his inquiry was understood, Joe rephrased the question, "I mean, in bed?"
>
> "Oh!" Herb realized the direction the conversation was taking. "I guess I can't really answer that. We've never 'made love.' In fact, we're both virgins."
>
> "You have got to be kidding! How old are you?"
>
> "I'm twenty-two."
>
> By the time the question-and-answer period had ended, Herb had managed to astonish his passenger. Joe stated he had never met a twenty-two-year-old virgin before. He took a small black book used for recording names of people who had provided him rides. He wanted something descriptive to remember the owner of the green bug. It was a simple task. The note read: "Twenty-two-year-old virgin."

The idea that "everyone is doing it" brings up two main questions: (1) Is it really true that everyone else is doing it? and (2) Are all those who are doing it enjoying it?

The feeling that certain teenagers may have — that they are the last virgins in the country — is based on a myth. True, many teens have been sexually involved. Statistics show the figure to be between 65 and 80 percent, depending on the statistics one chooses. Surprisingly, Christian teenagers are generally only ten percentage points or so behind the overall figure (i.e., 55 to 70 percent of them have been sexually involved).

From this we learn several things. First, our society is experiencing an almost complete breakdown of moral values and is passing its immorality on to our kids. Second, Christian teenagers are giving in to the world's standards in numbers unparalleled in Western culture. Third, those Christian teens who are not sexually active, rather than being left out, are some of the final holdouts against the tide of immorality: They comprise the group that has dug in its heels and refuses to be overrun. Fourth, as the statistics reveal, out of any one hundred teenagers, about twenty-five of them will not be sexually active (about thirty-five, if Christians). It simply can't be said that everyone is doing it. A significant minority of teenagers has not given in.

Teenagers who look around and think they see "everyone doing it" are looking in the wrong places. They have allowed themselves to come under the influence of peers, the mass media, and other elements of our culture that shamelessly promote premarital sex. Billboards, television commercials, locker rooms, slumber parties and classrooms abound with suggestions and direct commentaries on sex. Bumper stickers say: "Do it in a Datsun," "Nurses do it with patience," "Divers do it deeper."

However, even with all this outside influence, much of how a teenager perceives the world depends on his or her own family. A teenage girl who feels pressured and can look to abstaining siblings is able to make intelligent choices. She can say, "My older brother isn't doing it. My older sister hasn't given in. I don't have to either."

Friends are also of great importance in helping teens make decisions. So peer influences such as church groups provide opportunities to interact with people who may not be sexually active.

And of those the teenager knows who are "doing it," not all are finding sex as romantic as the movies say. Most find a temporary thrill in it, but without marriage it always ends up being unfulfilling. To some girls, sex is a physically painful process they go through for the gratification of someone else. They don't enjoy sex while it's happening, their moral conscience is hurt afterward, they have a weakened self-image that must be bolstered by the other person's approval, and so on. This doesn't happen in every case, but it happens often enough that the teenager feeling left out should note: The pain outweighs any gain.

Teenagers who are not sexually active and feel left out need to view themselves in a new light. Rather than feeling out of touch with their society, they need to realize that·their society is out of touch with God.

Teens can reply to "everyone's doing it" in a variety of ways:

"Well, I'm not everybody, I'm me. Besides, I don't really believe everybody is doing it. I think it's a lot of talk."

"If everyone's doing it, then you shouldn't have too much trouble finding someone else."

"Yes, I can see that the pregnancy rate of teenagers is fierce."

"Everyone is doing it is a mighty poor excuse for doing something. That pressure doesn't affect me for the simple reason that I don't want what 'everyone' else has. I don't want a sexually transmitted disease, a divorce, a broken home, or children bouncing from one parent to another."

"The frequency with which something happens does not accurately indicate its value. For example, let's say the majority of people develop cancer — does that mean I should be anxious to have cancer? That's as stupid a response as wanting to have sex because everyone else is."

We need to be realistic. Not many teens will have the courage to give the above responses to sexual pressure. Think of a thirteen- or fourteen-year-old facing the pain of being rejected. About all many teens think of is that they really want this guy or girl to like them.

In the kingdom of God, the Lord tells His people, "Be holy, for I am holy." Our culture tells us, "If it feels good, do it." One of these two kingdoms must fall, and we must, by word and action, choose which side we are on. A young woman told me how her boyfriend tried to pressure her into sex by saying everyone was doing it.

She looked him in the eye and replied, "Everyone but me."

Pressure to Conform

In their own words:

We are made to feel inadequate if we don't live up to the standards of our parents and teachers as far as grades go. The pressure from our friends to engage in sex is a lot like the pressure we feel to do well in school. *We feel inadequate if we don't live up to our friends' standards where sex is concerned.*

♡ ♡ ♡

Pressure is at a high point in the locker room. The little guy is usually picked on, and eventually rumors are spread about his virginity.

♡ ♡ ♡

The peer pressure by friends is probably the hardest to face as a virgin, because people will tease. "It's fun, you're missing out. Are you chicken or something? It's great. You won't get pregnant."

♡ ♡ ♡

The most important thing in life is how we are viewed by our closest friends.

———————— ♥ ————————

Friends are vitally important to teens. "Friends are to them what bread is to the hungry and clothes to the naked." 114/27

The need to conform is a particularly strong force in shaping teen choices. Shoes have to be of the right brand and style, hair must be cut and combed a particular way, clothing must conform to the swings of fashion and fad. Entertainment and possessions for which the young people spend their money are principally those that are in vogue among their friends. The desire to conform — to shape their words and actions to please a certain group — has a profound influence on youth behavior. 99/112

One teen wrote about her friend:

Karen was a virgin. She was insecure with herself and needed to be popular. She was tantalized by her friends who said, "You won't be in the group unless you have sex with John." She could not afford, so she thought, to lose the friendship she had with these girls. She gave in and had sex with her boyfriend, John. She also gave in to her friends because they told Karen she would have more dates with guys if they knew she would do whatever they wanted her to. Karen realized that those girls were not true friends and they had led her astray. She also realized the guys thought of her as a slut, not a good date.

Conformity is a familiar part of human nature. Few of us want to be noticeably different from our peers. Whether teen or adult, we hate to pay the price of being singled out for ridicule because of our individuality. In most cases conformity may be harmless enough — except when it becomes the determinant of our ethics and behavior.

One wife volunteered, "I was at lunch last week with eleven women. We've been studying French together since our children were in nursery school. One gal, the provocateur of the group, asked, 'How many of you have been faithful throughout your marriage?' Only one woman at the table raised her hand. That evening my husband looked crestfallen when I told him I was not that one.

" 'But I have been faithful,' I assured him.

" 'Then why didn't you raise your hand?'

" 'I was ashamed.' " 279/17

Kids Are Influencing Kids

Peer pressure as it operates among today's teens sometimes becomes a kind of "moral blackmail." The basis for this blackmail is the group's power to accept or reject. And in our permissive society, sexual activity is often seen as an important criterion for admittance into a desired group. Even Christian teens, who have grown up with biblical morality, find themselves discarding or ignoring those values because of their fear of rejection.

It is easy for us parents and church leaders to discount this peer blackmail and say to teens, "Be in the world, but not of it." However, we are not in the locker rooms. We are not being ridiculed for our lack of a sexual "track record." We are not feeling the pain of rejection.

The Hass report on teenage sex observed the difference between boys and girls when it comes to peer pressure:

> Years ago high school girls looked around them and thought, whether correctly or incorrectly, that most were virgins. Today they look around and their perception is that most girls are not virgins, and they think, "Is there something wrong with me if I'm still sexually inactive?" That change is pretty much limited to girls. For the boys there has always been pressure from peers and often from fathers to be sexually active, to gain some notches on their belts. 40/107-110

Can you think back to your teen years? The issues were different, but even then teen groups could be very cruel. I remember certain people being singled out for total humiliation. Personally, I remember the pain I suffered because my friends knew I had an alcoholic father.

Well, today teens are no less cruel . . . and girls can be as bad as guys.

"Be honest with me," Randy Alcorn asked a high school junior girl, "is there *really* that much pressure to go to bed with guys?"

"Let's put it this way," she said. "Yesterday the girl whose locker is next to mine lost her temper at another girl in our class. She was so angry that she screamed at the girl, 'You . . . you . . . you *virgin!*' She tried to think of the worst name she could call her, and came up with virgin. Does that answer your question?" 62/63

> "If you say no, you're a tease and if you say yes, you're a slut," complains a seventeen-year-old Atlantan. Yet in many instances, girls themselves are putting the heat on. Taking

a misread leaf from women's lib, they are becoming sexually aggressive and strutting a kind of locker-room swagger about their conquests. In her set, seventeen-year-old Victoria Sanchez notes, "Bragging is rampant. They'll brag about which jock laid them where. It's as if, now that we can be equal, we're going to be equally tacky." Debbie, a fourteen-year-old Berkeley, California, freshman, recalls a sexually accomplished girl friend, whom she idolized until "she began telling me I better get my butt moving, or I'd be missing out on the best thing in life. It got on my nerves. I wasn't ready." 22/51

Teens often assume that their needs for feeling loved, being popular with peers, or being more grown up, *can* be met by becoming sexually involved. Following the lead of peer pressure, however, is seldom rewarding or satisfying.

One reason peer pressure is so strong is that today's teens spend much more time with people their own age than they do with their parents. This is largely because of factors discussed earlier, such as two-income families and the breakdown of the family.

As a result, parents are influencing their children less today than ever before. Values are not being communicated effectively from generation to generation. We discussed earlier the fact that our young people often live in two cultures: the traditional culture of their parents, and the post-Christian culture of their peers.

With parents seldom available to their teens, it is not surprising that the teens are influenced most by the permissive culture of their peers. Rather than being an integral part of a family and a community, kids are growing up with kids. They have their own subculture. They talk to each other. They grow dependent on each other. Since their friends provide their main source of identity, teens cannot risk their alienation. So when the peer group moves in a particular direction, the individual teens within the group go along.

Even within church families, teens are in effect segregated from their parents — we segregate people according to age. Teens go to the youth group; parents go to various adult activities. What if our churches began offering activities and programs aimed at restoring intergenerational communication? It might help teens stand up better to peer pressure.

Much of the "don't get involved" pressure of years past resulted from the younger generation's carrying on values from their parents. But now that society is so much more segregated by age, that doesn't happen much. Without an inherited value system for determining right and wrong, teenagers are largely left to themselves to make choices. Tragically, most teens are totally unprepared.

Beneath the worldly veneer there are adolescent doubts and conflicts. Many teenagers are having sex as much because it is available and fashionable as because it is desirable. Once chastity was something to be guarded — or lied about when lost. Now an uncommonly virtuous teenager lies to protect the dirty little secret that she is still a virgin. There is more pressure than ever for a girl to "get it over with." 22/51

As parents and as youth leaders we must take the power of negative peer pressure seriously. It is a devastating force for sexual permissiveness.

What Can We Do?

Churches need to find ways to provide our young people with *positive* peer pressure. Christian teens need to function as support groups, helping each other stand up against the enormous sexual pressures they face. The problem is that many Christian teens are already involved sexually and can be of little help to someone who wants to go against the tide.

One of the most effective deterrents to peer pressure is a *good self-image.* The secure teen is usually the only one who can withstand peer pressure. We who are pastors and teachers must teach young people to see themselves as God sees them — with infinite worth and value because of God's creative/redemptive plan. Young people who find their acceptance in a loving/accepting relationship with God and with His people are well protected against moral blackmail from their peers.

As parents, we need to spend more time with our children, no matter what the cost. Perhaps we should consider the time spent away from our children when we choose the location for our next home. Perhaps a shorter drive to work is worth more to your children than a more comfortable house. Perhaps a promotion that requires a parent to be away frequently from his or her family may not be worth accepting. If you have a teen, or pre-teen at home, is that second income really needed?

Those are tough questions, but it is time we parents began giving high priority to our relationships with our children.

Remember:

- If our kids can't *talk* to us, they will talk to their peers.

- If we don't *spend time* with them, they will spend more time with their peers.

- If they don't have *intimacy* at home, they will seek it among their peers.

- If they don't get *hugs* from dad, they will get hugs from their peers.

- If we won't *listen* to them, their peers will.

- Teens respond to *relationships*. That is why they are so responsive to their peers.

6. The Media

Teenagers are growing up in a media-saturated society. Like the rest of us, they are surrounded by printed and moving words and pictures. The purpose of these is to either inform or entertain, and since most teens have their fill of information from school, they seek amusement in the media. (The word "amusement" literally means "without mind.")

People point their fingers at the media as being responsible for the sexual bombardment we endure on every page and every channel. The media point their fingers back at us and say they are only giving us what we want. "As a person thinks, so he is," say the Scriptures. So, as our minds fill with sexual thoughts, we buy magazines containing articles about sex, and we contribute to the ratings of TV shows with sexual encounters. Our minds become more filled with sex, and we demand more from the media. It is a snowball effect — a vicious cycle.

In a way, the amusement-without-thinking that teens — and we adults — so avidly seek is a denial of God's creation of us. We are created in His image: intelligent, clever, able to reason. By replacing mental nourishment with mental chewing gum, we turn our backs on one of the major elements that set us apart from animals.

When that mental sedative fills us with sexual suggestions and images, we associate sex with amusement.

From there, it is a simple step to seek out sex as a form of amusing escape, a sensory entertainment. Teenagers are doubly susceptible to this, because of the hormonal and emotional upheavals they are going through. Without a knowledge of right and wrong, without standards, without the Holy Spirit to fill the void, young people are open to the quickest counterfeit escape our society can provide.

Music and Lyrics

Another reason teenagers engage in premarital sex is the music they listen to. The lyrics in rock and country music are suggestive; they talk freely about sex. Countless song lyrics allude to one-night love affairs, part-time lovers, "this night will be a night of magic" and so on.

♡ ♡ ♡

Some teenagers may think nothing of it and say, "Oh, I don't listen to the words, I just like the rhythm and the tune." Subconsciously, though, they take in those suggestive lyrics. They may come to think any kind of sex is all right — which is not good.

♡ ♡ ♡

Over Christmas my brother cranked up the song "French Kissing in the U.S.A.," and to get me riled told me what a great song it was. The glorification of a song such as that leads teenagers to French kiss without even questioning it. This applies to music openly talking about having sex, etc.

———————— ♥ ————————

Music today is very powerful and very available through broadcast and sound reproduction technology. We don't just hear a song; we can be inundated with it through booming speakers. We can be persuaded by it through constant repetition. We can be influenced by it through suggestive messages that sneak into our subconscious thought.

When the music that teenagers find most appealing contains a barrage of encouragement toward sex, it is no surprise they are affected by it.

Psychologist Abraham Maslow researched what he called "peak experiences" in human lives. He pointed out that of hundreds of cases studied, there were many different experiences which people singled out as their life's highlight. "Peak experiences" involving music ranked second in the list — surpassed only by sex. From such a statement one can deduce the dynamics when sex and music are combined.

Frank Zappa wrote an article on the role of rock in the socio-sexual revolution. His conclusions were that rock music is sex. The big beat matches the body's rhythms.

A teenager's world view, his value system, and his attitude toward human dignity will determine the role music plays in his life. If he knows the effect the lyrics have on him, he must make a choice about which music he will allow to influence him. If he chooses to listen to music that degrades rather than dignifies men and women, he is not only showing what his true world view is, but which influences he wants to shape his future actions.

Television and Movies

When I was a youngster, the soap operas were a part of my daily entertainment. What a mistake to fill the young mind with such thinking! I also purchased sexual-type magazines at a very young age. My mother never monitored what we read. Thoughts of petting, kissing and sexual intercourse were planted in my mind during a very crucial point in my adolescent life.

By the eighth grade I was already acting out, by kissing and petting during recess, what had been planted in my thoughts. This continued during high school. When I moved away from home to go to college, I began having intercourse.

I know very well how important it is that we train up our children in the way they should go, especially concerning premarital sex.

♡ ♡ ♡

Many teenage girls and even a few boys are hooked on soap operas. In most soaps almost every person in the cast is involved in sex without marriage. Teenagers watch this and learn through those programs that premarital sex will make them happy and content.

———————— ♥ ————————

A guy's mind remembers scenes of sex so vividly that when he is with his girlfriend it is easy for him to act them out. "My mind is so vivid that I have to guard what I watch because I can easily recall those scenes," laments one student.

The sexual "freedom" portrayed in today's entertainment is a joke made at the expense of human dignity. Sex without marriage so often leads to self-doubts, diseases, unwanted pregnancies, shattered emotions, manipulation and exploitation. Such results are rarely portrayed on TV or in the movies because people don't want to hear about those things. They want to be told that somehow, someday, their promiscuity will lead to happiness, even though it hasn't up to this point.

And since our culture demands entertainment that reflects its hopes — not its realities — our TV and movie screens will continue to bring us lies about sex. Teenagers whose minds are filled with these falsehoods will be increasingly influenced by them.

A graduate student writes:

I did a research project on subliminal affects used in films and advertising. All that is needed in an advertisement or a film is a small inconspicuous picture or word in film. It is put in every 4th frame, which usually cannot be picked up by the conscious mind. In advertising they brush words and pictures into the pictures or shape things to look like sexual organs, etc. The mind takes a picture of everything it sees. The conscious mind takes about 1/1000 of the total information taken in, but the subconscious mind picks apart, deciphers, thinks about and files the information taken in.

David said, "I will set no worthless thing before my eyes" (Psalm 101:3, NASB).

The Scriptures admonish us to flee youthful temptation. If a teen knows that, and still takes his girlfriend to see an R-rated movie with plenty of skin, he will probably act out his aroused feelings when the movie is over. He can blame society all he wants, but he chose to see the movie, despite the warning in the Bible. Or if a teen girl invites her boyfriend over to watch an R-rated video or cable movie, she shouldn't be surprised when she violates her own limits of physical contact.

Parents have the task of bringing their children up in the admonition of the Lord and the influence of the Scriptures, yet they cannot go on dates with their teens to keep them in line. Parents must always be a resource of God's standards when a teenager needs an answer, but teenagers ultimately make their own decisions. The more they are taught from their early years to make proper choices, the easier it will be for them to stay on the right course when temptation comes.

Pornography

I do not believe most Christians make a single, willful decision to commit fornication. Rather, it is a series of smaller decisions which allow for improper thinking to enter in. Once the mind has been contaminated with impure thoughts and desires, it becomes much easier for us to make wrong decisions.

♡ ♡ ♡

Friends might happen to bring a pornographic magazine in, and the teenager might see it and be awed. Then once he or she has seen such things, fantasies start developing.

♡ ♡ ♡

This assertion is supported by Dr. Victor Cline, a professor at the University of Utah, who states there are four effects to viewing sexually explicit scenes: (1) they stimulate and arouse aggressive sexual feelings, (2) they show and instruct in detail how to do the act, (3) the acts in a sense are legitimatized by repeated exposures, and (4) they increase the likelihood that the individual will act out what he has seen.

As I grew older and began to date, I threw away the pictures in exchange for the real thing. To me, the excitement of casual sex was like a chess game. I learned to maneuver my opponent into a position where she couldn't say no. If I sensed there was a moral dilemma in her mind, I would play any role necessary to reach the point where sex became inevitable. This pattern of sexual conquest continued until I met Jesus Christ in 1979. Since that time He has totally transformed my perspective toward sex before marriage.

—————————— ♥ ——————————

Pornography promotes sexual promiscuity, incestuous sexual relationships, marital infidelity, sexual deviancy and "no-consequence" sex. Social scientific studies indicate that pornography is also progessive and addictive. 157/105 Soft-core porn has been termed the "marijuana" of pornography that leads its users to desire harder, more bizarre "heroin" versions of sexual explicitness.

Dr. Dolf Zillman at Indiana University and his colleague, Dr. Jennings Bryant at the University of Houston, in their 1984 research, sought to discover the effects of pornography on attitudes toward love, marriage and children. In the conclusion to their study, Zillman and Bryant stated: "The findings leave no doubt about the fact that repeated exposure to common, non-violent pornography is capable of altering perceptions of and dispositions toward sexuality and relationships formed on its basis." 128/7

They found that exposure to pornography clearly causes people to believe:
- the greatest sexual joy comes without enduring commitment;
- partners expect each other to be unfaithful;
- there are health risks in repressing sexual urges;
- promiscuity is natural;
- children are liabilities and handicaps. 125/25

Their research also substantiated their pre-study theory that "pornography projects access to some of the greatest unmitigated pleasures known, without indicating any restriction in freedom . . . Adoption of the values permeating pornography thus could undermine the values necessary to form enduring relationships in which sexuality, and possibly reproduction, are central." 128/7

It is reasonable to assume that those "unmitigated sexual pleasures" appeal not only to adults, but *also to teenagers.*

In another 1984 study, Canadian researcher James Check from New York University researched the effects of violent versus non-violent pornography. Check found that non-violent pornography increased the likelihood that subjects would commit rape and other forced sexual acts.

Pornography can lead to what is referred to as "date rape," the rape of a girl by her date. Dr. Zillman commented on Check's research:

> The investigation by Check has obvious implications for public health. It shows that, on the whole, common, non-violent pornography has the strongest influence on men's willingness to force intimate partners into forms of sexuality that are not necessarily to their partners' liking, and on the propensity to force sexual access. Violent pornography apparently has the same power to increase rape proclivity, although its influence on the coercion of specific sexual acts is limited if not negligible. 191/1

Check's findings reveal that exposure to non-violent pornography influences the acceptance and carrying out of the rape myth that when a woman says no she really means yes, and that ultimately she not only will concede to, but also will enjoy sexual advances made against her will.

This scenario can plausibly be linked to the rape or sexual attack of 27.5 percent of all university coeds nationwide. 305/162-170 It also can be tenably argued that increasing occurrences of date rape are linked to increasing exposure of males to non-violent, soft-core pornography. A Kent State University study attributes 57 percent of rapes occurring against its coeds to date rape.

I am convinced that the attitudes, perceptions, values, and sexual aggressiveness of teenagers are altered in the same or in an ever greater way than those of adults as a result of their exposure to pornography.

It is reasonable to assume that soft-core pornography and its themes promoting the "greatest unmitigated pleasures known" would be especially appealing to adolescents discovering their own developing human sexuality.

Some experts estimate that as much as 70 percent of all pornography ends up in the possession of children and teenagers.

The 1970 United States Commission on Obscenity and Pornography conducted a national survey of public attitudes toward, and experience with, erotic materials. The survey group consisted of a random sample of 2,486 adults and 769 young people, aged fifteen to twenty. Among other things, the commission found that about one in five males and about one in ten females had their first exposure to pornography by age twelve. By age seventeen, over half of the males (54 percent) and a third of the females had been exposed. Abelson found that "young adults, college-educated people, those with relatively liberal attitudes toward sex, and people who have experienced the most erotica recently are all disproportionately more likely than others to have had their first experiences with erotica at a young age." 164/249

Another more recent set of data based on a national probability sample of 1,071 respondents is available from Canada (Check, 1985). The Canadian results show that adolescents age twelve to seventeen report the *most* frequent exposure to sexually explicit fare. Check found in his survey that two in five twelve- to seventeen-year-olds view such material in movie theaters at least once per month; over a third (37 percent) see similar material on home videos with the same frequency. 191/1

In the 1970 sample, respondents were asked how many times during the past two years they had seen photographs, snapshots, cartoons, or movies of a list of sexually explicit items. *Adolescents reported more frequent exposure than adults, with three in ten saying they had seen such material six or more times in the last two years while the ratio was only one in four for adult males and one in seven for adult females.* 164/251/252

Present-day home video exposure will most likely increase with the ever increasing concentration of VCR ownership. It is estimated that VCR ownership will reach 50 percent by 1988 and 85 percent by 1995. 164/352

It can be argued that teenagers are, in fact, being massively exposed to pornography and its projection of the "greatest unmitigated pleasures" relating to sexual involvement. Moreover, their exposure to the themes of pornography would cause them to believe the same things Drs. Zillman and Bryant (1984) found that adults were caused to believe, which we listed a few pages earlier. 166/139

We could even conclude that the adoption of these beliefs by teenagers would cause disproportionately greater effects on them than on adults. Teenagers are undoubtedly less equipped and less experienced than adults to understand and properly control their developing human sexuality and related sexual drives.

Our actions are the result of our thoughts, and our thoughts are the result of what we have put into our minds. We cannot think something unless we have a basis for it in our minds. Granted, human beings are creative, able to think abstractly, able to stretch the limits of thought to new areas, yet we require pieces with which to build those thoughts.

If someone had never seen pornography, would he be able to conceive it and dwell on evil thoughts? Possibly. But if all he had ever heard of sex was how it forms a beautiful bond in a marriage, he would be hard-pressed to warp those thoughts.

But our society is spared the work of having to create evil thoughts. We just buy a magazine, go to a porno theater (and hope no one sees us), or pay for a cable TV channel which will bring degradation and exploitation into the comfort of our living room or bedroom. It all looks so professional and nicely done that we forget what we are really seeing: a gift of God being perverted for profit.

The pornographers walk away with our money. We walk away with the opinion that people are not dignified beings, but instead are objects to be used for personal gratification. The longer and more intensely we dwell on these thoughts, the more likely we are to act them out.

When our thoughts are out of sync with the truth, our actions will be also. That is why the Bible tells us to guard our minds, not to tempt ourselves, not to be conformed to the garbage the world offers us, but rather to be transformed by the renewing of our minds, that we may understand God's good, pleasing and perfect will. And when we get a grip on His will, we can act in accordance with it.

7. Alcohol and Drugs

In their own words:

Drinking alcoholic beverages or taking drugs can cause people to let their guard down and compromise values they intended never to compromise.

———————— ♥ ————————

The use of alcohol and other drugs causes us to do things we wouldn't do when thinking rationally. We lose control of our bodies because we lose control of our ability to make decisions. We go against our value system because it requires us to make intelligent choices, something we can't do when we can't think.

One researcher had this to say about drugs and teenage sex:

It's worth noting here that occasional use of marijuana doesn't seem to have a major effect on sexual activity; regular use — twice a week or more — is, however, associated with more frequent and more casual intercourse. Perhaps most striking, though, is the association between drinking and loss of virginity.

Perhaps because alcohol is the most socially acceptable drug, our interviewers found it associated to a great extent with teens' first intercourse. This was particularly true of unplanned intercourse (kids who were planning to have intercourse but were nervous about it frequently reported sharing a joint or two in order to relax.) Sometimes it was boys who were surprised (a 13-year-old who was "kind of counting on fooling around" lost his virginity after his date "had taken booze out of her parents' liquor cabinet so we got pretty drunk"), but it was more often girls. One New York 15-year-old who had not yet even been out on a date told us, "I had a party on Saint Patrick's Day in my house — my mother goes away every weekend and so I have a lot of parties — and so all of us were there, and all our mutual friends and stuff. And four or five people slept over that night, and we were both pretty drunk and sort of just fell asleep together and got more involved as the night went on. I don't think he made the first move; I'm pretty sure *I* did."

But especially because of the importance girls tend to place on continuing, loving relationships, girls can find the aftermath of alcohol-influenced "surprises" hard to bear. 45/79

This last point is underscored in the following excerpts from essays written by teenagers:

Let me quote an article from *Seventeen* magazine. The article is entitled, "Sex and the Teen-age Girl":

The first step is asking yourself if it's worth it. Let's talk to a few young women who have played the premarital sex game and see what they have to say.

Lisa is a sophomore at Kent State University in Ohio. When she was a freshman she developed a crush on a young man named Todd. One night Todd convinced her to "go all the way" after getting drunk. The next day Lisa woke up feeling very strange and very empty. She summed up her experience by saying, "It wasn't that great." Unfortunately, Todd must have felt the same way. As time went on, Lisa realized he no longer held any interest for her, and even went so far as to ignore her in public. Today they rarely speak.

♡ ♡ ♡

On a warm, sunny Saturday morning in June, a teenage girl with golden blond hair and light brown eyes rose stiffly and sleepily from her bed and tried with great difficulty to focus on the walls around her. She could not remember *all* the events of the previous night at her friend's graduation party, but she did remember some. She remembered playing drinking games with a group of friends around the kitchen table, and then taking someone up on the suggestion of skinny-dipping in the pool. She remembered her boyfriend Jesse kissing her, and even his hands all over her, and . . . what *had* happened that night? She was not sure, but as she fought off the alcohol haze and numbness, she knew there was a good chance she had had sexual intercourse.

If the paragraph above seems unrealistic and contrived, read it again because it is true. I know. The teenage girl was me two years ago. The night described was just one of many nights of my life that did not turn out exactly as I had planned. I never set out to hurt anyone, especially myself, and always thought of myself as a basically "good kid with decent morals." I told myself I just never wanted to deal with commitment and wanted my own freedom. I tried to achieve what I thought would be "maximum pleasure," but was becoming painfully disappointed when I found only guilt instead of freedom, pain instead of love, and suffering instead of pleasure. Instead of drawing my boyfriend and me closer together, a sexual relationship only drove us further and further apart.

8. Easy Access to Birth Control

In their own words:

Another reason premarital sex is popular is there isn't too much to be afraid of. If you don't want consequences, use birth control. If the girl becomes pregnant, hey, just get an abortion. If one of them contracts a venereal disease, no problem, just get a shot.

♡ ♡ ♡

Planned Parenthood's sex education, in my opinion, was the seduction of young minds. They filled us with curiosity about sex and supplied free contraceptives. Girls as young as thirteen were given the pill and other devices, often without their parents' permission or knowledge. I know. I had friends who did this. Planned Parenthood introduced a new form of peer pressure, but each person still had the free will to accept or reject what was being offered.

———————— ♥ ————————

It seems that the availability of condoms and medication would prevent or cure sexually transmitted diseases, yet we are being overrun not only by the old diseases, but also by a multitude of new strains that defy treatment.

It must be noted also that contraceptives, even when readily available and used properly, do not guarantee there will be no pregnancy or transmittal of STDs. The only real guarantee is abstinence.

9

PSYCHOLOGICAL REASONS

EXPRESSION OF NEEDS

1. Search for Security and Self-Esteem

In their own words:

Sins against God lead to ugly consequences. In the case of my girlfriend and me, premarital sex not only scarred us individually, but also damaged our relationship and ultimately hurt others outside the relationship.

Individually, I used premarital sex to deal with my lack of self-esteem. Because my partner was hesitant, I saw each encounter as a chance to be persuasive, domineering and accepted by at least one beautiful girl. Each session proved to me that I was a man and equipped me with good stories for the locker room. I looked to premarital sex to bolster my self-image instead of looking for worth in the eyes of my Creator. When my fiancé became pregnant, my self-worth deteriorated even further.

♡ ♡ ♡

People confuse sex with love. They think the compatibility of two people is in the pelvis rather than in the head. Insecurity breeds this type of thinking. An insecure person is afraid of losing the person of his (or her) affections and may see sex as a way to hold on to him. Using sex for manipulation and control is also typical of insecure people.

♡ ♡ ♡

Low self-esteem may drive teenagers to gain approval through sex rather than through acceptance of the truth that they are persons of worth because God says so.

♡ ♡ ♡

With a pizza face, a small frame and a germ-sized self-esteem I entered into puberty. I mention this in no way to inspire a pity party on my behalf or to make half-baked excuses for what followed in my life, but to show the interrelated nature of one's self-image and sexual behavior.

As a junior high student I bought every put-down that came my way, at a very high price. I became completely convinced that I was basically dumb, hopelessly homely, essentially a weakling and conclusively a reject. Once I bought that image, I set about to live up to the details of the contract — and others responded to me in kind.

Then, early in my high school days, a change began that brought with it both good news and bad news. The good news is that I finally found someone who really believed in me. A Christian math teacher became vulnerable himself to get through to me. It was through his persistent demonstration of Christ-like love that God began to form a new image for me to live up to. My freshman year in high school was definitely a mile marker, as things began to improve in every area of my life. By the time I was a senior, I was a leader in sports, a better-than-average student, and was elected student body president by my classmates. Even though this should have provided the much needed self-worth, I continued to have an undercurrent of doubt and fear.

Herein lies the bad news. I looked to female attention for proof of my worth as a male. The attention I received from a young woman became the gauge for my own worth. It didn't take long to discover the enjoyment of making out and the immediate gratification that comes in lustful exchange. As I got more physically involved, I found it more difficult to stop at necking and petting, and my life became increasingly filled with guilt. I was a miserable Christian, knowing that my dating was far from the biblical standard.

By the time I enrolled in Bible college I was tired of my double standard and resolved to establish a higher standard of behavior. Then I met Shirley. We began with a wholesome relationship centered around spiritual things, but it didn't last long. About halfway through the year we had decided we were made for each other and wanted to plan our wedding as soon as possible. To accommodate school rules we put our wedding off until summer break. With this mental arrangement we could justify anything.

"After all, we are practically husband and wife."

At this point we had also adopted a philosophy that stated, "It can't be wrong when it feels so right." I remember sneaking into one of the prayer rooms late one night after hours. Following a short prayer and an even shorter "sharing time," we became passionately involved. Then the back door of the chapel opened and closed. We quickly went back to praying, asking God to keep us from being caught in the position we were in. For being right, it sure felt wrong all of a sudden.

Only a short time after this experience I happened to catch Shirley feeling right with another guy. That closed the last chapter on the novel called *Shirley and I: The Couple That Felt Right*.

For close to a year I didn't date at all. Then I became interested in another young lady. This time I was aware that God had directed me to the one I was to spend my life with. This leading wasn't based on physical attraction or an insecure ego, but on a common calling and desire to serve the Lord together.

As much as I wanted a completely different kind of relationship with Melody, I led her, too, into a compromise of her standards, causing a breech of trust and a great deal of guilt. Once a physical standard is let down, it becomes extremely difficult to raise a new banner.

Never be fooled into thinking that getting what you want from a guy or a gal is going to increase your sense of self-worth. The Word of God says, "He that saves his life shall lose it and he that loses his life for my sake shall find it." I found that trying to bolster my ego through exploitation left me with an even greater sense of worthlessness. Since that time I have found that basing my self-worth on anything apart from the acceptance of God leaves me empty. If you want to find yourself, get to know God. In discovering Him, you'll discover yourself.

♡ ♡ ♡

In today's society, where the number of one-parent families is increasing, young people can easily become very isolated. It is more than likely that the single parent goes out to work during the day, leaving the child alone for long periods of time. The child therefore feels insecure and sometimes unloved, and he or she may try to find security and love in a sexual relationship.

♡ ♡ ♡

In addition to increased knowledge of oneself, physical contact reassures the participants they are desirable or "kissable"; and it matches the dating mores of the peer group.

♡ ♡ ♡

Being a jock, I had many sexual relationships, but the one thing that really stung me was the hatred that came out of these relationships later. Deep down inside I was really insecure about whether or not I was accepted by girls and whether or not I was a man . . . The pressures were very strong, so strong that I felt very lonely many times if I "failed" to attract a girl when all of my friends did.

♡ ♡ ♡

Sex provides some kids with a sense of security, a feeling of acceptance; it gives them the assurance they are liked and wanted.

For instance, a girl's family is really having problems and she needs someone to listen to her, care about her and, most of all, love her. In her eyes, she needs someone who will just make her forget her problems, someone she can hold on to for security. She meets the "perfect guy," but really this guy is having basically the same problems and is looking for security as well. Because neither one of them knows what real love is, they may mistake it for sex. This is where a lot of people my age get into trouble.

———————— ♥ ————————

The search for identity and security often takes the form of premarital sex in a relationship and is the result of a basic need every person has: the need to be accepted.

To understand clearly how this need to be accepted may motivate us to actions that can harm us, we need to be aware that true acceptance comes only from God. His grace toward us, the love He showers on us — even though we are completely undeserving of it — is the ultimate demonstration of total and unconditional acceptance.

God didn't create us because He needed us; He created us because He wanted us. In other words, God is complete in Himself. He is pleased when we respond to Him, but it is not a need for Him — it is a desire He has. On the other hand, human beings do need God. With Him, we live and can have an abundant life, both now and in eternity. Without Him, we are tossed about and separated from Him, both now and in eternity. It is *we* who benefit from the relationship with God.

When we realize that, we come to understand how valuable we are in God's eyes. Everything He does, He does for us. God calls you and me to fellowship with Him for *our* benefit, as well as for His.

Thus, our security is in God. He loves His children without conditions and without performance. We can respond to His love by loving Him back, but we don't have to keep pleasing Him out of fear of rejection. We are accepted; we have security.

Every person has individual significance in God's eyes. God considers us all so important that He sent His Son, Jesus Christ, to pay the total price for our sins and to open the door to our relationship with Him. In so doing, He said we are each so valuable that each of us is worth the life of His Son. All we have to do is respond to His offer of love. With a love so accepting and complete, how can we refuse?

Acceptance brings security. Appreciation brings significance. God doesn't like my shortcomings, but He loves me in spite of them and I feel accepted. When I am completely accepted in a relationship, I have the security to be myself, to let my guard down. I don't have to pretend. When I have security despite my faults, when I don't have to measure up to some standard to be accepted, I feel significant as a person. I am free to develop my God-given abilities because I want to, not because I have to do that in order to be accepted. I choose to do good work, to do the work of the Father, out of appreciation for Him, for his love, mercy and grace. I choose to live by faith. I know who loves me and has demonstrated His love by His actions. I am loved for *who I am,* not for *what I do.*

This is why true acceptance, security and significance can come only from God. All persons need the healthy sense of worth that God intended them to have — something defined in Romans 12:3 where Paul says, "Do not think of yourself more highly than you ought, but rather think of yourself with sober judgment, in accordance with the measure of faith God has given you" (NIV).

This tells us how God views us, which of course is how we should view ourselves. We are created in the image of God; we have talents and abilities given to us by God; we have been given the privilege of knowing Him personally if we so choose. Each of us is hand-crafted and dearly regarded by the Creator.

Yet we should not think more highly of ourselves than we ought. When we keep in mind that *all* we have and are able to do is a gift of God, we realize that our looks, musical talents, athletic abilities, powers of reasoning — *everything* — comes from God.

How do we then understand ourselves? We are caretakers of God's gifts, nothing more, and certainly nothing less. God has made each of us unique; no two people are alike. Therefore, God has unique plans for each person.

Security and significance are part of God's design for man, yet they were marred when man broke off the relationship with God. This means we have damaged our ability to understand a relationship with Him, which is why He sent Jesus. But it does not diminish the needs built into our lives by God. A person may not have a relationship with God through Christ, but that person still craves everything that such a relationship would fulfill. So, without a rational understanding of God and His truth, the person will seek to fulfill those desires in irrational ways.

Our needs are compounded by the breakdown of the family. God intends for our inner needs to be met by Him first, then by other people. In times past, even without a relationship with God, people could find a relative security and significance within the family. They had at least *one* place where they could be themselves and not have to perform. But that is not true in most cases today. Rather than being a haven from the world, for many teens the family setting is a place of discord and unrest, a place where spouses are put on a performance basis, knowing they will be discarded if they do not continually please the other. Any element of security the family may have held is removed, since people within the family are not loved for who they are, but rather for how they perform. Kids growing up in that kind of environment lack acceptance and security, which leaves them with an unhealthy sense of worthlessness. They don't feel free to be themselves. They believe that if they were, no one would like them.

> People feel vulnerable because of poor self-images: They feel they're not pretty, too short, too tall or not fully developed. They feel there is something wrong with them if their parents are divorced or because they are adopted. Some adolescents feel vulnerable because they haven't had intercourse or because they think it's wrong to feel sexual. 77/10

When young people seek acceptance, they will do what other people do in order to be like them. They have to perform, to do the right things, to live up to the standards of those whose acceptance they seek. Some may do it through joining gangs, others by being top athletes and keeping up with that crowd.

With a poor self-image brought about by lack of acceptance of them as unique individuals, teenagers may grab for the first thing that resembles security. Often this means sex. As one researcher discovered, "Without that self-esteem, people are open to exploitation, sexual and otherwise. They come to feel that even a poor relationship is better than none, and that a little caring — maybe contingent on sexual behavior they really don't want — is better than none at all." 223/B1

When a person discovers acceptance brought about by pleasing another person, regardless of how shallow and fickle that acceptance may be, it leads to a cycle of seeking security in performance and trying to impress others — as is brought out in the following study:

> The consequences of sexual debut suggested by our data are generally undesirable . . . Our results show no positive changes in self-concept as a result of becoming sexually active.
> Those who get deeply involved in sex also tend to lose

interest in school and are more involved in using drugs, drinking and smoking, driving recklessly and shoplifting, the study indicates. 223/B1

The security-through-performance cycle then continues into adult life, as these reports show:

> The promiscuous woman is usually in doubt of her own attractiveness and is seeking reassurance by repeated and varied experience with men. The fact of inferiority is also true of promiscuous men, who in such ways prove a virility which they secretly doubt. The promiscuous man or woman finds adjustment to monogamy almost impossible. 75
>
> Not infrequently, infidelity is the result of an "identity crisis" of one of the partners. A man may feel the need to test his virility. A woman may seek to reinforce her fading belief that she is still sexually attractive. 47/50

Often people get involved in sexual relationships because they are feeling lonely, depressed and like nobody really cares whether they live or die. They want, at least for a few moments, to be held and feel cared for or important to someone, even if it means having sex to get it.

Unfortunately, premature sexual involvement oftentimes makes things even worse. Lauren Chapin, who played Cathy Anderson in the TV series "Father Knows Best," describes a period in her life when she was desperately looking for happiness.

"I slept with many, many people trying to find love, to find self-worth," she said. "And the more people I slept with the less self-worth I had." 260/8

Before she became a Christian, Lauren Chapin had become involved with casual lovers, drugs and fast company. She had suffered through declining health, eight miscarriages, a mental hospital, prison, and welfare in what she calls Hollywood's "death zone." 260/8 She desperately and unsuccessfully searched for love until she found that most complete love, the love of God.

Casual sex not only failed to provide Lauren Chapin with the love and happiness she was seeking, but instead resulted in decreased self-esteem and even more unhappiness.

According to one study, women in general found casual sex lonely while men in general tended to find it meaningless. Sex alone, even "good sex," does not make a happy and enduring marriage relationship.

Jeanette and Robert Lauer researched successful and long-term marriages, and, in an article in *Psychology Today*, noted that sex was "far down the list of reasons for a happy marriage." 133/25 Less than 10 percent of the individuals with successful marriages thought good sexual relationships were important in keeping their marriage together. 133/25 Research data revealed, in this study of some three-hundred couples married more than fifteen years, that sex is not the key to a happy, fulfilled marriage.

But if good sex was not among the top reasons given for having a happy and enduring marriage, what kind of things were seen as important? According to their study the two top reasons given by both sexes as to why their marriage kept going were the same. They were:

(1) My spouse is my best friend.

(2) I like my spouse as a person. 133/25

One of the keys to developing personal significance is the freedom to fail, the freedom not to be perfect. Such freedom can be present only when a person feels security, when a person feels accepted for who he is, not for what he does. That kind of security is what young people need to develop in their relationships. And when they do, it will pay off in their marriage.

When two people are committed to each other, they both have freedom. They don't need to put on a show to gain the other's approval. Then, when they are married, they have the security to be themselves, to admit what they do not know. They don't have to be experts on their honeymoon because they are admitted amateurs. Part of the thrill of beginning a life together is learning about sex together, guiding and helping each other. It forms an extremely strong bond in the marriage, since, to a greater degree than anything else they will ever encounter, they are doing it together.

That is worth waiting for.

Apart from marriage, there is no security. There may be a spoken commitment, but if one partner refuses to make the commitment final through marriage, words are just words. Sex without commitment automatically bypasses the stages of acceptance, security and significance, and goes straight to putting someone on a performance basis. That person is not accepted as being a unique person who is loved no matter what, but instead has value only as he or she performs and puts out. It is degrading and dehumanizing. It is counter to everything God wants in relationships between people. It takes teenagers who are searching for security, and dangles in front of them a carrot they can never reach, no matter how hard they try.

2. Search for Intimacy

In their own words:

Another reason a teenager might rush into sex is that he is anxious to push this relationship into maturity in his search for intimacy. When they are making out, it gives him such a sense of security; he "knows" they are really starting to get close.

♡ ♡ ♡

The reason I see as the most common for sex before marriage is the overwhelming need to be close to another human being, to make emotional contact, to gain a sense of self-worth, to keep from being lonely and to feel cared for.

——————— ♥ ———————

One interviewer, in an effort to determine how peer pressure affects teenagers' sexual behavior, said the following: "I asked teenagers their motivations for engaging in sex, and the primary one was to express affection, intimacy, love and caring. Peer pressure is not, as far as I'm concerned, the primary motivation." 224/56-57

The excessive sexuality in our culture is indicative of our inability to experience true intimacy. An adolescent who has been involved sexually with various men wrote: "It is far easier to 'bare your bottom' than to 'bare your soul.' "

Emotional contact is the goal; sex is the means. When we see that on paper, it is obvious that a *physical* act cannot help someone reach an *emotional* goal, yet when you're an insecure teenager hungry for intimacy with another person, it seems plausible.

Emotional intimacy comes through recognizing and understanding our own emotions, and then sharing those feelings openly with another person in order to strengthen the relationship with that person. It means taking the risk of opening up to someone, not just unloading pent-up feelings or getting physically involved. It means letting our true self be visible, which holds the danger that our true self may not be found acceptable in the other person's eyes.

So to be able to be transparent with someone, we first have to be secure in ourselves. Then we must have a sense of security in the relationship that tells us our openness will not be abused.

As fallible beings, our security can ultimately be found only in the Lord. When our self-image is firmly rooted in a relationship with Jesus Christ, we are able to see in ourselves and others the dignity and worth God has given us.

If I am aware of my position in Christ and of the dignity God has bestowed on someone close to me, I am able to open up to that person and he can open up to me. He can tell me *anything* going on in his emotions, just as I don't have to hold back from him. We won't reject each other. We won't blackmail each other with the information shared. We won't condemn each other. Rather, we are there to strengthen one another and build our relationship. We are achieving emotional intimacy with each other.

One teen expresses it this way:

As I review my relationship with my fiancé, Jane, our most special times are when we have excellent conversations. Kissing is great enjoyment but we have found intimacy through conversations, talking about intimate things as well as working through problems. It sounds dull but it's not.

Without the security of knowing my position in Christ, without an understanding of the value and dignity of another person, I will be incapable of this intimacy. And even though I have a God-given desire for emotional closeness, I will close down my feelings rather than seek to open them up.

If I am unable to open up to another and allow another to open up to me freely, I am forced to resort to a substitute for intimacy. Since I can't go to my soul, I go to my body and my five senses. I turn to sensory closeness and become involved sexually.

The problem is that this false intimacy doesn't last. It proves itself to be shallow. People who discover this often fail to recognize what is happening, and instead of giving up the futile search for intimacy in bed, they intensify it. Time after time they achieve a type of closeness, and then watch it quickly fade. If this cycle is not broken, they will become numb to the idea of finding true intimacy. They settle for the cheap substitute.

Intimacy is built as a result of trust. Premarital sex easily breaks down that trust factor. Trust is built over time with a lot of communication as you work through problems. You see that the other person isn't going to "dump" you. You know that he or she is committed to you. Trust is established, and trust leads to vulnerability, and that leads to transparency, and that results in intimacy — a closeness to another person.

Intimacy, then, is twofold. First, having faith in Jesus Christ, we must be aware of our position in Him. When we know we are loved, accepted and deemed important by God *no matter what,* we have security and can develop a healthy sense of self worth.

Second, we must have love and acceptance from some person in our life, in order to see this tangible expression of God's love for us. We must see that it is possible for someone to accept us *no matter what,* that we in turn may be loving and accepting toward others. We must learn to love.

A healthy self-image arising from our relationship with God, combined with an experiential knowledge of how loving relationships work, makes us capable of emotional intimacy. It is God's design. When we achieve that intimacy in a dating relationship, we don't have to look to physical closeness. We know that it can wait until the relationship has been sealed.

3. An Escape From Relational Problems

In their own words:

Many people try to escape their problems — problems they may be having with friends, or, more likely, with their families — by having sex.

———————— ♥ ————————

Sex certainly can provide a short-term escape from a troubled teenage life. Once again, in this sense sex is like a drug, something to numb the pain. But sex is only temporary, and afterward the participants discover that the problems are not solved.

Two people may feel that their relationship is in trouble; they're starting to feel separated from one another. Having sex may give them a feeling of intimacy, of closeness — but only for a short time.

The questions teens need to ask themselves are: Is having sex a rational, legitimate way of dealing with my problems? Is it intelligent? Does it solve anything? (Actually, these are all the same question.)

Rather than try to blot problems out of our minds through sex or any other means, we need to deal with them. The first step is to acknowledge that problems exist and are having an effect on us. Next, we should try to understand why the problems exist. Then we need to seek counsel from someone who can help us through them.

God gives Christians three resources for bringing about change in our lives: the Scriptures, the Holy Spirit and the body of Christ. We need to utilize those resources as much as we can. They are free and come in unlimited supplies. They will help us resolve problems so we don't have to run from them or seek some other escape such as premarital or extramarital sex.

4. A Way to be Popular

Being Cool

Cool is a difficult term to define, yet we all more or less understand it. A cool person is popular, in, "with it." You don't even have to be likable to be cool. You just have to be cool.

This elusive state of being is foremost in the minds of many teenagers. The desire to be cool is the driving force behind many an action a teenager takes. It is ultimately a desire to be accepted, and since sexual involvement is often a prerequisite for acceptance, having sex becomes cool.

In their own words:

There were no feelings at all, not for each other and not for ourselves. We were basically doing it because it was cool . . .

♡ ♡ ♡

Someone asked me if I was still a virgin. I wanted to be cool, so I said no. Now that people have that in their heads about me, why should I wait?

———————— ♥ ————————

Being cool, being in, being faddish, is simply going along with others. A person who tags along just because something is cool says, "I don't know who I am; I don't have my own values, so I'll just do what everyone else does."

Rather than show the maturity of one who has internalized personal values and stands up for them, the teenager trying to be cool is a chameleon. He becomes what others expect him to be instead of who God created him to be. He lives out his life according to the minds and expectations of those he is trying to impress.

Being Macho or Liberated

"You don't want someone to think you're not a man, do you?"

"What's the matter, aren't you a liberated woman?"

Those views of sex show not only that many people have a low view of themselves, but also that they have a low view of what constitutes masculinity or femininity.

A high school girl trying to prove how liberated she is by having sex is caught in the mentality of a "liberation movement" that does nothing to make her free.

A woman may say, "I no longer want to be seen as a sex object for men; my worth should not be gauged by my appearance" — which is a valid way of thinking. However, instead of coming to an accurate, biblical view of herself, a woman may now say, "My worth is determined by how I perform and what I can accomplish," which is just as false a basis for self-worth as her outward appearance is.

Boys trying to be macho through sexual activity are caught in an equally self-defeating mentality. Their basic view of a real man is one who can drink everyone else under the table and make it with the women. A macho man uses others for his own pleasure and ego gratification, shows little respect for others as human beings and must continually perform. This means he considers himself of value only as long as he lives up to this warped standard of exploitation and conquest. Such a person does not have a healthy self-image.

Somehow we have been brainwashed into thinking that if you have sex you're a man. The opposite is stressed even more. That is, if you haven't had sex you're *not* a man.

If a fraternity brother stood up in his Greek house and said, "Brothers, I'm a virgin; I'm going to remain a virgin until I get married," what do you think the response would be? You're right. They would chide him and accuse him of not being a MAN. I ask, What in the world does sex have to do with being a man? A twelve-year-old kid can have sex. Does that make him a man? My dog can have sex. Does that make him a man? I can just see it. My German shepherd impregnates another dog, and a fraternity brother exclaims, "Wow, what a man!"

A sex education program used in Atlanta schools, titled "Postponing Sexual Involvement," gives some good advice to answer this kind of pressure:

> Some girls think having sex makes them grown-up. They think having sex will make them a "woman." In our society, a lot of boys think they have to have sex with a girl to prove they are a "man." They think it makes them "cool" or "macho" to other boys and girls. However, having sex has little to do with being grown-up. *Being grown-up means being able to develop and keep a long-lasting relationship. It means being able to take responsibility within that relationship for the consequences of how you act.* 85/11

How can kids reply to sexual pressure containing such innuendoes?

"If I let other people like you tell me what to do, that would show I'm *not* a man. I'll make up my own mind about what I want to do. That's being a man."

"Look, just because I don't want to have sex with you doesn't mean I'm not a man. I'm just not interested in getting more involved right now. I don't feel sex is everything in a relationship." 85/53

Girls trying to be liberated and boys trying to be macho need to come to an accurate understanding of who they are according to the descriptions given in the Bible. They need to recognize that the worth and dignity of a human being are not based on appearance, performance or proof of sexual ability.

When they begin to recognize that they are special in the eyes of God, they will begin to treat others as being equally special.

5. Living Together in Preparation for Marriage

Some people see cohabitation as a part of their *courtship*. They claim it provides a couple the opportunity to really get to know each other and thus be able to decide if they're compatible. Their assumption is that living together is a good sample of what married life is like and that, if a couple gets along well while cohabiting, they will have a good and long-lasting marriage. "On the surface," Dr. John Raney writes, "this would seem to make sense." 280/4

However, in a recent article, Dr. Joyce Brothers presents the view based on research data that the kinds of learning that occur during cohabitation don't particularly work for or against success in a marriage. 281/11 Some evidence, though, suggests that cohabitation may, in fact, have a negative effect on the quality of a subsequent marriage.

One study was made comparing couples who cohabited prior to marriage with those who had not. The findings showed that those who had lived together before marriage were more likely to disagree on such things as recreation, household duties and finances; they were more likely to seek marriage counseling; and they had broken up more often than those who had not lived together before marriage. 282/8 It should be mentioned that whether this difference related to the cohabiting experience or to the personalities, values and lifestyles of the individuals apart from the experience is still open to question.

In more recent research, Alfred DeMaris of Auburn University and Gerald Leslie of the University of Florida found that those who had cohabited prior to marriage "scored significantly lower in both perceived quality of marital communication and marital satisfaction. These differences were significant for wives in the area of communication and for both spouses in the area of marital satisfaction." 283/83 The differences persisted even when variables such as church attendance and sex-role views, which might have affected the outcome, were taken into account.

Communication

Apparently in living-together relationships, couples usually do not communicate their deeply held beliefs, ideas or fears. A psychologist, Dr. Matti Gershenfeld, president of the Couples Learning Center near Philadelphia, says, "To maintain their living-together relationship, couples often hide from each other important aspects of their true selves." 281/12

As one woman who had previously been in a live-in situation commented about sharing things like personal troubles, "It was too scary. I would never have told him how I really felt." 284/79

Dr. L. Mansell Pattison, professor and chairman of the Department of Psychiatry, Medical College of Georgia, in Augusta, puts it this way, "Good times are shared, and the good self is revealed; the bad times are hidden, and the bad self is concealed." 284/79

Pattison also states, "There is superficial sharing, but it does not extend to the core of the self that we spend so much time hiding from ourselves and others." 284/79

It appears that couples who are living together are afraid to look closely at issues, lest their differences hurt their relationship. 281/12 Their partner just might move out if significant differences arose, since living-together arrangements are much easier to dissolve than marriages. You don't have to go through the hassle and expense of getting a divorce. You can just walk out.

Decision Making

Living-together situations also allow a couple to avoid dealing with some of the joint decisions that married couples have to make. For example, money and property tend to be either *his* or *hers*, not *ours;* consequently, it isn't all that important how he or she spends his or her money. But once they're married, they will have to decide jointly how *they* are going to spend *their* money, when to save it, and how to invest it.

In-laws are rarely a factor in a live-in arrangement; they often disapprove and stay aloof from the couple. Only after marriage do in-laws intrude and cause disagreements, tears and divided loyalties. And then some joint decisions must be made by the couple as to how to handle this.

Nor does a live-in arrangement usually have to adapt to children, who require adjustments and sacrifices that some relationships can't accommodate. Married couples have to resolve these issues.

Sexual Dissatisfaction

If there are sexual adjustment problems, one member of the couple in a living-together arrangement easily can seek sex outside the relationship. In fact, "There's no real pressure on the couple," explains Dr. Raney, "to try to work out their sexual problems together, and in this regard it is of interest that the leading cause for the breakup of cohabiting couples is sexual problems or dissatisfaction." 284/70

Jacob Aranza, youth speaker and author, helps to clarify the issue about the need for sexual experimentation before marriage as a prelude to sexual enjoyment in marriage or as a means of resolving sexual problems before entering into marriage:

> But what if we don't get along sexually? Wouldn't it be better to make sure before we decided if we are "right" for each other?
>
> The answer is quite simple. The bodies of men and women are made to join together. There is no way that they couldn't be "right" for each other.
>
> The question I'm really being asked is, What if my partner likes sex one way and I like it another way?
>
> Sex, like any other part of marriage, is something you grow into. It's a learning experience for both people, a giving and taking. When you really love your husband/wife, you want to do what pleases them, and vice-versa. You learn to tell each other what you do and don't like. It's not like the passion they show on TV where it looks like every couple is in ecstasy!
>
> It's much better than that. You're getting to know each other intimately and can have a lot of fun in the process! 50/31

Pattison warns that "sex and love are not to be confused. Many partners are libidinally attractive, but sexual compatibility is different from life compatibility. A successful marriage combines sexual *and* life compatibility." 284/79

Similarly, a recent article in *Newsweek* states: "Sex alone cannot sustain a relationship — even Hugh Hefner has learned that." 285/51

Millions of people have been fooled by physical attraction or a "romantic relationship." A recent article in *Medical Aspects of Human Sexuality* points out:

> Many marry a "dream" hoping that strong magnetic sexual attraction means [living] happily ever after . . . They then find that good sex does not mean a good relationship, but that a bad relationship quickly may lead to bad sex." 286/73

A couple engaging in sex in the hope of helping their future marriage may find sex actually to be a barrier to the relationship. They may have a false sense of feeling good about each other because of a favorable sexual experience. They may overlook other weak spots in the relationship, which can lead to trouble after (or, more likely, even before) marriage.

Compatibility

"I wouldn't dream of marrying someone I hadn't lived with,"

young people frequently say today. "That's like buying a pair of shoes you haven't tried on."

Sounds logical, doesn't it? A couple has a trial period of cohabitation. If they find they are compatible, they get married. If not, they go their separate ways. They find out before they marry whether they'll get along. That should cut down on the divorce rate. Right?

Wrong, say sociologists Jeffrey Jacques and Karen Chason of Florida A&M University, who studied two groups of students married for at least thirteen months. In one group, the couples had lived together before their marriage; in the other, they had not. The researchers say they could find few differences between the couples. Satisfaction with the marriage was no higher or lower if the couples had lived together first. Neither was dissatisfaction. As many couples in one group as in the other seemed headed for conflict or divorce. However, both groups reported that they still found their partners sexually attractive and rated their sex lives as highly satisfactory.

Why doesn't a trial period of living together alter the marriage experience? For one thing, both people know that it's a trial. The man knows the woman doesn't have to put up with him if he mistreats her; the woman knows the man doesn't have to put up with a moody mate. So they both tend to be on their best behavior. Since it is a trial, each may be willing to put up with traits in the other that would be intolerable if a shared lifetime loomed ahead.

"Living together, it seems, prepares one only for future living with someone else. *It appears to have little correlation with happiness in marriage."* 34/4-7

Dr. Nancy Moore Clatworthy is a sociologist at Ohio State University in Columbus and has been studying the phenomenon of unmarried couples of the opposite sex living together. 282 Authors Charles and Bonnie Remsberg interviewed Dr. Clatworthy for *Seventeen* magazine. Following are excerpts from that interview:

> Q: *When you began your studies, what was your attitude toward unmarried couples living together?*
> A: I was intrigued. I saw it as a bold new step, a sensible thing, an extension of the old process of going steady. Some people were living together openly, some secretly. The couples usually reported how glad they were to be involved in the arrangement and how wonderful it was. I believed them initially.

Problems

Q: *What changed your mind?*

A: I began seeing girls so uptight that they couldn't be happy — constantly fearful of their parents' reactions, or disclosure of their situation, or pregnancy, or whatever. Then when we started testing couples who had lived together before marriage, we began to see other problems cropping up.

Q: *What did you find?*

A: The surface answers in favor of living together were not supported by underlying feelings. The most common problems were in the areas of adjustment, happiness and respect. There were specific questions designed to gauge the degree of those feelings. People who had not lived together before marriage showed a much higher degree of respect than those who had. The same was true for individuals' evaluation of their own degree of happiness and adjustment. It appears that the problems people say living together solves, are not.

Q: *Could you be more specific?*

A: One of the questions was, How often do you fantasize breaking off your relationship with your spouse? The only people who checked the "Often" answer had lived together before marriage. None of the people who had married first selected that answer.

Another question asked subjects to estimate their usual level of personal happiness. The only people who checked the "Extremely unhappy" answer were the ones who had lived together before marriage. You can't interpret this to mean that all people who marry first are happier, but you do have to conclude that it is a statement about living together before marriage.

Q: *But doesn't living together before marriage help to iron out some of the disagreements that every marriage inevitably must face?*

A: We asked questions about finances, household matters, recreation, demonstration of affection, and friends. In every area the couples who had lived together before marriage disagreed more often than the couples who had not. But the finding that surprised me most concerned sex. Couples who had lived together before marriage disagreed about it more often. You'd assume that this would be resolved in a living-together period. Apparently it isn't.

Q: *Don't couples who live together before marriage solve any of their problems?*

A: Almost half of the people who had lived together first said they had the same number of problems after marriage as before. Almost 20 percent said they had more. So you can't count on getting rid of your problems just by living with someone. You simply take them with you.

Commitment

Q: *One often hears: "We're in love with each other; we're committed to each other. We don't need a piece of paper to prove it." Would you comment?*

A: The other side of that argument is obvious. If there's no difference in your relationship, what's wrong with adding one more symbol to your total commitment? They are really saying they are not totally committed to each other.

Q: *Why is commitment so important?*

A: Commitment is what makes a marriage, living together, or any other human relationship work. Without commitment, one or the other party simply splits as soon as a problem arises. With commitment, you stay and try to work it out.

The problem most often encountered in living-together situations is a difference in level of commitment. One partner is more committed to the relationship than the other. Since that partner is frequently the girl, she runs more risk of being badly hurt.

Suppose I say to you, "I love you, so I'm going to make you a 60-percent commitment"? That's basically what many of those who live together are saying. However, if I say, "I love you, and I want to marry you," I'm saying, "I am making a 100-percent commitment to you. I'll do everything I can to sustain and protect our relationship." This "giving-ness" is what is missing when people don't make a total commitment.

A girl who was living with her boyfriend told me, "I know he's running around. If we were married, I wouldn't put up with it." She felt that if they were married, they would both be committed to an ideal of fidelity. Unmarried, she felt she had no choice but to accept infidelity, and naturally, she was very hurt.

Sociologists compiled statistics several years ago indicating that 75 percent of those who live together break up. If you think stability and security are important, you have to look at that figure and say, "That's not very good."

Q: *Take a given couple who love each other and who plan a permanent alliance. Do you feel they're better off to marry first rather than live together?*

A: They would be better off marrying. There are many problems involved in living together and also many problems involved in being married. But when you live together, and then marry, you're saying, "All right, we've worked to solve this set of problems; now let's trade them in for a whole new. set." 111

Consequences

Not all couples who "practice being married" actually live

together before the ceremony, but it is no secret that the number of them who do has risen drastically in the last two decades. One study of such couples shows, among other points:

> the most significant positive consequences for cohabitants are companionship, sexual gratification and economic gain; . . . the most significant negative consequences for cohabitants are the resolution of conflict concerning property rights upon termination of the relationship and the increased risk for female cohabitants due to their differing expectations with regard to marriage and sexual exclusivity in these relationships; . . . cohabitation does not seem to alter sex roles in marriage nor increase the quality of the mate selection process. 56/601

When people try to get the benefits of marriage without the commitment of marriage, it can be only for personal gain. Look at the positive consequences listed above: companionship, sexual gratification, economic gain. All are self-directed. They have nothing to do with giving to another or strengthening a relationship.

Look at the negative consequences: fights over material things, fights over sleeping around, emotional trauma caused by differing expectations about commitment. Again, the selfish nature of "playing married" is evident.

The Right Person

Finally, this research shows that living together will not help someone find the right person to marry. It all comes down to the basis for establishing a marriage.

If a person wants to find the right sex partner for marriage, he is going about it backward by living with someone. He could itemize qualities he demands in a mate, sexual prowess being among them, and begin to hunt, eventually settling for the person who best fulfills his "shopping list." But that person must continually live up to his expectations or be considered insufficient. That's no way to start a marriage, although it is done every day.

In 1986, there were around 11,000 marriages in the county I live in. There were around 13,000 divorces. Shopping-list marriages aren't working.

The secret to a lasting marriage is for each person to focus on improving himself or herself and the quality of his or her character. In that way, one can *become* the right person for someone else to find. There's no shopping involved.

This effort to be the right person for marriage must start early. Teenagers, rather than resenting their youth and its limitations, should be glad for the opportunity it presents. They have complete freedom to strengthen their character and begin to instill positive traits in themselves so that when the time comes to consider marriage, they don't have to go shopping. They don't have to practice sex. They don't have to worry about the quality of the relationship they are entering, because each of them already will have established themselves to be high-quality people.

For further information regarding the essential of *being* the right person in preparation for a fulfilling marriage, see my book *The Secret of Loving*.

MYTHS AND FAULTY BELIEFS

6. No One Will Be Hurt

In their own words:

Although the promiscuous lifestyle of the '60s is no longer in vogue, the popularity of sex before marriage is still on the rise. Why should we be surprised? Not only is sex a pleasurable experience, but with the proper care, two people can be reasonably sure that children will not result and also that disease will be avoided. So, if nobody is hurt, why wait for marriage?

♡ ♡ ♡

Teenagers tend to rationalize by saying it is better to be sexually involved than to be involved in drugs and alcohol. They think they aren't hurting themselves.

♡ ♡ ♡

There are also people who think premarital sex is OK because it doesn't hurt anybody. These people think, "Well, I can do what I want with my body and if both of us want to do it, it's OK."

———————— ♥ ————————

When teenagers try to rationalize sex by claiming that it doesn't hurt anyone, two main elements are at work: (1) These people willfully turn a blind eye to the pain that premarital sex has already caused in countless lives around them; (2) they give in to relativistic thinking and rely on situational ethics to guide them rather than an absolute standard of right and wrong.

A man decides to take a shortcut through a rough part of town. He has heard of the beatings and muggings that take place there, but as he looks ahead, he sees that the street is empty. He decides it is safe and proceeds. A woman in a third-floor apartment at the next crossing looks out her window and sees the man nearing the intersection. Around the corner, out of his sight, waits a group of young men. She turns a blind eye on the man's approaching pain, pulls away and shuts the curtains, having seen the inevitable mugging too many times.

It doesn't take a sociological genius to know how premarital sex hurts people. All we have to do is read a newspaper. Our society is hurting terribly from unwanted pregnancies, sexually transmitted diseases, abortion and so on. All a teenager has to do is look around the classroom to see broken relationships and emotional wreckage caused by premarital sex.

Teenagers who think they will be spared this pain are lying to themselves. They are being willfully ignorant. They think the rules don't apply to them. But just ahead, around the corner, the muggers wait to attack.

A Christian who understands God's system of values does not have to grope around to find right and wrong. God's standards are unchanging. They apply to any society and to any person at any time in history. There is no guesswork.

But those who do not accept the definitions of right and wrong as set forth in the Bible have to find some other way of determining their values. They have to be able to approach a situation and set a course of action based on *something.* If they listen to the relativistic thinking of our society, they will look to themselves for answers. They will say, "The right thing to do in this situation is to do what makes me feel good or is to my advantage."

This is situational ethics, a make-it-up-as-you-go morality that has no basis in anything. It allows a person to justify premarital sex by saying, "It won't hurt anyone," when he really means, "I think I can get out of this without being hurt, so it must be all right." Such ethics fly in the face of the righteous standards God has given us in His Word.

The extreme danger in this was spelled out by Paul when he said, "So I tell you this, and insist on it in the Lord, that you must no longer live as the Gentiles do, in the futility of their thinking. They are darkened in their understanding and separated from the life of God because of the ignorance that is in them due to the hardening of their hearts. Having lost all sensitivity, they have given themselves over to sensuality so as to indulge in every kind of impurity, with a continual lust for more" (Ephesians 4:17-19, NIV).

Christians who have fallen into relativistic thinking have two choices: (1) to turn back to God and to the truth, which has remained constant since time began; or (2) to continue as they are, in which case they will move further away from any semblance of righteousness, and their heart will become more and more hardened toward God.

7. It's All Right During Engagement

In their own words:

Many people feel that if they are engaged they can go ahead and have sex. If they're going to be married, why not just get started a little earlier?

♡ ♡ ♡

Lori and Jeff, a strong Christian couple, had been dating seven months when they fell into the trap of the enemy. "I thought it wouldn't be that bad to consummate our relationship, because, after all, we were engaged, and we knew we were going to be married." That was Lori's excuse. She didn't realize that God doesn't look at future promises when dealing with present sin.

The father of lies will try to convince you that if you really love a person, God understands your need to express that love in a physical manner. Not true. After a time of being sexually active, Lori and Jeff went through a terrible two-month period that could have destroyed their relationship. Although they repented, the scars are still there. Lori speaks of the time they were "engaged in sin." "Our prayer life went downhill. So did everything else. I felt, 'Now Jeff is coming over to see me — for just one reason.' "

———————————— ♥ ————————————

Studies show that 50 percent of people who get married have been engaged at least once before. So being engaged really means nothing as far as having the security of knowing that you will be married to that person soon.

One essay was written in the form of a letter to a friend:

Dear Kelly,
Congratulations on your engagement! You've just entered into a very special stage of life, no longer single but not quite married. Mike seems to be a perfect match for you. The more I get to know him, the more I believe that your match was made in heaven.

However, one area of your relationship has been troubling me for a while, but I haven't known how to talk to you about it. It's your increasing sexual involvement with Mike. You've told me he sometimes puts pressure on you to go further in your physical relationship than you feel comfortable with, and that you often give in because of your desire to please him. As a Christian, you know that God has reserved sexual intercourse for the marriage bed, so I have no worries about your becoming pregnant or contracting a sexually transmitted disease. What does worry me is this: I know from counseling many young women that the commitment of engagement often makes it easier to rationalize heavy sexual involvement that stops just short of what is expressly forbidden.

Let me warn you that by engaging in that kind of sexual activity you are risking spiritual, emotional and psychological consequences. Our vision always seems to be clearer in hindsight. For that reason, I want to tell you the story of a young woman I know who was once almost exactly where you are now.

Pat first had sex when she was sixteen. She became a Christian the next year, and although she eventually learned that sex outside marriage was wrong, she was often frustrated by her inability to break an established pattern of exchanging sex for "love." Finally, Pat decided to stop dating for a couple of years so she could get her thoughts together. It was a time of incredible spiritual growth and it seemed God was giving her victory in an area that had been a "thorn in the flesh" for so long. At last she felt ready to start dating again. After a few brief relationships, she met Bill.

A mature Christian and leader in her church, Bill was quite different from any guy she'd ever dated. He rarely touched her, but instead spent time discovering her secret plans and aspirations. For the first time, Pat sensed a genuine interest in herself as a person and not as a sex object. Bill even asked Pat's permission before he first kissed her. When they became engaged, Pat felt that her dreams had come true.

But even the sweetest dreams can turn sour. As their love intensified, so did their physical affection. Each kiss seemed a little longer than the last, each embrace a little more passionate. At first, Pat wasn't at all concerned. She thought, *Hey, I don't have a problem with lust anymore. I'm perfectly capable of controlling myself, and besides, Bill would never pressure me for sex.*

But just as the kisses were losing their excitement, Bill's hands started reaching down Pat's chest. The first time it happened, he apologized for losing control, but soon his fondling her breasts became a regular part of their romance. One night things went further than either of them planned. As they were making out, Bill reached for Pat's pelvis. She angrily broke away from him. When he tried to comfort her by saying that his goal was to give her pleasure by trying to manually bring her to orgasm, she tearfully replied she didn't want that kind of pleasure — not yet. They asked each other's forgiveness, prayed to the Lord for His forgiveness, and Bill promised, "This will never happen again." But it did happen, again and again and again.

Pat would try to resist Bill's advances gently. When his hands moved toward her most erogenous areas, she would firmly put them elsewhere. She explained why she didn't want to have her body sexually aroused, why she believed it was wrong, but Bill never seemed to hear her words. Pat often felt as if she was fighting a battle; their sexual involvement was most intense when she became too weary to fight.

At that point Pat came and talked to me. She expressed a desire to have a pure relationship, although she often fell short of that desire. She said, "Normally, I would advise someone in my situation to get out of the ungodly relationship, but how do you get out of the relationship when it's with the person you want to spend the rest of your life with?"

I met again with Pat two months later. This time her desire to strive for godliness was gone. In its place was strong rationalization. I sensed she had grown tired of fighting Bill, had given in and was desperately seeking to find some way to justify to herself the sexual activity she knew was wrong. She said, "I realize now that this is different from my past sexual activity. I used to buy love with sex. I know I don't have to buy Bill's love; it's already mine. Now I share my body out of my love for him. Plus, being engaged really makes things different. Bill and I love each other and we are committed to each other, and that's the context God wants sex in, right? Besides, we will be married in three months, and if we get familiar with each other's bodies now, we will feel much more at ease on our wedding night. We will also have some knowledge of what is sexually pleasing to each other so our sexual adjustment in marriage will be easy."

Pat's rationale sounded good on first hearing, but her life betrayed the lie she was living. The first thing to go was her spiritual life. She lost all desire to spend time in God's Word or in prayer. She no longer confessed her sin to God because she felt that nothing needed forgiving. Pat gradually stopped going to church and fellowship groups. She wasn't getting anything out of them, she said. I suspect it was because she felt like a hypocrite. When friends would ask if anything was wrong, she would answer, "No, nothing, I'm just going through a dry spell with God right now."

Mentally, Pat began to experience depression. Sometimes she would start crying for no apparent reason. The radiant joy that had once characterized her life was replaced by a lethargic "blue" feeling and a constant lack of energy.

Slowly, even the dream relationship with Bill began to change. She would get irritable and snap at him without provocation. She was increasingly critical of him. It became difficult for her to trust him or to believe his promises. Though Pat and Bill still verbally professed their love for one another, the feelings they once had were slowly growing cold and were at times replaced by revulsion and even hatred.

Throughout that time, the whirl of wedding plans and parties offered a convenient busyness into which Pat could throw herself. Occasionally, when her schedule slowed down enough to allow a quiet moment alone, she would wonder if she was doing the right thing by marrying Bill. But she attributed her fears to pre-nuptial jitters.

When Pat's sister Karen came home from college a month before the wedding, she noticed a marked difference in Pat. Lovingly, Karen began to question her sister until she got a full account of the relationship. Karen convinced Pat that starting a lifetime commitment under the present circumstances could be disastrous and the best thing to do would be to postpone the wedding. It was good that Pat had the courage to follow Karen's advice. She realized it would be better to put the relationship on hold than to terminate it years later in divorce court.

Pat and Bill never did marry. It has been several years now, and Pat only recently has acknowledged that sexual involvement was the root of the problems. She told me, "As I think back, I know that the effects of our unwise sexual activities were deadly. The mutual loss of respect, the guilt, the anger at myself and him, were all things we tried to ignore but eventually could not. Using our engagement as a rationale was never enough to excuse our actions, though we often tried to do so. I thought I could isolate my sex life from the rest of my life, but I quickly learned that, like a rope woven together, all the areas of my life are intertwined and affected by each other. I still wonder how something that started off so great could become such a nightmare. Where did we go wrong? It's hard to admit, but I'm now convinced that our premature sexual intimacy ultimately caused our engagement to be broken."

Kelly, I hope you can see why I've taken the time to write all this to you. I want to help keep you from making similar mistakes and suffering the same pain as Pat. I do get worried about you because I see many similarities between you and Pat in situation, background and mindset. However, I know that at this point your basic desire is to live a life pleasing to God. That's why I believe you can avoid taking the path Pat took.

——————— ♥ ———————

If every engagement ended in marriage, it might be hard, apart from the Bible, to refute sexual activity during this period. But, as has been noted, the reality is that over half of all engagements are broken off.

God established sex for the marriage relationship. As a couple builds toward the point of officially sealing their commitment in front of God, friends and family, they find more and more opportunities to strengthen that commitment. The engagement period should be a wonderful time of supporting, loving and honoring one another.

Sex before marriage doesn't build up, it breaks down. It doesn't show love, it shows selfishness and self-centeredness. It doesn't honor, it uses. In one sense, a rush for sex before marriage embodies everything an engagement *shouldn't* be.

The Bible could not be clearer about the need to reserve sex for marriage. As Vance Havner says, "We do not really break the Law of God, we break ourselves against it. We do not break the law of gravity by jumping from a skyscraper, we break our necks. Benjamin Franklin said, 'He who spits against the wind spits in his own face.' Our sins find us out."

The story of Pat and Bill was included here in its entirety because it gets the point across better than a hundred sermons could. People can argue and justify themselves all day long, but the pain brought about by consciously violating God's command is terribly real. Sex before marriage cannot help the marriage in any way.

Those who insist on "becoming familiar with each other's bodies" for the sake of the wedding night are not only denying themselves the thrill of discovery on that night, the first night in which they can do what only a husband and wife may do, they also disregard a basic knowledge of anatomy. In the words of Tim Downs, a Christian cartoonist and speaker, "Rest assured — the plumbing works." There is no need to try it out in advance.

But despite the pain that sex may have brought to almost-married couples, there is good news. God heals.

Dick and I have counseled a number of couples who were involved sexually, and we have seen great things happen when they gave control of the relationship back to God. We have seen couples in much the same situation as Pat and Bill reestablish trust and mutual respect by totally abstaining from physical contact. Even though they may have felt they couldn't go back to a non-physical relationship, they knew they had to choose between putting off gratification for the moment and losing each other. We have seen engagements turn from being a time of insecurity and distrust to a time of purification. It can be done.

When trust is rebuilt in such a close relationship, it causes the individual partners to trust themselves again. Whereas the sexual activity had caused each to feel insecure and to have a poor self-image, stopping the activity brought about a new sense of self-control, responsibility and dignity. As they each experienced a new, healthy self-image, they were able to view the other also as a person worthy of dignity and respect.

8. "I Owe It To Him"

In their own words:

You feel you owe it to your boyfriend or girlfriend. Perhaps they have been really nice to you, and you think sex could repay them. First, your date or steady is probably nice to you because they want to be. Second, you don't owe them anything. If they try to say you do, that may have been the reason they were nice in the first place. You have to stick to your own personal morals; you don't owe sex to anyone.

———————— ♥ ————————

If a girl thinks she owes a boy sex (it is rarely the other way around), it is because he wants her to think that. Otherwise, she would know by his words and actions that he cares for her regardless of how she responds. He either cares for her and acts in a loving and respectful way, or he is concerned about himself and acts in a manipulative way.

It all comes back to the dignity of each person and how our world view influences our actions. To treat people with dignity is to show them God's love by our actions. The Christian world view is not compatible with manipulation; manipulation indicates people are there to be used, not loved. God's love longs to give, not get.

A graduate student about to be married writes, "God has gracefully given Jane and me physical self-control in our three years of dating. I have never asked or expected her to perform in any way. She owes me nothing, especially her own body. By my having that attitude, she respects me and in marriage will want to give herself totally and freely to me. It is a love with no strings attached and no wrong and deceptive motivations. She knows that I respect her and this builds her up as a woman of God."

The story is told of a man who approached a woman and asked if she would go to bed with him for a million dollars. She said she would.

He then asked, "Would you do it for ten dollars?"

"No!" she said, "What do you think I am, a prostitute?"

"Well," the man said, "we have already established that. Now we're just haggling over the price."

In a sense, we prostitute ourselves when we allow others to manipulate us. We give them what they want in order to get what we want. A girl manipulated by a boy into sex because "she owes it to him" is selling her body for whatever she wants out of the relationship, be it security, popularity, or some semblance of love. God is grieved when we thus destroy the dignity He has given us.

The cause of this mentality of "giving something in order to get something" is insecurity. If a boy feels he *must* have sex with a girl, regardless of how he gets her to say yes, he is showing insecurity. He has made sex a requirement for feeling right about himself or feeling good about her. Likewise, a girl who gives in to his manipulation in order not to lose him does not have a self-image grounded in the Word of God. She values the relationship more than her own importance, and she acts out her insecurities.

Sex is not a chip to be bartered with. You don't buy it in the market. When it becomes something to be obtained by making strategic moves, sex becomes an end in itself.

A manipulative boy does not want sex with this particular girl, he just wants sex. When he indicates that she owes it to him if she wants to keep the relationship, he shows that he is out to take, not give. He's not seeking to cement a lifelong commitment of love and sharing and looking out for the other person's best interests; he wants to make it with anyone who will say yes. A girl who offers herself at such a price doesn't feel she is of great value, which is tragic in light of so much that God says to the contrary.

9. It Proves One's Love

In their own words:

People worry about offending their girlfriend or boyfriend. For example, the boy may believe that having sex is the only way to prove your love. If the girl doesn't have sex with him, it is the same as saying she doesn't love him. Even though to her that isn't true, her boyfriend may believe it. When such a situation arises, the girl has to decide who is more important to her, God or her boyfriend. The other solution would be for her boyfriend to change and realize that a good relationship is more important than having sex.

–––––––––––––––– ♥ ––––––––––––––––

Nowhere in the Scriptures do we find an example of showing someone love by manipulating and causing that person to sin. When the Bible talks about love, it always refers to actions and attitudes that draw people closer to God and demonstrate His character.

Sex without marriage can never demonstrate the love of God; people who fall for "proving their love" with sex are buying into a lie with their bodies and emotions. They are squandering something priceless on a cheap product.

But what about non-Christians, people who don't measure right and wrong by God's standards? Perhaps their personal definition of love allows for this kind of activity.

Such a question can be answered only by that person's value system, which, without an absolute standard as its base, is foggy to begin with. If a non-Christian girl believes that the most loving thing she can do is give somebody something he wants, she is caught. If he wants sex, she can give him that. But what if he wants her to help him commit suicide? Must she, out of love, push him off a cliff?

A deficient value system is one that contradicts itself. It lets people think, in some instances, that right and wrong actions (or loving and non-loving actions) are based on how they will make someone feel, yet it also may prohibit certain actions because they are "just plain wrong." Without a measuring rod to determine right and wrong, standards become arbitrary. And when right and wrong are arbitrary, they are meaningless.

Christian teenagers who think sex is a way to show love have lost sight of God. They aren't filtering their thoughts and actions through the Bible. If they were, they would know that acts of love can only do good and draw others to God. Premarital sex does not fit that description.

10. It Shows Passage From Childhood to Adulthood

The teenage years are times of transition from being a dependent child to becoming an interdependent adult. *Interdependent* persons believe that they have something worthwhile to give to others, and that others have something worthwhile to give to them.

While this transition from childhood to adulthood involves every facet of a young person's life, we must remember that the different areas of that individual's life develop at different rates of speed.

For example, one person may seem more "mature" than another of the same age because he is more mature socially and emotionally than the other. But, the second person may be more mature physically than the first.

Regardless of a teenager's actual level of development, to many of them sex seems a way to speed up their total passage to adulthood. After all, sex is not something *children* do. It is for adults. The logic behind this way of thinking is not hard to see.

In their own words:

Many young people, even though they are still in school, view themselves as fully mature. Because of this feeling, they want to engage in so-called "adult activities," such as smoking, drinking and having sex. It would be tough to explain to them why they shouldn't be involved in sex if they see themselves as adults and then look around and see what other adults are doing. Still others may have sex to *become* mature. They think if they have sex they will somehow magically become adults.

♡ ♡ ♡

A feeling of maturity is a final reason kids engage in premarital sex. Teens feel that having sex makes them adults, but they don't realize that being an adult means having certain attitudes and accepting all consequences. Many teens think they can handle their sexuality, and in turn handle the consequences of their actions. A feeling of maturity leads teens into thinking they are mature. This is not the case.

♡ ♡ ♡

The belief that sex is a passage from childhood to adulthood makes it difficult to resist: Boys want to become men; girls want to become women.

———————— ♥ ————————

The author of a magazine article recently received this letter from a young man who sincerely believes that maturity is acquired through having a sexual relationship:

> Dear Beth:
> I am a senior in high school, and Molly is a junior. We have been very close in every way, and have great respect for each other as well as love. Last fall we decided, after long discussions, that the time had come for sexual relations. So Molly went on the pill a month before, to be ready.
> My parents went away for a vacation, and Molly stayed overnight. We were a little shy and awkward, but it was a wonderful experience just the same. It has brought us even closer together.
> We aren't just "sex-crazed kids." We are both on the honor roll, good athletes, and well liked by our friends. We both have big plans for the future, and I hope Molly is a part of mine, but even if she's not, I'll have no regrets. I just wanted you to know that for kids who are willing to take responsibility, this can be the right choice. — One Who Knows. 275

A youth worker observes:

> High school girls I know try to act like married persons in a relationship, and having sex is one of the ways they do it. Girls have dreamed of marriage and the perfect man from an early age and they often like to pretend. I, however, have heard girls say that when they gave away their virginity they felt they gave away their youth, which they are very sorry about. This is especially true if they got pregnant.

Our culture makes the transition from childhood to adulthood difficult for the American teenager. Just a few generations ago, young people came into physical development around age thirteen or fourteen and were married by sixteen or seventeen. Today's young people may well be on their way to physical maturity before even reaching thirteen, yet the marrying age often gets pushed into the twenties and even further.

Although teenagers may be interested in instant physical maturity, they often ignore or are unaware of other aspects of their lives that need to be developed in order to mature as a whole person. They usually don't realize that those facets of their lives are just as affected by sexual activity as the physical aspect is, if not more so.

One researcher at Western Washington State College determined that more than half the teenagers who engage in sex do so

> to feel more like adults — yet the attempt backfires. George Cvetkovich, whose two-year study involved 273 Bellingham [Washington] area high school sophomores and juniors, learned that rather than improving the teenager's self-concept, sexual activity more often leads to immature behavior. 223/B1

Another report shares the following story and insight:

> "I first had intercourse with my girlfriend when we were fifteen. I'd been going with her for almost a year, and I loved her very much. She was everything I wasn't — friendly, outgoing, charismatic. We'd done everything but, and then one night she asked if we could go all the way. A few days later, we broke up. It was the most painful time in my life. I figured sex was the problem. I opened myself up to her more than I ever had to anybody, even my parents. The next year I went to high school. I was depressed and moody and nervous. My friends dropped me because l was so bummed out. In junior high, see, I'd been the star football player. But when she and I got serious, I stopped playing football. I had better things to do. By high school, I felt like a failure. I wasn't in sports any more, I didn't look like Donny Osmond, my grades weren't terrific. When I was seventeen I had intercourse again. A bunch of guys I knew went to a girl who was sort of a slut. That was awful, too, fast and frustrating. I felt like I'd malfunctioned. I'd read those things in *Penthouse* about how some guys go all night, for hours. I wondered if other girls — girls I really liked — would hear about it and say I was a lousy lover. I didn't go out again until I got to college. I've had mostly one-night stands in the last couple of years. I'm afraid of falling in love." — A College Senior.

I heard happier tales from other teenagers, but this boy's story illustrates some of the pain and lingering harm of too-early sex. Like most fifteen-year-olds, he did not yet have a firm sense of identity, and sought it in a girl he idealized as having all the virtues he wanted. Once their relationship progressed to intercourse, a despair about his sexual adequacy eroded his fragile sense of self-worth and haunted him for years.

Sex researchers know (as do most of us) that the first

experience with intercourse usually is disappointing for both male and female. But when it happens to a vulnerable, uncertain, young teenager, he or she may actually get turned off to the whole idea of sex and relationships in general. 38/158

The physical ability to have sex cannot make up for a lack of maturity in other areas of a young person's life.

One type of maturity needed is moral maturity. Dr. Urie Bronfenbrenner of Cornell University has done extensive research on adults' inability to transmit moral values to their kids. He points out that part of the reason is our cultural tendency to segregate people by age groups. This segregation has happened as a result of the mobility of our society, lack of extended-family influence, single parenting which has created latch-key kids and so on.

A young person is forced to spend time with his (or her) peers, whose influence shapes his moral thinking (among other things). Combine this peer-exposure with an educational system that does not teach moral values, the lack of contact with preceding generations and the desire of teenagers to achieve adulthood through sex, and you have young people who are physically *capable* of sex, yet with little more moral understanding of it than two dogs in an alley.

The intellectual maturity of today's youth seems to have surpassed that of previous generations because of the enormous amount of information available, but many educators are questioning the validity of what passes for intellectual maturity in our educational system. Memorizing data and repeating it does not bring about intellectual maturity. Young people need to be challenged to reason, to deduce, and to be creative.

Yet this type of maturity — the ability to solve problems, to reason through and foresee the consequences of one's actions — is not necessarily taught in schools. Educators call it intellectual or cognitive maturity; everyone else calls it common sense; the Bible calls it wisdom. Many teenagers are trying to become adults without it.

Young people are also making their transition to adulthood with less emotional maturity than in years past. Our society affords less freedom to express emotions. It doesn't mean that emotional outbursts are not possible; it means that teenagers do not often find help in understanding how they feel and so are unable to develop the maturity needed to handle emotional stress and to be responsible for emotional reactions.

Family tensions contribute to teens' immaturity. School counselors are seeing more and more students with behavioral problems and self-image problems caused by such stress in the home as fighting or absent parents, lack of love and acceptance by parents, a single parent (usually the mother) having a live-in lover, and so on.

Marla Isaac, a psychologist and director of the Families of Divorce Project with the Philadelphia Child Guidance Clinic, concludes from a recent study that

> . . . children whose mothers live with a new man after a separation have significantly more problems than kids whose moms remarry, become involved but don't live with another man, or who casually date or don't date at all. In three years, kids of moms living with a new man were more likely to have trouble with social relationships; the troubles got worse after five years. They were also more likely to have school problems. 232/D1

Such students are generally referred to the counselor by a teacher, since the parents do not communicate with their kids and are unaware of the stunted emotional growth caused by family stress.

Regrettably, these emotional and self-image problems make it difficult for a teenager to go against what the crowd is doing. Conformity is a haven for emotionally immature and insecure people, and it is hard for such people to say no to sex, even when intellectually and morally they know it is wrong.

A sign of emotional maturity, then, is enough confidence in one's own self to stand up for one's own values.

A person's value system is a vital part of his (or her) *world view*. To understand someone's world view, one observes that person's behavior, and from that behavior one can determine what his value system is — because one inevitably acts out the values they have.

If a person does not live out his own stated value system, then he doesn't really believe in it. If he says God designed sex for the completion of marriage, yet is sexually active before marriage, his true world view is in conflict with his claimed beliefs. One's physical maturity overrides one's lack of emotional, intellectual, social and moral maturity.

A *Time* magazine cover story warns about teens rushing their sexual maturity:

> Can teen sex be harmful, apart from causing such problems as illegitimate pregnancy and disease? Manhattan psychoanalyst Peter Blos believes that the early adolescent, however physically developed, is psychologically a child and lacks the emotional maturity necessary to manage sexual relationships. If a child tries to grow up too fast, Blos says, he may never grow up at all. Says Catholic author, Sidney Cornelia Callahan: "Sexuality is very intimately related to

your sense of self. It should not be taken too lightly. To become an individual, the adolescent has to master impulses, to be able to refuse as well as to accept" . . . Experts also detect a frequent sense of shame and incompetence at not enjoying sex more. "A great many young people who come into the office these days are definitely doing it more and enjoying it less," says [Arizona] Psychiatrist [Donald] Holmes. According to [sociologists] Simon and Gagnon, sexual puritanism has been replaced with sexual utopianism. "The kid who worries that he has debased himself is replaced by the kid who worries that he isn't making sex a spectacular event." 231/37-38

One of the hallmarks of any kind of maturity is the ability to delay gratification until a future time. When a small child is given two pieces of candy, he wants to devour both of them. He doesn't understand why he should put one aside for later — he is not mature enough to understand. Likewise, a physically mature yet otherwise immature teenager does not understand that sex does not make instant adults.

We see in our culture today a great deal of sexual immaturity. Feeling that we have to express sexual desire right now indicates that immaturity. The basic issue is not sexual expression, but rather the whole personality development. Somewhere along the line, our teens have to start establishing some healthy patterns in their lives and relationships. One might summarize that maturity is the ability to FEEL — THINK — ACT, instead of just FEEL — ACT. 244/10

11. There's No Way Back

In their own words:

Adolescents sometimes believe that once they've participated in sexual activity, there's no use stopping. They feel they have already messed up and there's no way to change that. This is a common feeling.

---------------- ♥ ----------------

A Christian who is sexually active before marriage and falls into that kind of thinking has given up on God's forgiveness. it doesn't mean that God's forgiveness no longer applies, or is no longer complete; it means the Christian has developed an improper view of God the Father.

The beauty of God's forgiveness is that it is never-ending. We can come to Him in repentance at any time, for any reason, no matter how long we have been straying from Him.

Sexually active teenagers know that once they have started down a path, it is easy to keep going. But God offers us the opportunity to leave the old ways behind and start on a new path: a renewal that can start at the time of our choosing. If we have walked ten steps away from God, He has already walked nine steps toward us. But we have to take that final step to a restored relationship with Him.

Continuing to have sex often tears down one's self-esteem. You feel cheap, used and unworthy of God's love. A girl commented that she felt God could not use her because she wasn't a virgin — and so she might as well blow it again. She was miserable. She had more trouble forgiving herself than accepting God's forgiveness.

Reestablishing a damaged relationship with God requires two things: repentance and forgiveness. Both of these simply mean to agree with God. *Repentance* means to agree that sin is sin, with no rationalizations and no intent to commit it again. *Forgiveness* means to agree that God's grace — evident in Christ's death on the cross — is sufficient payment for our sins.

To reject God's forgiveness is to say that His grace is inadequate to cover our sin, and nothing grieves Him more than such an attitude. When we consider ourselves beyond forgiveness, we say that God is not almighty, that He is unable to cope with the magnitude of what we have done. Nothing hurts Him more than the rejection of His grace, when He has paid such a tremendous price for it.

Once we agree with God unconditionally that our sin is wrong (we repent) and agree that His grace is sufficient to erase the sins of His believers (we receive forgiveness), we are able to leave the path we are trapped on and can start over.

God forgives, and He doesn't keep a scorecard.

Viewed in a different light, continued premarital sex presents a real danger, something everyone needs to consider. The path of teenage sex is full of all kinds of traps, and the longer you stay on it, the less likely you are to escape unharmed. Emotional trauma, ruined relationships, ruined reputations, ruined self-image, unwanted pregnancies, sexually transmitted diseases are all there — the path is dangerous. To emphasize those consequences is neither sensationalism nor an attempt to panic anyone. It is the hard truth. Staying on the wayward path simply because one is already there means taking a foolish gamble.

For a more in-depth look at what it means to forgive and to be forgiven, see the section entitled "Forgiveness" beginning on page 415 of this book.

CONFUSION

12. Curiosity

In their own words:

Curiosity is one of the reasons teenagers become sexually active. They want to know what it is like. They hear about it in songs, read about it in books and magazines, and watch it on TV and in the movies. With their curiosity aroused, they go out to try it for themselves.

♡ ♡ ♡

With all the movies, TV shows, books and public lifestyles portraying sex as something exhilarating, it is no wonder that teenagers are curious. "What does it feel like?" "Is it really as great as they say?" When such questions bother young people long enough, they are going to seek answers.

———————— ♥ ————————

People have a natural curiosity about the unknown, which is the basis of the problem here. If teenagers had a healthy, biblical view of sex, they wouldn't have to do their own research.

A young adolescent may have begun maturing physically but may still be emotionally and intellectually immature. This puts a child-like curiosity about sex into the body of an individual capable of sex — the result of which is not hard to foresee.

Parents, then, must assume the responsibility of educating their kids and regulating what the kids are exposed to. It doesn't mean the children should be sheltered; rather, it means that kids should not be repeatedly exposed to false views of sex or allowed to have their curiosity aroused inappropriately. Sex needs to be discussed in the home.

Prohibition often leads to rebellion, and certainly leads to curiosity. If parents say, "You can't watch this, and don't argue with me," the kids may sneak out and watch it at a friend's house just to see why. Their curiosity, rather than being toned down, intensifies when a subject is considered hush-hush.

Parents can use the scheduling of an undesirable program as a platform from which to share why they question the value of their child's viewing it. That kind of occasion can become a positive influence in the child's life and help to satisfy his or her curiosity as well.

Another way to satisfy this curiosity is to let kids know that their parents enjoy sex. It would be difficult for parents who have rarely or never discussed sex suddenly to be candid with their teenagers, but it is possible. Such honesty and openness is better when started early. It will help take the mystique away from sex and will keep the children from feeling that they are being robbed by their parents of something they should have.

Teens need to understand that sex is so beautiful that it is worth waiting for. Its beauty is worth protecting by keeping it within the commitment of a loving marriage.

Our goal as parents is not to keep sex among teenagers unknown, just unexplored.

13. Skepticism About Commitment

In their own words:

Another reason for sex before marriage would be a personal choice not to be married due to a distrust of marriage, inability to make a commitment, or being the child of a divorce. Such a person might choose to become involved in short-term relationships, or even a long-term one which does not include marriage but does include sex. Another reason would be the lack of ability to make an emotional commitment to another person, and therefore using sex for personal gratification.

♡ ♡ ♡

People are very skeptical about committing themselves to another person for the rest of their lives. They won't risk giving up the freedom of being their own person.

♡ ♡ ♡

I hear two main things from teenagers: (1) I never want to get married because I never want to go through what my parents have gone through, and I don't want my kids to go through what I've gone through; or (2) I am determined to have a great marriage and not be like my parents. (This is what my fiancé says.)

I was talking with someone two months ago who said he couldn't see himself getting married because too many bad habits from his parents have developed in his character. His sense of self-worth is low and he blames it on his parents. He felt that there was no way he could change.

———————— ♥ ————————

I hurt the most for people who have given up on the committed relationship of marriage, because, as it usually turns out, they have good reason to feel that marriage doesn't work. It usually means they haven't encountered a positive, successful marriage that has affected their lives in a constructive way. To them, all the talk about commitment and marital happiness is hogwash. They have yet to see it.

Without a working model, they have no means of understanding commitment. To them, a relationship is worthwhile only as long as the feelings are good and personal satisfaction results. As soon as conflict arises, they abandon the relationship. They have learned to do this by watching others.

The solution to the feelings these people have is not found in a lecture or in giving them quickie answers. These young people need models. They could read a library full of books on the joys of commitment and marriage, but until they see it, it will remain a theory without credibility.

Responsibility for showing young people the results of solid relationships lies in part with the church. Kids from broken homes need to spend time with other families where committed relationships are visible. They need to see people give to one another in love without wanting anything in return. They need to see unselfish love in action.

Poor family relationships make kids wary of commitment and contribute to their poor self-esteem. Healthy marriages have the opposite effect. Families within the church, both with good marriages and with broken marriages, need to reach out to each other for the effect it will have on the kids. This can be a great unifying and healing force within the body of Christ.

When teenagers settle for sex as a substitute for committed relationships, they are acting on their emotions regarding relationships.

As Christians, we sometimes forget the enormous power our emotions have over us. We like to quote Romans 8:28 at people who are in emotional turmoil and expect them to see the light instantly. We think that an intellectual grasp of Scriptures automatically outweighs an emotional reaction.

But our emotions, the way we understand and react to life, are an integral part of our lives. When we look at the experiences in our lives, the greatest emotions we feel — good or bad — are in the context of relationships. And these become deep-rooted in our lives, affecting the way we view current and future relationships.

If we listen to the secular world view about relationships, we will feel despair. But God has given us the Scriptures, the Holy Spirit and the church as the tools for developing a proper world view and living it out.

Christian teenagers who have given up on relationships are caught between what God says to be true and what they have seen to be true so far. When we encounter someone whose flesh is at war with his or her spirit, we have stepped onto a battlefield where emotions play a big part. As the body of Christ, we are equipped by God to show this person a model of how that war can be won. We can help bring those raging emotions under the lordship of Christ, not by quotes and lectures and a wheelbarrow full of Christian literature, but by examples of God's truth, by marriages that last.

14. Confusion and Disillusionment

In their own words:

Another reason some people have premarital sex is that they get confused. They get in the wrong crowd and are brainwashed by the group until they believe things are right that they know are wrong. Pretty soon they don't know any better.

♡ ♡ ♡

Teenagers today are confused and disillusioned. Virtually every relationship leaves them stabbed in the back. They wonder, "Who can I trust?" The big difference between this generation and the rebellious generations before is that the previous rebellion was for a cause. This generation has no cause. We have given up. We have no vision.

———————— ♥ ————————

In one sense, the young man who wrote the preceding passage is correct: The generation currently coming into adulthood does not have a crusading cause, a unifying point. But in another sense, teenagers today have a very real cause. *Survival.*

In a dangerous, fragmented society where there is no truth, and right and wrong are interchangeable, teenagers feel tossed about like driftwood. And so we see their actions. They are saturated with information, but told there are no real truths. They are told they are the result of a cosmic accident, but to think positively and feel good about themselves.

Their actions are the result of the contradictions swirling in their minds. Unable to come to any conclusions about their lives, they resort to things they *can* understand — to sensory pleasures.

Throughout most of history, man has had only one question to answer: What am I going to do? Faced with survival or death, his day-to-day thought process dealt with actions he would take. Only a few elite, whose needs were taken care of, had time to ask: Who am I?

Modern Western society is unique in history because of its enormous affluence. No longer faced with mere survival, hundreds of millions of people now have time to ask Who am I? before deciding what their actions will be.

But modern men and women are faced with a dilemma.

Unwilling to accept God's truth, they turn to dozens of other concepts now on the market. Overwhelmed and disillusioned, they come to the conclusion that they are nothing more than a fluke of chemical happenstance. Whether they recognize such a conclusion or not does not matter; their acceptance of it is played out in their actions.

Those actions reflect a lack of form in their individual world. Without a recognition of right and wrong, or good and bad, without a structure by which to measure themselves and their actions, they are left in despair. To placate the despair, they look to entertain themselves. They look to amusement ("without thinking"), which always leads to seeking pleasure in temporal, sensory ways.

Materialism.

Drugs.

Sex.

People are trying to put together the jigsaw-puzzle fragments of their lives. What they don't know is that someone has switched the boxtops. We should be looking at the boxtop of our Creator, the Word of God that points to significance, individual worth, truth, meaning — all the things that give us the dignity God designed us to have.

But the pieces given us by our culture — materialism, drugs, and sex — are so dehumanizing and degrading that we eventually quit trying to figure out the puzzle. We lose ourselves even further in temporal pleasures.

Teenagers feel this confusion acutely. As they grow increasingly attracted to the opposite sex, they feel the God-given desire for true intimacy with another person. The world, however, offers them a cheap substitute for that intimacy. What's worse, with most kids coming from homes where biblical values are not taught and modeled, the cheap substitute is all they will ever know about.

Kids need role models at home to teach them right and wrong. If they're instructed in the ways of right and wrong but do not see the parents *living* this way, they will reject their parent's words as hypocrisy. They need the anchor of God's truth to make sense out of the mayhem confronting them. They need a basis, a standard by which to make decisions. They need a world view they can put into words.

A caring youth pastor observes that "there just aren't many good role models left and very few positive heroes. Because of this, teenagers model themselves after rock stars, movie actors and athletes. They are being led by people who are incapable of leading, and they are suffering from it."

The desire for parental role-modeling was expressed by a young teenager whom Dick was counseling (along with her parents). The father made a profound statement on "godly parenting" and his daughter replied in all sincerity, "Dad, I wish you could hear what you just said, and do it." This father later left his wife and children for another woman.

It is not what parents preach; it's what they do. All parents are role models. Modeling is not the question. The question is, What are they modeling? Are they dispelling teens' confusion, or are they adding to it?

10

EMOTIONAL REASONS

1. Need to Love and Be Loved

. . . According to [a] survey, most teenagers said they had been in love. But when they tried to tell their parents, parents replied, "What can you know about love? You're only sixteen." Teenagers' feelings are just as intense as adults.

If you ask ten adults what love is, you get ten different answers. So a teenager's concept of love is no less valid. Whether their definition of love corresponds to their parents' definition is irrelevant. 45/48-49

In their own words:

I trusted Bobby to know how far we could go without making love. He was in the driver's seat. He was also insecure, and he would tell me over and over how he loved me, how he was sure I didn't love him as much as he loved me. It was then that I set out to prove it. I was his — 110 percent his. The first time we made love, I had no idea what was going on. Afterwards, he didn't speak — he passed out. I was *so* alone. I've never hated myself more. But it was done, my virginity was gone. Never could I get it back. It didn't matter after that, so sex became an everyday occurrence. My only fear was losing Bobby — he was the first — and even if he treated me badly (and there were those times) I

159

was going to do anything I could to hang on to him. Slowly we drifted apart. He wanted to go out with other girls. I loved him and he fooled me into thinking he loved me too.

He didn't love me. He tricked me into thinking he loved me. Bobby's "love" was a conditional, selfish kind of love. We learn from 1 Corinthians 13:4-7 what real love is:

> Love is very patient and kind, never jealous or envious, never boastful or proud, never haughty or selfish or rude. Love does not demand its own way. It is not irritable or touchy. It does not hold grudges and will hardly even notice when others do it wrong. It is never glad about injustice, but rejoices whenever truth wins out. If you love someone you will be loyal to him no matter what the cost. You will always believe in him, always expect the best of him, and always stand your ground in defending him. (LB)

---------------- ♥ ----------------

From beginning to end, the Bible shows us God's definition of love, the only accurate definition available. Love is an attitude we have, resulting in action, that makes the security, happiness and welfare of another as important to us as our own. This type of love is selfless, considers others more important than ourselves, and seeks to guard and strengthen the dignity God has given each person. It is a reflection of God's love for us.

Unfortunately, since we as a society have lost sight of God, we have lost the understanding of His love. As a general rule, we have reduced love to one of two things: (1) a warm feeling or emotional reaction; or (2) a positive response to a relationship that makes us feel good. Both of these are self-directed, not outer-directed, and stand in juxtaposition to the biblical model.

It is no wonder teenagers become confused about love. Teenagers are in the process of maturing and establishing their own identities, yet they must contend with a force that baffles and defies definition even by adults.

Love, however, seems to be a justifiable cause for premarital sex, perhaps more so than any other reason. Even Christian teenagers, lacking a solid understanding of love, may be firmly convinced that unmarried people who are "in love" may engage in sex. As one researcher states,

> Kids believe that love carries moral weight . . . Yet the "in love" standard is extremely encompassing. Even at the age of thirteen, more than half of all teens (53 percent of boys, 52 percent of girls) say they have been in love, and the percentages rise to include 85 percent of eighteen-year-old boys and 83 percent of seventeen-year-old girls.
>   . . . A fifteen-year-old New York City girl, a virgin only because

her father called downstairs to her at a crucial moment and interrupted her last night with a summer boyfriend she felt she loved, told us that once she "wanted to have sex with someone I loved. Right now, I don't think it really matters if I have sex with someone I love. I think after I have sex for the first time, then it'll matter." Later on in our interview, she added that "if I was to go out and have sex with someone whom I didn't love, I wouldn't be a virgin anymore, but I still wouldn't have made love."

This distinction, though it is perhaps a rather tortured effort to justify some future scratching of an itch caused as much by curiosity as anything else, also represents a not unusual effort to establish *some* standard for right and wrong in a world where inherited rules seem unconvincing.

. . . We have to remember what the survey showed about teens' conservatism. Teens do want their friends to think well of them, and most do want to be "good." That combination can make the generous standard of love a flag of convenience. In the absence of notions like commitment and responsibility, horniness can look an awful lot like "love."

The pressure on young adolescents today is intensified by confusion. Teens look at love and sex as being synonymous. Much of this confusion is encouraged by television, videos and movies.

This confusion about sex and love can cause a young adolescent to feel acute pressure to have sex when he feels he loves someone. Another danger of this confusion is the pressure to respond sexually when the other person says "I love you" to a teen. The conclusion of many teens is, "If you don't have sex with me, you don't *really* love me."

The chart on page 162 is a breakdown by Search Institute of how young adolescents responded to the question: Are you in love now with someone of your age who is of the opposite sex? 98/16

Most of the books I read at age sixteen were Harlequin romances and gothic love stories. I fantasized I would meet a man like the ones in the novels, a man who would embrace me and I would melt into his arms and feel beautiful, warm and loved. Once, on a trip, I met a boy on the beach. It was just like I had read in the books. He told me I looked like a movie star and we walked hand in hand along the shore.

He took me out to dinner, and afterward stopped along a deserted road. He began kissing me and telling me how much he loved me, and kissing me again. He ran his hands all over my body and I tensed. He told me he loved me, and so I relaxed, and he kissed me again.

♡ ♡ ♡

Finally, one of the most common reasons people have premarital

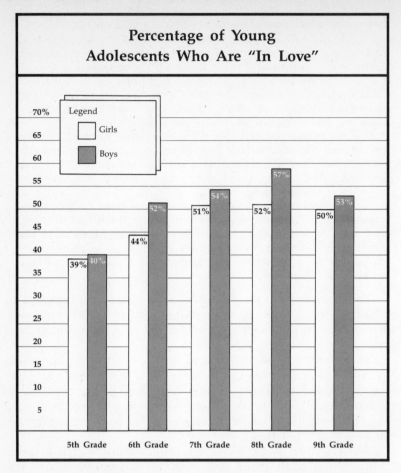

Percentage of Young Adolescents Who Are "In Love"

Legend
- ☐ Girls
- ▓ Boys

	5th Grade	6th Grade	7th Grade	8th Grade	9th Grade
Girls	39%	44%	51%	52%	50%
Boys	40%	52%	54%	57%	53%

sex is because of love or what they think is love. Wendy and Kevin mistook their feelings for true love. They began as acquaintances and became good friends. He invited her to the school's Winter Formal, which was enough for her to consider him the perfect male, since this was her first time for such a special occasion.

After the dance they became boyfriend and girlfriend. Their relationship became deep and they were very open, honest and sympathetic with each other. Wendy thought these feelings had to be true love. Since she was so open and trusted him with her deepest secrets, she decided it was all right to have sex with him. She thought he wouldn't leave her after having intercourse.

Unfortunately, it ruined their relationship, separating them instead of drawing them closer. He began dating other girls. Now she tries to avoid him, not because of resentment or hatred, but because she opened herself completely to him and she feels betrayed. Now she's afraid of trusting anyone else in a relationship.

———————— ♥ ————————

A university counsellor relates that one of his clients, a college student, discovered "she was pregnant after having casual sex with a friend. Both had been drinking too much, she said. After weeks of painful deliberation, she decided to have an abortion. As she waited in the clinic, another student whom she knew entered the lobby. Both were embarrassed to see the other, but when they began to talk, they discovered to their mutual horror that *the same man had fathered their children. Were the two tiny bodies that were expelled that day and tossed into an incinerator the result of love?"*

Consider the above stories in the light of the following statement: "Promises of lifelong love and commitment flow freely in the heat of passion but often turn to indifference and even contempt." 62/232

The *pressure line* is: "If you love me, you will have sex with me," or "If you love me, you'll prove it." Sex is never a test of love. The true nature of love is seen in how we treat people (1 Corinthians 13:4-7 again). The result of this pressure is that the person pressured begins ot feel that his or her willingness to take the next step into sexual involvement becomes a test of true affection or love for the other — not trust, respect, caring, sensitivity, but sex.

Usually the two discover later that what they thought were feelings of love were only charged up sexual sensations and now they must live with the consequences. The "I love you" of one person can be significantly different for another. Sex is often given in the name of love with the anticipation of marriage and commitment. But, for the partner, sex is simply saying "You're someone very special" and with no anticipation whatsoever to marry.

That *pressure line,* "If you love me you'll have sex with me," should be considered in the light of the following replies by teens:

"If you love me, you'll respect my feelings and not push me into doing something I'm not ready for."

"Having sex doesn't prove you're in love. I have too much self-respect to get sexually involved before it's right. I've decided to wait."

"OK, prove how much you love me by understanding and respecting my feelings."

"Love or no love, any way you slice it, it can result in a baby and that does matter."

"I love you. But I'd feel better showing you in another way."

Many young people today are so desperately crying out for love that they will *believe anything and fall for anyone*. The truth is often ignored in the heat of the moment.

The Scriptures tell us that we are made in the image of God. The Scriptures also tell us that, among other things, God is love. As finite images of the infinite Creator, we therefore have a part in each of us that seeks love.

The prototype of the love God offers us should be found in the family. God established the family as a way of representing His image, yet as families break up and children feel a lack of love at home, the image and understanding of God's love grows weaker. God desires the family to point a child to Himself.

A Christian's relationship with God is based on trust; a child needs to grow up knowing nothing but trust in his parents. A Christian has security in a relationship with the Father; a child finds its security in the home. Just as with a child of God, children love their parents in response to the love the parents first have for them.

That is how it should be. When the image of God in the family breaks down, there is a tremendous price to be paid.

Parents need to wake up to the fact that if they don't show love to their kids, their kids will find love somewhere else — which might lead into premarital sex.

♡ ♡ ♡

I think it's time kids get the love they need at home, instead of in the back seat of an old Chevy.

♡ ♡ ♡

It is obvious that the emotion teenagers fear most is loneliness. The thought of being without love leads most teenagers to believe that sex leads to love.

♡ ♡ ♡

The next place people go to find love is in a relationship. A boy-girl relationship provides a feeling of security and love that often is not to be had elsewhere. It is within this relationship — a person wanting so badly to be accepted — that sexual relationships begin. Many times teenagers are not even aware that they are searching for love, and yet they want to be loved so much that they will do anything the other one wants them to for the security of the relationship.

♡ ♡ ♡

Rejection is another cause of premarital sex. In most cases, females feel unloved or unwanted. And so to reverse those feelings, they engage in sex. It gives you a temporary feeling of being loved. Later you find out how temporary that feeling is as you begin to hate yourself and feel very unlovable.

♡ ♡ ♡

In this day of so many broken homes, kids are not getting all the love they need from their parents. In many cases there is only one parent, or, if both parents are there, the relationship may not be all that great. Teenagers feel the need to be loved and cared for, yet many are not receiving the love and attention needed. They do not feel they fit in anywhere; they are looking for love in all the wrong places. They are trying to belong somewhere. Sadly enough, they turn to sex, thinking they are receiving love, but usually they end up adding to their hurt.

♡ ♡ ♡

It was near Thanksgiving, and she was babysitting. "Mind if I come over?" Well, one thing led to another, and in a strange house on an old beat-up sofa I was no longer a virgin.

Virginity gone, innocence gone, the floodgates of immorality were now open, and in poured masturbation, prostitutes, marijuana, speed, a couple of acid trips, crabs, and a few bouts with gonorrhea. Love and acceptance were all I was looking for.

How could the world be so rotten? I hadn't found love. I'd found casual sex with all kinds of strings attached. Acceptance? No one really cared. They were too worried about getting burned themselves.

———————— ♥ ————————

Teenagers will not sit idly by and feel unloved. They will look for love wherever they think they can find it, even in the back seat of a car with someone whose name they don't remember.

Experiences like that are a poor substitute for the love that God desires for our lives. They lead to false understandings of what love is.

The important consequences of these different ways of thinking and feeling about love is that each person loves according to his or her own definition. This may be the one situation where the Golden Rule is not the right approach. Most of us love our partner the way *we* want or expect to be loved, not the way our partner wants or expects to be loved. When partners' definitions conflict, each is likely to feel unfulfilled. 55/54

Different definitions of love can be categorized in the following way:

> *Romantic love* seeks a total emotional relationship with the partner and expects that relationship to provide a constant series of emotional peaks. There is a powerful physical attraction to the loved one, usually from the very first meeting.
>
> *Self-centered love* views it as an enjoyable game and employs a wide range of tactics and strategies to keep the game interesting. Persons who define love this way usually show a good deal of self-control and self-sufficiency. They make few demands on the loved one, and do not like demands made of them. Such persons do not look for an "ideal"; they can love a variety of types. Their approach to an intimate relationship is almost casual, and they tend to avoid intense expressions of love.
>
> *Intense-dependency love* justifies making enormous demands on the partner. A person in this category reacts to the smallest emotional slight with fierce jealousy or anxiety, for he or she seems to have an insatiable need not only for affection but also for reassurance. "Tell me you love me" is a frequent plaint.
>
> *Thou-centered love* is unconditionally giving: "There is *nothing* you could do to make me stop loving you." The partner need not return affection in the same way as it is given or to the same extent. This kind of lover often is considerably self-sacrificing; yet the result is not martyrdom but a pleasurable "better-to-give-than-to-receive" attitude.
>
> *Best-friends love* is emotionally predictable, companionable and mutually supportive. It is usually slow to develop. Sex is not important in the early stages of a "best friends" relationship.
>
> *Logical-sensible love* emphasizes the practical values of a stable relationship. Such lovers often know exactly what kind of a partner they are looking for, and will wait patiently for the one who meets most (not necessarily all) of their requirements. 55/54-58

Of those listed, only "Thou-centered love" reflects God's love for us; and regardless of how we may approach others, it is the type of love each of us seeks. Accepting, forgiving, no-matter-what love. Yet when teenagers don't receive it at home, they are soured. They don't think it really exists.

Roger Simon's *Chicago Tribune* column, "Muffled Scream of Ruined Dreams" is a heartbreaking account of one woman's search for love:

> "Takes two to tango, doesn't it?"

"Yes," she said. *"But I was looking for love. That's all I was looking for."*

Her name is Jane. She is in her twenties and floundering somewhere in the backwash of the sexual revolution.

"When I was twelve, my mother told me about sex and how it wasn't right until marriage," she said. "My mother got married when she was sixteen and had children right away. She had eight children and she let us know what getting pregnant and accepting responsibility was all about. She let us know it is not some easy thing."

If you read the surveys, kids are not supposed to even care any more about things like virginity and what Mom would think. But I have a feeling there are thousands of kids out there who care very much.

"So what happened?" I asked her.

"I fell in love," she said. "But I let the guy know I wasn't going to have sex with him. That was for marriage."

"And?"

"And he said: 'How am I going to marry you if we don't find out if we're compatible first?' That's what he said. Compatible."

"And you fell for that?"

"I liked him," she said. "I loved him. So I did it. And he liked it. And we got engaged. And then he dumped me."

"And you felt used."

"I felt hurt and used," she said. "I never should have done it. If I had held back, he would have respected me."

"So why did you do it?"

"You know how many women are out there?" she said. "And he was a good-looking guy. There were plenty of women who were willing. I did it because I wanted him to love me. And that was stupid of me. *Making love doesn't make them love you.*"

"From now on, no sex until I get married," she said. "I'm not giving myself any more. I feel like what I've done is wrong. Before you can love someone else, you have to love yourself, you have to respect yourself. If I had respected myself, I would have remembered what my mom told me."
190/5

Our society, to a great extent, has stopped passing biblical morality on to its kids. Without clear standards of right and wrong, teenagers are left to find their own. Many come up with "love" as the justification for sex. But they don't know what love is.

Read the words of teenagers who have given the matter some serious thought:

Even though you may be 90 percent sure you will marry this person, there is no excuse to go ahead and have sex. In fact, there should be even more incentive to wait. 1 Corinthians 13 talks about real love. This kind of love is patient (able to wait) and wants the best for the other person. It is not selfish. Love doesn't sacrifice long-term good for immediate pleasure.

♡ ♡ ♡

In the book of James, the deadly equation is even more carefully spelled out: "But each one is tempted when he is carried away and enticed by his own lust. Then when lust has conceived, it gives birth to sin; and when sin is accomplished, it brings forth death" (James 1:14,15, NASB).

Lust, then, is no one's friend. In fact, God says it is the mother of sin. Nowhere is that more clear than in the case of Tamar, David's daughter. Her half-brother Amnon lusted for her and finally raped her (2 Samuel 13:1-19). Note that not only did the lust spawn the rape, but that Amnon's feelings for his half-sister quickly changed to *hatred* after he had raped her. Quick reversal in feeling is a principal characteristic of lust and a good way to differentiate between it and love.

In the heart of 1 Corinthians, chapter 13, we read: "Love is patient, love is kind, and is not jealous; love does not brag and is not arrogant, does not act unbecomingly; it . . . does not take into account a wrong suffered, does not [delight in evil,] but rejoices with the truth; bears all things . . . endures all things. Love never fails" (13:4-8, NASB).

Love doesn't break God's rules. Love does what is right, what is honest, what is pure, what is good. Love doesn't produce sorrow, sadness, guilt or fear.

2. Loneliness

High school girls are the loneliest people in the USA, a study released today shows.

And the more activities they join, the lonelier they are likely to be — lonelier than alcoholics, unwed teenage mothers and even the elderly, says researcher John C. Woodward, of the University of Nebraska.

"That doesn't mean the elderly aren't lonely or that all adolescents are," says Woodward. But as a group, high school girls are more "abjectly lonely" than anybody. Woodward has researched loneliness for twenty years and studied nearly 3,000 people. 98/1D

In their own words:

Loneliness — which may be caused by not having many friends, parents who are divorced, or parents who don't spend time with their children — causes a lot of adolescents to seek a cure in premarital sex.

♡ ♡ ♡

I used to think it would be OK to have sex with a steady boyfriend; at least then you would be doing it with someone who really did care about you. I thought that until I lived with my roommate, Liz. Liz dated Chris for two years. They went to high school homecomings and proms together, they drank beer and ate Oreos together, and they made love together in the back of Chris' car.

And afterward, Chris would drive Liz back home, and sometimes Liz would cry, because she was in her bed back home, and she was alone. When Liz found out she was pregnant, she was alone, too.

Chris said he couldn't marry her because he had a good football scholarship, so Liz went to a clinic to have an abortion, and she went by herself.

Once again, she was alone.

♡ ♡ ♡

What some people think is a desire for sex is really a reaction to loneliness. Since many people think having sex brings an intimacy that can't be achieved any other way, they feel this is the only way to escape their loneliness.

—————————— ♥ ——————————

Usually the quest is for a steady relationship, not sex. Yet the fear of losing that person and being lonely again prompts one to have sex to keep that person. Some girls want to have a baby in hopes that their boyfriend will marry them, and then he and the child will take away her loneliness. Even in the case of teenage pregnancies where marriage does not follow, approximately 96 percent of teenage unwed mothers who do not have an abortion end up keeping their children. This is generally done in order to meet their own emotional needs — that is, to have a child to love and to return love to them.

The latter aspect of desiring children to return love to them is often a cause for child abuse. The vast majority of parents who abuse a child come from families of violence themselves, and often wanted to escape that environment by having children. When the infant or child does not respond to them in the ways they deem desirable, the young parent may become frustrated and deals with that child in the way that he or she saw modeled in their family of origin. That is, with violence. I agree that many teenagers are very lonely; some will do anything for the person who takes them out of this loneliness.

God created a number of needs in human beings; one of them is our need for companionship. In fact, one of the first things God said about us was, "It is not good for the man to be alone." Loneliness was not part of God's design for us. Today it is a result of the fallen nature of the world, which is an alienated nature.

When God gives us a need, He also gives a way for that need to be met. To deny the need, mask it or run away from it is to avoid God's plan for fulfilling it. Such responses are self-defeating, and can only be unfulfilling.

A teenager looking for companionship through sex is legitimately lonely. It is a real condition, not something he cooked up in his head.

When we admit we are lonely and have a relational need that must be fulfilled, we are on the way to fulfilling it. Our next move must be in the direction of God, though, because a God-given desire can be met only in God's way.

Sex cannot eliminate loneliness. It can merely displace it, and only for a very short while. When the spiritual need of companionship is not met in an intelligent, rational way, the only recourse is an irrational attempt. Sex, drugs, alcohol, or anything that affects the five senses and numbs the spirit, can become a painkiller for loneliness. That type of escapism leaves us void of the blessing God would bring if we would let Him fulfill our need.

3. Fears

Fear of Rejection

In their own words:

When he wanted to have sex with me, I didn't want to disappoint him. We were in love anyway. What was the harm?

♡ ♡ ♡

Today's teens are faced with a decision that will affect them the rest of their lives. If they choose to give in, the outcome may destroy them. If they choose to stand steadfast and not give in, they may still feel rejection or loss of self-esteem.

───────── ♥ ─────────

When our lives are based on a knowledge of our acceptance and security in Christ, we are able to have a healthy self-image. Without a healthy self-image, we need something else to make us feel good about ourselves. When that is found in a human relationship, we become dependent on it. We feel good and accepted as long as the relationship is going smoothly. We feel afraid and rejected when things get rocky. In such a position, we are open to manipulation and abuse.

That type of dependency on others is dangerous. If relationships are based on performance, the ones being made to perform are not in a loving bond; they are in a living hell. They never know from one minute to the next if they are keeping up with the other's expectations. They can never feel contentment and security. They are never allowed to make a mistake or fail. They can never be themselves.

It is little wonder that people who need a relationship to bolster their self-image are terrified of rejection. They have become so accustomed to playing the chameleon to make others happy that they have lost their own identity in the process. The longer this ambivalence continues, the harder it becomes for them ever to reestablish a healthy self-image.

Teenagers in such a relationship need to get out *now*. Those who "give sex" out of fear of rejection are trying to buy security with their bodies and self-esteem, a price God never intended anyone to pay. They need to turn to Christ, and to His truth, to find where real security lies. They need to begin seeing themselves through God's eyes.

Fear of Missing Out

In their own words:

Some people become sexually active not out of need, but out of fear. There is the fear of physical deterioration and emotional abnormality. There is the fear that time is running out. Another fear may be that of losing a treasured relationship. And there is a common fear in our crowded world — loneliness.

♡ ♡ ♡

Being in my late twenties and no longer sexually active, I must reflect on my younger years when I was so promiscuous. When I asked myself about the traps that ensnared me into premarital sex, I was faced with some interesting revelations.

The basic human emotion involved in my sexual explorations was fear; fear of not knowing something (or anything), fear of missing out on the "fun," fear of getting old and fear of commitment.

So many times, the idea of sex had challenged me. What was it really like? Will I know how to perform with approval? Would I know something about pleasing a man and being pleased? And, what if I never knew what sex was like? I mean, I could die and never have "known" a man. What a wasted life! I was afraid, afraid that all the excitement in life was passing by my door, afraid that, should I get married, I would end up getting divorced because I wouldn't know what I was doing in bed. I surely didn't want a divorce!

There was a desire to go along with the crowd so I wouldn't feel left out and strange when the conversation turned to sex. But most of all, at the gut level, there was a desire for intimacy, a desire for marriage, a desire for commitment, a desire for fulfillment and a desire to hear the words "I accept you." With all of those desires, fears arose. What if *none* of these needs was met? Frustration set in.

The "what if" rationalization was absorbed into my thinking and decisions. As an attempt to find fulfillment and acceptance, "rolling into and out of bed" became a common pattern for me, a balm to cover my fears. Fulfillment took the scope of a few hours instead of what I had imagined — a lifetime. The fears surfaced again and produced the truth: I had become bored *and* boring; I didn't find any lasting acceptance of me; I didn't find my ideal mate from bedroom gymnastics.

♡ ♡ ♡

Teens don't want to miss what their friends are experiencing, and marriage just seems too far away.

———————— ♥ ————————

Teenagers have inherited a world that demands instant satisfaction, a world in which the events of an entire day warrant only thirty minutes of news, 300 years of history fits into a one-week miniseries, and food is tossed through the car window as we drive by a restaurant. It is a world in which pocket calculators rescue us from having to think. Video tapes rescue us from having to read. Abortionists rescue us from taking responsibility.

The TV says we can have it all. And we want it all. Now. And the TV says if we don't get it now, we're out of step and behind the times and no fun.

Little wonder, then, that young people feel gripped with fear that they may be missing out on something. When that something is as all-pervasive and hip and exciting as sex, the fear is multiplied.

I used to be amazed at how many teenagers say they are terrified of dying a virgin, but I can see where that fear comes from. Their culture deifies sex and scorns those who have not experienced it. They have been conditioned to believe that sex is the ultimate in life and without it they risk dying unfulfilled.

So they have sex — and come away empty, wondering how the ultimate in life could leave them so hollow. Then they have more sex to keep up with everyone else. They get quickie gratification and little else, but they have been told that gratification is enough.

Without God and His word, they don't know any better.

Our culture is one in which people feel powerless. We elect politicians who don't do what we want once they are in office. We work, save our money and invest; then the economy changes course and leaves us awash. We try to stop wars in other countries, but we're afraid to go outside at night.

We are overwhelmed and helpless. And in helplessness we resort to mindless pleasure. We may not make it home alive tonight, but by golly we'll make sure we feel good first. Sex, as the writer above so accurately put it, is a balm for covering fears. But it doesn't make the fears go away.

Fear of Never Getting Married

In their own words:

As young people approach the marrying age, they may lose hope of ever finding a compatible mate. These thoughts are reinforced both by the person who rarely dates and by the person who dates often, yet never seems to find the right person.

Another reason for premarital sex, then, would be this loss of hope in finding a permanent partner in a world where people and things are always changing. This can lead to a "live for now" or "get it while I can" mentality.

———————— ♥ ————————

Fear of not finding a suitable mate is actually a problem of inner contentment. When people think that by changing their circumstances, such as by getting married, they will find happiness, they are kidding themselves. If they are not at peace in their present state, they will not be at peace when change comes.

Many teenagers think *When I get married, I'll be different,* yet married couples stress that when you get married you are the same person.

A person who has never established a ministry in his own surroundings does not *become* a missionary by going to the Maldive Islands. If he can't reach out to people at home, a plane ride won't change anything. Just so, a person who doesn't have God's joy in present circumstances will not have instant joy after a wedding ceremony. Inner peace is a reflection of character, not circumstances.

People clearly have a desire to get married. God gave that desire to nearly everyone, and marriage is in the normal course of most people's lives. However, the Bible also says that absolute contentment is indeed possible without marriage (read 1 Corinthians 7). God alone is able to provide inner peace. Marriage is not necessary.

As a male who did not marry until age thirty-one, I know this from experience. I hate to think how my marriage would have turned out if I had counted on my wife suddenly to provide contentment for me. I would have been placing impossible expectations on her, and then would have become frustrated with her whenever she didn't come through. By allowing the Holy Spirit to provide contentment in my life as a single man, I was able to enter my marriage with realistic expectations.

Young people who seek sex *now* for fear of not having it in marriage are trying to solve the wrong problem. They think the problem is sex and marriage. The real problem is their reaction to their circumstances.

4. Pressure From Boyfriend or Girlfriend

In their own words:

This pressure is harder not to succumb to because we're dealing with someone we really care about. Teenagers feel they owe their partner some sort of allegiance, and feel obligated to have sex with them. They also feel if their partner wants to have sex and they object, their partner is going to break up with them.

♡ ♡ ♡

Shauna and Bryan, her boyfriend, were on a date to the movies. On the way home, Bryan drove them to a dark secluded area where most couples went to "park." Bryan turned to Shauna, looked at her with very serious but loving eyes, and asked, "Shauna, do you love me?" Shauna chuckled and said, "That's a dumb question. Of course, I love you! You know that." Bryan then said, "If you love me you'll prove it by having sex with me. *If you won't then I will no longer be able to be your boyfriend."*
What could Shauna do? She would never want to give up Bryan, but she knew that sex before marriage was wrong. She decided she loved Bryan more and gave in. Within a week Bryan and Shauna had broken up and neither had respect for the other. Did Shauna really love Bryan? Not really, but she thought she did. However, her fear of losing Bryan overcame her moral views.

♡ ♡ ♡

I started going with this real neat guy when I was fourteen. He was a real nice guy and we had been brought up in Christian homes. I thought he was a Christian and I thought I was a Christian too. This guy was fun and nice looking and very honest. I thought what I was feeling was really love, but it wasn't. I found that out too late. One Saturday we decided to go out for the day, but that was a very wrong decision. After we picked him up, my father dropped us by the movies and told us he would pick us up at 10 P.M. The movie was over at 9, so we had an hour. After we left the movies we went out the back; he said he had something he wanted to show me. When we got there, he started kissing me and then a lot more. It really scared me because it was the first time a guy had ever touched me like that. I told him I was a Christian and thought he was too. *He told me if I didn't do what he asked, he would never see me again* and he would tell my parents I had asked him to make love. So I did what he told me. After that he and I didn't speak for about three months. Then he called and said he had changed. He came over to my house for dinner, and when my parents were gone, he said he wanted to see my stereo (which was in my bedroom). Well he hadn't changed: he did the same thing again. But this time I stopped him. I said I did love him but I was not about to ruin my life because of premarital sex. After that he did not call again for a long time.

♡ ♡ ♡

I was scared. My first concern was to please him so I wouldn't lose him. After the first time (the biggest mistake of my life), the craving for love and intimacy became almost an obsession.

♡ ♡ ♡

And while you're considering those consequences, how about asking yourself the question: Why am I doing this anyway? Are you so insecure that you're afraid of losing the relationship if you don't go "all the way"? Let me assure you, if you lost a relationship for that reason, you really didn't have any kind of a strong relationship in the first place. Check your motives.

♡ ♡ ♡

Some teenagers have sex because they are afraid of losing their boyfriend or girlfriend, or of not being asked out for a second date. Also, when a relationship is in jeopardy, most people will go against their principles to save it — especially if they still love that person.

♡ ♡ ♡

A lot of my friends tell me how their boyfriends want them to do sexual things. When a girl's boyfriend asks her to do these things, she's afraid to say no. She thinks if she doesn't go along with him, he will want to break off the relationship.

———————— ♥ ————————

Nothing is more condemning and degrading in a relationship than to be put on a performance basis. When one of the partners says, "You have to do certain things or I won't love you," that person no longer has an honest and unconditional love for the other. The one being made to perform will spend the remainder of the relationship jumping through hoops. For now, it's sex; later, there will be other requirements.

This situation is almost exclusively arranged in such a way that the boy manipulates the girl. When a girl allows herself to be pushed around and emotionally abused for the boy's gratification, she is depriving herself of her God-given dignity. She is allowing herself to be robbed of something very precious.

Part of the problem here is the heavy emotional attachment that can come in dating relationships. If a boy threatens to dump a girl because she won't give in, she may be fully aware that she is being manipulated, yet she has become so dependent on him emotionally that she does what he wants.

Teenagers who are aware of their identity in God don't need acceptance by others to feel secure. They recognize the dignity each of them already has, and they will protect the dignity of the other as vigorously as they protect their own.

The pressure line is, "If you won't have sex with me, then we'll have to break up." Or, "If you don't have sex with me, someone else will." If anyone really cares about a boyfriend or girlfriend, that person will respect the other's feelings and not put the pressure on them to have sex. Such pressure shows that the relationship isn't a very good one to start with. Most of these couples break up later anyway. Relationships should be based on caring and respect, not on sexual performance.

Candy, a seventeen-year-old, remarked, "Deciding not to have sex can mean the end of a relationship, though usually that means the relationship wouldn't have lasted much longer anyway."

Consider this pressure in light of the following replies by teens:

I just explain I'm not ready for sex by saying, "It's quite easy for you never to call or speak to me again, but I have to live with myself in the morning."

Well, if that's the way you feel, I'm going to miss seeing you, but that's the way it's got to be.

If all I mean to you is a body to have sex with, maybe we'd better take a closer look at why we see each other. *You have no right to use me.*

Our culture has come up with a number of definitions for love, one of which is: "I give to you in order to get." This is the kind of "love" that allows one partner in a relationship to manipulate and coerce the other into sex — that is hardly the selfless, giving love described in the Bible.

When, for example, a boy pressures his girlfriend into sex, he has a number of weapons he can use against her. He knows she wants acceptance. He knows she wants security, companionship and the emotional boost the relationship gives her. He knows she will give in to his pressure because she wants to keep all of those things. And he does it all in the name of love.

But love seeks to give and encourage. It shows respect and it reaffirms a person's dignity. It does not force another to violate his or her conscience. And, perhaps above all else, it takes into consideration the consequences an action would have for another and acts in light of that person's best interest.

5. Rebellion

In their own words:

Jessica liked to be around her friends, because when they were together, she didn't have to think about all the hurt her mom had caused her.

One night Jessica had a party at her house. She met Joe, a cute, intelligent guy, and was immediately attracted to him. They talked a lot and got to know each other over the course of the evening.

Nearly everyone at the party was paired off in different parts of the house. Jessica led Joe to her parents' bedroom and they had sex that night in her parents' bed. It was the ultimate way Jessica could think of to rebel against her mother and the hurt.

♡ ♡ ♡

Many times young people engage in sex out of spite or rebellion against parents or authority. They simply choose a lifestyle based on what Mom and Dad *don't want from them.* This is an act of the will, not of the intellect, I am convinced. Usually, the young person learns a lesson from this rebellious attitude somewhere down the road.

♡ ♡ ♡

The people in my age group become sexually active before marriage mostly because of peer pressure or rebellion against parents. From what I see at my school, most parents [I would say *some* not "most"] don't care about their children, much less whom they are with and what they are doing. The kids, not totally excluding me, rebel by doing something they think will harm their parents, not realizing they are harming themselves more than anyone.

♡ ♡ ♡

The main attraction to premarital sex, I think, is that it is not allowed. Many teens do things just because Mom and Dad said no.

————————— ♥ —————————

A youth pastor writes:

One of my high schoolers is an only child, whose mother writes books and speaks on family relationships. He once told me that he could greatly hurt his parents and ruin his mother's career if he rebelled. Since then he has been in trouble with the law, switched schools for his own personal safety and has greatly grieved his parents. Even though his parents are wonderful he seems to be rebelling to hurt them.

Rebellion is a form of reaction generally caused by a lack of relationship. Counselors see again and again how the "rebellious child" in question is reacting to poor relationships, both between the parents and child and between the parents themselves.

One marriage and family counselor estimates that in as many as 95 percent of the cases regarding a rebellious child, marriage counseling for the parents is required before long. Family counseling is included, too, but the marriage counseling is the crux. He reports that amazing results in the children's behavior take place once the parents get their act together.

Imposition of rules on a young person will not work if a positive relationship has not been established between him and the one making the rules. The teenager will rebel against authority, since he is not convinced the authority figures have his best interest in mind. To counter the rebellion, parents often lay down even more rules. It becomes a battle, with parents and children pitted against each other rather than working together toward understanding. Remember that "rules without relationships lead to rebellion." That rebellion can take the form of active resistance or passive indifference.

A teen's sex as a form of rebellion signifies faulty relationships within the teen's family. However, concerned parents can take some initial steps to re-establish the relationship.

Steps for Change

First, back off on as many rules as possible, especially grounding. Let the kids know you want to rebuild the mutual trust you need. You are still in charge, but you can't show your kids you trust them if they have no opportunity to prove themselves trustworthy.

You need to exercise caution, though, because a sudden switch from rules can lead to anarchy and could confuse the situation. Don't overplay the suspension of rules. Relationships that have eroded over the course of years won't instantly change, and kids won't respond just because you expect them to.

What needs to happen now is what should have been happening all along: You need to focus on the kids and *listen to them.* One of the most powerful ways to build a relationship is to listen. You have to know what is going on in their heads. In some ways it is no different from establishing a friendship.

When you listen to someone, you are letting that person know he or she is important to you. As you and your teenager become more important to each other, you will want to spend more time together. When you feel you are reaching this point, begin working on some activities together.

As the relationship and trust are gradually (sometimes quickly) reestablished, the rebellion will become less of an issue. They don't have to hurt you now, because they like you, and may even love you. They don't have to rebel against what appears to them as your stupid rules any more, because now they know you love them and have their best interest in mind. They don't have to have sex with someone now just to be rebellious — they trust your judgment more.

Getting Attention

Here we must consider the phenomenon of *negative attention-getting.* Often we think of hatred as the opposite of love. In reality it's not. The opposite of love is indifference. The greatest affront to another human being is to act as if he doesn't exist. Dr. James Dobson has characterized the post World War II period as an era of permissiveness in the raising of children. Many of the "baby boom" children are now the parents of our current youthful generation. Children who were raised permissively often become self-indulging parents. And self-indulging parents often seem indifferent to their children. Their children then, in seeking attention, often will go to negative extremes in their behavior. It is their way of crying out, "Hey, I'm here; does anybody care?"

Young persons who get caught in crime, drugs or pregnancy will generally catch the attention of their parents. I have heard several young women say that they didn't know if their parents really cared what they did until they got pregnant. In some cases the parents came down on them, but in other cases the parents became supportive. I remember one young woman saying, "I didn't know my mother really loved me until I had to tell her I was pregnant. Then, for the first time in my recollection, she put her arm around me and said she was with me regardless of what was going to happen." What a tragic way to find out that a parent cares.

11

SPIRITUAL REASONS

1. Negative Perception of God

In their own words:

An obstacle to the discussion of Christian arguments against premarital sex is theological, and has to do with our negative perception of what God wants for us. Many Christians don't believe that God wants good things for them.

————————— ♥ —————————

"Thou shalt not . . ."

Why not?

Christians have always been quick to give the *what* about the biblical view of premarital sex: Don't do it. What has been lacking is the *why,* which is just as important. People don't realize how God uses such commands to protect and provide for us.

Without an understanding of God's loving nature, we could easily come to view negative commandments as being to our detriment, rather than to our benefit. If we don't have a relationship with one who claims to be in authority over us, we won't understand the motives behind that person's orders, and we won't want to co-operate. We must know our position in Christ.

Rules without relationships lead to rebellion. That's how it is in the family. That's how it is in the spiritual realm.

I recently read a study in which some 40 percent of "Christian" and Jewish leaders think that fornication is all right for today. When those we look to for spiritual guidance tell us the opposite of what the Scriptures tell us, we are confused. If those who supposedly are leading us to God reject His commands, how are the rest of us supposed to feel about God's authority?

We are failing to look at God's commands in light of His character. He loves us so much He sent His Son to suffer on the cross, a punishment that should have been dealt to us. Everything about God's character reflects the deep love and concern He shows for His people. When someone loves a person, he will do two things: He will protect that person, and he will provide for him.

Why do parents give their children new shoes when the old ones wear out? They want to provide for them. Why do parents tell their children not to run into the street? They want to protect them. Why do the children respond and obey? They have a relationship of trust with their parents. And even if the children disobey, they know they are taking a risk (Mom and Dad must be saying "don't" for a reason), and they know they will be in trouble afterward.

It's easy to see how this principle applies to families, but for some reason we have a rough time admitting that it also applies to our relationship with God. So many of us see Him as just a big killjoy, hovering in heaven with a rolled-up magazine, waiting to clobber us as soon as we have a little fun. We ignore the biblical account of His character and we rebel. Then we get mad at Him when there are consequences!

Part of the breakdown of our culture has come through certain psychological schools of thought about child-rearing. Adherents of these ideas say that any negative injunction is unhealthy. They admonish parents to say only nice, uplifting things to their children, not to put any prohibitions on them, not to forbid anything.

This false (and illogical) philosophy has gained a significant foothold in child-rearing; even Christians are buying into it. The Bible says: "Train up a child in the way he should go." Our society says: "Let them do anything they want." And our kids are paying the price.

Teenagers who have lost sight of God's plan for them, and are sexually active because of that loss, need to reevaluate the trendy philosophical and theological ideas they have absorbed. They need to hear the words of one of their peers who wrote, "At some level, people often feel that God's commands are there to deprive or hold them down. We need to hear Christ's answer to His own rhetorical questions in the Sermon on the Mount:

> Which of you, if his son asks for bread, will give him a stone? Or if he asks for a fish, will give him a snake? If you, then, though you are evil, know how to give good gifts to your children, how much more will your Father in heaven give good gifts to those who ask him! (Matthew 7:9-11, NIV).

2. Longing for Spiritual Oneness

In their own words:

> From a female point of view, I know that the spiritual oneness, not the physical oneness, is the main reason girls today long for sexual union.

---------------- ♥ ----------------

Because the Bible tells us that sex is a spiritual as well as physical act, this mystique may draw people to attempt spiritual oneness through sex. They may continue having sex, even after feeling the negative spiritual effects that have resulted from its improper use. They may even deny that sex is the cause.

But oneness of spirit with another person can be legitimate only if it is based on a spiritual oneness with God. People who long for spiritual intimacy with another to the point where they will violate biblical standards and their own consciences are totally sabotaging their relationship with God.

God wants people to draw near to each other spiritually. That is why we pray together, encourage each other in our walk with Christ and discuss spiritual matters. Jesus even tells us He is in our midst when two or three gather on His behalf.

But to do something completely opposed to the righteousness of God, with the supposed aim of a greater spiritual good, makes for an impossible juxtaposition of goals — the two are incongruous, even mutually exclusive.

Who has ever felt guilty after prayer? Who has ever felt separation from God after encouraging someone in Christ? Who has ever felt cheap and debased after sharing the gospel with another? There are certainly spiritual ramifications to sex, but sex can be a blessing only when it is part of God's plan, when it is an act of love within a marriage.

Teenagers seeking spiritual depth in their lives through sex need instead to turn to God and be firmly rooted in Him.

The following is a clear example of the encouragement of teenage sexual promiscuity. In her booklet *Your Engagement,* Dr. Eleanor Hamilton states:

> Young people today are believing that positive sexuality

has another and perhaps even more important function,
communication of feelings of love. Furthermore, they find
that when they are fulfilled sexually, they are aware of a
new and creative approach to life. They feel themselves
washed clean, transmuted from the daily humdrum that may
have worn them down. They are psychically ready for a new
day. For them positive sexuality brings such loving connected-
ness with their partner that they feel "at-one," and through
this personal at-oneness, they tend to feel at-one with the
universe and with God . . . The sum total of damage done
because of sexual negativity will doubtless be referred to by
future historians as one of the greatest of the inhumanities
that the elders of a society have inflicted upon their young.
196/22-25

In *The Christian Mind,* Harry Blamires notes:

The psychologist, by the very nature of psychology, tends
to reduce the significance of youth's romantic experiences to
the physical level. Aspiration, love, and delight are presented
in terms of appetite and sensation. This limited interpretation
does scant justice to the spiritual aspect of youth's passions,
and provides no sound basis for moral guidance. Moreover
it tends to develop a self-conscious and calculated attitude
to one's personal experiences of pleasure, which provides a
convenient foundation for cynicism, self-indulgence, and in-
sensitive exploitation of others. 197/165

3. Lack of Biblical Understanding About Sex

In their own words:

I guess you could say I was a direct by-product of modern
secular society. I grew up in a non-Christian family, and when the
divorce phenomenon began in this country in the 1970s, my parents
jumped on the bandwagon.

My mother completed her master's and got a job, and my brother
and I began to come home in the afternoons by ourselves. We got
our own snacks and watched TV until Mom got home. We were
very mature kids for our age (about eleven and twelve), and we
enjoyed being on our own.

As I got into high school, I started to make plans for college,
and I wanted to be far enough away from home to "be my own
person."

I remember my visions of an exciting, jet-setting career, complete
with expense account. My favorite magazine was *Cosmopolitan,*
and I dreamed of being just as elegant and attractive as the women
pictured in it. Not exposed to anything but the world's view of
sex, I naturally assumed I would be sexually active before I got
married, *if* I got married at all. Since sex outside of marriage was

acceptable, marriage seemed to be a somewhat old-fashioned option.

Despite growing up in the Bible Belt and having many Christian friends, no one ever told me premarital sex was wrong. Not even my mother. She didn't want to bias me with her opinion, so she never told me one way or the other.

I believe this is one major reason people of any age participate in premarital sex. They are never given God's definition of love, marriage and sex. I had people tell me sex before marriage was a sin (what's that?) and that God had told *them* He wanted *them* to wait, but they never explained what sin was, and they never said God didn't want *me* to have sex before marriage either.

I was asking questions about Christianity and not having them answered. I was asking (looking) for reasons *not* to have premarital sex, and I didn't receive any answers I could apply to my situation.

--------------- ♥ ---------------

God admonishes parents to instruct their children in a healthy, biblical view of sex. This is not a simple task, and you may even find it embarrassing to teach your kids about the proper place of sex. But if you don't teach them, who will?

Raising a family is not a simple task. Although Western society is the result of Christianity, our culture now attacks and erodes its influence. Rather than reinforce Christian morals as was done in generations past, our schools disavow God's truth and teach a relativistic outlook, i.e., there is no absolute right or wrong, only what seems right at the moment.

As the influence of Christianity diminishes in our society and families, the devastating results will continue to show up in our kids. Without direction, they clutch at false securities. Without the solid self-image of a child of God, they grab at anything to make them feel a little better about themselves. Without a knowledge of God and His love, they settle for anything that resembles love, even if they are exploited and hurt by it.

Without the Word of God taught in the family and the love of God shown in the family, kids are adrift. They have no basis on which to make decisions. They have no security.

Even kids from Christian homes make wrong choices about sex. As we have seen, they become sexually active for a number of reasons, each of them valid in their minds. These kids need to know they can turn to their parents. They need to hear their parents say, "No matter what you've done or what you do, we love you and will never turn our backs on you. Nothing you have done wrong is beyond repair. We will help you through any trouble. We are here for you to turn to. Talk to us."

PART 3

REASONS TO WAIT

INTRODUCTION

GOD GIVES POSITIVE PRINCIPLES
TO PROTECT US AND PROVIDE FOR US

"You take sex too seriously" is often the response to the emphasis on waiting for a loving, committed relationship in marriage. Yes, we do take sex seriously. As loving, deeply concerned Christian men and women, we consider it extremely serious. Sex is serious business. Most people take it too lightly, and then they pay the awesome consequences.

This section, "Reasons to Wait," shows why Dick and I take it so seriously — especially as responsible husbands and fathers who deeply love and cherish their wives and children.

Premarital sex is risk-taking. There is no way you can get around it. As you ponder all the reasons to wait, ask yourself: Is having sex before marriage really worth the risk?

The results of premarital sex are not always seen at first. They often are not even thought about because a relationship can "feel so right." But how we feel doesn't change the consequences. The wise author of Proverbs talks a lot about sexual relationships, for example: "Stolen waters are sweet and bread eaten in secret is pleasant . . ." (Proverbs 9:17, NASB) — yet he concludes that the eventual consequences are neither sweet nor pleasant.

Let's enter the world of a college freshman, Dana, and watch her as she faces a life-changing decision: to wait or not to wait. Dana lives on campus. She is an honor student, active in student body affairs. This year has been especially exciting for her, mainly because of the guy she has been dating, Troy. Troy is handsome. He is a member of the university debate team and has aspirations of becoming a lawyer some day. But best of all, he is crazy about Dana. They have been dating for eight months, and things seem to be getting better and better. Sometimes when they are alone it is hard to hold back because their feelings are so strong for each other. Dana is beginning to wonder why she should still hold back.

Dana is facing an important moral decision. Resources available to help her make that decision are:

a. her own moral standards;

b. the moral standards presented to her in the media;

   c. her boyfriend's opinion;

   d. the opinions of her friends and people she respects;

   e. the standards of morality established by her parents.

Dana knows that her parents don't approve of premarital sex. But she is away from home and her parents no longer have the influence on her they once had. Dana's best friend and roommate, Marie, advises her to go ahead if she really loves him and plans to marry him. At first Dana feels she would be violating her own moral standards by becoming sexually involved with Troy, but as she falls more deeply in love with him, she begins to compromise her standards. The media, including her favorite magazine and soap operas, cement her position by asserting, "It's your body, so it's your decision."

God's Viewpoint

There is, however, one viewpoint Dana has not considered yet: God's viewpoint. You might be thinking, *Oh, now you're going to give me a lot of ancient, outdated rules from a book that never made much sense to me anyway. We're talking about love here, not some pious standard set up by a God who I'm not sure even exists.*

My response is that I am also talking about love — not human love, but superhuman, divine love. I am talking about God's love for us. The God who created the universe also created you and me. In Psalm 139:13, David says of God, "You created my inmost being; you knit me together in my mother's womb" (NIV). God knows what makes us tick. In Psalm 139:1,2, David marvels at God's knowledge of him: "You have searched me and you know me. You know when I sit and when I rise; You perceive my thoughts from afar" (NIV).

Not only does God know us intimately, but He also loves us dearly. John 3:16 tells us of the extent to which God loves us: "He gave his one and only Son, that whoever believes in him shall not perish but have eternal life" (NIV).

The statement above points out one of the most exciting principles of biblical reality I have ever encountered: Not only does God know us intimately, but He also loves us dearly. Whenever God does something, He does it out of love for us.

As everyone knows, the Bible is full of negative commandments. They may look imposing and dreary on the surface, but that is where the exciting part comes in. Behind every negative commandment in the Bible are two positive principles: One is to *protect* us; the other is to *provide* for us.

In other words, when God says, "Thou shalt not commit adultery," He is not being a cosmic killjoy. He is a cosmic lovejoy.

He is saying, "I don't want you to do something that will bring you and others pain; I have better things planned for you." Inherent in every negative commandment is a positive principle that gives us intelligent and practical standards for making decisions in our lives.

Please remember this: One of God's main motivations in dealing with His children is love. He seeks our wellbeing at every turn. When we read the negative commandments of the Bible in this light, they don't look ominous and threatening any more.

Can we be sure that God really acts out of love for us? Read the following explanation of two Greek words, *agapao* (godly love) and *phileo* (brotherly love), as they are used in the Gospels.

Jesus is not recorded in the Synoptic Gospels [Matthew, Mark, Luke] as using *agapao* or *phileo* to express God's love for men. Rather He revealed it [God's love] by His countless acts of compassionate healing (Mark 1:41; Luke 7:13), His teaching about God's acceptance of the sinner (Luke 15:11*ff.*; 18:10*ff.*), His grief-stricken attitude toward human disobedience (Matthew 23:37; Luke 19:41*ff.*), and by being Himself a friend (*philos*) of tax-collectors and outcasts (Luke 7:34). This saving activity is declared in [the Gospel of] John to be a demonstration of the love of God, imparting an eternal reality of life to men (John 3:16; 1 John 4:9*ff.*). The whole drama of redemption, centering as it does around the death of Christ, is divine love in action (Galatians 2:20; Romans 5:8; 2 Corinthians 5:14). 65/753

Evidence of God's Love

Those ideas may look like deeper theology than most people are comfortable with, but the point is actually very simple. God *demonstrates* His love for us. We can question His motives all we want, but the only evidence we have is evidence of His love. He does nothing that will bring us any harm. Instead He sets boundaries, limitations to our activities, to keep us from doing ourselves harm. As one young man wrote:

> Let me clear up a misconception you may have. God is pro-sex! He invented it and thinks it's beautiful when enjoyed within the correct framework: lifelong marriage commitment. His rules about sex are not there to deprive us of something fun, but are a sign of His love to protect us from harm.

Unwritten and Written Laws

In another look at a pair of Greek words relevant to our lives today, a doctor who treats many patients with sexually transmitted diseases (STDs) had the following to say about God's standards protecting us from our own foolishness:

> The Greek word *ethos* refers to a way of expressing unwritten laws. In the United States, the *ethos* is constantly changing. Societal norms come and go as any fashion or fad. Sexual promiscuity, or as the humanists call it, "sexual freedom," is an *ethos* that currently pervades much of Western society.
>
> Contrast *ethos* with *nomos,* a law set up as the standard for administering justice. Humanists say that their *ethos* equals *nomos.* Christians say no; humanistic *ethos* is contrary to God's law.
>
> This is an essential point for us as Christians. Sin should not be an emotional issue tied to *ethos;* rather, sin is based solely on *nomos,* the unchanging Word, written in stone, etched into hearts by the Holy Spirit. As the STDs graphically and prophetically demonstrate, if the *nomos* is defied, payment and punishment are demanded. *Nomos* was given to man not for God's edification but rather for man to protect himself from destroying his own kind. 78/25-27

Think of a swimmer who has trained, competed and proven herself, after many years, to be a world-class athlete. She is ready to take part in the Olympics and go for the gold. When she gets there, she goes to the starting block to start her race. Some of the blocks are on one end, some are on the other, some are on the side, some of the competitors are already in the water. There are no lanes — only arrows painted on the bottom, pointing in various directions. Everyone takes off at different times in different directions, bumping into each other, splashing and cursing.

Is that how races are set up? Of course not. You wouldn't have a race; you'd have a demolition derby. For a swimming race, the pool must be marked in lanes. There must be someone watching to make sure everything is fair. There must be a specific starting point and time so the competitors can know when to dive in and swim. Without those parameters, no one can win.

Rules Protect

The rules, the lanes, the specific starting time and so on provide our swimmer with the opportunity to win; they protect her from anyone else in the race who might hinder her. Similarly, God has established rules to keep us in our lanes and to keep others in their lanes.

With reference to sexual activity, there is one basic rule: *Wait until marriage.* Of course, a number of subheadings fall under that, such as, "Be holy, for I am holy"; "Control your body in a way that is honorable"; "Honor God with your body"; and so on. Out of His boundless love and wisdom, God has given us boundaries for our protection.

When we see those boundaries as limitations on our fun, we are like a fish in a fishbowl who sees the big exciting world happening around him and feels left out. "I want out!" he says. "I don't want to be stuck in here!" He flops out of the fishbowl and onto the floor, where he dies. Inside the bowl he had been fed and taken care of. The bowl was there to provide for him and protect him, yet he couldn't accept it that way. When his owner found him dried up on the floor, he was sad.

God says, "I love you. For your own sake, stay within the bounds of My provision and protection." When we transgress those bounds, we are hurt — and when we hurt, He hurts.

When we recognize God's loving plan for us — a positive plan for our welfare, not a negative plan to limit or frustrate us — our response should be one of loving obedience to Him. As one author said:

> If God loved us enough to send His Son to die for us and to provide us with eternal life in heaven and an abundant life now on earth, can we be motivated to do any less than totally obey Him?
> True, we are no longer under the law. But as Peter reminds us in 1 Peter 2:16, "You are free from the law, but that doesn't mean you are free to do wrong. Live as those who are free to do only God's will at all times" (TLB).7

Our Creator is not out to get us, yet when we want to cross a protective line, we twist His love around to make it seem as if He is trying to spoil the fun.

> Consider the irony of it all. The same God who spoke the world into existence also masterminded our physical relationships, and yet the world acts as if He were some prudish old maid ready to give us a slap on the wrist for holding hands. God has declared that all He had made was "very good" (Genesis 1:31) . . . The world has a shortsighted, painfully inadequate understanding of all that God meant sex to be. 109/11

God Provides

> Though it might appear that God would like to thwart all of our fun, nothing could be further from the truth. "For I know the plans I have for you . . . They are plans for good and not for evil, to give you a future and a hope" (Jeremiah 29:11). 109/8

God says that His commands are for our good (Deuteronomy

10:12,13). He knows that waiting for marriage to experience a sexual relationship is in our best interest.

God's commands are not arbitrary; they have the stated purpose of keeping us safe from harm. They are not random, but are targeted to provide for us in specific ways. They are not there to frustrate us, but are a reflection of the freedom we have in Christ. The lanes on a swimming pool may appear regimented and stiff, but those lanes can be used for freestyle, breaststroke, backstroke, butterfly and so on. There is a freedom of style and movement within those limitations, just as with God's limitations.

God's commandments are a reflection of His character. The Bible instructs us to be transformed to the image of Christ: We are to be holy, for He is holy (1 Peter 1:16); we are to be truthful, for He cannot lie (Titus 1:2), and so on. The picture of what God is like is in the Scriptures. We become like Him by obeying His commandments. We were originally created in His image, but even though we fell away, He gives us the provision for turning back to Him.

Freedom Is Not Free

But what is God protecting us from? Is it really that *bad* outside the fishbowl? What many young people fail to consider in their quest for "freedom from rules" is that such freedom has a price tag. Actions have consequences.

> Imagine a man learning to skydive. Just before the plane gets to the jump area he starts taking off his parachute. The instructor demands, "What are you doing?" The skydiver replies, "I want to be free! I want to experience the freedom of soaring with no strings attached." The man would be a fool to jump without the parachute. He is free to do as he wishes and to jump without any strings attached but he is not free to escape the consequences. 117/79

In the "Write Your Heart Out" essay contest, I asked young people across the country to write about various aspects of premarital sex. Some of the more than 1,000 entrants described the consequences of premarital sex, the things God is protecting us from by His commandments.

God's negative commandments are there to protect and provide for our young people. Our task in communicating that to our kids was well stated by this young man:

> I firmly believe that curiosity is very dangerous in a teenager's mind regarding sexual immorality. Parents need to teach children the "whys" for living their lives pleasing in the sight of the Lord, not just "because I said that's the way it's going to be." There are

a hundred "good" worldly reasons to have sex in your life as a teenager. Parents need to have a thousand better reasons for waiting. Most important, each of those reasons must have love behind it.

12

PHYSICAL REASONS

PROTECTION

1. From Sin Against One's Body

In their own words:

The main reason I feel sex before marriage is wrong is that the Bible says it is a sin against the body. In 1 Corinthians 6:12-20, a passage on sexual immorality, verse 18 says, "Flee from sexual immorality. All other sins a man commits are outside his body, but he who sins sexually sins against his own body" (NIV).

Believe me, there are repercussions from willful disobedience. I went through a lot of unnecessary, gut-wrenching pain and heartbreak when I separated myself from the Lord. I should have heeded the word of the Lord. I discovered that, as true children of God, everything in Scripture is absolutely vital to us.

♡ ♡ ♡

Obviously, God gives us a choice. He says everything is permissible, but not everything is beneficial. None of us likes to do anything not beneficial for us and our bodies. After all, we exercise and try to go easy on high-calorie foods in order to take care of our bodies, so why shouldn't we guard them from harm in the area of sex, too? God says that when we get caught up in sexual immorality, we are committing a sin against our own body. Why do something that obviously causes harm to our very own bodies, to what the Bible refers to as the "temple of the Holy Spirit"? It is just not worth it to be so diligent in every other aspect in taking care of our bodies if we do this. We flee from impurities such as fattening foods, why not flee from the impurity of misused sex? If we do flee, we will be obeying God and the results will be totally pleasing. You know why? Because obedience brings blessing.

♡ ♡ ♡

Sinning against your own body means that you lose respect for your body, as well as for the body of the one you're involved with. Once you lose respect for your body, it becomes increasingly easy to indulge in promiscuous sex. Your attitude toward this divine gift becomes practically as casual as a handshake.

Losing respect leads to a warped view of love and centers your definition of love around the physical. You get caught in a deceitful illusion of seeking love in a sexual relationship. The needs of security, commitment and oneness then reach paramount heights because those needs *cannot* be met by the world's definition of love.

God created these emotional needs. The felt need of wanting someone to hold you was put in you by God, but God's gift of sex cannot be enjoyed ultimately until it is placed in the framework of marriage.

———————— ♥ ————————

God created each of us as a total being, and therefore is interested in each of us as a total being. Most important, He wants to see us grow near to Him spiritually. He also wants to see our minds challenged. He wants to see us emotionally and physically healthy. He is interested in our moral conscience, desires, speech, social relationships, plans for the future. He is no less interested in our physical wellbeing and how we treat our bodies. The body is the vehicle for all the rest.

The owner's manual for a car I bought was entitled "The Proper Care and Maintenance of Your Vehicle." If car manufacturers, who already have my money, are so interested in how I care for my vehicle that they print a sixty-page booklet about it, how much more is God concerned about how we care for the "vehicles" He has placed us in?

We don't put gas in the radiator or water in the engine. Why? Because we know it will ruin everything. Even people who know very little about cars know that much. And even if they don't know such things, all they have to do is check the manual to find out. Yet even though we see the awful damage premarital sex continues to cause in lives all around us, millions of people engage in it nonetheless. They may even glance through the Manual and claim a knowledge of the subject, yet they continue to take part in sex out of the context God established. If God tells us sex is wrong because it wrongs our bodies, He knows what He is talking about. Remember, this vehicle is His design.

God wants us to be good stewards, good caretakers, of what He has given us. That goes for money, possessions, talents, spiritual gifts, our bodies, everything entrusted to us.

Just as true love displays love for the whole person, counterfeit love in the form of premarital sex is detrimental to the whole person (perhaps to a greater degree than anything else). Sexual immorality harms the emotions. It clouds both the intellect and our ability to make godly decisions. It causes social uneasiness. It wreaks spiritual havoc. It can have permanent damaging repercussions physically. Nothing is safe from the damage it can do.

If we want our cars to keep going, we check the oil and radiator and rotate the tires now and then. It's all spelled out in the manual. If we want to keep bad things from happening to our bodily vehicles, we avoid overeating, we exercise and we stay away from sexual wrongdoing. It's all spelled out in the Manual, God's Word.

2. From Addiction to Premarital Sex

In their own words:

I won't try to pretend passionate physical exchange isn't enjoyable. But I do want to say that outside of marriage, the enjoyment is short-lived. And when it is over you are left disappointed, looking for another fix to appease your lust, much like a drug addict craves another hit.

♡ ♡ ♡

A girl I know who used to be heavily into drugs told me, "Sex is like drugs. You keep wanting bigger highs. In fact, I think it made me do more drugs, too. I'd get high, and then I'd do some weird, kinky stuff. Regular sex wasn't enough. I'd do things I felt horrible about. Then I would do more drugs to take away the pain. It was a vicious circle."

♡ ♡ ♡

Many people are totally unaware of the sexual trap young couples can fall into. The desire for repeated sex can grow into a strong drive which can control the relationship. They become addicted, and it becomes harder (and eventually impossible) to leave sex out of the relationship.

♡ ♡ ♡

The more sexually involved I became, the more I thirsted for this "ultimate experience." Looking back on that part of my life, I feel I really was addicted to sex. I never found a balance, I never found real love, and the more I searched, the more miserable I became. I also got into other vices because of my sexual involvement. This may all seem extreme to some who are just "experimenting" with sex, but in the eyes of our gracious, righteous God, sin is sin. And because of His holiness, it is impossible to please Him when we willfully engage in sin.

♡ ♡ ♡

I began to notice that the more I had, the more I wanted. I had always heard the excuse that having sex was the way to get rid of sexual tension, but the opposite was true. Having sex increased the desire. It was like a drug. I couldn't stop myself, yet at the same time I wasn't satisfied at all. The people I knew who were outright promiscuous were even worse than I was — it was all they ever talked about and evidently all they ever thought about. It controlled them; they never controlled it. Sex was an all-consuming fire that never burned out, but instead burned them out.

———————— ♥ ————————

Many modern views of man maintain we are nothing more than primates in tennis shoes, beings whose physiology is no different from any other mammal. Science books often equate our sexuality with animalistic instincts, and this is where the concept of the "sex drive" comes in. Sex is seen as a primitive force required for survival, just as food, water and shelter are required. If human beings are only smart monkeys and our sexuality a primal urge we cannot control, sex could legitimately be considered a drive. That view was expressed by Desmond Morris, author of a best seller, *The Naked Ape:*

> It must be stressed that there is nothing insulting about looking at people as animals. We are animals, after all. Homo sapiens is a species of primate, a biological phenomenon dominated by biological rules, like any other species. 294/308

Such a view robs us of dignity and the value of life. Consequently, many biologists say infanticide [the killing of infants] is as normal as the sex drive . . . It is hardly a comforting thought, but then, neither is the realization that infanticide can no longer be called "abnormal." It is, instead, as normal as parenting instincts, sex drives and self-defense. 293/78-79

To understand human sexuality and how it differs from the

sexuality of lower creatures, one must have an understanding of the uniqueness and dignity of man — created in the image of God. One must understand the *humanity* of man, to understand human sexuality. If man does not have choice, he has no freedom, sexual or otherwise. Derek Wright, a senior lecturer in psychology at Leicester University said,

> The much-vaunted sexual freedom that the sex researchers and their disciples insist we share is turning out to be a new bondage . . . At the heart of the new ideology is a misplaced metaphor . . . It is the idea that sex is a "biological force," an impersonal energy, one of nature's coercive pressures which is there whether men like it or not . . .
>
> When one studies the research into animal and human sexual behavior . . . it becomes increasingly clear that this notion of sex as a biological force is seriously inadequate and even misleading, especially when applied to human beings. The far more likely possibility is that human sexual behavior is in the nature of an acquired habit, appetite or even addiction . . .
>
> Sexual motivation is to a very large extent cultivated. We could, therefore, progressively decondition ourselves and considerably reduce our sexual desires if wished. In a society apparently bent on developing it to its most intense level, this might not be easy, but it is certainly possible . . .
>
> The biological force idea encourages people to develop the appetite and at the same time provides an excuse for disowning responsibility for it. Hence, today [we have] sex addicts and all the new-styled anxieties.
>
> If we are to be truly liberated . . . then we must evolve a way of thinking about sex which sees it as embedded in a personal context. 292/4

As Christians we know that God desires to give us the dignity of choice. His desire is motivated by love; He wants to both protect us from hurt and provide for us in abundance.

We are far more than primates. We are created in the image of God and we have the capacity to know God personally. Our temporal needs are for food, water and shelter, but we have both a temporal and eternal need for a relationship with God also. When any one of those needs is not met, our survival is threatened, and we go after what we need. In the United States, food, water and shelter are generally available, but when it comes to seeking God, many of us get caught. In order to establish that relationship, we have to admit our failings and acknowledge our need for God, something that most people refuse to do. So instead of having that basic need met, they look for fulfillment in other ways.

Often, people look for fulfillment in physical relationships. They take the spiritual need they sense within themselves and switch it over to a physical need. Once they proclaim sex as a basic desire, they allow themselves the freedom to fulfill it as often and with as many people as they wish.

The result? They come up empty time after time, because they are trying to fill a spiritual vacuum with physical pleasure. Rather than change their actions, they become swallowed up in their sexual pursuits. The sexuality which had started out as a desire now becomes the master, demanding to be sated. As the writer quoted above put it, sex becomes an all-consuming fire that never burns out. Instead, it burns people out.

Premarital sex is inherently unfulfilling, since it is outside God's will. It is sin, and "not only does sin have consequences, [but also] each time we sin we reinforce a pattern that becomes harder and harder to break. If we persist in sin with the thought that one day we will get right with God, we should remind ourselves that God may still be there to forgive and restore . . . but *we* may not be." 62/243

One of the "greatest dangers of petting in a dating relationship is that it very easily becomes the pattern for every date. Other aspects of the dating relationship suffer; the couple only go through the formalities, waiting for the parking session at the end of the evening." 27/74

God, in His love, gives us His command to avoid sexual immorality to protect us from the destructive, self-defeating cycle of sexual addiction. When we are obedient to His wise edicts, we are spared the frustrating habit of seeking temporary and illegitimate physical highs.

God's provision for dealing with sex in the manner He prescribed is sexual fulfillment in a marriage relationship. This does not mean that sex will be continually available, nor does it mean that each lovemaking session will necessarily be great. It means that the couple is able to have the proper attitude about sex. Rather than see each other as objects to be used for a personal high, they see each other as God sees them: unique creations of the Master who have an inherent dignity and who deserve being ministered to.

Only in marriage is it possible for the sexual relationship to reaffirm the dignity and uniqueness of each partner. Sex strengthens the marriage bond. It brings pleasure to one's spouse. It can create a new life that is welcome in the family. It brings personal pleasure. It displays patience, maturity and understanding. Sex, as God intended it to be, makes you *want* to *give* to your mate, not *take*. That's an addiction you can live with.

3. Sexually Transmitted Diseases

In their own words:

If you have multiple sex partners or the person you sleep with is promiscuous, not only have you reduced the value of a human being to nothing, using sex only for pleasure, but you also open yourself up to many kinds of diseases. They may be bothersome or chronic or fatal, depending on what you get, but if you sleep around enough, you will probably get *something*.

♡ ♡ ♡

Waiting until marriage also gives you peace of mind, knowing you will not catch diseases that could cripple you or your children. This makes waiting worth it.

♡ ♡ ♡

Having sex simply because you enjoy it is probably the worst reason to be sexually active. It means you will take your pleasure when and where you feel like it. The person you end up in bed with will probably be as easy as you. With such a high percentage of people having venereal diseases, only a fool would take such a risk just because it feels good.

♡ ♡ ♡

Yet in the midst of all the tragic psychological, emotional and physical consequences of premarital sex, I see a golden opportunity. The vast secular world, reinforced by the media, is beginning to awaken to the horrifying reality of what sexually transmitted diseases have in store for our generation. People will be gearing up highly publicized programs to teach kids how to protect themselves against this new wave of STDs. But we can be there first — on the cutting edge — offering the Christian alternative to the costly price of "free" sex.

I believe the sexual revolution has come full circle. The "do your own thing" and "if it feels good, do it" philosophies are taking their toll. Millions of kids are waking up to the reality that "free" sex has not only demanded a very high price of them psychologically and emotionally, but is now costing them physically also.

—————— ♥ ——————

One of the most destructive and permanent results of pre-marital sex is acquiring a sexually transmitted disease (STD). STDs get more play in the media now that people are afraid of them. They have always been around, but they can be spread only through promiscuity, something our society did not accept until this generation.

The birth control pill became available in the 1950s but

didn't catch on until the '60s. Some medical authorities call
the pill the single most important development in human
sexuality. It freed women for the first time from the fear of
pregnancy, allowing sex to be separated from procreation,
thereby ushering in the age of recreational sex. 25

The medical experts never dreamed that the freedom the
pill would provide also would usher in a devastating epidemic
of sexually transmitted diseases.

People are paying the price for abusing their bodies and
God's gift of sex, reducing it to a form of entertainment. God
designed sex to take place in the intimate commitment of marriage.
In so doing, He has provided for us an environment in which
we can experience true sexual freedom. After all, sexual freedom
means the ability to let down all barriers, to be completely
vulnerable to another, knowing we can trust the other without
reservation. It means the partners have *nothing to fear in any
way* by participating in sex. All of this is possible in marriage —
and only in marriage.

The secular view of sexual freedom means the ability to
sleep with as many people as one wishes as often as he (or she)
wishes. This automatically excludes intimacy from the relationship,
since it is not possible for anyone to be free and vulnerable
around someone whom he doesn't know well, whom he doesn't
know he will see tomorrow, and whose sexual history is an
unknown threat. This type of sexuality may make the body free
to do as it pleases, but it puts the person inside in emotional
bondage.

One reason people can't be free in casual sex is the constant,
looming threat of taking home a permanent reminder from a
temporary tryst. This is what God is protecting us from. In His
perfect plan for sex, everything about the sex act should be
beneficial, edifying, unifying, pleasurable. That is why His command to remain pure until marriage, although it may seem like
a negative command on the surface, is actually a positive command. He has set aside something so valuable and wonderful
that He doesn't want us to spoil it in our immaturity and impatience.

Yet despite the growing threat of sexually transmitted diseases, despite the explosion of STD cases among those under
age twenty, teenagers often do not recognize the danger. "Too
many students come away with the idea that if they do get VD,
a shot or two will cure it, or, if not, at least they have plenty of
company." 123/H1

Dr. Ronald Taylor, a professor of obstetrics and gynecology,
has hit out at sex educators for their reluctance to warn against
the health risks involved with early or promiscuous sex: "Sexually

transmitted infections now cause more long-term damage in chronic ill health, sterility and tubal pregnancies than ever before, despite stronger antibiotics." 63/6

> Sexually transmitted diseases are no longer reserved for prostitutes or wayward GIs in foreign countries. They are infecting people from all economic and social strata at the rate of 33,000 people a day in the U.S. alone. 33/53

That means 12 million cases a year, up from 4 million in 1980. At this rate, one in four Americans between ages fifteen and fifty-five eventually will acquire an STD.

Anyone who has sex outside of marriage is at risk. STDs do not recognize a person's religious or moral beliefs, only his or her actions. As one researcher said, "Unless you're monogamous for a lifetime, with a monogamous partner, you're at risk. And the more partners you have, the greater the risk." 48/1672

The United States is currently seeing an outbreak of STDs unprecedented in history. The statistics are staggering.

The Minnesota Institute of Public Health warns that "there are twenty sexually transmitted diseases which are not prevented by contraception." 101/5 They emphasize that fifteen million people now get a sexual disease each year.

Dr. Edward Weismeier, director of the UCLA Student Health Center, warns students that, "Even an honest answer to an intimate question is no guarantee that a person is safe. While dormant in one person, an STD can be transmitted to another." 33/54 He admonishes then that "one chance encounter can infect a person with as many as five different diseases." 33/54

A survey that the U.S. Centers for Disease Control conducted in 1984

> showed that 62 percent of graduating physicians were going into specialties where they might expect that 5 percent of their practice — one of every twenty patients they see — would have an STD. It's a concern . . . that's now cutting across the mainstream of American medicine. 48/1672

What are these diseases that God wants to protect us from? There used to be a handful. Now there are dozens. The major ones will be addressed here in detail, because this is a subject that cannot be passed over lightly. STDs are changing the nature of our society, and those who are concerned about showing that the unchanging message of Jesus Christ is relevant to this culture must be informed.

Until recent years, public-health experts counted barely five types of sexually transmitted diseases. Now, they know that more than twenty-seven exist. Research shows that the number-one concern of women — ahead of even war and peace — is sexually transmitted infection. 48/1665 Causing the most concern is AIDS.

AIDS

Acquired Immune Deficiency Syndrome, since first reported in the U.S. in 1981, has each year doubled its number of new victims. AIDS damages the body's immunity against infection, leaving its victims without a defense against a host of serious diseases.

Cause: A virus called HTLV-III/LAV. However, not everyone exposed develops AIDS. Many of the estimated one million people infected by the virus so far have no AIDS symptoms.

Symptoms: Tiredness, fever, loss of appetite, diarrhea, night sweats and swollen glands.

When do these symptoms occur? From about six months after infection to five years or possibly longer.

How is AIDS diagnosed? Doctors look for certain kinds of infections; they do tests to reveal AIDS antibodies and damaged white blood cells.

Who gets it? The three largest groups are: sexually active gay men, 73 percent of cases; intravenous drug users, 17 percent; blood-transfusion recipients, 2 percent.

Treatment or cure: None as yet. 33/54

Dr. Ward Cates of the U.S. Centers for Disease Control concludes that anyone can see the potential for this disease being much worse than anything mankind has seen before. 124/38

It could become one of those infectious diseases that change history. 124/38

Dr. Teresa Crenshaw, president of the American Association of Sex Educators, Counselors and Therapists and chairperson of that group's task force on AIDS, reports, "We have more heterosexuals infected today than we had homosexuals infected five years ago." 176/16

A lot of people believe that a condom is a safe shield against AIDS. Dr. Crenshaw argues:

> It is an overstatement. Condoms are certainly better than nothing . . . but basically, they're Russian roulette, and we already have two reported cases of women who have gotten the AIDS virus from their partners, who were depending upon condoms. 176/22

As it spreads to heterosexuals, "The disease has become the number-one public health menace." 124/38

Dr. Michael Coplen warns that "AIDS is the greatest human

threat since nuclear war." 20

The number of cases is increasing geometrically, doubling every ten months. 126/44

It's estimated that 1 to 1.5 million Americans are currently infected with the virus.

By 1991 AIDS patients will need 4.6 million days in hospitals. That's more beds than are currently used by lung cancer or traffic accident patients. 176

Dr. C. Everett Koop, Surgeon General of the United States, was asked if in his long medical career he had ever seen anything as menacing as AIDS. His answer: "After almost half a century in medicine, I can say that nothing is more frightening to me than the specter of AIDS in the future on public health." 176

Babies with AIDS are becoming increasingly common in the hospitals of big cities. At present 70 percent of children diagnosed with AIDS die within six months. 176

It will probably prove to be the plague of the millennium. "If you were the devil," says Dr. Avlin Friedman-Kier, AIDS researcher at New York University, "you couldn't conceive of a disease that would be more disruptive and disturbing than this one, a sexually transmitted disease that kills within a short period and for which there is no treatment." 200/A19

The Secretary of Health and Human Services, Dr. Bowen, recently said this (and it has been confirmed by PEOPLE WHO ARE INFORMED), "If our predictions are correct for global statistics, there could be from fifty MILLION up to one hundred MILLION die by the end of the century." We say that because it is rampant in Central Africa. The figures there represent between 9 and 11 percent of the entire population. 208

Chlamydia (Pronounced Kleh-mih'-dee-uh)

The "disease of the '80s," chlamydia hits between three and ten million Americans a year. It is the number-one STD in America. 33/54

Cause: The bacterium *chlamydia trachomatis,* spread to adults by sexual contact and to babies of infected mothers during birth.

Symptoms: For men, discharge from penis or burning sensation during urination. For women, vaginal itching, chronic abdominal pain, bleeding between menstrual periods.

When do these symptoms occur? Sometimes two to four weeks after infection. But many men have no symptoms. Four of five women won't notice anything until complications set in. Victims can go for years not knowing they have it.

Complications: In both sexes, possible infertility. In women, pregnancy problems that can kill a fetus and, occasionally, the mother. In babies, infections of the eyes, ears and lungs, possibly death.

Diagnosis: For men and women, a painless test at a doctor's office.

Cure: Usually the drug tetracycline or doxycycline. 33/54

A Pap smear can detect it, and antibiotics can cure it. If not treated, it can cause pelvic-inflammatory disease (PID), which can lead to ectopic, or tubal, pregnancy and bring pneumonia and eye diseases to children born to infected mothers.

> One of the most striking characteristics of the current crop of STDs is that, with the notable exception of AIDS, their most severe consequences are visited upon women and babies. A prime example is chlamydia, a disease that strikes both sexes, but with very different repercussions. Unlike AIDS, syphilis and gonorrhea, chlamydia is not among the STDs that doctors are required to report to health authorities, but no one doubts that the infection is spreading rapidly. One reason that numbers are hard to pin down is that until recently the diagnosis (made by culturing suspected chlamydia cells in the lab) was so cumbersome, time consuming and expensive that it was seldom made. But a simpler, cheaper test has just been developed that doesn't require the culturings of cells and should make accurate diagnosis more common. 20/72-73

Pregnant women with sexually transmitted infections are more likely to have premature deliveries and newborns with serious abnormalities, say two studies.

The studies, in the *Journal of the American Medical Association,* are among the most definitive to make that link.

One study of 534 women, by University of Washington at Seattle researchers, found 19 percent had bacterial vaginitis, a vaginal infection caused by several kinds of bacteria, and 9 percent had chlamydia.

Women with bacterial vaginitis had twice as many premature deliveries as women who didn't and women with chlamydia infections had almost three times as many.

Among women with chlamydia, 32 percent had low-birth-weight babies compared to 15 percent of uninfected women.

In the second study by University of Alabama at Birmingham researchers, it was also found that 2 percent of 16,218 pregnant women had active infections with a herpes virus called cytomegalovirus (CMV).

About 36 percent of infants born to CMV-infected women were also infected, and one-third of those infants developed hearing loss, mental retardation and other handicaps within three years. 127/D1

Chlamydial infection is also increasing on college campuses. Robert B. Jones, MD, PhD, associate professor of medicine and of microbiology and immunology at Indiana University School of Medicine, Indianapolis, who studies the disease under a grant from NIAID, says that rates of infection vary in persons across the country but are reported by some student health services to be as high as 17 percent in undergraduate women. 48/1665-72.

Gonorrhea

The number of cases of this ancient disease rose [in 1985] for the first time since 1978. The case load for gonorrhea doubled between 1968 and 1973 to 2.5 million cases for that year. The U.S. Centers for Disease Control estimates that in 1986 the number was 2 to 3 million cases. 304/A1

The *Medical News and Perspectives* warns:

> Teenage girls with very recent memories of cheerful family-oriented sex education classes, where the subjects of intercourse and parenthood were inextricably coupled, may find without warning that they can never become mothers. Because gonorrhea is often asymptomatic in women, it can progress painlessly until the result is pelvic inflammatory disease with its sequelae of infertility or ectopic pregnancy. 48/1665

Cause: The bacterium *neisseria gonorrhoeae.*

Symptoms: For males, a pus-like discharge. Most infected women show no symptoms.

Complications: Many, from back pains and urination problems to arthritis and sterility. Babies of infected mothers may be born blind.

Diagnosis: Cell-culture tests.

Cure: Penicillin works in most cases. A sharp increase, however, is occurring in a strain of gonorrhea, called PPNG, that resists penicillin. 33/54-55

Genital Herpes

Twenty million Americans have genital herpes. Recurrences are frequent in some, rare in others. Some persons have only one outbreak in a lifetime.

Cause: Herpes-simplex viruses in skin-to-skin contact with infected area.

Symptoms: Blisters in genital area form and become open sores. Initial outbreak sometimes is accompanied by swollen glands, headache or fever, and its lesions may last weeks. Later outbreaks are shorter and less severe.

Diagnosis: A physician can make a test while sores still exist.

Cure: None is known. The drug acyclovir reduces severity of flare-ups. 33/55

Part of the pain for herpes patients is the conviction of being damaged goods. George Washington University's Elisabeth Herz reports "intense guilt feelings" among women who get the disease, and hears again and again the feeling that they are unclean, dirty. "We're all looking for someone to love," says a New York woman, a freelance artist. "In this world our chances seem so slim anyway. Then you add herpes and you think, 'Why should anyone want me now?' " A doctor in Amityville, New York, says the same glum view has invaded the ranks of teenage herpes sufferers, who come into his office, cry, and say, "No one will ever want to marry me." 11/65

Joe Blount, statistician for the U.S. Centers for Disease Control, says that an estimated 500,000 new cases of genital herpes occur every year and that the total number of cases may be as high as twenty million. 129/D5

Although an epidemiologic association between HSV-2 [herpes simplex virus affecting the genitals] and cervical and other cancers has been shown for some time, there is now much more interest in building evidence that human papilloma virus (HPV) [also known as venereal warts] is more important in a variety of genital cancers in both men and women.

Dr. Jonathan Zenilamn, a specialist with the division of Sexually Transmitted Diseases at the U.S. Centers for Disease Control, said that HPV "was thought to be just a nuisance — get rid of them [venereal warts] and that's the end of the story." However, he concluded that new research shows HPV to be a cause of cervical and anal cancer. 304/A8

Dr. Alan Lawhead, Assistant Professor of Gynecology and Obstetrics at Emory University and a specialist in HPV, states that "HPV is probably going to be the disease of the '80s and '90s . . . If it wasn't for AIDS, I think HPV would be one of the big topics . . . [infection] appears to be spreading in epidemic proportions." 304/A8

Approximately 80 percent of genital cancers have now been shown to be associated with HPV, so if herpes is at fault, it must be as a cofactor with HPV.

According to Director Cates of the U.S. Centers for Disease Control's STD division, the three (of forty-five) known types of HPV that have been found to be associated with cancer of the vulva, vagina and cervix — types 16, 18 and 31, of which any or all may cause a tumor of any area — usually become seeded in the female genital tract during adolescence because "the cervical epithelium is so vulnerable at that time. Then certain triggers can later set off their growth." 48/1672-73

Andre Nahmias, MD, of Emory University School of Medicine in Atlanta, who is conducting research on many aspects of herpes, has collected data (not yet published) that may profoundly alter thinking about the disease. His data, which is corroborated by ongoing research at other institutions, suggests that the true prevalence of HSV-2 infection is much higher than the 10 percent of Americans previously recognized. And, in addition to its capacity of being harbored without symptoms (which was known), the virus may be transmitted asymptomatically. 48/1667

Dr. Steven Strauss, a scientist at the Laboratory of Clinical Investigation, has shown that the herpes virus (HSV-2) was transmitted to another person through sexual intercourse during an asymptomatic state. 48/1667

"Researchers believe HPV can spread even when warts are not obvious; as many as 10 percent of women who show no symptoms of HPV-related disease may be infected . . . scientists have recently learned that, contrary to a long-held belief, herpes is contagious when it is dormant and no lesions are present." 304/A8

The data suggest that, depending on age, sex, socioeconomic group and race, the prevalence of HSV-2 infection in this country ranges from 20 percent to 60 percent. The average male adult in this country, it seems, has a 40 to 50 percent chance of having been infected with HSV-2 — and may have unknowingly infected his sexual partner(s). 48/1667

Strauss looks forward to seeing controlled trials of anti-HSV-2 vaccines within two years. "Given the fact that genital herpes is already a very common disease," he suggests, "one might consider administering a safe and effective vaccine before or during the age of beginning sexual activity," that is, in childhood or adolescence. 48/1667-72

Scientists have discovered a new virus they suspect could cause some forms of cancer.

The discovery is reported in *Science* magazine. The virus is related to the five already known herpes viruses. It was isolated from six patients with disorders of the blood or immune system, including two who also were infected with the AIDS virus.

But, researchers say, the new virus is not believed to be linked to AIDS.

The virus is being called HBLV, for human B-lympho tropic virus, a reference to the type of blood cells (called B-cells) it seems to attack.

Dr. Robert Gallo, whose National Cancer Institute team was primarily responsible for isolating the new virus, says it is not yet known whether it causes disease or how easily it is transmitted. "All known human herpes viruses cause disease. We expect that will be true of HBLV." 131/D1

Speculation is that it may cause a type of blood-cell cancer called lymphoma. It's also thought the virus could cause an illness characterized by fatigue and muscle weakness.

The puzzling illness has been associated with another herpes virus, called Epstein-Barr, which causes mononucleosis.

Like other herpes viruses, the new virus could have the ability to remain dormant in the body for long periods, then be triggered to cause illness. 131/D1

Why the dramatic rise now in the incidence of herpes? Sexual freedom is obviously implicated. "With herpes, every new case is added to the pool," says Dr. Yehudi Felman, a New York City VD specialist. "The increase is exponential after awhile." Not only are more people indulging in sex, they are also more active — starting younger, marrying later, divorcing more often. The wider acceptance of oral sex has also played a role. Richard Hamilton, a San Francisco family physician and author of *The Herpes Book,* thinks science has wrought the herpes epidemic: penicillin allowed greater sexual contact with little risk, and the pill and other contraceptives largely replaced condoms, which prevented direct contact with sores.

Women often have a harder time than men. They appear to suffer more physically in both the initial and subsequent episodes. During recurrent attacks of herpes, they have more lesions than men do, and the pain lasts twice as long. On the other hand, to complicate matters further, some women are barely aware of their herpes outbreaks and the periods during which they are high transmission risks. They sometimes have internal, hard-to-see lesions, they may be carrying the virus in their genital secretions, and a few may spread the disease via shedding from the cervix without showing any overt symptoms. For many women, the disease exacerbates their doubts about casual sex; they feel they were pushed into it by a permissive culture, then made to pay a heavy price. 11/65

Trichomoniasis

Some three million men and women get trichomoniasis each year.

Cause: The parasite *trichomonas vaginalis.*

Symptoms: For women, a frothy discharge, itching, redness of genitals. Men usually have no symptoms.

Diagnosis: Pap smear or microscopic examination.
Complications: None in men, gland infections in women.
Cure: Drug metronidazole. 33/55

Venereal Warts

Although often painless, these growths on and around the genitals can be dangerous and need medical attention.
Cause: HPVs, the human papilloma viruses.
How are they found? Some look flat. Some look like tiny cauliflowers. Some only a doctor can see. It takes a Pap smear to detect warts on the cervix.
What harm do they do? Babies exposed during childbirth may get warts in the throat. Some researchers believe that venereal warts caused by some types of HPVs increase risk of cancer of cervix, vulva, penis and anus.
Cure: Doctors can remove with the drug podophyllin. Some require surgery. Over-the-counter drugs for other skin warts should be avoided. 33/55

Syphilis

This once rampant disease is now on the decline, but still can be life-threatening.
Cause: The bacterium *treponema pallidum,* an organism that can be killed with soap and water.
Symptoms: In two stages and usually in three weeks. First a painless pimple, blister or sore where the germs entered the body. Then, a rash, hair loss, swollen glands.
Diagnosis: Blood test, microscopic examination.
Complications: Brain damage, heart disease, paralysis, insanity, death. Babies born to untreated women may be blind, deaf, or crippled by bone disease.
Cure: Penicillin. 33/55

Of course, people became optimistic that the battle against these diseases was won, and in fact, the incidence of infectious syphilis in the United States dropped from a high of more than 100,000 cases in 1947 to a low of 6,516 cases in 1955.

That decline, however, sparked two reactions. First, health care officials relaxed their attempts to control syphilis because it seemed that eradication of it was at hand. Second, sexual promiscuity in the United States increased. As a result, in 1977, an estimated two million cases of gonorrhea and seventy-five thousand cases of syphilis were reported in the United States. 78/25-27

PID

Pelvic inflammatory disease is described by the U.S. Centers for Disease Control as the "most common serious complication" of STDs.

Causes: Infections from any of several diseases, including chlamydia and gonorrhea, that result in inflammation and abscesses of a woman's Fallopian tubes, ovaries and pelvis.

Possible harm: One in seven women with a PID attack becomes infertile. After three attacks, up to 75 percent cannot conceive.

Diagnosis: Examinations of abdomen and pelvis, laboratory tests.

Cure: Antibiotics for some cases. Severe cases often require surgery that results in infertility. 33/55

U.S. Centers for Disease Control researchers believe that a large proportion of the 70,000 ectopic pregnancies — mostly in older women — occurring annually in this country are related to pelvic inflammatory disease. "Partially blocked Fallopian tubes allow sperm to get up," says Dr. Guinan, "but the fertilized egg can't get back down, so there's implantation in the tube." The problem has increased dramatically over the past decade, she says, and is now a leading cause of maternal death among black women. 48/1665-72

> Infertility following the development of pelvic inflammatory disease occurs in about 10 percent of those who get the disease — or approximately 100,000 American women each year — and the rate is much higher in sexually active teenagers than in older women, according to Cates. Moreover, if a woman who has had pelvic inflammatory disease does become pregnant, the result may be disastrous. 48/1665-72

Other Physical Risks

In addition to pregnancy and the growing list of STDs, there are other, less-known physical consequences to premarital sex.

> The earlier a girl begins having intercourse, for example, the higher her risk of developing cervical cancer as an adult. Cancer specialist Dr. Hugh R. K. Barber, director of obstetrics-gynecology at New York's Lenox Hill Hospital, believes that the trend toward earlier intercourse is too new to know what other physical risks may turn up. "We know a fair amount about females," he says, "but I suspect that boys aren't going

to get off scot-free, physically . . . There's no data, but I wouldn't be surprised if boys eventually get cancer of the prostate at an earlier age than now." 38/60

God is good to us. Not only has He provided a means of bringing pleasure and total unity through sex, but He also has given us boundaries in which to enjoy His gift fully. He has told us to wait until marriage because He loves us and wants us to have an abundant life. When we choose to ignore God, we leave ourselves open to the consequences.

One young person included the following piece in an essay:

S. I. McMillen, in his book *None of These Diseases* says, "Medical science with all its knowledge is inadequate to take care of the world's venereal disease problem. Yet millenniums before the microscope, and before man knew the method of the transmission of venereal diseases, God knew all about them and gave to man the only feasible plan of preventing these universal and blighting killers. Jesus clearly stated that, from the beginning, our Father ordained that one man and one woman should constitute a family unit. This plan of two, and two alone, constituting a family unit is so unique, so different from human plans, and so effective in the prevention of the vast complications of horrible venereal diseases, that again we are forced to recognize another medical evidence of the inspiration of the Bible." 132/44

Is it any wonder that those informed in the medical profession and other related areas are advocating monogamy? This conclusion in the *Medical News and Perspectives* bears repeating: "Unless you're monogamous for a lifetime, with a monogamous partner, you're at risk. And the more partners you have, the greater the risk." 48/1672

Safe Sex

Surgeon General Koop, in a personal interview in his office with the authors, strongly emphasized that the only safe sex today is between "a monogamous man with a monogamous woman in a monogamous relationship."

The president of the American Association of Sex Educators, Counselors and Therapists agrees. "I define safe sex as celibacy or masturbation, with the next best thing that could be completely safe as monogamy with a trustworthy partner, who's not already infected." 176

Time magazine, in an extensively researched article on herpes, "The New Scarlet Letter," concludes that "herpes cannot be defeated, but only cozened into an uneasy, lifelong truce."

It is a melancholy fact that [premarital sex] has rekindled old fears. But perhaps not so unhappily, it may be a prime mover in helping to bring to a close an era of mindless promiscuity. The monogamous now have one more reason to remain so. For all the distress it has brought, the troublesome little bug may inadvertently be ushering in a period in which sex is linked more firmly to commitment and trust. 11/65-66

Many STD researchers "have little to offer in the way of prevention. With effective vaccines a long way off, the best protection against STD, it seems, just might be a return to that old-fashioned safeguard: monogamy." 20/73

The joint report by Surgeon General Koop and Secretary of Education Bennett warns that "AIDS education (as part of sex education in general) should *uphold* monogamy in marriage as a desirable and worthy thing . . . Young people should be taught that the best precaution is abstinence until it is possible to establish a mutually faithful monogamous relationship." 208

One concludes, "Young people must be told the truth — that the best way to avoid AIDS is to refrain from sexual activity until as adults they are ready to establish a mutually faithful monogamous relationship. 140/A3

4. Unwanted Pregnancy and Abortion

In their own words:

When you are a teenager and you become pregnant, you have several options open to you, none of them favorable.

♡ ♡ ♡

Although precautions can be taken, pregnancy is always a possibility. There is no 100 percent protection. Many think they won't get caught, and they use that as a cop-out. They think, *God won't allow me to get pregnant and ruin my life,* as though He were in the business of helping us sin.

There is a price to pay for sin. Even David was caught, and he was a man after God's own heart. The Bible records the consequences of his actions: His son died and his family was disgraced.

Abortion is also a so-called "way out." But do two wrongs make a right? Should murder be added to fornication to make everything OK? Many women who have abortions are later unable to have children; that risk alone should be enough to prevent premarital sex.

A friend of mine had an abortion when she was sixteen. Now she is married and anxious to have her own family. After a period of time of trying to get pregnant and not succeeding, she went to the doctor. Evidently the abortion had caused scar tissue to build up and had closed the Fallipian tubes leading to her womb. Her body had formed its own defense against any future abortion. The doctors had no other explanation.

♡ ♡ ♡

When I left my baby at the hospital the day after he was born, I left part of me with him. The problems and hurt caused by premarital sex far outweighed the benefits. I learned this the hard way. The one good thing that happened because of my pregnancy is that I received Jesus as my Savior.

♡ ♡ ♡

The very consequences of sex prove that it is not intended for anyone other than a husband and wife. Creating another life (or engaging in activity with that potential) is an awesome responsibility that cannot be borne by any who are not committed to each other fully. The bond between the parents must be stronger than the bond between parent and child. The couple's relationship must be the foundation for all others, both in and out of the home.

♡ ♡ ♡

I wonder about the pregnant girls I see at school. What are they feeling? What are their desires, hurts, frustrations? What will their lives be like? And aside from the obvious biological aspect, *why are they pregnant?*

If two people don't have the love needed to raise a family (if they did, they would be married), they have no business taking the chance of getting pregnant outside marriage.

♡ ♡ ♡

The tragic reality among pregnant girls at my school is that many believed they would not conceive because they had sex only once, or they felt that only bad girls get pregnant.

♡ ♡ ♡

God made sex not only as the most intimate expression of love for the one you're committed to, but also as the means of reproduction. If you're ready to have sex, are you ready to have kids? Girls, what will you do if you get pregnant? Will you get an abortion and murder an innocent person? Or will you have the baby and try to raise it without a father? Regardless of the choice, three lives are permanently marred for the sake of a few minutes of self-gratification. Is it worth it? God made sex, among other reasons, so a godly man and woman could share the joy of bringing up children in the admonition of the Lord. Do two selfish teenagers in the back seat of a car live up to that high calling?

♡ ♡ ♡

My friend is now married, but she still lives with regrets, especially of her past abortion: "Even after you're married, you have
so many scars. It follows you everywhere, even though it has been
forgiven. You go to the doctor and are required to write out your
medical history, and you have to write *Abortion.* The thought
patterns, too, do not suddenly go away. They have to be erased
over and over."

♡ ♡ ♡

Our society is basically two-faced. If you don't go all the way
before marriage, you are "chicken" or a "goody-goody," but if you
get pregnant outside marriage, you are shunned as being "loose."
It seems to me the opinion of the population at large should have
no control over such an important decision in your life.

♡ ♡ ♡

Abortion resolves one situation for the moment, but it never
resolves the guilt or breaks the bond between a mother and her baby.
Recently I read these statistics by Anne Catherine Speckhard,
Ph.D., of the University of Minnesota, on the long-term manifes-
tations of stress from abortions (five to ten years after):

> Eighty-one percent reported *preoccupation* with the aborted
> child.
> Seventy-three percent reported *flashbacks* of the abortion
> experience.
> Sixty-nine percent reported feelings of *"craziness"* after the
> abortion.
> Fifty-four percent recalled *nightmares* related to the abor-
> tion.
> Thirty-five percent had perceived *visitations* from the
> aborted child.
> Twenty-three percent reported *hallucinations* related to the
> abortion. 296/89-92

In Dr. Speckhard's findings, 72 percent of the subjects said they
held no religious beliefs at the time of their abortions, and 96
percent in retrospect regarded abortion as the taking of life or as
murder. 296/69

♡ ♡ ♡

Adoption seemed the only way for actual survival for Rita who
gave up her two children. Today, twenty years later, although she
has a new family, Rita cannot forget the two she gave up. She
told me she thinks about them continually, every day, wondering
where they are, what they are up to, if they will ever want to
know her, if they will ever understand. Her letters to the adoption
agency, are they in a file somewhere, unopened?

♡ ♡ ♡

The price, however, for the rampant sexual promiscuity today is overwhelming. Abortions exceed the number of deaths caused by the Holocaust, and teenage mothers are proving to be a sad counterfeit for the real thing. With all the changes in our society, one thing remains constant: The wages of sin is death. No amount of technological breakthroughs concerning the reproductive system will change that.

♡ ♡ ♡

I heard the following statements from a group of young mothers I spend time with:

"Everyone kept asking, 'Did you lose your virginity yet?' and it finally got to me. They don't ask any more."

"I was going to have an abortion, but I spent the money on clothes."

"I used to think, *Ten years from now, I'll be a woman of twenty-four.* Now I think, *I'll be twenty-four, and my child will be ten.*"

♡ ♡ ♡

God did not give us the ability to have sex, and then want us to misuse it. He wanted it to be right, so He told us the place for sex, which is marriage. He meant it to be an act of love. If you're not married and you think you're "making love," you run the risk of creating a new life, and I would ask you: Would you kill something that was made in an act of love?

♡ ♡ ♡

Even if a couple decides to marry after conceiving a child, the woman often feels cheated and carries resentment toward her husband. I know someone like that. It's my grandma. Their marriage was the pits. And the child, my aunt, still throws it in Grandma's face. Even after all these years, the reminder is still there.

♡ ♡ ♡

Men traditionally are responsible for initiating the relationship. But when the relationship leads to sex, which, by design, is meant for reproduction, look what happens: The woman has to bear the child. And she only has to be a woman in the biological sense to have a child, which is why four out of ten teenage girls in the U.S. wind up pregnant by age twenty.

550,000 American teenage girls gave birth in 1981, but the mortality rate for teen births is extremely high. If the mother does keep the child, she is not prepared psychologically, intellectually or financially to be a parent; thus, 60 percent of teenage mothers drop out of school.

———————————— ♥ ————————————

We live in a culture that deceives itself daily. We have surrounded ourselves with amazing drugs and technology that should take all responsibility out of casual sex, yet look at us. We have the pill and think we are safe, and as a result the nation is infested with dozens of sexually transmitted diseases. We have, readily available to anyone, creams and foams and gadgets to prevent pregnancies, yet the illegitimate pregnancy rate is going up, not down. We have developed a handful of methods to "terminate" pregnancies (with euphemistic language to accompany them), yet millions of women are wracked with guilt and anguish over having taken the life of their child. The deception goes on.

At the same time, we are becoming callous to the pain we cause ourselves and others. Many people who contract STDs seek revenge on society by deliberately passing on the diseases. Men and boys get girls pregnant and abandon them. Some women and girls genuinely suffer after an abortion, others simply become hardened.

In this strange society, young people are caught in the crossfire of opposing and often nonsensical views on sex. As one young writer above noted, our society is two-faced about sex. If young people aren't sexually active, they are outcasts and prudes. If they are sexually active and suffer some consequence as a result of it, they may find people to be unsympathetic and judgmental.

If society is reluctant to tell the negative aspects of premarital sex, the church must be willing to speak up. Kids must have the knowledge to make intelligent decisions. They must be taught what God says about sex, why He gives commands concerning sex, His provision and protection for those who obey, and the potential consequences for those who don't.

One of the consequences, of course, is the potential for a new life to be created. The girl has one of four choices: give the baby up for adoption, marry the father of the child, raise the child alone, or have an abortion. Regardless of her choice, she will probably have to make it alone, since "more than 85 percent of boys who impregnate teenage girls will eventually abandon them." 77/9 She may not even be able to turn to her family:

> Nearly a million teenagers run away from home each year in this country. Girls account for almost half this number; as many as 40 percent of them do so because they are pregnant. When interviewed later, they make statements such as "My father said that if I ever became pregnant he'd kill me," or "My mother said that if I ever became pregnant I shouldn't come home." These runaways face horrors that are simply beyond belief. Many end up the victims of pimps who immediately turn them into prostitutes. It may also be

appropriate to add that pregnancy is reliably reported to be the most prevalent reason for suicide among teenage girls. 110/104

Social stigma and family problems aside, the health risks for teenage mothers and their babies are enormous. Girls still in adolescence find the energy they need for their own growing bodies being diverted to the baby, leaving the mother open to a number of health problems.

An adolescent is more likely to begin premature labor and have a more difficult labor, thereby increasing hazards to herself and her baby. Non-fatal anemia and toxemia also are more likely for pregnant adolescents.

A baby born to a girl under age fifteen is almost 2 ½ times as likely to die in its first year as is a baby born to a woman in her early twenties. Babies born to adolescents are 1 ½ to 2 times as likely to be of low birth weight and almost 2 ½ times as likely to have brain and nervous system disorders as are babies born to women in the early twenties. Low birth weight is associated with a greater risk of infant mortality, childhood morbidity, and such complications as blindness, learning disorders, cerebral palsy, and learning and behavioral disabilities. Generally these babies also have lower IQs, do less well academically, and repeat school grades more often than do children of older women. 32

(Author's note: As we mentioned before, many pregnant adolescents do not take care of themselves physically, so the problems with babies born to teens are often due to poor health care rather than age.)

Another report shows the high risk of poverty, school failure, unemployment and marital instability for teenagers who keep their babies:

• Pregnant and parenting teens are less likely to obtain a high school degree or equivalent than are women who delay childbearing.

• Families headed by young mothers are seven times more likely to be living below the poverty level than other families.

• Teen mothers suffer higher rates of marital separation and divorce than women giving birth at later ages. In 1983, 35 percent of all divorces involved women who married in their teens. The risk of marital dissolution is carried on through later life, showing up in increased risks of marital dissolution in second marriages.

• An SRI International study estimated that each of the 442,000 first teenage births in 1979 would cost federal, state and local governments an average of $18,700 every year over the next twenty years in additional health and welfare costs. 32

As the values in our country continue to change, and moral standards once generally accepted are ignored, young people will continue to pay a high price in unwanted pregnancies. "Free sex" came on the scene in the 1960s, and as a result of that freedom, "the percentage of out-of-wedlock births to women under twenty years of age has dramatically increased over the last twenty years, from 15 percent to 51 percent." 215 Even an increase in sex education from a secular point of view has not stemmed the tide. "If present trends continue . . . 40 percent of today's fourteen-year-old girls will be pregnant at least once before age twenty." 35/79

"Those who choose to try to parent the child themselves," explains Dr. John Raney, "often find after the first glow and excitement of parenthood wears off that being a single mother (or father) is far more demanding and difficult than they ever imagined. Even with an involved spouse or mate the young couple who are still trying to mature themselves can 'frequently feel woefully inadequate to face the responsibilities of parenthood.' " 287/25

Many come to feel very much trapped by their parenting role and by the fact that they're missing out on the fun other teenagers are having. To a considerable extent this is often sadly true.

"The teenage years can be a wonderful and exciting time in which individuals grow and mature physically, emotionally and mentally into adulthood. It's a time when their identity tends to solidify as they discover more of who they are and attempt to answer questions as to what life is all about and how they are going to spend their lives. It is a time when they think about or settle on particular vocational pursuits and on what kind of husband or wife they would like. A time when they prepare to make their own way in the world." 288/71 Unfortunately, becoming a parent as an adolescent can short-circuit this whole process. 287/22 In commenting on this, one author succinctly puts it: "Committing to adult responsibilities at such an early age creates victims of what psychologists term identity foreclosure." 287/22

"This is not to say," says Dr. Raney, "that people's personalities don't grow once they have children or get married, but that the responsibility of adulthood prematurely faced because of single parenthood or an early marriage changes the quality and extent of the type of growth that does occur." 289

The alternative to parenthood and adoption is abortion. In the United States an abortion is performed every twenty-two seconds; that is more than 4000 a day. In many states, a thirteen-year-old girl cannot receive aspirin from the school nurse without parental consent, yet the same girl can receive an excused absence from school officials to have an abortion performed without her parents' knowledge.

> Since the Supreme Court decision of Roe v. Wade in 1973, in excess of 15 million abortions have been performed. This is an unconscionable moral and ethical dilemma. In speaking of the Roe v. Wade decision, President Ronald Reagan said, "Our nationwide policy of abortion-on-demand through all nine months of pregnancy was neither voted for by our people nor enacted by our legislators — not a single state had such unrestricted abortion before the Supreme Court decreed it to be a national policy in 1973. But the consequences of the judicial decision are now obvious: Since 1973, more than 15 million unborn children have had their lives snuffed out by legalized abortions. This is over ten times the number of Americans lost in all our nation's wars." 218/18

The answer to the problems of teenage pregnancy is not to make contraceptives more available. It is not to promise food and housing for life to single mothers. It is not to take the life of an innocent child for the sake of convenience. The answer is to take God at His infallible word and realize that His wise commands are there for our own good.

He has provided sex so married couples can have children and raise them in the ways of the Lord. The book of Proverbs says children are a blessing, and in a committed and loving marriage, that's just what they are. As fathers of six and four children, Dick and I know the reality of that truth.

God's commands are also there for our protection. He doesn't want anyone ever to have to make gut-wrenching decisions about unwanted pregnancies, so He tells us to wait to have sex until marriage. He gives a solution that is so simple it confounds the modern mentality.

The Bible promises that God can work all things to the good for His believers (see Romans 8:28). He can even take something as disastrous as premarital pregnancy and make something good come of it. But knowing this is no excuse for continued premarital sex. The life-changing pain of such pregnancies is immeasurable. As one young woman wrote:

> Of course, the adoption and marriage alternatives are better than abortion, but the point is that few people enter into a sexual relationship for anything other than the pleasure of the sport where both teams win. Some even keep score. But let it be known: there are no winners, and the game is never over. The players must continue what they have started, injured or not.

PROVISION

5. Beauty in the Marriage Relationship

God has set sex aside for marriage for the protection and happiness of people. Sex within marriage brings increased unity and an opportunity to give pleasure to your spouse, as well as to find pleasure yourself. Sex outside marriage brings a momentary thrill, a release, a way to block out problems, but it brings with it an avalanche of negative consequences.

Simply said, sex within marriage is within God's design and is good; sex outside marriage is outside God's design and cannot ultimately be good. It might *feel* good for a moment, but sin can never be a good thing.

By reserving sex for marriage, God protects us from emotional hurt, from disease, from damaged relationships, from the misery that accompanies sin. Sex needs the commitment, trust and longevity that a marriage can provide. In the words of young people who wrote on the subject:

> God has set aside physical intercourse to be shared by a husband and wife. In years past, marriages were consummated once the conjugal rite had been performed. You became "one" after this act, which is why it was designated to take place *after* marriage. I am no longer with my sexual partner, but I consider it one of my most foolish acts to have someone walking this earth who was "one" with me but is no longer with me. He has a part of me that I cannot get back.

♡ ♡ ♡

> How can you lose the true meaning of making love? It depends on how you classify "true meaning." I believe making love was created and perfected by God as a method of enabling a woman and a man to share total intimacy, to let all the walls down and to enjoy in the mutual giving — a total giving of each person to the other. When this intimacy is attempted before marriage, the depth of its meaning is easily lost. It is easy to involve oneself in the sexual act for the pure physical enjoyment with no real thought of the exchange which could be taking place. In addition, when the partners do not love each other, the act becomes very self-centered and focused on "how well does the other person please me?" What could be further from the way God intended than an act of total giving being used as one for self-centered satisfaction?

♡ ♡ ♡

Is it, in the end, really worth all the pain, especially when you know it's wrong? The Lord didn't give us this command to hurt us or restrain us from something enjoyable. He did it to protect us and keep us safe. So let's listen to Him. He knows what He's talking about.

♡ ♡ ♡

God has placed a fence around our freedom, and inside those boundaries there are countless possibilities for innovation. Outside the fence lie chaos and perversion. God doesn't put that fence around sex to smother it, but to keep it safe there.

♡ ♡ ♡

I found it very interesting to study God's plan and purpose of sex. You see, God isn't against sex, as long as it is within the marriage relationship. That just didn't seem fair to me at first. I mean, surely it must be OK if you really love someone. Can't we express our love? But after studying God's perspective further, I found out that God says NO to premarital sex to protect us. He wants to keep us from experiencing the pain I felt with my boyfriend. I saw in 1 Corinthians 13 how love involves compassion, patience, truth and trust, not envy, anger and self-centeredness.

———————— ♥ ————————

Just as sex is safe and free within the limits of God's protection, it is also able to reach its fullest and most exciting potential within those limits. There is no fear of rejection, no need to pretend, no need to sneak around, no guilt, no fear of a baby ruining your life. This is God's provision for sex within the marriage. In the words of the young writers:

> To begin with, I think it's important to note that God has ordained the sex act for couples who have committed themselves to a lifetime of marriage. Any sex outside this relationship is forbidden by God. Now I have to be honest and admit I knew this long before my first sexual encounter. Unfortunately, I misunderstood God's intent for my sex life. I figured He was just trying to deprive me of having any real fun in life. What I didn't understand was that He created me with a sex drive; therefore, sex itself was not wrong or dirty. It simply needed to be confined to the marriage bed.

♡ ♡ ♡

God does not want us copying worldliness or giving in to pressure just because everyone else is doing it. The Bible makes it very clear that God wants Christians to have the most vibrant, exciting sex life possible.

♡ ♡ ♡

The first reason is to increase our joy in the marriage relationship. God wants two virgins, free from guilt or shame, to enter into marriage undefiled. God does not want people burdened down with emotional scars entering into marriage. God desires two people who are so committed to His rules that they will abstain from premarital sex, entering into marriage with the certainty of each other's purity. That is definite joy!

♡ ♡ ♡

I believe that sexual intimacy is the nearest we, as finite human beings, can come to experiencing the unique love relationship of our triune God while we are on earth. This partially explains the joy and attractive power of sex — the two people together become greater than they were individually. This is the way sex builds the marriage spiritually.

———————— ♥ ————————

This spiritual side of sex is often overlooked. Even many Christians are not aware of the profoundly spiritual nature of their sex lives. A person will feel acute spiritual pain and separation from God when engaging in sex outside marriage, but may not even realize how spiritually beneficial and unifying sex is within marriage.

13

SPIRITUAL REASONS

PROTECTION

1. From God's Judgment

In their own words:

Hebrews 13:4 says that "marriage should be honored by all, and the marriage bed kept pure, for God will judge the adulterer and all the sexually immoral." If that is true, and I believe it is, then how much more should the marriage bed be honored before one is married! Wouldn't we also be judged and punished by God for something this important? When the Bible says we reap what we sow, it would certainly apply to immoral acts.

♡ ♡ ♡

However, if we choose to ignore what God says, we are placing ourselves under His judgment, and we are subject to the natural consequences of living outside the limits He has set for His children.

Because of our corrupt society, most find it difficult to wait to experience sex. From everything I've heard and read, sex sounds great. That's why I believe it is worth waiting for!

♡ ♡ ♡

But in His wisdom, God has restricted this intimacy to the

bounds of marriage. There are strict judgments against people who engage in premarital and extramarital sex.

———————————— ♥ ————————————

The Bible paints a clear portrait of God as being just. As a just God, He must act when His unarguable laws are broken. If He allowed His people to flaunt unrighteousness, doing damage to themselves and others, He would not be a fair judge.

Please remember that God's discipline comes out of His love for us — just as parents, out of love, discipline their children for playing with matches after being told not to. God created us with dignity and value and freedom to make choices, but He hasn't set us adrift. He has given us a framework, a value system within which we are to make our choices. A spiritual law of cause and effect is at work, so that choices made within God's value structure bring blessing, and those that transgress His boundaries bring negative consequences.

We first see this law in effect in the Garden of Eden; the results of the irrational and selfish choices made there are still being felt. In fact, as one author has documented, the Scriptures are full of examples of how sexual transgressions have brought about the wrath of God:

> Genesis records sexual sin in the lives of the people of Sodom (19:1-29), Lot and his daughters (19:30-38), Shechem (34:1-31), Reuben (35:22), Judah and Tamar (38:1-26), and Potiphar's wife (39:1-20).
>
> Consider the consequences of these sexual sins. Sodom and Gomorrah were obliterated by God's judgement. The incest of Lot and his daughters produced two nations: the Moabites and the Ammonites, wicked people who plagued Israel for many generations. Revenge on Shechem's rape of Dinah resulted in the murder of every man in his city. The sins of Reuben and Judah brought shame to the house of Jacob. The uncontrolled lust of Potiphar's wife sent Joseph, an innocent man, to prison.
>
> Samson was God's "man of the hour," but his lust after beautiful but unrighteous women led directly to his tragic downfall (Judges 14 — 16). Not only Samson but his entire nation suffered because he satisfied his desires rather than obeying God's word.
>
> David was as godly a man as Scripture portrays, yet 2 Samuel 11 documents the lust that brought him catastrophe. What began as relief from boredom ended in adultery. Actually, it didn't end there. David attempted to circumvent the consequences of his adultery — to cheat the law of the harvest — by covering up. In doing so his sin of adultery expanded to the murder of a righteous man and the death of

David's infant son.

David's model of immorality was not lost on his family. When David's son Amnon lusted for his half-sister Tamar, he took what he wanted, just as his father had. This prompted Absalom's murder of Amnon, followed by David's banishment of Absalom. That in turn led to the bitterness that divided David and Absalom and eventually divided the nation.

The final blow was the death of Absalom, for whom David grieved inconsolably (2 Samuel 18:33). Three sons dead, his daughter raped, his family name disgraced. David fulfilled his own words by paying for his sins four times over (2 Samuel 12:6).

True to form, even Solomon, the son in whom David put most hope, eventually let his devotion stray from God to ungodly women. In trying to please his seven hundred wives and three hundred concubines, Solomon built altars to their false gods and brought divine judgement on himself and all Israel (1 Kings 11:1-13).

Sometimes God's judgement on sexual sin is immediate and obvious. Paul warned the Corinthians to learn from the example of Israel in Moses' day: "We should not commit sexual immorality, as some of them did — and in one day twenty-three thousand of them died " (1 Corinthians 10:8). When twenty-three thousand people in one place are struck dead for sexual sin (among other things), the message is not a subtle one.

. . . While the physical consequences of immorality may be circumvented, the spiritual consequences are inevitable. Antibiotics will prevent or cure some venereal diseases. The pill will lower the chances of pregnancy. Abortion is a way out of an unwanted pregnancy. But no scientific or medical breakthrough ever changes the fact that I will answer to God for my moral choices. Medical science may eliminate some consequences of my sin, but it cannot remove my accountability to God.

It was to religious people that God said,
"When you spread out your hands in prayer,
I will hide my eyes from you;
even if you offer many prayers,
I will not listen" (Isaiah 1:15, NIV).

When the adulterous people of Israel sought God they would not find Him, He said, for He would withdraw Himself from them (Hosea 5:6). Similar statements are found throughout the Old Testament.

To those living in immorality, here is the message: Husband, don't bother praying at meals — God isn't listening. Wife, don't lead out in prayer at a women's Bible study — God won't hear you. Young couple, don't pray that God will bless the wedding ceremony — His ears are deaf to you. Pastor, don't ask God's anointing on Sunday's sermon. If you are living in sexual sin, there is one prayer He is waiting for — the prayer of sincere confession and repentance. He longs for you to start fresh with Him again.

"I wanted to pray that I could share the gospel with my friend. But I knew God wouldn't hear me because of what I was doing." This young man was sexually involved with his girlfriend. Without knowing the Scripture quoted above, he sensed his prayers were being blocked by his sin. He was right. By the grace of God he repented, and God was once again pleased to hear and answer.

Our sexual lives cannot be isolated from our spiritual lives. The believers in Corinth tried to separate the two. They still participated in the idolatry and immorality they grew up with and thought they could somehow remain spiritually unaffected by it. Paul told them they were wrong (1 Corinthians 6:12-20; 10:14-22). God is concerned with what I do with my body, for it is the temple of my spirit — and His. 62/230-234

There are consequences for sin, the Bible leaves no doubt. We may sometimes wonder, however, where justice is when we see evil in the world. We read the papers and we think that crime really does pay. But there is always justice in the spiritual realm. Civil laws are often arbitrarily established and can be circumvented with tricky legal maneuvers, but God is not impressed with clever arguments. His laws are an expression of His righteousness, protection and provision for us. They are not arbitrary, not designed to benefit one person over another. Although He understands our frailty, He doesn't listen to excuses, and He can't be bought off. Sooner or later, those who transgress His holy statutes will pay the price.

God doesn't want to watch us suffer. He wants only one thing: sincere repentance and obedience. One young person wrote the following in a letter to a friend:

I hope that God has truly spoken to you through this letter. He desires the very best for you. He designed you and He loves you so much. But He is also a righteous and just God. He will not tolerate sin. The sexual freedom you desire brings with it a high price tag. I sincerely pray that you consider the facts and turn to your Father. He is waiting. He earnestly seeks to restore to you the newness and purity you once possessed. His promise to you: "Therefore if any man is in Christ, he is a new creature; the old things passed away; behold, new things have come" (2 Corinthians 5:17, NASB).

2. One's Walk With God

In their own words:

[Letter to a friend] Alice, you told me you sometimes wish you could erase the past. I know the thing that haunts you most is the daily struggle you told me about. I couldn't help crying when you told me that since you and Jay started sleeping together your relationship with God has deteriorated. You even told me how helpless you feel, knowing that sin looms between you and your Maker. I think you'd agree with me when I say the biggest problem I see with premarital sex is not wondering if you'll get caught, catch something, or even get pregnant. The tragedy is the feeling of separation from fellowship with God. You have discovered that, like any other sin you engage in for any length of time, you become a slave to it.

♡ ♡ ♡

I then shifted the flow of the discussion. "You all have been away from sex for a while now, at least since you've been here. What is different for you now? How have your feelings changed?"

"Well," said Lisa, "I have a cleaner conscience. I have a better relationship with God because I don't feel so guilty."

♡ ♡ ♡

If you are a Christian, the Holy Spirit dwells within you. If you try to mix worldly lusts with the Spirit of God, you will fail. My friend Sally had a sexual relationship while she was backslidden. She said, "It destroys your relationship and fellowship with God. I knew He still loved me, but He seemed very far away."

♡ ♡ ♡

Another example was when the men of Israel committed fornication and they died in the wilderness, never seeing Canaan and missing God's greatest blessing in their lives. Many times we see people underdeveloped and weak in character, unable to reach their potential because of their sexual sins. Sexual sins prohibit people from becoming what God intends them to be and nullify His plan for their lives.

♡ ♡ ♡

Since making love entails such intimacy and sharing, it is very easy for one to become committed to someone they cannot or should not marry. Making love is very personal and requires much trust of the partner. Therefore, after a time, the feelings of attachment become very strong. The next thing you know you are "in love." Being in love is great, but it can quite naturally promote the desire for marriage. God calls us to love Him first and to marry only a believer. Engaging in premarital sex may skew those beliefs, and before you know it, you could end up married to a nonbeliever and none the better for it.

♡　♡　♡

Julie and her boyfriend were both brought up in Christian homes where they learned they should wait for marriage to have sex. They had heard from the "old folks" that they would get carried away if they let their emotions get the best of them, but they both felt they could control their urges.

After eight months of dating, they began to have sexual contact with each other, and a couple of years later they finally had intercourse.

At one time they had both been very close to God and had good relationships with Him, but their indulgence interfered terribly with that relationship. The feelings of guilt have been there since they started going too far and are still there.

———————— ♥ ————————

Whenever we exercise an act of our will that goes against the will of God, it will affect our walk with Him. Since the Bible is adamant about reserving sex for marriage, choosing to have sex outside marriage will put us in conflict with God, thus damaging our relationship with Him.

Prolonged sin such as unrepentant premarital sex not only clouds the relationship with God by itself, but it also leads to a downward spiral in a person's spiritual life. One teenager told me that his sexual activity made him "uncomfortable" in the presence of God. When we are uncomfortable with someone, we avoid them. This leads to a cooling of feelings, and if not checked, will lead to indifference.

As we begin this downward spiral, we are more apt to fall into other types of ungodly behavior. I have frequently seen how young Christians who are sexually active are more likely to cheat in school, drink, and become involved in drugs, and are less likely to attend church, pray, seek out fellowship and read the Scriptures. When sex becomes more important than God, priorities in general will change.

God wants to protect us from that. After all, every Christian was at one time lost and separated from God, but then made a decision to respond to Christ's calling and enter the Kingdom. There is safety in God: safety from the repercussions of sin, safety from an evil world charging ahead with no direction, safety from the uncertainty and fear of being adrift in a society that knows no right and wrong. When God calls us to righteousness and a daily walk with Him, He is doing it for our benefit.

At the same time, God provides for us by never breaking

off the relationship. He allows us to come back to Him at any moment. His patience in the midst of His anger is a remarkable thing; His willingness to forgive even our foulest sins is even more remarkable. *He* is the one who, by His grace, seeks to restore our damaged relationship, even one hurt by repeated sexual sins. It is a great deal of damage to repair.

Sin drives a wedge between us and God. Isaiah 59:2 says, "Your iniquities have made a separation between you and your God, and your sins have hid His face from you."

Sexual sin will cause a person to lose his desire for spiritual things. Jesus said that "everyone who does evil hates the light, and does not come to the light, lest his deeds be exposed" (John 3:20). Everything that has to do with God, such as prayer, Bible study, witnessing, and strong Spirit-filled preaching exposes our sins and brings guilt, and so we begin to shun such things. And after awhile, even though you know that what you are doing is wrong, you don't care. You have become enslaved to your passions (2 Peter 2:18,19). Apart form the grace of God at this point it is impossible to repent and come back to Him. 117/81

When a Christian becomes involved in an improper sexual relationship, he begins to feel "uncomfortable" with God. This initial discomfort eventually will lead to unbelief and to a cold, calloused relationship with his creator.

3. Being An Undesirable Influence on Others

Brothers and Sisters in Christ

In their own words:

> Christians have the responsibility of making sure they are not causing a weaker Christian to sin. If a Christian is heard to have had premarital sex, another Christian may easily be influenced into making a wrong choice when confronted with a sexual situation.

——————————— ♥ ———————————

A basic principle of the Bible is that we should not cause others to violate their moral consciences or do things detrimental to themselves. Premarital sex can cause other members of the body of Christ to stumble in their walk with the Lord in at least three ways.

First, someone who has been a Christian awhile who becomes physically involved with a young Christian will hinder that person's spiritual development. Remember that Christ doesn't always make instant changes in people's lives, but may make changes through a gradual process. He works in the way most appropriate for that person. If another Christian fouls up the maturing process through sexual involvement, God's handiwork in that person's life is damaged and the body of Christ is weakened.

Second, a Christian who persuades a more mature Christian to do something they both know is wrong has violated that person's moral conscience. This causes that person to have to account for a deliberate sin, and once again the body of Christ is weakened.

The purpose of a Christian dating relationship should be to build each other up in the Lord. To determine whether a relationship is good or not, each must ask, "Am I growing in my walk with the Lord through this? Is the other person growing closer to the Lord?" If the answer is no, the relationship is not edifying, and the people are not ministering to each other. It may be the relationship is based on manipulation, which is "giving in order to get."

Third, a Christian can cause another to stumble by his example. For instance, Paul has been a Christian for a long time, but he also has been sexually active for some time. Steve, who has never dated before, has just started going with a girl in his youth group, and is very happy about it. While talking to Steve, Paul reveals his sexual activity, and because Paul seems, on the surface, to have his act together, Steve begins to wonder if it would be all right for him to have sex with his new girlfriend.

Paul needs to realize that he is not in a right relationship with God. He is not growing consistently, and he cannot be filled with the Spirit. Unrepented sin makes those things impossible. In addition, he may even be causing his Christian brother to stumble, which would be further evidence of how far out of God's will he is.

Paul may have hurts or needs in his life, such as family problems or a poor self-image, and he may be endeavoring to deal with those through sex. However, he needs to know that this is an irrational attempt to mask his problems through physical release, and he is hardly a desirable role model for Steve.

On the other hand, rather than follow Paul's example, Steve should encourage Paul to walk according to God's principles. Depending on Steve's level of spiritual maturity, he may be able to motivate Paul to study the Scriptures concerning sex and to be in prayer about living righteously. Such opportunities to build up a brother in Christ and turn him from a pattern of sin can be key in strengthening the body of believers.

But if Paul continues to live in bold contradiction to God's commands, there comes a time when Steve must decide if Paul is to remain an influence in his life. The longer Paul is sexually active and talking about it, the more likely Steve is to feel the influence of it and be tempted to sin.

If Steve continues a relationship with Paul without speaking up, he is intentionally putting himself under a bad influence.

God protects us from the bad influences of others when He admonishes His followers not to cause one another to stumble. He knows we may be swayed when a fellow Christian is involved in a sin, since we then can more easily rationalize the sin in our own lives.

Non-Christians

As Christians we are a witness to non-Christians during our lifetime. As we go through life we need to remember that our actions will *always speak louder* than our words. Premarital sex is a very "loud" action; therefore, it would not be good for our testimony as Christians.

———————————— ♥ ————————————

A life of contradiction, of inconsistency in words and actions, is a poor testimony for Christ. This lifestyle verbally proclaims Jesus as Lord, yet conforms to the world in contradiction to God's standards.

When we live contrary to the principles of God, there are serious consequences. We send mixed signals to those who are observing our faith. As one author points out, perhaps there is no more tragic consequence to the sexual sin of Christians than its effect on non-Christians. Nathan said to David, in the wake of his sexual sin, "By doing this you have made the enemies of the LORD show utter contempt" (2 Samuel 12:14, NIV).

The damage is done when non-Christians become aware of Christian's consistent sin. This can be in a relationship between Christians, or between a Christian and a non-Christian. I have known many young people who got involved with nonbelievers in the hope of bringing them to Christ, but instead wound up in sexual relationships with the non-Christians. On the one hand they were trying to witness; on the other hand they were conforming to the non-Christian's lifestyle.

This creates conflict, first within the Christian, who more than anyone else is aware of the inconsistency involved, and second within the non-Christian, who receives a double message. The Christian seems to be saying, "Jesus Christ has cleansed me of my sin, so in return I'm going to sin some more."

God knows that young people are in a fallen and tempting world, but He calls them to a consistent witness and provides the means by which to maintain their convictions: the Scriptures, the Holy Spirit, the body of Christ.

"Excuse me! Are your values showing?"

"Say what?"

"Your values? Are they showing? Do others know that you are a moral person? Do your values identify you as a Christian?"

When David was confronted with his sin of adultery, he went to God in repentance. His prayer of confession is recorded in Psalm 51.

PROVISION

4. God Blesses Purity

In their own words:

God has provided limitations for certain activities, for our protection, and sex is one of them. Sure, we have birth control methods that are somewhat reliable, and one may even think it is all right to pursue sex outside marriage if both partners are responsible. But the one who created us has ordained that we should wait.

♡ ♡ ♡

It says in Proverbs 4:23, "Above all else, guard your heart, for it is the wellspring of life" (NIV). Regardless of how we have strayed from God, we can regain our innocence and keep it forever. As Romans 16:19 says, "I want you to be wise about what is good, and innocent about what is evil" (NIV). "But if you will not do so, behold, you have sinned against the LORD, and be sure your sin will find you out" (Numbers 32:23, NASB).

♡ ♡ ♡

"It is God's will that you should be holy; that you should avoid sexual immorality; that each of you should learn to control his own body in a way that is holy and honorable, not in passionate lust like the heathen" (1 Thessalonians 4:3-5, NIV). Clearly, God in His Word forbids any type of sex outside the marriage relationship. Not because it isn't pleasurable, but because it has a far greater purpose than simply pleasure.

♡ ♡ ♡

If I was given the opportunity to engage in premarital sex again, I wouldn't do it, because God calls us to moral purity and obedience. The first step in responding to God's will is recognizing that a spiritual warfare exists and that Christians must look at the world from a spiritual perspective. Second Corinthians 5:16 says, "Therefore from now on we recognize no man according to the flesh; even though we have known Christ according to the flesh, yet now we know Him thus no longer" (NASB). So, based on Christ's death and resurrection, no one should be regarded from a human perspective. The responsible Christian must look at the world in a biblical context.

In this perspective, the Christian knows that the will of God is that we "abstain from sexual immorality" (1 Thessalonians 4:3, NASB). "God has not called us for the purpose of impurity, but in sanctification" (1 Thessalonians 4:7, NASB). God also calls us to obey Him, as Samuel says, "Behold, to obey is better than sacrifice, and to heed than the fat of rams" (1 Samuel 15:22, NASB). God provides the way we should go, even during temptation: "No temptation has overtaken you but such as is common to man; and God is faithful, who will not allow you to be tempted beyond what you are able, but with the temptation will provide the way of escape also, that you may be able to endure it" (1 Corinthians 10:13, NASB).

Chuck Swindoll says, "It is impossible to come to terms with moral purity without dealing with some practical facts related to the body." Some of those facts include presenting our bodies as sacrifices to God (Romans 12:1), knowing that the Spirit of God dwells in us (1 Corinthians 6:19), glorifying God in our bodies (1 Corinthians 6:20) and knowing our bodies (1 Thessalonians 4:4).

This last fact is extremely important in dealing with the sin of premarital sex. We must know when our bodies can endure and when they are in danger of falling into sin. A Christian must recognize the position he is in, and if he is in danger of engaging in sexual immorality, he must flee. For if he rejects purity, he will be rejecting "the God who gives His Holy Spirit" to him (1 Thessalonians 4:8, NASB).

———————— ♥ ————————

Sexual purity is also a way to show our respect for others and to confirm their dignity and value as human beings. When we abstain from immorality in a relationship, we are able to minister to the other person. When we are sexually immoral, we are manipulative. That is, the reason people are sexually involved before marriage is for some kind of personal gain, which reflects a selfish concept of love. It is impossible to show someone the love of God while engaging in immorality with them.

When we maintain sexual purity, we are channels of God's love. We can accurately represent Him to others.

Sexual purity protects us from the awful consequences of abusing the sacredness of sex. It protects us from misusing our bodies, the dwelling place of the Holy Spirit. It protects us from making a mockery of our position as ambassadors of Christ, allowing us to represent Him in truth. It protects us from the pain Solomon described in Proverbs 6:27,28, when warning his son not to lust after an immoral woman:

Can a man scoop fire into his lap

without his clothes being burned?
Can a man walk on hot coals
   without his feet being scorched? (NIV)

In sexual purity we have the provision and the promise of God's blessings, both in our sex lives in marriage and in all areas of our lives.

5. Patience Is a Fruit of the Spirit

Patience is a fruit of the Spirit. The Bible says: "Against such things there is no law." The action of waiting for something builds excitement. The longer you wait and dream of it, the greater your response will be when it finally arrives. That's why birthdays are so great. All year long we wait for that special day. We don't know exactly what will take place, but we know that it is a day set aside for us. The fact we've waited so long and finally reached it adds energy to the events of the day.

In their own words:

Sex is something we wait our whole lives for until we finally partake of it.

♡ ♡ ♡

A godly character is the result of patience and perseverance in times of trial. Had I been patient and waited to consummate my marriage at the proper time, my character would have been developed and my self-esteem could have been built up. I would have anxiously anticipated my wedding date instead of dreading it. Fortunately, God can use even my mistakes to conform me to Christ's image, but that's no excuse for exhibiting impatience as I did.

♡ ♡ ♡

On the positive side, waiting will help one to subject his or her physical drives to the lordship of Christ and thereby develop self-control, which is an important fruit of the Holy Spirit.

——————— ♥ ———————

Patience is indeed a characteristic of one empowered by the Holy Spirit. So when Christians are involved in sexual activity before marriage, they should realize, in addition to everything else, that they are not living in the power of the Holy Spirit.

The passage the writers above referred to is Galatians 5:22,23: "But the fruit of the Spirit is love, joy, peace, patience, kindness, goodness, faithfulness, gentleness, self-control; against such things there is no law" (NIV).

The characteristics of the Spirit-filled life are not the same as spiritual gifts. It is not possible for someone to say, "I have love, joy and peace; he has patience, kindness and goodness; she has faithfulness, gentleness and self-control; and we're all Spirit-filled." The fruit of the Spirit is the visible evidence of God at work in someone's life. If that person deliberately chooses to rebel against God, the Spirit is unable to work fully in that person's life, and he will be hampered as long as the sin is unresolved.

The Spirit and the traits He works into our lives show God's provision for us. When we have self-control, we will have goodness and peace; when we exhibit patience, we will have love and joy. In fact, each time one element of the fruit of the Spirit is evident in us, other elements surface. When the Spirit is at work in our lives, God gives to us so fast and in such abundance that we can hardly take it all in.

At the same time, the workings of the Spirit are there to protect us. God keeps us out of trouble when we keep our minds on Him, and we have to be thinking about Him when we are living in the Spirit.

In other words, the fruit of the Spirit goes against everything our sinful nature would automatically stand for. As fallen people, our immediate reaction is irritation and impatience when things don't go our way. For kindness, gentleness, patience and the other fruit to be evident, we have to make a conscious choice to react as God would have us react. So when something hits me, rather than fly apart I can say to myself, "Patience . . . keep calm . . . measure your words carefully . . . don't say anything that's not edifying . . .remember — you are a witness for Christ in this situation too." That *makes* me think about God all the time. And the more my mind is on Him, the less I stray from Him. In this way the working of the Holy Spirit in my life protects me from hurting myself or others.

Teenagers who are continually striving to be filled with the Spirit will find premarital sex to be less of a temptation. (For a full explanation of the filling and the power of the Holy Spirit, see "Doing What Comes Supernaturally" in Part 5 of this book, pages 404-409.) When they are in a position to act out an impatient urge for sex — i.e., on a date, at someone's house, etc. — they won't have to fight the urge, because patience will be an integral part of their lives. Self-control will be evident in the choices they make. They will have joy and peace, knowing their patience is not only paying off now, but that it also will pay off in the future, and in an even more significant way.

6. Waiting Builds Trust

God knows that marriages need to be built on a basic trust factor. Suspicion of a spouse's potential infidelity undermines that trust.

"I know how difficult it is to stop having sex once it becomes part of your relationship," a college student writes. "There is pressure from friends to continue, and society endorses it. But I've already seen how my sexual involvement with my former boyfriend affects my present dating relationship with Scott. Scott feels as if I have betrayed him and he doesn't have as much trust in me as he would like to. Just think — I betrayed God too! For a long time I felt guilty for what I had done, but I finally asked the Lord to forgive me and help me live the way He wants me to."

♡ ♡ ♡

"On a more personal note," a wife remarks, "I know the temptations of premarital sex — the physical desires, the emotional desires, the peer pressure — and all the good excuses. I was teased through high school and two years of college about my sexual abstinence. At one time I was even accused of being homosexual."

♡ ♡ ♡

God introduced me to Mr. Right and we struggled through a fourteen-month engagement to refrain from premarital sex. And at the age of twenty-three, after three years of marriage, I have never regretted the no's or the reasons for the no's. I firmly believe that waiting until after the "I do's" to experience sex can only enhance the marital relationship. Our doing that established a trust that cannot be equaled. We both loved the Lord and each other so much (even before meeting) that we wanted our first time to be with our partner for life.

♡ ♡ ♡

A single woman warns that "if you have sexual relations before marriage, you are involved with someone's spouse-to-be. And what if you think *you* will marry this person? Does that make it all right? No. In 1 Thessalonians 4:3,4, it says: 'It is God's will that you should be holy; that you should avoid sexual immorality; that each of you should learn to control his own body in a way that is holy and honorable' [NIV]. No matter how much your spouse loves you, we are all human, and lurking somewhere in the back of her mind you will probably find the question, 'Was I the first, or has he given in before?'

"How can you base a marriage on that kind of doubt? It might never show up until someday it comes out in the middle of an argument. Suddenly there is a great big hole in the relationship."

———————————— ♥ ————————————

God's command that we reserve sex for marriage is an expression of His love for us. He wants to protect us from the damaging effect that distrust or suspicion has on a marriage. At the same time He wants to provide us with the most fulfilling sex life possible.

Marriage counselors, therapists and psychologists tell us that a key factor in producing a maximum, fulfilling love, marriage and sexual relationship is *trust*. Trust becomes the fertile ground for vulnerability and transparency to develop in the relationship, and these lead to intimacy. Suspicion or distrust works against, or undercuts, intimacy and vulnerability in relationships.

Sexual involvement almost always, and often very subtly, wipes out trust in a relationship. Sex, the way God intended it, calls for a 100-percent abandonment to your mate. It doesn't take a genius to realize how distrust prohibits such abandonment. This is what God wants to protect us from.

One person who felt the emptiness of a lack of trust was Gretchen Kurz. A student at San Jose State University, Gretchen talked very candidly in *Mademoiselle* magazine. She entered school, she said, ready for the "decadent life."

> There I was, well equipped with my No. 2 pencil, student service card and an adequate supply of birth control pills. But somehow, I missed the boat on the pleasure cruise to carefree, guilt-free sex. Actually, I now believe it's all a myth perpetuated by a lot of disappointed students too afraid to tell the truth. But then again, how are you supposed to admit it's all a crock after you couldn't wait to get out and break all the rules?"

Gretchen never doubted that when she got to San Jose State she'd "share" sex. But she says,

> To put it mildly, "share" was a gross misnomer. My first encounter with Mr. Variety-Is-the-Spice-of-Life left me utterly confused by a number of things. Do I leave now or spend the night? What will I say in the morning? Is it kosher to borrow his bathrobe? Was I any good? He wasn't. Does this mean we've started something somehow permanent? [She discovered it didn't.] To say that I was overcome by guilt would be a lie, but the experience was far from euphoric. The most positive description I could use to label the exchange would be "dull." It was void of emotion, or perhaps any trace of emotion was deftly disguised as avant-garde nonchalance. I soon found this cool and detached approach characteristic of any future encounters.
>
> This lack of emotion not only baffled me, but it also infuriated

me. I wanted to know why it existed and why it was so instrumental in the sexual liberation of my college friends. Obviously, it was the all too common basis for an active sex life.

Disturbed, Gretchen began to ask the many men in her life why this detached unemotionalism existed. What was their view of sex? The answers were similar. Sex is "fun and games," "a natural reaction," "consenting adults and a good time."

"Words like *love, share* and *happy* never entered the conversation," she admitted.

She decided to return to her "celibate, but happy, style of life." Some time after making this decision, she talked to a close male friend who was airing his gripes about the free and easy college sex circuit. In describing what he felt was the thinking of a majority of college males, he said,

> Most of the times I found myself in bed with someone, I usually wished it never had gotten that far. After I reached a point where I knew I would wind up spending the night with her, it was all downhill. I just went through the motions. There were times when all I wanted was to hurry up and get it over with. I finally stopped messing around when I realized sex is no good unless there is a true trust and love involved. Without it, it's just not worth the hassle.

Gretchen concluded her article with these words:

> Now, with all this fuss about sexual freedom, it's a little hard to stand up and admit it's not what everyone imagines, especially to an anxious world that refuses to let the subject die. Consequently, here we sit, tight-lipped, and too embarrassed to say we couldn't find it. We can't admit it to the world or, worse yet, to ourselves. Perhaps we could all begin to set the record straight — by saying that *without love and trust, "it's just not worth the hassle."* 212/19-21

When I was single and dating, I never dreamed how powerfully my date life years ago would affect my marriage right now. Many people have found painful, negative consequences of premarital sex, which now must be dealt with in marriage. Because I waited, I found something great and positive: the blessing of God's provision through trust.

I dated a young woman named Paula when I was in graduate school. We dated for three and a half years and almost got married. Even though we were very compatible and enjoyed and respected each other immensely, the fullness of a love given by God was missing. We finally broke up and continued to be the closest of friends.

Three years later I met Dottie, and not long after we were married, Dottie met Paula. They became good friends and started spending a lot of time together. Eventually Paula moved close to our home in California, where her parents and sister also live. We practically became neighbors.

One morning I arrived home from a trip and Dottie wasn't there. When she returned, she told me she had spent the morning with Paula. She came over, put her arms around me and said, "Honey, I'm sure glad you behaved yourself for three and a half years."

I took a deep breath and asked hesitantly, "Why?"

Dottie responded, "Paula told me this morning that she was so in love with you that there were times she would have done anything for you, but you never once took advantage of her." Needless to say, there was a big sigh of relief from me. I was profoundly glad I had never pushed Paula in the area of the physical.

Can you imagine what that conversation with Paula meant to my wife? It affirmed, "I can trust my husband!" In an interview, Dottie shared this:

> You must build your relationship on trust. I trust Josh to be a good provider for my children. I trust him to be faithful to me. I trust him to be our spiritual leader and to have his own relationship with Christ. And I trust him as a person who is going to take care of our finances.
>
> He can trust me to be a good mother while he's gone. He can trust me with feeding the children properly and nutriti- ously. As he travels he can trust me not to be spending lots of money or having wild parties. Everything you do, every step you take in a relationship together, has to be built on trust. It is the foundation for your marriage. It is easy to abandon yourself to someone when you trust him.
>
> The reason I totally trust Josh is because he has a trustwor- thy track record. 213/89-90

Much of establishing trust comes by not putting oneself in a position where sex is accessible. Here is an example of one father's wisdom:

> Psychologist Henry Brandt's young son was upset when his father didn't permit him to go out alone in a car with a girl. "What's wrong, Dad? Don't you trust me?"
>
> "In a car — alone at night with a girl?" Brandt replied. "I wouldn't trust me. Why should I trust you?" 62/266

Trust is built by consistency and commitment backed up by sacrifice, a sacrifice demonstrated by a desire to meet the need of the other person, not merely to get our own needs met. It is built by showing love in action. We can trust God because we not only have the spoken message of His love, but we also have tangible evidence of it in His actions. We know He seeks what is best for us. Marriage relationships, as mirrors of spiritual realities, are built in the same way.

As one young writer said:

> The command to wait until marriage to become sexually involved not only protects a person from destroying himself by linking harmful emotions to the sex act, fracturing his inner self, but it also presents him as a gift to his marriage partner. It promotes the greatest fulfillment in sex by paving the way for trust, emotional satisfaction, joy and passion unthreatened by mental battles. How good and intelligent the Creator is.

Premarital sex lays a foundation of distrust and lack of respect. "Mature love," observe Stacy and Paula Rinehart in *Choices,*

> is built on the security of knowing that your love is exclusive. There is no one else. Premarital intimacy chips away at the cornerstone of trust as you wonder, "If he has this little control with me, maybe I won't always be the one. Maybe there were others before me." As suspicion and distrust increase, you slowly lose respect for the other person. 109/94

7. Jesus Can Fill the Void

In their own words:

> Since becoming a Christian, I have realized that the spiritual emptiness I thought could be filled only by another person could actually be filled only by Jesus Christ. I can feel deep, intimate love without sex. I also see that because the sexual union *is* so sacred, and you do become *one* with the person, God has reserved it for the sanctity of marriage. Sex is the greatest display of love possible other than dying for someone. It is to be shared only by those who have made the commitment to love each other for better or worse for the rest of their lives. I am *very* grateful to be forgiven and released from my guilt, and to have a new beginning by being a virgin again in God's eyes. I am grateful for the opportunity to *wait* this time and share that intimacy *only* with my husband.

———————— ♥ ————————

In the book *Sexual Freedom,* Mary Stewart says: "The need to be always in a sexual relationship with someone really did not have that much to do with the release of sexual tension. Rather, it was a desperate fight against a rarely admitted loneliness and isolation." 135

A lifelong relationship between a man and woman is something to be held in awe. When two people overcome all forces that would drive them apart, and devote themselves to mutual edification and giving for life, we need to remember that something very powerful is at work here. This relationship, in effect, goes against all that our flesh would have us selfishly pursue. It is a bond of love that defies an egocentric and uncaring world.

But there is a bond of love even greater than that. Most people are not aware of it, either because of ignorance or because of refusal to take part in it. And even many of those who enter this bond do not enjoy it to its fullest.

It is the love that exists when a person repents of his sins, turns to Jesus Christ, and accepts a relationship with Him. God calls each person to this relationship. He extends love. The only thing people have to do is respond. They don't have to initiate the relationship.

Once the relationship is established, only we can break the fellowship. God never turns His back on anyone or acts selfishly. He never does anything to harm those He loves — something that can't be said for even the best human relationships.

As teenagers move into that part of life in which relationships with the opposite sex become important, they may come to feel that those relationships will bring the greatest feeling, the greatest fulfillment, the greatest joy they will ever find. When that turns out not to be true, they may try to increase their search for joy and fulfillment through sex.

But they always come up empty — they always experience a void. They are looking for intimacy in relationships that lack the cornerstone of building intimacy: commitment.

Each person can be fulfilled only by a right relationship with God. We are then loved and accepted as a complete person, faults and all, which gives us security; we don't have to earn God's love. We are free to do what we were created for: to glorify God by doing the work of the Father in ministering to others. This gives us significance. We know we are loved because of who we are, not because of what we do.

That kind of understanding inspires obedience to God's authority, which in turn strengthens our relationship with Him. It is a synergistic, growing love, a relationship in which we are complete and fulfilled.

God may, of course, give us a mate to love and be loved by, but marriage is not meant to be the goal of a Christian's life. It is icing on the cake.

To understand why a Christian is truly complete in God, we need to take a look at the nature of God and His relationship to man.

"God is love," say the Scriptures, but for love to exist, it must have an object. It must love *someone*. Not even God's love is possible without a recipient. But what is beautiful is the uniqueness of the Trinity. God's need to love someone is satisfied within the Trinity: the Father, Son and Holy Spirit.

So God did not have to create man in order to love. Instead, He created man so that man could have the blessings of God's love. In other words, He didn't create us in order to receive, He created us in order to give to us.

God didn't need us. He wanted us. Let's personalize it. God doesn't *need you,* but He sure does *want you.*

Not only did He proclaim His love for His creation, a people who stubbornly turned away from His offer of love, but He also proved His love by sending Christ to redeem us. It was the greatest price that could be paid in behalf of another.

It means that each person is of infinite value to God. Each person is worth the life of Jesus. When we realize that, and make it a part of our lives, we live as people of great value. We become aware of being accepted, aware of having security, aware of our enormous significance in God's eyes.

Dr. Francis Schaeffer so aptly observed:
                "The chief end of man
                    is to glorify God
                and to enjoy Him forever."
Commenting on that statement, Schaeffer noted:

It would be scripturally false to leave out the second phrase,
                "and to enjoy Him forever."
            The men who formulated this showed
                great wisdom and insight in saying,
                "and to enjoy Him forever."
        Nevertheless, the first phrase is the first phrase:
                "The chief end of man
                    is to glorify God."
    And in Christianity we have a non-determined God
                who did not need to create
    because there was love and communication within the Trinity,
    and yet having been created, we as men can glorify God.
        But we must feel the force of both sides of the issue.
        If we fail to emphasize that we can glorify God,
                we raise the whole question
                of whether men are significant at all.
            We begin to lose our humanity
            as soon as we begin to lose the emphasis
                that what we do makes a difference.
                We can glorify God,
        and both the Old and New Testament say that
                we can even make God sad.
                That is tremendous.

Adam was complete in his relationship with God. He had all he would ever need. But God gave him icing on the cake, because He wanted him to be happier still.

Each Christian, having established a personal relationship with the same God whom Adam knew personally, is just as complete as Adam. Every need is met in Christ.

So we find our security in a relationship with Him. We find our significance in doing all that we do, whether it is mundane or earthshaking, to the glory of God — in carrying out the work of the Father, which is to minister to others.

Why wait until marriage for sex? Because premarital sex won't bring the fulfillment we are looking for. That fulfillment is in Christ. It is in ministering to others on His behalf that we will become aware of our significance, of the honor we have of representing the King of kings on earth.

Ultimately, marriage is meant to be a ministry to another person, a one-on-one relationship of commitment and love for the edification of each other to the glory of God, in sickness and in health, "till death do you part."

It is worth waiting for.

14

EMOTIONAL REASONS

PROTECTION

1. From Being Put On a Performance Basis

Sexually active people also suffer from comparison and the performance syndrome. Debora Phillips, author of *Sexual Confidence* and director of the Princeton Center for Behavior Therapy in New Jersey, states, "Due to the instant sex of the sexual revolution, people perform rather than make love. Many women can't achieve a sense of intimacy, and their anxiety about how well they perform blocks their chances for honest arousal. Without genuine involvement, they haven't much chance for courtship, romance or love. They're left feeling cheated and burned out." 295/121

When people are put on a performance basis (which means they are accepted only when they act or do something the way another person expects), the value and dignity given to them by God are lost. They are not considered important because of *who they are,* but rather are deemed acceptable because of *what they do.* How degrading and dehumanizing that is, yet it is characteristic of the "free sex" in our society.

Without the committed bonds of marriage, sex is inherently a selfish act done for personal gain. For the relationship to go

249

on, the sex partners must continue to be pleasing to each other. As soon as one partner no longer lives up to what the other wants, the relationship is in trouble. The partners are kept in a state of perpetual insecurity, a state that symbolizes much of what true love is *not*. Couples in this circumstance experience an unspoken element of fear: the fear of rejection. Such a relationship is totally contrary to God's plan for us. God protects us from being put on a performance basis by reserving sex for the commitment of marriage.

One young couple went for counseling because of sexual difficulties. The wife had been a victim of incest as a child, but she hadn't told her husband that until it came out in counseling. Her background had caused her to be very inhibited about her sexuality, which in turn caused her husband to feel rejected.

After the problem came to the surface in counseling, they could look forward to beginning a normal sex life. The husband was able to encourage his wife in the freedom of her sexuality. In the process of wanting to help her, however, he went out and bought the book *The Joy Of Sex.* His wife went back to the counselor and said, "I appreciate what he is trying to do, but this book just makes me feel more inhibited. All it deals with is physical positions and things two bodies can do to each other. After I looked through it, I felt like a piece of meat, something to be used for another person's pleasure."

Although the husband's intentions may have been good, his purchase was way off base. A book that deals with sex primarily on a physical level (as most books on sex do) can put a person on a performance basis, even if that is not the intention. Fear of inadequate sexual performance is the major cause of sexual dysfunction. What needs to happen is an edification of the partners, a mutual building and encouraging that lets both know they are free to fail, to make mistakes. They need to know they are on solid ground emotionally, intellectually and spiritually, so that the physical expression of their love can be free.

That, of course, is possible only within the commitment of marriage, and even married couples need to work continually at edifying each other. God has provided marriage as the lifelong training ground for sex. It is a school in which a person cannot fail, because the only criterion is to reach out in love to the other.

2. Guilt

In their own words:

Another problem that results from premarital sex is the feeling of guilt. You have adult problems without having the maturity of an adult or mate with whom to share them.

♡ ♡ ♡

Another consequence of violating God's standard regarding sex before marriage is guilt. One of the worst feelings many sexually active people experience is to get up the next morning and realize that the person lying next to them is a total stranger. This "morning after" syndrome robs a person of a healthy self-image and a clear conscience, which decreases his ability to experience the transparency needed to cultivate an intimate relationship. On top of that, flashbacks from past sexual encounters can haunt a person the rest of his life, which can leave him feeling "grimy" in the hands of his current lover. It has been said that "a good conscience is a continual feast, while a bad conscience is worse than a thousand enemies testifying against you."

The hurts, fears and feelings of guilt associated with premarital sexual involvement are real. When people are hurting they want relief; they want their fears removed; they want to be free of guilt. A firm commitment to rules on morality is not the only answer. They need a committed relationship to Jesus Christ. They will find true happiness and fulfillment in that relationship alone.

♡ ♡ ♡

Guilt is another effect to be reckoned with. The conscience is trained by God to give warning signals when an action is not right. When the negative side of the conscience is triggered by deliberate sin, the effects can be emotionally torturous.

♡ ♡ ♡

For a Christian woman, the results of sexual immorality are often felt even more strongly than for a non-Christian. I was very much affected by this when I became sexually involved with my fiancé We had convinced ourselves that sex outside of marriage was all right for us since we were engaged, but the Holy Spirit was convicting me that it was wrong. I felt incredibly guilty, but I was so carried away by my fleshly desires that I felt there was no escape.

♡ ♡ ♡

Just that one small period of time that you have sex could destroy a year's worth of fun, happy times and good memories because of the guilt.

♡ ♡ ♡

This may also explain why you feel you get nothing out of church. You feel guilty about seeking the love you need with someone other than God. You know He can supply it best. You are reminded of this at church, so you endure it rather than enjoy it, and find it easier to evade. No one can get much out of church that way.

♡ ♡ ♡

People can also promote a free, unhindered passion in marriage if they abstain from premarital sex. Passion expressed in physical arousal and emotional excitement is very much a result of the mental activities of the moment. Nothing is more dampening to one's passion than to have to fight mental battles each time the sex act is approached. To have the sex act linked with guilt in one's emotions from patterns of premarital sex is like pulling the stopper from a basin of water. The joy is drained, robbed, clouded away by the oppressive feeling that guilt imposes. To have to fight washes of memories or a sea of faces from the past totally drains the mental energy that should be reserved for the enjoyment of the moment. Abstaining from premarital sex prevents any such battles and allows for freedom and abandoned enjoyment.

♡ ♡ ♡

Not having any bad memories and guilty feelings make it worth waiting for.

——————— ♥ ———————

Guilt is one consequence of premarital sex that may haunt a person longer than any other. It is a nagging, gnawing feeling that seems to surface at the least appropriate times. If not dealt with, it can be a great hindrance to spiritual growth and emotional wellbeing.

When sex is entered into casually and without commitment, no concern is shown for the other person. People get hurt physically and emotionally. Sex without meaning damages the self-image of those taking part, rather than boosting it. But it is all around us, as one young girl told her father when she said, "When I see how casually sex is treated by my classmates, they make it all sound so natural and inevitable, there are times when I wonder what I'm waiting for." Her father answered, "You are waiting to be free — free from the nagging voice of conscience and the shadow of guilt." 146/A8

Guilt is the awareness of having transgressed a standard of right and wrong. Or it is the lingering doubt of thinking that perhaps some act was wrong. Our society is plagued by those two kinds of guilt. The first is a moral guilt, one that Christians are subject to, which tells us specifically when we have stepped outside God's boundaries. It is a conscious awareness of specific transgressions.

The other kind of guilt can be called a floating sense of guilt. Psychologist Erich Fromm says, "It is indeed amazing that in as fundamentally irreligious a culture as ours, the sense of guilt should be so widespread and deep-rooted as it is." 221/181 He was pointing to the floating guilt that comes from a relativistic society, a society that says there is no right and wrong. Rather than being free, people in such a society are constantly questioning: "Are these things I'm doing right or wrong? How do I decide?" Regardless of whether they are aware of those questions within themselves, the questions are there. Such people have no form to their lives, no standards by which to measure actions. They have a feeling of being adrift, they continually have a floating sense of guilt about doing things wrong — yet they are not able to nail it down.

Christians have the Bible, which, in addition to telling us the character of God, His redemptive plan for man, and our ability to have a relationship with Him, also gives us a basis for determining right and wrong. It tells us which actions are pleasing to God and which are not. It doesn't leave things open to debate. In this way, Christians have *form* to their lives, a framework for understanding good and evil and making decisions accordingly.

Dick once asked a farmer if it was better to raise cattle on open grazing land, in a pasture or in a corral. The farmer said, "Well, on open grazing land they are always subject to attack from wild animals, or they could wander off for good. In a corral they are safe, but somebody has to take care of them. In a fenced pasture they have everything they need. They are protected, yet they have the freedom to graze."

The Bible defines our pasture. God has put intelligent boundaries around us to keep us "home" and to keep away those who would prey on us, yet within those boundaries we have freedom to make a variety of choices. Persons without God's boundaries are wandering aimlessly and feel lost. Persons in a legalistic system of beliefs are in a corral where they are fed and hosed off but are unable to move.

For example, God has provided marriage as the place for sex, and persons moving within God's limits are free to marry or not marry. Should they decide to marry, they are able to express their sexuality in a context where no one can be hurt. The husband and wife won't catch diseases from each other. They won't use each other and then run off to the next sex partner. Since sex is an open and unabashed part of their lives, they are free to discuss their sex life. They can plan ahead for their family, should they decide not to have children for the time being. If they do have children, the children become part of a family, not reminders of a grave mistake.

There is no guilt in any of this. God protects us from destructive, shattering guilt by reserving sex for marriage.

3. Misleading Feelings

In their own words:

There are all kinds of reasons not to have sex before marriage. Misleading feelings is a big one.

♡ ♡ ♡

[Letter to a friend] Looking back, I think you will realize how misguided your feelings were. You thought you were in control of your life because you did what you wanted — you were "living fast and loose" with no thought for anyone but yourself. You see now it was more like "selfish-control" than self-control; your desire for sex led you into false emotions about your situation.

Now, you feel only depression over your experiences. At the age of fifteen you professed your belief in the salvation of Jesus Christ; now, at age seventeen, you feel lost and empty and you want to die.

♡ ♡ ♡

Let's look at the effects premarital sex has on people and relationships. Two people get to know each other, and at some point in the relationship decide to have sex. The relationship stops growing right there, because physical gratification becomes more important than emotional, mental or spiritual cohesion. They can't stand to be in one another's company without having sex. The majority of their conversation is spent discussing the next time they can get together for sex (even though they may not come right out and say it). They can hardly take part in leisure activities because the need to have one another is so strong.

I remember when the "love" I had been waiting for came along. Three months after we started dating, we began having sex. Suddenly we avoided friends and social activities as much as possible in order to be alone, but our goal was only to satisfy our physical hunger. Ironically, we actually referred to this misplaced passion as love!

———————— ♥ ————————

One of the reasons I hear most often for sexual involvement taking place is the confusion between sex and love. Premarital sex can take a person who may actually have had a legitimate understanding of love and confuse him or her terribly. As one writer put it, "Sexual encounters outside of marriage, whether or not they include intercourse, give an illusion of intimacy that can be mistaken for the lasting commitment that makes a marriage work." 102

Sex before marriage is outside God's will, so it shouldn't exist in the first place. When it does, it turns relationships upside down and mixes emotions to the point where a person can misinterpret feelings. That is what happened to the young lady in the above quotation.

When we mix sex and love, we have confused the simple concepts of giving and taking. Love always gives and always seeks the best interests of the other person. Premarital sex takes. Each individual has his or her own goal in having sex before marriage, but each is in it for personal reasons. The problem is, the taking can sometimes look like giving. This is where the water gets muddy.

A girl may "give her boyfriend what he wants," thus making it look as though she is giving to him in love, but she does it from a personal motive. She may want the security he provides. She may want to achieve popularity by being his girlfriend. She may have one of a dozen other reasons, but her "giving" is actually a form of taking. She is manipulating him for her own ends. It takes maturity and understanding to realize this, something a girl who behaves like that does not have. She is misled by her emotions.

Not only are these mixed-up feelings destructive in a dating relationship, but they also can have tragic consequences if the relationship continues on to marriage.

> Studies show that a relationship based on physical attraction may hold itself together for three to five years. During that length of time two people are fooled into thinking, "Well, we've been going together for so long, surely we can make it for a lifetime. This must be love." On the other side of marriage, they wake up to see they had little in common and no basis for a quality relationship. 109/95

Colleen Kelly Mast, creator of *Sex Respect*, points out that premarital sex can fool us into marrying the wrong person: "Because sex is so powerful, it creates very strong emotional bonds between partners. These bonds can make us believe the relationship is deeper than it really is, that we know our partners (and our partners know us) much better than we actually do. Or, because we've had sex, we may be tempted to hang on to the relationship, not out of love, but just to 'save face.'" 244/23

By restricting sex to marriage, God protects us from the devastating effects these confused emotions can have.

Our goal as Christians is to grow in *agape* love, the kind of love God has for us, the kind that gives with no expectations of getting something in return. As sinful people, we will always fall short. Consciously or unconsciously, we will put some conditions on our love, meaning we give in hope of getting something in return. But as we grow in Christ and continue to mature, we should get closer and closer to *agape* love. We will never be sinless, but as we grow we will sin less.

Love is a series of choices. It is an emotion expressed by acts of the will. The description of love in 1 Corinthians 13 does not describe emotional feelings but rather acts of the will. And even though love is primarily an act of the will, it has tremendous emotional overtones, because it has to do with how we relate to people. Our actions of love — the choices we make in dealing with people — are deeply tied to our emotions because relationships automatically have emotional bonds.

Likewise, sex has a powerful emotional aspect, because although sex is a physical act, God meant for it to be a joining of the soul and mind and moral conscience and all the other intangibles about two people. That's why premarital sex can leave us feeling good for a moment, and not just physically. It gives us an emotional rush. But when the wave of good emotional feeling is over (however long that may take), bad emotions set in. When we deal in the moral realm, we are faced with moral consequences.

Even though sex and love both have strong emotional components, those components are not the same. Rather, they are parallel; they cannot be one until two people have been made one through the commitment of marriage. In that context, sex and love can be expressions of the same emotions. Marital sex becomes a model of God's provision and selfless giving, drawing us closer to each other and to Him.

4. Hardships of Breaking Up

In their own words:

Although having sex does hurt a relationship, it also makes it harder for a couple to break up. Breaking up when you've had sex together can be a terribly tearing experience emotionally. Sex creates an emotional bond so powerful it must be reserved for marriage.

————————— ♥ —————————

Sexual desire drives many couples apart, yet it makes others stay together. The problem is, they are together for the wrong reason.

So often I've talked to girls who don't know why they can't seem to break up with the guys even though they're unhappy with them. I truly believe this has to do with their sexual union. Then, when they finally do break up, it's full of heartache. 50/51

A person with a moral conscience who has gotten caught in the trap of premarital sex may find ways to justify the relationship. If it is a young woman who thinks she has found her future husband, she will continue to give in to her partner in the hope that all of the wrong they have done might still turn out all right, since they are getting married. She knows it won't actually be right; she just hopes it won't be as wrong as sleeping together and then breaking up would be. So she holds on to the relationship.

So many people have said to me, "When I walked away from that relationship, I left a part of myself behind." Sex forms a bond that can exist no matter what the rest of the relationship is like. Even if communication has broken down and emotions are strained, sex forms an almost unexplainable bond. It locks people into relationships. The longer it goes on, the harder it is to break it off.

But for the problems in the relationship to be resolved, the couple must break up. They may be able to start over after they have cooled off, or they may not. In any case, they are better off spiritually, emotionally, mentally and possibly even physically after they break up. Trying to stop the sexual aspect while continuing the relationship is nearly impossible. Once a couple has gone all the way, it is no small task to go back to holding hands.

In reserving sex for marriage, God protects us from emotional traps. He knows how easily we can fall into a rut of sin and not see a way out, so He gives us guidelines to keep us out in the first place. God's provision for us is this, that once we are married, that same sexual bond strengthens the marriage and makes the partners want to stay together.

5. Psychological and Emotional Distress

Premarital sex has a serious adverse effect on the self-image of the person engaging in it. Emotionally crippling guilt, not joy, seems to be the companion of permissive sex. As Manhattan sex therapist Shirley Zussman says, "Being part of a meat market is appalling in terms of self-esteem." In fact, Dr. Elizabeth Whelan, in her 1974 book *Sex and Sensibility*, cites a study of unmarried women which showed 86 percent of those under psychiatric care were sexually active, as opposed to 22 percent sexually active for those not under care. It is obvious that premarital sex and emotional instability are directly related.

Part of what God wants to protect us from by limiting sex to marriage is the devastating emotional consequences that premarital sex can bring. Those effects may be immediate or they may not show up for some time. The person may find that through prayer and support of friends the emotional distress can be dealt with and put in the past, or it may drag on for years. Regardless of how each individual may be affected, God doesn't want that kind of distress to happen in the first place.

Christians acknowledge that human beings are made in the image of God and that broken relationships with Him are the root cause of so many problems. We recognize the wisdom of His commands and the value in keeping them. While secular researchers may try to ignore the spiritual ramifications of our sexuality, they are forced to acknowledge that something more than a physical act takes place during sex. They see the emotional consequences of premarital sex as clearly as we do. As the Rineharts point out,

> There is no possibility of having sexual intercourse without meshing a part of your non-physical self. Sex is such a definite experience that a part of each of you remains forever a part of the other. How many times and how casually are you willing to invest a portion of your total self and accept such an investment from another person, with no assurance that the investment is for keeps? 109/92

The effects a "casual investment" have on the mind and emotions can take many forms. "Some [sexually uninhibited people] felt humiliated after sleeping with people who never called back. For others, the sexual revolution eventually meant boredom." 33/55 Premarital sex also produces guilt, because God has wired us together in such a way that we know we've violated His intentions. "Marriage should be honored by all, and the marriage bed kept pure, for God will judge the adulterer and all the sexually immoral" (Hebrews 13:4, NIV). Whether the offenders acknowledge God's laws or not, they feel guilty because they *are* guilty before a holy God. As Dr. Joe Aldrich says, "There is no prophylactic [condom] for the conscience." 109/93

In addition to inward emotions, such as humiliation and guilt, outward-directed emotions are also affected. One partner may see sex as a sign of love, direct his love toward the other sex partner, and then feel anger and rejection when love is not returned. Rejection can make the person feel a desire to strike back at the one rejecting.

Another common emotional effect of premarital sex is resentment, which can lead to bitterness. "You may secretly become bitter toward the other person for causing you to violate your own moral standards. You blame your boyfriend or girlfriend for what has happened and so become secretly bitter toward him or her." 117/84

But some might ask, Don't premarital sexual experiences in these and other relationships increase the quality of later marital sexual relationships through practice and experience? Though on the surface this again might appear to be a valid argument, it does not appear to be the case from the limited data available. In fact, in the case of young teenagers who have negative premarital experiences, the adverse effect on a later marriage relationship might be quite significant.

Dr. Mary Calderone says: "No one knows what effect sex, precociously experienced, will have on the immature mind. Sex experience before confidentiality, empathy, and trust have been established can hinder and may destroy the possibility of a solid, permanent relationship." 113

In a study of the reaction of college women to their first sexual experience, Dr. David Weis found that for a third of them it was quite negative, involving little or no pleasure and high levels of guilt and anxiety. In another third of the women the reaction was rather mixed, but they still often experienced a considerable amount of guilt and anxiety. 290/60HH-LL Interestingly enough, one third of the women in the study felt exploited during their first sexual intercourse. 290/60GG These are hardly the kinds of initial experiences upon which to build a positive, satisfying marital relationship later in life.

Emotional damage is a result of premarital sex that nearly everyone can count on, since an act of such spiritual intensity — an act so expressly forbidden by God — entails rejecting the established spiritual order of things. It flies in the face of what is beneficial to us. When this emotional damage goes unchecked, the problems could last for life. Worst yet:

> In 1965, perhaps a little too soon to reflect the changing attitudes about sex, there were 21,560 suicides in the United States, with a rate per hundred thousand members of the population of 11.6. In 1977, twelve years later, 28,500 people committed suicide with the rate of 12.6. Even if we cannot equate the rise in suicide with sexual activity, it is obvious there has been no decrease in the rate as a result of the sexual revolution. Surely the expert opinion has not proved that only the celibate or sexually denied are committing suicide.
>
> The suicide rate has increased in one age group that has become increasingly sexually active as the pregnancy, abortion and venereal disease statistics indicate. In the last twenty-five years the rate of teenage suicides has doubled. We are not

suggesting, of course, that sexual promiscuity is the only factor operating in the teenage suicide picture, but it is certainly one factor, and the therapeutic effect of sexual liberation on the suicide rate is not apparent. 42/18

God wants to protect us from the psychological and emotional trauma we inflict on ourselves through premarital sex. I have included here a number of quotes from young people, all of whom have a unique insight into the subject:

God does not forbid premarital sex to harass the hormones or vex the sex drive. He simply warns us against those things capable of destroying us. He created sexuality; therefore, it is good. But just as drugs are capable of healing, the same drugs used incorrectly are capable of killing.

♡ ♡ ♡

The physical reasons for waiting can be rationalized away by saying, "It won't happen to me." What about your emotions? There isn't any way of knowing how you will feel after you've had sex. Sue explains it this way: "After you've done it, you're really attached to that guy. It's as if he's your life; you feel really vulnerable." When I asked her how she felt when the relationship ended, she said, "Really awful. I can't describe it. About a week after we had sex, we broke up because I found out he was dating other girls. It really hurt." Another friend, Sally, who had an experience similar to Sue's, said, "You feel that you can't trust anybody ever again." I asked them if they wished they had waited. They both said yes.

♡ ♡ ♡

The issue of sex before marriage can cause emotional conflict and change which are not easily straightened out and may never be.

♡ ♡ ♡

When a man and woman who are not married begin to engage in physical relations, they lose perspective on the relationship. They judge everything from the outlook of their emotions. Their intellect becomes clouded and they become slaves to the self-gratifying impulses of their wills. Therefore, they allow themselves to become intimately vulnerable in a relationship which is based solely on the physical. They, in turn, feel trapped in a vicious masquerade of continuing to interest their partner physically in order to maintain the relationship. But in truth, they are unhappy because the real fabric they want in the relationship is not there. It takes the essential threads of commitment and unconditional love to weave a durable fabric — a lasting covenant between two people with Christ as the center.

♡ ♡ ♡

Many couples break up after sex enters the relationship; after that the people may have trouble emotionally and find it hard to establish other relationships.

♡ ♡ ♡

Most of those interviewed [for a *Cosmopolitan* survey] said they got involved to meet emotional needs such as closeness, self-worth, needing to be involved with another human being. But the end result was the loss of their ability to give emotionally or to even feel much at all. Men as well as women stated that the emotional toll was not worth the sex.

♡ ♡ ♡

Within a marriage, a holy and permanent commitment to one another, the act of making love can be a physical expression of your love and "oneness." The "first time" is an especially holy act, as it consecrates or seals the marriage. When you give this outside of marriage, it creates a void, a feeling of having lost something. These painful emotions can cause a rift in the relationship, and fear and insecurity. The distance created will allow suspicion, anger and even hate to take root and begin to grow. Feelings like this can damage you emotionally forever.

♡ ♡ ♡

A study done at the University of Wisconsin-Madison showed that 86 percent of the psychologists' patients who were interviewed had engaged in premarital sex. The main problem they had was the guilt caused by premarital sex.

♡ ♡ ♡

Sexual relationships also need to be protected from being associated with harmful emotions. When a young person is involved in premarital sex, his body associates sex and arousal with the emotions of guilt and the fear of getting caught. These emotional bonds can become very strong, so strong that they constantly plague any future sexual relationship, robbing it of joy or prohibiting arousal. It can cause a person to follow an endless chase to find those same emotions in order to stimulate physical arousal, leading to extramarital affairs. Waiting until marriage to engage in sex protects a person from linking detrimental emotional responses with their sexual expression.

───────────── ♥ ─────────────

Sex without marriage not only brings destruction to the persons involved but also to the society. As the saying goes, "History repeats itself." An anthropologist, J. D. Unwin, conducted a study on eighty-eight civilizations that have come and gone in world history. In every one of those eighty-eight civilizations, the morals and strict sexual conduct started off the same, but then things became lax giving the people more and more freedom to express sexual desires whenever they pleased. 216 That freedom began the destruction of the civilization. First came venereal disease, then breaking up of homes. Children were brought up in unstable environments and patterned their behavior after their parents' behavior, making each succeeding generation more degenerate than the last. Thus those civilizations eventually were destroyed.

Dr. James Dobson, in his book *Emotions, Can You Trust Them?* reviews the historical facts above and makes the following points:

> Who can deny a society is seriously weakened when the intense sexual urge between men and women becomes an instrument for suspicion and intrigue within millions of individual families;
> when a woman never knows what her husband is doing when away from home;
> when a husband can't trust his wife in his absence;
> when half of the brides are pregnant at the altar;
> when both newlyweds have slept with numerous partners, losing the exclusive wonder of the marital bed;
> when everyone is doing his own thing, particularly that which brings him immediate sensual gratification! 215/66-67

In addition, George Leonard, who once used his position as senior editor of *Look* magazine to spearhead the sexual revolution, has now written a book called *The End of Sex* (1983). In it he states that the revolution has caused as many problems as it has cured:

> While they sought to bring joy and social happiness through permissive sex, they failed and brought only guilt, unhappiness and dissatisfaction with relationships. The mores the revolutionists wanted to replace were there for a reason; displacing them brought about social failure. 207/27

Therapist Peter Marin expresses this opinion, when he writes, "The simple fact is that many of the obstacles to sexual life are not merely the function of repressive attitudes or mores. They are grounded in the complexities of human nature and in the everyday difficulties of living together and all these natural . . . difficulties are intensified by the disappearance of traditional sex roles . . ." (Marin, 1983)

One teen writes:

In taking this chance, you run the following risks:

(1) The breakdown of your relationship with the Lord Jesus Christ, who forbids premarital sex;

(2) The chance of pregnancy, even with the use of contraceptives;

(3) The chance of getting one of the many sexually transmitted diseases, including AIDS;

(4) The chance of great emotional damage. You may feel you are physically ready for sex but you may not be emotionally ready. If you give your heart and your being to another person and you end up getting dumped or used, you're stuck with feelings of hurt, anger and rejection.

All four of these risks are consequences you must be prepared to face if you choose to engage in premarital sex.

But what about those who consider the costs and proceed anyway? It is their right, just as a child, given the choice between a piece of candy and a ten-thousand-dollar savings bond, has the right to choose the candy. God doesn't force us to live a certain way, He just tells us what's best. But when we make a choice, we choose the consequences also.

Many teens are aware that boys are no more emotionally equipped than girls to deal with sex:

If a girl says no (and many do), the rejection can distort his attitude toward women and sex.

Also, with more girls taking the initiative these days, a boy who finds himself unable to perform may suffer a terrible blow to his self-esteem, a wound not quick to heal in men of any age.

The masculinity he is trying so hard to project turns into confusion and disappointment.

It seems to be our emotions that rule our lives sexually. "There aren't going to be any huge reductions in sexually transmitted disease cases," Arthur Block, program manager for New York City's Venereal Disease Bureau, says. "Emotions, not rational thinking, seem to be carrying the day when it comes to sex." 266/3

"If our heavenly Father," writes a teen, "stripped the desire for sex from us, we would very quickly die out." By the same token, we must be able to trust Him enough to turn our sex lives over to Him without necessarily knowing why, as was illustrated in the following story I heard:

Not long ago, my two-year-old son was walking through the kitchen. He reached up on the counter and grabbed a sharp carving knife by the blade. He came running into the living room, chuckling, "Look, Dada! Look what I have, Dada!" He thought he had found a treasure, nice and shiny. I gasped! As I reached for it, his little fingers grabbed the razor-sharp blade tighter, and he pulled it back, saying, "No, Dada, mine!" He was right; it was his at that moment. But even though it was in his grasp and highly appealing to him, it was also highly dangerous. If I had stripped it out of his hands, I would have sliced through his tiny fingers and maimed his hand for life, exactly the scenario I wanted to avoid. As his father, I had to communicate to him to give it over to me, even though he would not understand why. Finally, he gave it over to me, and I have since been able to teach him the uses and abuses of knives.

Waiting until marriage for sex produces many benefits. Emotional freedom is one important one. Refraining from premarital sex prevents the potential effects of guilt, fear and self-deprecation. For example, the Sorenson report, the most complete sociological study of teenage sexuality available, discovered that girls who had had their first intercourse before marriage chose words like "afraid," "guilty," "worried" and "embarrassed" to describe their reaction to that experience. These negative emotions hamper one's relationship with God, with the sex partner and with everyone else.

The person who decides to practice premarital sex often encounters many problems. The following letter is an example of how sex can hurt a relationship:

I went with a guy for four years, and we really loved each other. All through the four years we were sleeping together. During that time, I was a Christian and knew it was wrong.

Then we had a falling out. The breakup hurt so bad I knew I could only get rid of it by turning to God. We then got back together and my strength as a Christian has helped, except for not having enough faith to say no to sex. Since we've gotten back together, sex has been an uphill battle for me. My boyfriend is a Christian, too, but he sees no wrong in us making love as long as we love each other.

Another thing is I'm not sure if I love him. But I feel we need to stay together, because it says in the Bible that when two people make love they become one in God's eyes. Does that mean if I am to do God's will I should stay with him?

I know the logical answer to my question about sex is to have more faith. But how can I get that through my boyfriend's head? And how can we pull together and fight this urge? We have talked about it a million times and it never helps.

As one can see by this example, sex has confused this girl's life. The answer, however, is not "more faith." The logical answer — at least the practical answer — is for her to break up. The pull of sex, particularly when it has long been a normal part of their relationship, would be extremely difficult to resist, even if they both agreed it was wrong.

Another aspect of premarital sex is the abuse it causes. One teen listed four kinds of abuse:

(1) *Emotional abuse,* which can be subtle; withholding affection

or giving the silent treatment until one gives in and engages in sex.

(2) *Verbal abuse* is often linked to emotional abuse. According to one girl, "He always used to tell me I wasn't attractive enough to get anyone else; I could never live on my own." By his saying these things and her believing them, she would have sex with him, do anything he wanted, just because she was afraid she would lose him and be on her own.

(3) *Physical abuse* means any unwanted and hurtful physical act. Initially, there may be pushes, shoves or light slaps on the face or other parts of the body. This may not seem that bad at first, but when ignored, problems may quickly become severe.

(4) *Sexual abuse* is any sexual contact that is unwanted. It may also be subtle — an unwanted kiss or fondle, or, in extreme cases of premarital sex, rape (and date rape is far more common than rape by a stranger).

These four abuses show how selfishness often takes over. Deep-set emotional problems often turn into abuse. People strive for control and become possessive.

One element is almost guaranteed to be a part of any sexual relationship outside of marriage: unequal levels of commitment by each partner. This can be particularly devastating emotionally for women and girls, as one researcher reports:

> Sexual intercourse has a psychologically binding effect, particularly for females. The act itself increases the feeling of closeness. In uncommitted and temporary relationships where sexual intimacy, with its psychological bonding effect, is shared, there is considerable risk of hurt. Nearly always, one partner has become more deeply involved than the other. And there is no recognized religious or social influence to hold a temporary "mate" or "friend" to the other. All that these temporary partners share is the dangerous freedom of "for as long as it feels good." Either partner is always vulnerable to rejection, which happens more often than not in such relationships, and the break is very hard for one or both. One can *say* "no strings," but that is not possible. There always *are* strings and tearing them away hurts, inflicting injuries that may take years or a lifetime to heal. 99/91

This point was carried further by the following essay:

> . . . Then one day I was listening to the radio, and one of those "five minutes for science" spots came on that give updates on new research or interesting discoveries. That day they talked about a study being done regarding teenage girls and why they are so often severely affected by sexual relationships (specifically, why teenage girls are more prone to attempt suicide when a relationship ends than boys are). The study went into the mechanics of sex and particularly of the orgasm, and noted a similarity in muscle contractions between orgasm and labor before childbirth.

It was found that when a woman goes into labor, the muscle contractions trigger a nurturing instinct in the mother (they didn't say whether it was chemical or neurological) that makes her want to protect, love and nurture whatever passed through the birth canal.

They concluded this was insurance for the survival of the species, because, for example, if a woman had been raised out in the woods and had no knowledge of what was happening to her body as she carried a child for nine months, her reaction would be either relief or anger at delivering this child who had caused her so much pain and discomfort. Without the nurturing instinct associated with the birth canal, she would have no desire to care for this noisy pink thing that had hurt her. The instinct overrides logic and feelings, and is put there to insure that a mother doesn't leave her baby in the woods somewhere.

The study went on to point out that, similarly, when a woman has relations with a man, the sex act and orgasm cause those same muscles to contract. With the contractions, the same instinct is triggered to love and nurture whatever passed through that opening, which in this case is a man, not a baby. Therefore, a woman's feelings often run deeper than a man's in a sexual affair, because a deeper set of feelings are tapped, feelings that go beyond the merely emotional or intellectual. So, the study concluded, once those feelings are activated, it becomes all the more devastating if the relationship ends.

I've thought about this information a lot since that afternoon, It hit me that if this is accurate, it would explain a lot about God's laws and how that relates to much of what has gone wrong in our society. If a woman's primal instincts to love and nurture are triggered every time she engages in sex, then, conversely, every time such a relationship ends she must reprogram herself to ignore those deeper feelings of longing for that man — the object of those reactions — and move on to someone else.

This is more than just breaking a habit; it involves playing with biology and deep primal urges. For a woman who has had, say, ten affairs over a five-year period, that's ten times she has had to train herself to ignore those nurturing instincts for the previous man in her life.

If God designed these strong, built-in feelings to be the glue that holds together marriages and families, then each affair, each lesson in negating those feelings, weakens the bonding power of marital and familial emotions. The result is obvious in view of the divorce rate in our culture. After all, how is the body supposed to know (after being conditioned to reject feelings of attachment) that this is the "real thing?" When a person destroys over a period of years the glue intended to bond her to someone, what is left to hold the relationship together once the glow of the honeymoon fades?

By the same token, this can be seen in the effects on the family. If the nurturing instincts were meant to bind a mother to her children, yet through a series of premarital sexual affairs she has destroyed the power of the feelings, it will affect her ability to nurture her children as well. Again, look at our culture. To me, this explains much of the high incidence of child abuse, abandonment and even abortion.

By pursuing what we thought was love, we have reduced ourselves to a loveless people that idolizes sex, is incapable of commitment and considers children an inconvenience.

And what about men? I wondered what the incentive was for men to be monogamous, when I went to a seminar given by John and Paula Sandford. In it, John said the first time a man has sex, he gains a sense of knowledge he did not have before. Each time he lies with that woman, it deepens the bond between them as they "know" each other and themselves in a way brought about only by sex. However, if he breaks off the relationship and finds another woman, confusion sets in. He cannot completely commit to her because his soul is still searching for that first woman. Though he may be physically and even emotionally distanced from that first woman, a spiritual bond has been established between them that is still recognized in God's eyes — the two are still spiritually one. It takes specific prayer to break those bonds before a person is truly free to love someone else; otherwise there will always be a sense of restlessness, longing and comparison.

This suggests why so many men are confused and hesitant to commit to a relationship. They are a multitude of restless souls, searching for their first love, long since abandoned, becoming more confused as more bonds are created and abandoned.

What all of this seems to say is that we, as a culture, have vastly underrated both the complexities of how we are created and the wisdom of God's laws. Too often we see the Bible as a rule book rather than an owner's manual. God created us; He knows how we're put together, why we break down, and what we need to run efficiently. He doesn't always give us the scientific reasoning behind His laws — we are merely asked to trust and obey.

Yet we are often rebellious children who think we know better than our Father. Just as the first man and woman chose to eat of the fruit because it didn't seem harmful — they trusted their senses and intellect rather than God's word — so we trust our intellects and emotions and enter into things that appear harmless. We thought we had it all figured out when we introduced the pill, so sure that the only reason God would limit sex to marriage was a lack of contraceptive technology available when the rules were being drawn up. Nobody counted on an epidemic of herpes to make us reconsider. Nobody counted on AIDS. The scary thing is, after all these years we are still finding new consequences.

—————————— ♥ ——————————

If God's protection is against the emotional suffering brought about by sexual immorality, His provision is for emotional and psychological wholeness brought about first by obedience before marriage, and then by a loving and giving sexual relationship after marriage. In the words of more of the young writers:

My celibacy — which was not always my preference — has played an important role in the success I enjoy today. I've been able to start a career without the problems and worries encountered by Christians and non-Christians who couldn't wait any longer: the bouncing baby who is really a bundle of tragedy; the loss of respect for another when the relationship is revealed as infatuation or a one-night stand, and the sense of being used that accompanies it; the emotional responsibility of maintaining a predominantly physical relationship; dealing with a person's true feelings once the new wears off and it's time to move on; explaining ourselves to those who look to us as examples; AIDS, herpes, and all the rest.

♡ ♡ ♡

What it comes down to is a matter of choice. Gratification of the immediate says, "Sleep with him!" After all, most anyone else would. But looking beyond that to what I would have to live with keeps me saying no. I would be paying a much higher emotional price for that sex than it would be worth. I choose, instead, to invest in loving, caring relationships that don't include sex but do include the kind of emotional support, gratification and challenge that keep me going in life. Sex alone just can't do that.

6. Self-Esteem

In their own words:

I was talking with a former girlfriend, and she boldly stated, ". . . At least I'm still a virgin. I didn't lose it to some hooker like you did!" I was deeply hurt by that statement. I wondered, if I were to have married her, what, in her eyes, did I have to offer? My self-esteem began to wane. I wondered if my girlfriend or any other woman would hold my past against me.

♡ ♡ ♡

I think my heart became hardened. After a while, I didn't care whether or not I loved the guy. I didn't like doing it that much, and I didn't even care who I did it with. My self-concept went way down. I quit caring about myself.

♡ ♡ ♡

I finally got a girl into bed (actually it was in a car) when I was seventeen. I thought I was the hottest thing there was, but then she started saying she loved me and getting clingy. I figured out that there had probably been a dozen guys before me who thought they had "conquered" her, but who were really just objects of her need for security. That realization took all the wind out of my sails. Worse yet, I couldn't respect someone who gave in as easy as she did. I was amazed to find that after four weeks of having sex as often as I wanted, I was tired of her. I didn't see any point in continuing the relationship. I finally dumped her, which made me feel even worse, because even I could see she was hurting. At least one of her parents was an alcoholic (maybe both were), her home life was a disaster, and just when she thought she could hold on to someone, I ditched her. I didn't feel very cool after that. I felt pretty low.

♡ ♡ ♡

Every teenager must wrestle with this issue. A teenager is not a child, nor is he an adult. He is just beginning to form ideas about who he is and how acceptable, normal and desirable he is perceived to be. Sex is often used to gain acceptance, and if he does score, he will find himself overwhelmingly accepted for the moment. But once that wears off, he will see what really happened. He entered into an act requiring emotional and spiritual commitment and love, yet he tried to keep it on a purely physical level. When those elements are missing, the human spirit is punctured, and growth, maturity and self-acceptance spill out.

♡ ♡ ♡

When a girl becomes sexually active before marriage, she very often feels she is merely being used by the guy to fulfill his physical desires. Her self-esteem is lowered. I was one of those girls. I sometimes felt my boyfriend didn't care about me as a person, but that he wanted me only for sex. Such hurt runs deep, and it is almost certain to have repercussions in the relationship.

The young woman's lack of self-esteem can put a strain on other relationships as well. She seeks constant reassurance of her worth from family and friends, reassurances they are often unable to provide.

At the other end of the spectrum is the girl who feels loved when guys desire to have sex with her. She can begin to view herself as valuable only when guys find her sexually attractive. If a guy doesn't take her to bed, she wonders why he doesn't care for her. This creates a desire within her to become more sexually active to prove her worth.

♡ ♡ ♡

No matter what the reason is for beginning to have premarital sex, the issue becomes more clouded instead of less clouded. I thought that once I tried it, I would better be able to make a decision about whether it was right or wrong "for me." But instead I became more and more confused, until whatever good sense I had to begin with was of no use to me. I was entangled in something I couldn't get myself out of.

I actually reached a point where I decided I would no longer have sex until I got married, but I was never able to follow through. I had turned on mechanisms that weren't so easily turned off, and I suffered a lot of self-hate because of my weakness.

---------------------- ♥ ----------------------

A much publicized report on teenage pregnancy by the National Research Council of the National Academy of Sciences draws one conclusion that many would agree with: Sexual activity among teenagers is intimately connected with issues of self-image. As the report states,

> Several studies of social and psychological factors associated with adolescents' sexual behavior conclude that self-perception (not self-esteem) — that is, the sense of what and who one is, can be, and wants to be — is at the heart of teenagers' sexual decision-making. 175

People who see themselves the way God sees them — as unique creations of the Master, made in His image, having talents and personality traits that set them apart from everyone else, valuable and significant to God — are free to be themselves. They have a healthy self-image, one that lets them stand on who they are in Christ and not have to depend on another person in order to feel good about themselves.

Without a healthy self-image, people are insecure. "Indeed, low self-esteem is reported by many to be the number-one psychological problem in contemporary society. People who do not believe they are lovable often find they are incapable of liking others and of functioning productively in society." 107/5 These people will need some kind of boost, some kind of infusion of self-esteem from another person in order to feel right about themselves. Sex is a common tool used in the effort to bolster a weak self-image. An insecure guy may try to be macho and prove to himself and others how masculine and attractive he is. An insecure girl may try either to hold a guy's affections by giving him sex, thus making her feel secure, or to be sexually appealing to a lot of guys, thereby proving to herself she has value in their eyes.

The problem is, those strategies backfire. Sex as it should be, in marriage, is based on security. In God's plan and provision for sex, there is total love, trust, companionship and freedom in giving sexually. The marriage is designed to be a permanent commitment in which the partners are completely secure in the relationship. There is no need to prove anything, no need for ego-boosts, no cause whatsoever for insecurity. Yet even though

God has provided that perfect arrangement, people think their plans are better. They think they can buck the system, play by their own rules, and somehow come out ahead.

People place terrific expectations on sex. They think sex in itself can work miracles, giving them a better view of themselves, making them look better in another person's eyes. One of the greatest expectations people place on sex is that of establishing intimacy. Many people have low self-esteem because they feel unable to establish intimacy with another. They feel unlovable and incapable of truly loving anyone. They hope that through physical intimacy they can find emotional intimacy and thus feel better about themselves. But, as the following report shows, even when people find sex physically pleasurable, it doesn't make them more capable of intimacy:

> A pathetic paradox of these sexually "free" times is that Americans are making love more but enjoying it less. The average young man and woman experience their first sexual intercourse at an increasingly early age. Fewer brides, and even fewer grooms, are virgins at their first wedding. And marital sex takes place more often. One study of 10,000 wives found that between 1965 and 1970, coital frequency increased from an average of 6.8 times in a four-week period to 8.2 times — a 21-percent jump. Extramarital sex is also on the rise.
>
> Yet at the same time there is marked dissatisfaction with the rewards of all this sexual activity. William Masters and Virginia Johnson, the pioneer sex therapists, estimate that half the married couples in the U.S. have sexual problems. Marriage counselors say that four out of every five couples they see report some sexual difficulties. True, one reason for these statistics is the freer sexual climate itself: People expect more from sex and are more willing to seek help when they are disappointed. And some of the problems result from physical difficulties, or ignorance, or negative conditioning about sex during childhood. But much sexual unhappiness grows directly out of the fear of intimacy. In fact, some couples develop sexual problems as a result of the stress one or both partners feel about being emotionally committed. For these people, sex may be good before and early in marriage. But when they realize that a good marriage demands ever-higher degrees of closeness, there may be a retreat from sex. 45

When God commands us to reserve sex for marriage, He does it to protect us. He knows that a person's self-esteem can only be damaged in the long run through premarital sex. He knows that the artificial "high," which people feel about themselves after physical intimacy, will wear off leaving no sense of emotional intimacy, and that they will crash hard when they realize how empty their "freedom" is. So He protects us by establishing boundaries within which sex is good and edifying and brings lasting pleasure.

As a person grows nearer to God in a personal relationship with Jesus Christ, he understands that he doesn't need the temporary, fickle acceptance of others to have a healthy self-image. She knows she is complete in Christ and is accepted by God just as she is, and is free to be her own person. He is free to give to people and doesn't have to take. She is free to minister and doesn't have to manipulate. They are both free to say no to what is not within God's plan for their lives.

For a more thorough understanding of the concept of a healthy self-esteem, see my book, *His Image . . . My Image,* published by Here's Life Publishers.

PROVISION

NOTE: In this section, and through the remainder of the book, we are presenting some of the material in a form you can use with your teens; thus, in places, we have spoken directly to them. You also could let them read it themselves since it is addressed to them so personally.

---

7. The Richness of Maturity

Maturity of Patience

In their own words:

A patient couple who realize they are in God's will and want to achieve God's purposes together can experience a fulfilling sex life in its proper setting: marriage. Sex can unify a couple, be a time of ecstasy and pleasure, and result in a child who is loved. Because I didn't have those three functions of lovemaking in mind before marriage, I couldn't experience everything God intended for sexual relations. Only those who are united for God's purpose, who realize they are united by God, and who are willing to accept the responsibility of a child can experience healthy sex.

♡ ♡ ♡

People should wait until marriage to engage in sex, because waiting gives your mind and body the time they need to mature.

——————— ♥ ———————

One of the marks of maturity is the ability to delay immediate gratification. Nonetheless, we live in a microwave society, a culture that insists on instant pleasure and a fast fix. In other words, our society is immature as a whole, and it encourages teenagers to live in the same way.

If you give a small child a pack of gum with five sticks and say, "One is for now, the others are for later," you can be fairly sure that when you come back a few minutes later the child will have a huge wad of gum in his cheek and five empty wrappers. Because children are not mature, they do not display the characteristics of maturity. They are seldom able to wait for anything.

Life is a process, and developing maturity is part of that process. It doesn't happen overnight. Just as God protects us from the consequences of immature sexual behavior — the demand for immediate gratification — He also provides for us in the process of waiting until marriage. He builds character and maturity in our lives as we display self-control and obedience.

Physical gratification is fleeting. Maturity is a quality of character that can never be taken away.

Maturity of Discipline

And there's something to be said for discipline, that old-fashioned virtue that gives backbone to a person. The strength to say no will do one of two things to your relationship. Either it will win you the respect of your loved one and increase confidence and trust in the relationship (by making it obvious you care about him as a person, not a body), or the relationship will end. If it does end, be glad its true colors were shown at last. For if that was the basis of your love, it was very shaky.

To continue in a relationship based on sexual attraction is to be continually insecure. There is always someone sexier than you, always someone more attractive in some way. If sex is the focus, then one of you may be tempted to give in to the lure of one of those sexier people. It is easy to lose a sexual relationship to such outside forces, because once the door is open to sexual sin, other things can easily get in.

———————— ♥ ————————

When the intense emotions of a young couple's love lead them into physical contact, one or both of them may feel that sex is a natural expression of their love. After all, the movies tell us that sex and love are the same thing, and even if young people don't quite buy that, they may persuade themselves it is true once the windows start getting steamed up.

Genuine Love

Physically expressing your love for one another may seem acceptable now, but what is your rush? If you are counting on marrying him and you will be spending the rest of your lives together, why does sex need to enter the relationship at this point? Marriage is an institution in which a man and woman share in every facet of each other's lives, and it is only when they are united in the legal and social sense that they may be united legitimately in the physical sense. If you are really in love, you will recognize this.

———————— ♥ ————————

But love always, in every case, with no exception, seeks the best interest of the loved one. That is why we can be secure in God's love — He will *never* do or say anything that is not in our best interest. When He says, "Wait until marriage for sex," He is doing it to provide a solid basis for our relationship.

One particular passage of Scripture, 1 Corinthians 13, always comes up when Christians start talking about love. There is a reason. Its brief lines about love encapsulate many of the qualities of an emotion people often find hard to define. Instead of just saying, "Well, it feels like love, so it must be," this passage gives us something we can sink our teeth into, a standard by which we can measure our actions and feelings.

Look at what verses 4 through 7 (NASB) say:

Love is patient,
love is kind,
and is not jealous;
love does not brag
and is not arrogant,
does not act unbecomingly;
it does not seek its own,
is not provoked,
does not take into account a wrong suffered,
does not rejoice in unrighteousness,
but rejoices with the truth;
bears all things,
believes all things,
hopes all things,
endures all things.

Teens, as a test to see if your feelings for someone are really feelings of love, go back and substitute your name for the word *love* in this passage. (Be careful — it might hurt!) Are your actions and thoughts directed for the benefit of the other? Do you put the other person's happiness and well-being on a plane equal to or higher than your own?

If you are in a dating relationship, go back and substitute your partner's name in place of *love*. How accurate is the description? If you are in a premarital sexual relationship, this list won't fit you or your partner very well. Examine each quality listed and see how any sexual relationship that goes against God's commands compares.

Respect for One's Body

Your body is something you should save for your mate-for-life, not some one-night-stand. If you think you've found the one you really love and he says he loves you, he will wait. Don't fall for the old line, "If you love me, you'll do it." If he tries that, just say, "If *you* love *me*, you'll wait."

——————————— ♥ ———————————

Our bodies are described in the Bible as being temples of the Holy Spirit. How is it possible for one person to claim love, but then cause another person to misuse his or her body, that tabernacle of the Holy Spirit? One young essay writer put together the following study:

Our bodies are the dwelling place of God, and sexual immorality disgraces God's temple. In Exodus, the tabernacle was a dwelling place for God (Exodus 25:8; 40:34; Leviticus 26:11). In 1 Kings 6:11-14, we see that Solomon's temple was a dwelling place for God among the Israelites. The presence of God was shielded by a curtain in both the tabernacle (Exodus 26:31) and in Solomon's temple (2 Chronicles 3:14). God's throne was represented as the Ark of the Covenant (Exodus 25:21,22; 1 Kings 6:19), and contained in the Most Holy Place (Exodus 26:33,34; 1 Kings 6:16).

Hebrews 10:19,20 indicates that this curtain which shields us from God's presence has been torn down by the blood of Jesus Christ, and through His blood we may confidently enter the Most Holy Place (God's presence). Taken a step further, 1 Corinthians 6:19 states that our bodies are a temple for God (the Holy Spirit).

Look at 1 Corinthians 6:19,20: "Do you not know that your body is a temple of the Holy Spirit, who is in you, whom you have received from God? You are not your own; you were bought at a price. Therefore honor God with your body" (NIV).

For Christians, our bodies are the dwelling place of God, a Most Holy Place, made holy because we have been purchased with the blood of Christ (Revelation 5:9). Shall I take this temple (my body) and join it to someone outside of the marriage union which God has established (Genesis 2:24; Matthew 19:5; Ephesians 5:31)? Is that honoring God with my body? Of course not!

When premarital sex is given the title "Love," things once

considered black and white start turning gray. If you have doubts about whether your relationship shows love for one another and respect for each other's body as a temple of the Holy Spirit, take time to look up and study the above verses. Study the passage on love in 1 Corinthians. God has provided us with clear guidance in His Word to keep us from becoming confused. That way we will not let our temporary emotions override His unchanging truth.

8. Affirmation of Dignity

In their own words:

I was very naive about sex (the only information I was able to get was from booklets and listening to friends). I had the usual crushes on boys who didn't notice me. My ninth grade year, though, I found out what it's like to stand up for your morals. The first kiss was not all that enjoyable and the hands up the shirt shocked me. The next time we were alone, the boy tried to go all the way. After saying no and explaining my position, he took me home in complete silence. I was hurt when he no longer wanted to see me, but I was confident I had done the right thing.

♡ ♡ ♡

One of the greatest misunderstandings in premarital sex is the idea that sex in itself constitutes love. Sex outside marriage can be nothing more than a selfish desire for sensual pleasure. When we engage in sexual activities we are affected personally — *very deeply.* We try to maintain proper dignity and self-worth. But when we share physically with another simply for the fulfillment of sexual desire, we give away part of that dignity, and in return expect something rewarding, meaningful, lasting and valuable. When we don't find meaning in the relationship, we sense that our dignity has been stripped away and that something is messed up. Since God created sex, He wants it to be enjoyed to the fullest extent, but according to His Word this can occur only in marriage. When used outside God's purpose, it produces an unfulfilled emotional need that leads to frustration and bitterness. These emotional conflicts cause damage that cannot be corrected except by the wonderful grace of God.

♡ ♡ ♡

God loves you and me so much that he wishes for each of us to be true lovers, faithful to our partners in a stable marriage, living our lives in dignity and honor. One reason God gives us His loving commands is so our dignity will be preserved. Dignity is the sense of nobility, worthiness and honor God puts in everyone. It is a concept unique to human beings; it makes us more than animals. Dignity is part of the nature of God and we are created in His image, so our awareness of dignity results from our awareness of being created in God's image. Satan, on the other hand, enjoys manipulating people into the belief that they are basically run by passion and lust rather than the power of God. Satan's desire is to make a mockery of God. Remember that!

♡ ♡ ♡

And God created man in His own image, in the image of God He created him; male and female He created them (Genesis 1:27, NASB).

♡ ♡ ♡

For through the grace given to me I say to every man among you not to think more highly of himself than he ought to think; but to think so as to have sound judgment, as God has allotted to each a measure of faith (Romans 12:3, NASB).

♡ ♡ ♡

Therefore if any man is in Christ, he is a new creature; the old things passed away; behold, new things have come. Now all these things are from God, who reconciled us to Himself through Christ, and gave us the ministry of reconciliation, namely, that God was in Christ reconciling the world to Himself, not counting their trespasses against them, and He has committed to us the word of reconciliation. Therefore, we are ambassadors for Christ, as though God were entreating through us (2 Corinthians 5:17-20, NASB).

———————————— ♥ ————————————

The Bible spells out in numerous passages the inherent dignity and value in each person. We are valuable because we are handmade by God in His image. We are not chemical accidents. We are not monkeys who have learned to use tools. We are living sculptures, the finest handiwork of the Master.

The essence of God is love. He doesn't grow in it; He *is* it. The nature of His love (*agape*) requires an object; it *has* to give. But God does not need us. He can completely satisfy His expression of love within the Godhead (the Father, the Son and the Holy Spirit). In His sovereignty it pleased God to create us so that He might love us and that we might have fellowship, a relationship, with Him. He did not need us, He wanted us.

Because He created us in His image, we have worth in God's creative plan. He provides us with redemption, with salvation — and that has nothing to do with any human merit. Rather, it is the result of God's divine sovereignty.

When we come to realize these truths, we will not think

more highly of ourselves than we ought to. We will accept our looks and talents and brains for what they are: gifts of the Master, added in just the right measure for our benefit and to His glory. We will not be conceited, but at the same time we will not be self-effacing. We will think of ourselves correctly, knowing we are unique and of great value in God's eyes.

Those of us who have recognized the truth of Christ's words, accepted His forgiveness, and given our lives to Him, have an added measure of dignity. We are royal envoys, ambassadors of the King of kings, called to live in a manner worthy of our high office.

Human sexuality is a reflection of the dignity God has given to us, a dignity that, in the right time and place, can be expressed in sex. It is precisely this dignity which our sinful nature destroys. When we are impatient for sex, when we fill our minds with pornographic garbage and dwell on it until we are moved to action, when we act immaturely and demand instant gratification, we degrade ourselves and the calling we have been given. The young woman quoted at the beginning knew that, which is why she could write, "I was confident I had done the right thing." She had held to her standards and not let herself be degraded by someone trying to use her for his lust.

9. Only One First Time

In their own words:

If you jump into sex for the first time before marriage, you will remember that time for the rest of your life, regardless of whether you remember it as good or bad. Sex after marriage will be extra special to me because it will be new and exciting, and the result of our love. We won't have to worry about listening for footsteps of returning parents, tattletale brothers and sisters, or uneasy feelings around the house.

♡ ♡ ♡

Why wait? Because you're playing with fire. The consequences are for life — there's no turning back. Once you give away your virginity, you can never, ever get it back.

♡ ♡ ♡

If you decide, that night, to be "with" this person even though you are not married, you are essentially saying, "My will be done." You're taking a very precious part of yourself and giving it to someone (who is more than willing to take it) who, for all practical purposes, is not committed to you or the relationship. This gift, once given, can never be taken back, even though you will realize you have made a mistake.

♡ ♡ ♡

Emotional scars often accompany premarital sex. There is only one first time to have sex. If you share it with someone other than your partner for life, it could turn into something you want to forget.

♡ ♡ ♡

The idea of virginity as a lost gift can apply even to those who end up marrying their original sex partners. One who gives away virginity in a relationship without the commitment of marriage gives a gift which implies far more love and commitment than either person is prepared to deal with. A once-in-a-lifetime blessing, which echoes the very relationship between Christ and His Church, is thus squandered.

———————— ♥ ————————

A teen from T. C. Williams High School in Alexandria, Virginia, says of some of her friends: "I get upset when I see friends losing their virginity to some guy they've just met. Later, after the guy's dumped them, they come to me and say, 'I wish I hadn't done it.' " 175

In the true physical sense, there is only one first time. And unless a person has a memory loss or was extremely drunk that night, the first time is indelibly stamped in her or his memory.

What a joy it is to be able to share that first time with the one committed to you for life! God's provision for marriage is that first-time bond, the memory of an act of love that made the relationship complete. Even if the wedding night is awkward, rushed, or maybe a little painful, the memory of having first made love with one's lifelong partner often overrides all of that.

God instructs us to restrict sex to marriage in order to provide freedom from memories of past sexual activity. He knows the power that "first time" has in influencing our view of sex and its relationship to the past.

If someone has had sex but is not yet married, he (or she) can't technically be a virgin again. But the forgiveness and regeneration of being a new creation in Christ make it possible for a sense of innocence to be restored. God always meets us right where we are — no matter where we are — and offers us a fresh start. He can instill forgiveness where there is guilt; self-control where there is none; a healthy appreciation of sex where there is either obsession or aversion.

If an unmarried couple is sexually active, they may feel that since neither of them is a virgin any more, they may as well continue right up until marriage. God, however, can work in a person's life at any time. If the couple stops sleeping together, they can begin to reestablish their self-control and their appreciation and respect for themselves and each other, aspects of their relationship which they have ignored. They can show one another they are capable of submitting to God and of controlling themselves, each for the sake of the other.

Many people have thanked me for encouraging them to cool their relationship for awhile — maybe even break up — in order to stop the sexual activity that was controlling them. Almost 100 percent of those couples who went on to get married have written or called to thank me. They were able to use the waiting period to build their commitment to each other and regain the trust they had forfeited through sex. They were able to approach their wedding night as a new "first time."

God provides us with a fresh start if we are willing to obey Him.

15

RELATIONAL REASONS

PROTECTION

1. From Communication Breakdowns

In their own words:

Not only does premarital sex cloud the issue of true love, it tends to thwart the communication process. Most of us by nature gravitate toward what comes easily and is pleasurable. Therefore, sex offers an easy out to those who have never learned to communicate intimacy apart from the physical. Many people think that sex produces intimacy, but as William McCready of the School of Social Work at the University of Chicago says, "Sexual activity only celebrates what's there. Sex cannot deliver what doesn't already exist."

♡ ♡ ♡

Like many others, I have learned that if there is too much touching in a relationship, it can cause uneasy feelings which lead to lack of communication. This will lead to fighting, boredom and eventually to a breakup.

♡ ♡ ♡

Another situation to consider — communication. You are getting

281

to know and enjoy a person, their likes and dislikes. You appreciate
it when they let down their walls and allow you to see them as
they really are. But when sexual activity starts, the lines of communication break down.

♡ ♡ ♡

Premarital sex can also inhibit communication, especially when
each person's view of the other is lessened. He figures, "Who else
has she slept with? She's not worth much." She thinks the same
about him, and wonders, "How do I compare with his other
women? Does he tell anyone how I perform in bed?" Each then
becomes less willing to talk, and communication is destroyed.

—————————— ♥ ——————————

Hunger for an intimate relationship is built into each of us.
We all want to love and be loved. Sex is merely the physical
expression of that intimate love we seek, not the source of it.
That is why premature sex will shortcut an immature relationship.
It tries to express something that isn't there yet.

When we delay physical involvement to its proper time, we
allow the relationship to grow and mature. Then, once that
relationship has developed into a lifelong marriage commitment,
sex can become meaningful, constructive and beneficial to the
relationship. Until that commitment is sealed, however, the couple
needs to spend time discovering each other, finding out what it
is that makes the other unique and attractive. This forms the
friendship that lays the foundation for love, which leads to the
personal intimacy each seeks.

It is a building process, and cutting it short by getting into
sex before marriage may make it impossible to put the process
back on course. Communication breaks down.

In one survey of 730 sex therapists and counselors, 85
percent said the number-one complaint they hear is about the
lack of communication in relationships. 121/83 This same survey
asked 30,000 women about their choice of their husbands. Most
of them said they had chosen their mates based on sex appeal,
but 80 percent said if they had to do it over again, they would
choose a husband based on his ability to communicate. 122/90

Waiting until marriage to have sex requires that the couple
develop some basic qualities. A commitment to obey Christ and
His word will mean exercising self-control, discipline and patience.
Those same qualities are necessary to form a lasting intimate
relationship. Our society is facing a crisis in the ability of its
members to form intimate relationships, a crisis caused by disregard for commitment and faithfulness, the cornerstones of intimacy. A commitment to Christ to be faithful to His commands

regarding sex lays the groundwork for building intimacy.

Still, many couples who *are* committed to each other cannot enjoy true satisfaction in sexual relations because they have not learned self-control, discipline and patience. They have weakened the communication that had made them strong in the first place. God's provision for those who obey is the opportunity to develop these basic qualities that are valuable not only in forming solid friendships now, but invaluable in marriage in the future. As one young man said:

> By obeying God and waiting to have sex until marriage, a couple can discover other ways to communicate that will facilitate a healthy relationship. The patient couple can really get to know each other and start to discover God's purpose for their marriage before they ever sleep together.

2. Difficult Courtships

In their own words:

Premarital sex makes a courtship more difficult. Courtship is a critical period of time — the potential stakes involved are the many years ahead in a lifelong marriage. In view of the tremendous investment a lifelong relationship represents, many aspects of a relationship need to be worked out before a commitment is made.

During the later periods of courtship, the time a couple spends apart can be as important as the time they spend together. Time apart can give each person perspective on the relationship and time to work alone on various issues that need to be resolved to make a wise decision about a potential mate.

Premarital sexual involvement wages war against responsible courtship in two powerful ways. First, it has a binding effect on the partners. In sexually active courtships, many issues surrounding the relationship are often not weighed or dealt with adequately. Once the initial blast of sexual involvement tapers to a more stable flame, unresolved issues become far more pressing. Very often issues that are not resolved during courtship become issues that shipwreck a marriage later on.

Second, sexual involvement makes it more difficult for couples to have adequate time away from each other. The intimacy developed by sexual union can be so compelling that a couple finds it more and more difficult to spend time apart.

———————— ♥ ————————

One of the gifts God allows us to give another person is a demonstration of self-control. When we establish a relationship, self-control must be evident for trust to be built, and trust is the foundation for any continued growth in the relationship.

Premarital sex undermines such trust by proving that a person is not in control of his or her desires, but instead is controlled by them. When both become controlled by their desires, sex controls the relationship. When they become victims of their own inability to put off gratification, the relationship suffers and may end. According to Robert O. Blood, Jr., in one of the most careful surveys on the subject, sexual "intimacy produced more broken relationships than strengthened ones." 220/82 More engagements were broken by Burgess and Wallin's couples who had intercourse than by those who did not, and the more frequent the intercourse, the larger the proportions of rings returned.

As the single person above noted, once the physical aspect takes root, it takes over. The people lose the ability to communicate and learn about each other. They don't develop the social, intellectual, moral and emotional aspects of the relationship. Instead of growing stronger, they grow weaker. So, rather than being the culmination of a mounting intimacy between two people, marriage (if it happens) becomes a permanent seal on an incomplete relationship.

God's commandments against sex before marriage are there to protect us from hurting our relationships. If a couple is sexually active, they may find themselves hooked into a relationship, but the wise move, regardless of how close they may be to marriage, is to break it off and reestablish the self-control so vital to a marriage. If the couple is able to get back together without sexual involvement and continue on to marriage, they have a major accomplishment that will strengthen rather than weaken their marriage. The sooner they can break it off, the better.

It's hard to end a steady relationship, harder to end an engagement, harder still to end a marriage and even harder to end a marriage with children. The further you go, the harder it gets, and the more pain results. That is why God commands us to "flee immorality" — He knows we need to run from a bad situation as fast as possible.

God's admonition to wait as protection does not guarantee a smooth courtship, but provides an opportunity for an *intelligent* one. When issues are not clouded by sex, people are able to understand each other in many aspects, and can know with certainty if they are making the right move in getting married. I discovered this when I dated a young woman for three and a half years. Even after all that time, we were able to understand that marriage was not right for us. We are still friends to this day. By being obedient to God's commands concerning sex before marriage, we were under God's protection and able to partake of His provision.

3. Involuntary Comparison of Sex Partners

In their own words:

There could also be a tendency to compare the sexual performance of one's spouse to previous sexual partners, especially if the "experienced" partner is left unsatisfied by his or her spouse. This has the potential to drive a wedge between husband and wife, preventing them from experiencing God's plan for true intimacy and love in their marriage. Mental flashbacks to earlier sexual experiences are common. The flashback can happen during idle thinking, at work, while trying to have a quiet time with the Lord, or in the passion of a sexual embrace with one's spouse. I know the frustration and disturbing effects of those flashbacks. I regret having had any kind of sexual involvement with anyone other than my wife, and I wish I could completely erase those memories from my mind.

♡ ♡ ♡

If I had sex with another girl, there are two things I know would happen. I would never be able to forget her, and because of that, I would compare her with my wife in the future. This would make it harder not only in my sexual relationship with my wife, but I also wouldn't be able to accept her for who she really is. But if there are no past memories on which to base a comparison, then acceptance of my wife is so much easier.

♡ ♡ ♡

In the book *Choices,* it says, "Sex causes you to compare one person with another." If you have premarital sex, you could find yourself comparing your spouse to the person you had sex with before. Regardless of whether you say your spouse is better or worse than the previous person, you are still concentrating on that person and not on your spouse.

♡ ♡ ♡

My two friends must also deal with the problem of *comparing* their husbands to the men of their past relationships. Although guilt makes them feel hesitant or inhibited, they also fight the attitude of scorn or rejection for their husbands, who always seem to fall short, not measuring up to idealized memories of previous sexual encounters.

♡ ♡ ♡

First, there is no guarantee you will marry the girl you're engaged to and be her sole sex partner. About half of all engagements are broken off (I know). Thus, if you have sex and she ends up marrying another, her future partner will have to compare himself with you, wondering if he pleases her as much as you did. That will hardly enhance *their* sexual relationship. If you really love her, how can you be willing to take such a chance with her future happiness?

♡ ♡ ♡

Frankly speaking, I am looking forward to having sex when it comes time for me to be married. But I want to be a virgin on my wedding night and go through all the excitement, vulnerability and uneasiness of being united with my husband physically. I am so glad I will not have someone else to compare my husband with and that I can totally concentrate on making him happy.

——————— ♥ ———————

The power of sexual interaction is a force a person may have to deal with for years after the actual sexual contact. I have had people in counseling who can describe a number of sexual encounters and remember in detail exactly what happened, yet they don't even remember their sex partners' names. Such is the influence sex has on our emotions and memories. Abraham Maslow describes sex as the peak human experience.

Why do memories and comparisons of past sexual experiences haunt people so mercilessly? Simple. God created the sexual experience to give us automatically the most unforgettable, vivid, and often-recalled memories we will ever have. Let's look at how memory works and why this is true.

There are two basic approaches to understanding human memory: (1) the neurobiological approach, which studies the molecular brain processes (like studying the circuits of a computer); and (2) the practical approach, which examines the functions and principles of memory (like studying the software for a computer). We will look at the practical approach, as it is more applicable to our purpose.

Scientists have discovered a number of principles that help us understand why sexual memories are so intense and permanent. One principle involves what is called "consolidation" of memories, that is, how short-term memories become long-term memories that can be recalled in the future. There are at least two important factors involved in long-term memory: (1) the intensity of the experience; and (2) how much we rehearse or review the experience in our mind. Sex is likely to involve both of these, as it is by any measure intense, and we are likely to rehearse the experience often because of the emotions involved. Our sexual experiences seem to be written in "indelible ink" in our memories, never to be erased.

Another memory principle, which applies to sexual experiences, is that people tend to learn and remember more clearly

when they are alert 106/76 and stimulated, 82/345 when their
bodies have large amounts of adrenalin in them, 39/49 and when
emotions are involved. 39/50 It is difficult to imagine any experience that involves as many of these factors as sex does. Few
experiences leave us with memories that are as vivid.

Our five senses are involved also in learning and remembering. Specifically, the more different senses we involve in an
experience, the more likely we are to recall it later. One highly
effective Scripture memory method illustrates this. The method
includes reading the verses out loud three times from the text;
writing them three times; reading the verses out loud three times
from what you just wrote; and saying them three times as you
now remember them. This method involves three senses: sight
(reading); hearing (as you speak); and touch (as you write).

These same three senses can be involved in an even stronger
way in sex, and the other senses can be as well.

In addition, memories are called to mind by association.
Something from within us (thoughts, feelings, actions) or from
without (through our five senses) reminds us of something similar
from our past. Think of what can be associated with sex: anything
from any of the five senses; any of the automatically strong
positive, negative, or ambivalent emotions involved in sex; anything related at all to the person one was with at the time;
anything about the location or the time of day . . . and the list
goes on.

In considering these various principles, we realize that someone who has had previous sexual encounters probably will have
the same feelings in subsequent encounters, such as in marriage,
as were experienced before. This is especially true if the earlier
occurrences involved hurt, exploitation, mistrust or guilt. (That
is one reason rape and incest can devastate people's lives — permanent scars are left.) When past experiences are transferred into
marriage, there is trouble.

We can see that the most important sex organ God gave us
is our mind, and, actually, that is good news! Since God created
sexual experience in such a way that we automatically have the
most unforgettable, vivid, and often-recalled memories, think of
what happens when two people learn about sex from their first
time — *together* — within marriage. Indelible, extremely *positive*
memories are formed, which can bind those two people together
in a loving, trusting unity, without any interferences from the past.

> One young husband admitted that his relationship with
> his new wife wasn't what he had hoped it would be. "It's
> really my fault," he admitted. "Before we were married I
> had several physical relationships with girlfriends. Now,

whenever I kiss my wife or engage in love play, my memory reminds me that this girl could kiss better than my wife, that girl was better at something else and so forth. I can't concentrate on loving my wife with all that I am — there have been too many women in my life to be wholly committed to one." 109/94

A married woman observes, "When sex is explored before marriage, future sexual problems arise, and love in the marriage relationship is hurt. Walter Trobisch illustrates this idea in this way: 'Premarital sex is rather like picking blossoms in spring. It seems beautiful, right and natural. But when autumn comes, there is no fruit.' Often there may be more sexual satisfaction at first in marriage, but that may be short-lived as there may be a tendency to compare past performance with other sexual partners. Sexual pleasure decreases."

Fears and concerns often will develop about how one matches up or compares to a previous lover. In quarrels or fights, unfortunate comments or comparisons can be made that will be detrimental to the marriage.

God has given us His commands to postpone sex until marriage in order to protect our minds. When we are disobedient and shun His protection, our sexual experiences start to condition us mentally. One man who discovered this was a worker in a Christian organization. He offered to drive me to the airport after a conference.

On the way there, he said, "I need your help. I am married to one of the most wonderful women I've ever met. I love her. I would do anything for her. But before I became a Christian, I was very active sexually, to the point where my sexual adventures became distorted and rather depraved." At that point he began crying. "I would do anything, ANYTHING, to forget the sexual experiences I had before I met my wife. When we start having intercourse, the pictures of the past and the other women go through my head, and it's killing any intimacy. I'm to the point where I don't want to have sex because I can't stand those memories. The truth is, I have been married to this wonderful woman for eight years and I have never been 'alone' in the bedroom with her."

The Bible says in Hebrews 13:4 to let "the marriage bed [be] kept pure" (NIV). Pure means to be void of any foreign substance. The moment a foreign substance is added to something, that thing becomes diluted or adulterated, i.e., impure. For example, if we add Nutra-Sweet to sugar, the sugar is no longer pure. A foreign substance has been added.

As for the marriage bed, premarital or extramarital sexual relationships defile it. They so affect our minds that we carry a foreign element, the memory of those past relationships, into the marriage bed with us. One woman, relating the effects of her previous sexual relationships on her marriage, referred to the "ghosts" of relationships past. Another referred to the negative "reruns in the theater of the mind." For each of these women, the foreign element had entered her marriage bed and it was no longer pure.

You can give back the ring, return the pictures, and throw away the mementos, but you cannot give back the mental pictures or the memories. You carry them with you.

The mind is the number-one sexual force to be reckoned with. God has given us His wise and loving commands to protect our minds, not to frustrate us or ruin our fun.

Another young man approached me one time and said, "I used to be sexually involved and look at a lot of pornographic magazines, and it has messed up my marriage. I got so hooked on being turned on by those pictures that I still have to have them. When I go to bed with my wife and have sex with her, I can't even have an orgasm without a foldout next to her head on the pillow." As if that weren't evidence enough of the hold this had on their marriage, I was approached some weeks later by a woman who told me her self-image had been shattered. I asked her why.

She said, "Every time my husband has sex with me, he has to have a pornographic foldout on the bed next to me. He can't even come to a climax without it."

This young woman's self-image was destroyed. Her husband was having sex with her, but was making love with the person in the picture. Like the man who took me to the airport, he had filled his mind with so much junk and so many salacious memories that he was paying the price years later in his marriage. Neither of those men wanted it that way. But they were reaping the consequences of their earlier disobedience.

When one partner fears comparison to the spouse's previous lovers, he (or she) begins to seek assurance that he is actually good enough to compete. That kind of unhealthy need for affirmation certainly does not allow freedom and self-expression in the bedroom. It creates insecurity, which comes from a feeling of being threatened. Further, fear of an outside threat can lead to jealousy — a strange kind of jealousy that pits a person against "competition" that has not been around for years. It is not so simple as an attractive person at the office making a pass. It is a memory that enters the bedroom with the spouse.

Although most teenagers think about sex and even fantasize (boys more than girls), they fail to see the power of their thoughts on their sexual activity and the power of their sexual activity on their thoughts. They don't realize that the way they live their lives now has a direct bearing on how they will live later. If they remain in line with God's instructions and keep themselves pure, they will reap the reward in marriage of being able to concentrate fully on their spouse when making love. If they are sexually active before hand, they are setting themselves up for future mental battles. This is not mere hypothesis. It is a reality played out every day in the fear and insecurity found in countless marriages.

God provides a way for those who have been sexually active and are haunted by it to be free. Since He commands us to be transformed by the renewing of our minds (Romans 12:2), it must be possible for our minds to be renewed. In specific instances in my own life I have prayed for a certain memory to be blotted out. It's hard to imagine that such a thing is possible, but it is. I remember being bothered, needled by something out of my past, something I knew intellectually God had forgiven but I was unable to shake. I remember praying that God would relieve me of the burden of that memory. Incredibly, I became aware at some point after praying that a burden had been lifted. I didn't recall exactly what it was, but I wasn't supposed to remember. All I knew was that another area of my thoughts was transformed and renewed, no longer weighed down and haunted.

So many of us need to be brainwashed. We need to have our brains washed by God. We need to bring our memories and past experiences under the Lordship of Jesus Christ and allow Him to repair the damage. We need to begin *today* building relationships that will leave good memories, relationships we can look back on with appreciation as we see personal and spiritual growth, not look back on in regret and self-disgust. God always meets us right where we are and offers us a fresh start.

The Father knows what is best for our minds and has set up boundaries around sex to protect and provide for our minds. One young bride who found this out wrote:

> The first benefit I am experiencing as a result of obedience is freedom from the jealousies I would be experiencing had my husband been with another woman before me. I would be haunted by the possibility that sex was better, more exciting with her. I could never be fully assured that he is as satisfied and fulfilled in our physical love. The second benefit is, I have no guilt to deal with, no conviction by the Holy Spirit for having been disobedient.

4. Sex Becoming Dominant and Burying Love

In their own words:

It was different for me. My boyfriend was the only one I ever had sex with. I loved him and needed him. I wanted to keep him, but it didn't work. Our communication broke down. Pretty soon we were fighting a lot. He tried to patch things up by having sex, and I gave in because I wanted him to love me. We both got really selfish. We stayed together, but all the love was gone from the relationship.

♡ ♡ ♡

The development of the relationship is inhibited because much of the couple's time together will be dominated by sex. A couple can stop investing energy into exploring the many facets of each other's personality, explorations that deepen the relationship. With the curiosity gone, and the mystery gone, boredom sets in.

♡ ♡ ♡

I think premarital sex buries love, or maybe even kills it. You can either have sex or love in a relationship. If you're not married, you can't have both. I don't think it's possible, because if you loved someone, you wouldn't risk their being hurt through sex.

♡ ♡ ♡

Often the entire focus of the relationship shifts to physical gratification. Many times a couple has a great friendship going, but then sex enters the scene apart from permanent commitment. They get into "*my* desires, *my* wants, *my* pleasures" without regard for the other's needs. When a relationship hits that point, why should they consider the needs of the other first?

♡ ♡ ♡

In the vast majority of instances, premarital sex clouds the true issues concerning the relationship. It is by the physical that each partner expresses himself or herself, to the exclusion of honest communication. When a problem in the relationship arises, they comfort one another with sex, leaving the relational problem to plague them in the future. Sex takes precedence over all else and the two become nothing more than passionate creatures seeking self-gratification.

This is not the self-giving and self-sacrificing love Christ taught, but rather the hedonistic theme running through the rest of society today.

♡ ♡ ♡

I remember two long-term relationships I had. I knew they would never amount to anything, but the excitement of sex made me a slave to pleasure. Like a drug, sex demanded heavier dosages to satisfy my desires. I began to use and exploit my girlfriends rather than love them.

♡ ♡ ♡

[Letter to a friend] I hear you and Greg are getting married after college. Do you know the odds of a relationship lasting that long? It doesn't matter whether you two get married or not — when you sleep together, you are still sinning against God. Premarital sex is premarital sex, no matter who you are having it with.

You have no idea how you are hurting your relationship by doing this. Pretty soon, you and Greg will concentrate only on the physical aspect of the relationship until the emotional respect is lost. When the emotional growth is stunted, your relationship will be built totally on physical attraction. What kind of Christian relationship is that?

♡ ♡ ♡

Sex is so powerful that it overwhelms the heart. If Mr. Right won't openly commit his life to you forever, how can he be Mr. Right? If you are sexually involved with someone who is not Mr. Right, your heart will not know what to do. Your body is doing something that calls for total commitment, yet your mind knows the commitment is not there. If it were, you would be married.

So when people tell you to wait, it's easy to misunderstand them. It is not because they are stuffy or think sex is wrong, it is because they know sex is overpowering. If your heart is confused and you don't know what you feel any more, how can you know when you are in love? The implication is that you can never come to that grand moment of deciding to marry him, since your heart will be too mixed up to tell you it is time. That is why former live-in lovers who do end up getting married respond so unenthusiastically when you ask them about their wedding, honeymoon, or married life. There was never a distinct moment of spontaneous decision.

Remember when you first came to Christ? Such moments of sudden realization become rare as you get older. It's the type of situation in which one moment you didn't know something that could change your life, and the next moment you did. Your heart was joyful and sure in its decision. That is the way it should be in a relationship that could lead to marriage, and then to physical oneness. But the moment of sudden joy is lost forever when you become intimate with Mr. Could-Have-Been-Right.

———————— ♥ ————————

The very nature of a male-female relationship is that of companionship, friendship and intimacy. The marriage relationship is supposed to last a lifetime, and to make that possible, people get to know one another in the period leading up to the marriage. They are not committed to one another legally, morally or otherwise. They do not live together and do not have mutual responsibilities. They are free to spend time together and learn what makes each other tick, free to question and discuss and debate. They are able to make clear-headed choices about spending their lives together. When the growing intimacy between them leads to the altar, they know what they are getting. After the wedding, they are free to seal the relationship as only a husband and wife can do.

The above process comprises the foundation for building a lifelong relationship. When sex enters the scene too soon, the foundation is weakened and frequently collapses completely. As many of the young writers in this book have stated, sex takes over dating relationships like wildfire. It consumes everything built to that point.

One of the first casualties is communication. When a couple has found a quick way to be "intimate" by having sex, they don't bother taking time to become mentally and emotionally and spiritually intimate. They become lazy in their attempts to grow closer, opting for what is easy over what is lasting.

The next casualty is trust. When people have revealed their character to each other by having sex before marriage, there is distrust on both sides. Each knows the other is incapable of controlling physical desires. What will happen if they should be apart for awhile? What is to keep each from seeking out other opportunities for gratification? Frequently, nothing. Whether they say it out loud or not, they know it.

One by one, the vital mutual concerns needed to build a lasting intimate relationship are consumed by sex. Sex displaces and then destroys love.

> Many young people try to prove their love by sexual surrender. But when a relationship has no more unexplored dimensions, boredom usually sets in along with loss of respect. Sexual compromise is actually the surest way to end a good relationship. Ironically, it is also an effective way to prolong a bad relationship — many people end up marrying the wrong person because of the sexual involvement (a disastrous consequence that affects the rest of their lives). 62/233

God's provision for a couple committed for life is a relationship that grows with the years, not one that falters under pressure. Sex is only one of many, many bonds that hold together a permanent relationship. It is not the focal point. Too many couples have discovered that sex doesn't make their mortgage payments go away. It doesn't resolve the crises that are normal in the course of a lifetime. Premarital sex prevents development of those aspects of a relationship that must be present for a marriage to work.

Although the physical is the most direct route of communication and the easiest to learn, it is only the tip of the iceberg of a good relationship. Anybody can kiss, but not everyone can carry on a meaningful conversation. Often a relationship begun on a plane of physical attraction is never able to reach the deeper intimacy of mind and spirit.

Believe it or not, *your* skin is going to sag, and eventually you will have bulges in mysterious places — and in fewer years than you think. If someone's attraction to you is based mostly on what is sensually appealing, what kind of future does that project for your relationship? It's God's gracious intent to replace some of your physical attractiveness with a deeper inner beauty. As God develops those qualities of character in your life, your marriage will mature, not just endure with age. So you must think ahead to decide which aspects of your relationship will be most important over the long haul. 109/92

God's protection for us, seen in His command to restrict sex to marriage, is to keep us from hurting ourselves and those we care about by ruining our relationships. A young couple making cow-eyes at each other may not see the terrible pain that can come from a relationship that dries up because of sex. The Father knows how nearsighted we can be, so He tells us which road to take. He takes the guesswork out of relationships by giving us clear instructions about the place of sex. If we stay within His boundaries, we are protected. If we leave His protection, we are open to whatever consequences may lie outside.

When we look at the Bible and its commandments, we can see that God is not out to spoil our fun. Everything He says and does is rooted in His love for us. He seeks the best for us at every turn. When He says to wait, He wants us to use our time wisely, to get to know others as friends, and become lovers only after we make a relationship permanent. As one author says, "You don't want to end up having a lover but needing a friend." 87/89

5. Damaged Family Relationships

The Couple

In their own words:

Premarital sex can also harm one's future marriage. *Premarital Sex in a Changing Society* by Robert R. Bell [203] explains that premarital sex increases the chance of extramarital sex, which often leads to divorce. Still, some ask what the importance of the piece of paper is to marriage. Studies shown by *Family Life* magazine say that "[premarital] intimacy produces more broken relationships than strengthened ones. Love can wait to give, but lust cannot wait to get."

♡ ♡ ♡

A man who was sexually active before marriage may often find himself being driven by his fleshly desires after the wedding. Because sex is not that special an act to him, he is more open to having problems with lust. Due to his earlier sexual immorality, it will be easier for him to seek sexual fulfillment outside his marriage. This progression is clearly stated in James 1:14,15: "But each one . . . is carried away and enticed by his own lust. Then when lust has conceived, it gives birth to sin; and when sin is accomplished, it brings forth death" (NASB).

♡ ♡ ♡

Some studies show that twice as many engagements are broken among couples who have had intercourse . . . Furthermore . . . [these couples] are more likely to be divorced or separated or to indulge in adultery. One way or another, premarital intimacy is more closely connected to broken relationships than to solid ties.

♡ ♡ ♡

Guys, think about your future wife. Do you really want the best for her? The best sex for her? Then you will wait. If you wait to have sex only with her, she will be convinced you will not seek sex elsewhere outside marriage; therefore, she will be able to give herself freely and completely to you, unafraid that she has to share you with someone. Nor will she be concerned about her ability to match up to your past partners. In short, your waiting for her will communicate self-sacrifice and love for her that cannot help but cause her to love you more.

———————————— ♥ ————————————

One of the things God protects by reserving sex for marriage is the trust and assurance of fidelity that a proper sexual relationship brings. That assurance provides peace of mind for both spouses when they are apart (for whatever reason). Both know they are deserving of trust. Both know the other is deserving of trust. Why? Because, in the period before their marriage, they have proven their character, their maturity and their self-control.

When a man says, "I do," remember that he is answering a question. The question is "Do you take this woman to be your wife?" When he says yes, he means he takes *this woman,* not some future ideal, not an improved version of her he has pictured in his mind. He is saying, "I take her and accept her just as she is, and I know what I'm getting." The same holds true for the woman's answer of "I do."

That's why premarital sexual activity can be such a source of distrust in a marriage — according to statistics, the spouse has good reason to be suspicious. A person is generally not changed by marriage; rather, one's personality traits are intensified. People who can't control themselves before marriage will have a hard time controlling themselves after. *Redbook,* reporting on a study of 100,000 women done by a professional sociologist, puts it like this: "Premarital sex . . . does not necessarily lead to extramarital sex — it simply increases the odds that it will." 298/40

How accurate are those odds? We know that at least three quarters of all unmarried people today are sexually active. But does this really have an effect on sex after the marriage?

> The most widely accepted figures . . . indicate that more than half of all husbands and about one third of all wives have been unfaithful at least once. And those percentages are on the increase, particularly among working wives and couples under thirty. 47/50-54

Our society has taken its nonchalant attitude about sex to such extremes that some people actually enter marriage agreeing that both are free to have affairs. They want commitment as long as it is not a bother. They offer love and security in portions designed only to please themselves. Instead of the true view of marriage, which is designed for each to give 100 percent without expecting a return, or even the cheaper but widely accepted view of "I'll give 50 percent if you'll give 50 percent," these couples have reduced marriage to an opportunity for *taking* 100 percent of the time and *giving* only when they feel like it. One study took a look at such relationships and the effect of "sexual freedom":

> The "open marriage" described by psychologists George and Nena O'Neill emerged from attempts to combine committed relationship with unabridged personal freedom . . .
> Individuals involved in open marriage believe that jealousy is destructive in marriage, and struggle to free themselves from its effects. Social traditions and conventional morality are set aside; after difficult negotiations the ground rules are set based on the values, beliefs and needs of each individual. The partners may then be freed to establish extramarital platonic, social or sexual friendships. The theory sounds all right, but in 1978 Nena O'Neill reported that most stable marriages are based on sexual fidelity. She also reported that among the 250 couples she studied, those relationships that ended within two years tended to be the ones that included some planned extramarital sex. 87/118

One woman who thought that sex outside marriage was all right suddenly found herself with a new attitude after marriage. She wondered why this was (and please note that the respondent's idea of a "sophisticated couple" is one that allows promiscuity outside the relationship):

> *Q:* My husband and I lived together for a year before we

were married, and during that time each of us had occasional sexual relationships with other people. We agreed to continue that arrangement after marriage, but something strange seems to have happened. I can't imagine having an affair now without feeling guilty. And I'm consumed with jealousy when I suspect my husband may be out with someone else. Why have my feelings about sexual freedom changed so much?

A: Many unmarried women and men who can accept sexual freedom within a close and loving relationship are surprised to find how dramatically their attitudes change after marriage. The fact seems to be that a wedding certificate is, for most people, more than merely a legal requirement or "just a piece of paper." It symbolizes a different level of commitment. Even the most sophisticated couples may find the traditional values accompanying marital commitment hard to shake off — especially sexual values, which are so often tied to ideas about loyalty, fidelity and feelings of security. 47/50-54

To a great extent, the desire to pursue sex outside marriage comes not from a physical yearning for continued sexual release, but from the established habit of trying to solve problems with sex. When a couple becomes physically involved before marriage, sex can easily become a panacea, a way to feel good instantly when problems arise. It becomes a mask, a glow that makes the problems go away for the moment.

The same mindset carries over into marriage. When the responsibilities of children and mortgage payments pile on top of rough points in the marriage, a person who has learned to look to sex for an answer will do it again. When sex with the spouse leaves the problems unresolved, tension in the marriage mounts. The couple begins to back off from each other physically and emotionally, and one or both may go looking for the "good feeling" somewhere else.

People who look to this escape and allow the affair to become serious — to the point of changing their lives to accommodate it — find themselves in for a rude awakening. We have seen it happen many times, where people find a sexual release outside marriage to be just the medicine they needed. No demands, no responsibilities, no entanglements. They then become enamored with the situation, divorce their spouses, marry their sex partners — and suddenly find themselves back in a relationship with demands and expectations. When tension returns, they go looking again.

Premarital sex can cause a rift in a relationship before or after marriage. Many unmarried couples break up because of sex, but other couples are able to quell their insecurities, distrust, lack of respect and loss of love long enough to complete the marriage ceremony. However, those same forces that destroy unmarried couples often come back to haunt married couples.

The commands of the Bible are there for our protection. The Lord knows how devastating the effects of premarital sex can be, so out of His love for us He has established parameters for sex to keep it from being destructive.

By insisting that we wait until marriage for sex, God protects us from that destruction. He wants our sex lives to be a point of strength and unity in the marriage relationship, not a point of division. His wisdom supersedes all our rationalizations and excuses.

Children

One of God's provisions for sex within marriage is the blessing of children. A married couple is complete without children, of course, but as the father of four, I know the great joy children add to a marriage.

This blessing can be tarnished when the children are conceived outside marriage. One young woman told me about a marriage conference she had gone to, where the speaker had said, "Ladies, one thing you can know for sure is this: Out of all the women in the world, your husband chose you because he wanted you." She told me, "I went out of there with a sick feeling. I had gotten pregnant and we had to get married, and I don't have that confidence in our relationship."

While such a couple must deal with the guilt, financial stress and other problems brought about by a premarital pregnancy, the child can also pay a heavy price.

When an unmarried couple conceives a child, they have a number of options. First, and one often taken by Christian couples, is the "shotgun wedding," the marriage that takes place quickly out of a sense of responsibility (and usually under a fair amount of pressure from the families).

These marriages do not necessarily turn out bad, but instead of beginning in joy and anticipation, they begin in guilt and stress. Such marriages cause two people to begin a family when they are often really too immature to handle the responsibility.

The child, rather than being a symbol of the self-perpetuating love in the marriage, becomes a reminder of a big mistake. There may be a subtle, if unconscious, resentment toward the child, as though the child were the one who forced the marriage. If such resentment is present, the child grows up with it and is aware of a kink in the parent-child relationship, even when the parents are not.

A second option is giving the baby up for adoption. Although we see it being done less in our culture, it is often the most loving thing to do, especially when the couple (and the mother in particular) is too immature to raise a child. With so many childless couples desperate to adopt, it is a tragedy that so many young people are raising children they may not even want, and who are often the victims of child abuse. Both of the authors have experienced the joy of having adopted children just as our heavenly Father has (Galatians 4:5).

A third option is single parenthood. If the mother is a teenager, chances are she is still living at home. She will eventually move out and be on her own, but according to statistics, her chances of remaining below the poverty line for life are very high. Immature mothers who insist on raising a child without a husband often do so in an attempt to establish a loving relationship. They want the baby as an object for their love, and they want to be loved and accepted by the child. As the baby grows, the mother may find that the child does not fulfill the requirements of love and affection she has placed on it, and the child becomes a victim of the mother's immaturity.

A fourth option is abortion. Taking the life of the child may be the quickest way out, but it may also have the most damaging repercussions. What it does to the mother is so extensive and complex that we cannot deal with it here. But the abortion of one child can have an effect even on future children. In some instances, the presence of a child in a marriage becomes a continual reminder of the sibling the mother aborted before. She is constantly aware that the family is one person short, and the psychological battles she endures are felt by her living children. Again the children become victims of the parents' premarital sex.

God can work all things to the good of those who believe in Him. He can take the most embarrassing, destructive situation, such as an unwanted pregnancy, and somehow make things turn out right (Romans 8:28). That won't make the premarital sex right, nor will it make the child magically go away. But God does respond to the repentance and prayers of His people. His amazing grace is greater than our worst mistakes.

Better still, when He reserves sex for marriage, He protects us from even getting into these situations. By limiting sex to marriage, He protects everyone involved, including those not yet born.

Parents

Sadly enough, they [young people] turn to sex, thinking they are receiving the love they seek but don't get at home. However, they usually just end up adding to their hurt. They create more problems than they solve. If the girl gets pregnant, the relationship with her parents usually is made worse and she still does not receive the love she was looking for. She just drifts further from them.

♡ ♡ ♡

The last reason for not having sex before marriage is that it would hurt my mother's feelings. This may not seem important to most people, but it is very important to me.

——————————— ♥ ———————————

When parents have convictions of biblical morality and therefore desire to raise their children understanding God's principles, they are going to be hurt when the children knowingly violate those principles.

Their hurt takes several forms. First, the parents may feel that the child is bringing them embarrassment; they feel hurt for themselves. They take the child's disobedience toward God as a personal blow. Second, the parents may be genuinely hurt on the child's behalf, since they want the best for their child at all times. They know that straying from biblical boundaries will bring pain to the child's life. Parents may also feel personal hurt because of what the unplanned pregnancy takes away from their expectations or desires.

Teenagers trying to please their parents by avoiding sexual immorality are under the protection of God's blessing. But there is something better. When young people have established a personal relationship with God and keep His commandments as a willing response to His love, they have internalized God's values. They are showing maturity and independence, and they are free to become the unique persons God created them to be.

God's provision for seeking to maintain His standards are described in the words of this young woman:

> When I lay down next to my husband on our wedding night, I did not need to sneak away before dawn. My parents knew where we were. We had their blessing. Friends and family had sent gifts and cards of congratulations. It was right in "my crowd's" eyes as well as my Lord's. I had waited long for my wedding day and I have been enjoying the relationship ever since.

PROVISION

6. A Special Relationship Found Only in Marriage

A Unique Oneness

In their own words:

A young man went into a rose garden and chose a pretty young bud to be his own. While waiting for it to mature and open, he walked around in the garden, touching and smelling other roses. He gradually grew more careless and even crushed a few flowers. Eventually he wandered back to his rose. It had opened. It was the largest, most fragrant rose in the garden.

He picked it and tried to savor its fragrance, but his sense of smell had been dulled to the point where he found pleasure only in the envious glances others cast his way.

♡ ♡ ♡

When a person engages in sex prior to marriage, he cheats himself of a uniqueness found in marriage in previous generations but almost unknown today. In decades past, the two usually entered marriage with no sexual experience, and therefore had no basis on which to draw comparisons. They learned from each other and had to refine the techniques necessary to please only one person — their spouse.

♡ ♡ ♡

I never realized that I felt cheated until my wedding night when we got to our hotel room. As I was getting ready for the most romantic evening of my life, I looked in the mirror and realized I had already done this. What a letdown. What was there to be excited about? This was nothing new. It was as if all the life had been drained out of me.

As months went on, we got frustrated and uptight. Sex used to be so much fun before we got married. What happened?

Sex had been just a game before. Now, when it should have been the ultimate expression of love between a husband and wife, it had no meaning.

We struggled with this for almost a year. It was about to destroy us when we finally went to some close friends and received counseling, prayer and forgiveness from the Lord. Now things are as they should be.

♡ ♡ ♡

Premarital sex can make something unique into something every-day and casual. It destroys the timing required to make sex what it should be.

♡ ♡ ♡

If a person is sexually active before marriage, he has a mental attachment to past partners that takes away the uniqueness of sex with his lifelong mate. This is like the story about the young man who found a locket he liked at a jewelry store and gave it to his girlfriend. They later broke up, but he still liked that locket so much he began buying one to give to each successive girlfriend.

When he finally found the girl he would marry, he went to look for a present for her. Sure enough, he got her the same locket. She was thrilled when she opened the box, but even though he liked the locket, it was no longer special. He had given the same gift to a lot of girls.

♡ ♡ ♡

If I could give any reason as my most persuasive, it would be this: Many have given in to passion, as I did, in the heat of the moment. I have heard many say they regretted this. Other people have waited until they were married. I have yet to hear *one* of them say they are sorry.

———————— ♥ ————————

Have you ever searched around the house to find a present with your name on it and peeked in to see what it was? There was a sense of daring and espionage about it, but when it came time to open the present in front of everyone, you had to fake surprise. The gift itself was still just as valuable, but the most important part — the giving and receiving — was tarnished.

God does not want our wedding night to be just another occasion for sex. He has given us His commands to wait, so we won't experience a big emotional letdown.

At the same time, His provision for sex in marriage is exactly this uniqueness, this specialness. He gives us the opportunity to learn the ways of sexual pleasure with the one we will spend our lives pleasing. This learning process forms one of the strongest bonds in the marriage.

The special nature of sex within marriage is clearly seen when we remember what marriage is: a lifelong opportunity to minister to another person. Sex within this context of giving and meeting the needs of the other then becomes a matter of emotional, spiritual and psychological oneness, as well as of physical oneness.

No Disappointment Because of Lost Virginity

"I'm not a virgin, and now that I've found the man I want to spend the rest of my life with, I wish I were," says Lisa regretfully. "He's a virgin so we've talked about it and he accepts that I'm not. We've decided not to have sex until after we're married and are comfortable with that decision."

♡ ♡ ♡

Fact: Many men do not want to marry a woman who has had intercourse with someone else.

♡ ♡ ♡

I guess one thing that would keep me from premarital sex is this: I would not want any man to have had sex with the girl I plan to marry; therefore I would not want to destroy another man's dream by being sexually involved with the girl he will someday marry.

♡ ♡ ♡

God planned sex in marriage to be an expression of love between a husband and wife. Society, however, has truly exploited sex and tarnished God's great plan. My uncle gave me some excellent advice once. He said, "When a man is ready to marry, he wants a woman who is pure and unstained by immoral behavior. That's why he does not marry a harlot. He wants a woman who will be a faithful and loyal wife and a good role model for his children to be raised by." That's why when peer pressure is overwhelming to conform, one must remember that one's virtue is to be guarded.

————————— ♥ —————————

Virginity is something that can be lost only once, and many (possibly even most) people feel some degree of regret when it is lost too soon. This is especially true with girls, since girls are

> more likely than boys to feel that their relationship with their first partner improved after intercourse. Their lingering regret, despite the improved relationship, suggests that girls place a higher value on virginity *per se*. About half, for instance, want to be virgins when they marry, while only a third of the boys want to marry a virgin. Rather poignantly, 15 percent of the girls who'd already had intercourse said they had wanted to be virgins when they married. 45/73

Regret is a terrible thing to have to live with day after day. We can't change the past, no matter how much we want to. The value that people place on virginity, even people without biblical beliefs, makes us know it has inherent importance.

When we lose something we know is valuable, we feel regret. God wants to protect us from that, so He has reserved sex for marriage. There is no chance of regret when our first sexual experience is with the person we will spend our lives with.

Part of God's provision is that new attitude we are able to have about virginity: It is not something we lose in marriage — it is something we are free to give.

Cindy, twenty-four, is a high school swimming coach from the southwestern United States. She lost her virginity to a man she didn't know or care about, "just for the heck of it." She has drifted in and out of love affairs and one-night stands ever since,

304 ♥ PART 3 — REASONS TO WAIT

not really sold on intercourse as a casual activity but figuring you don't miss a slice from a cut loaf.

"I wish I were still a virgin," she says, echoing a common sentiment. "It would be nice if I could marry someone and we could grow in all ways together as whole people; to have nothing bad to look back on. But I guess I had to get where I am now to know that."

Part of God's provision for sex within the marriage is the openness, honesty, and freedom the permanent relationship brings to physical sharing. This is what He wants us to have, yet when we are sexually involved before marriage, it is exactly what we don't have.

When we forego God's provision and seek sex outside its intended bounds, we not only open ourselves and our sex partner to hurt, we hurt our future spouse, possibly someone we haven't even met yet. As the young woman quoted above said, we may even forget this is a person with feelings, someone who will one day be hurt by our present actions.

The disappointment one's spouse (or spouse-to-be) feels because of the other's inability to wait is a real and understandable emotion. It is something the couple will have to talk about and pray about so that it does not become a point of friction in the future.

Sex in marriage is designed to be a loving act of giving, not an act of taking. God wants us to be able to say, "I have something to give to you regardless of what you have to give to me."

Although sex is an irrevocable act, God can take even the worst situation and make it good. He is able to heal any wound, no matter how deep. But God doesn't want us to have to deal with that kind of resentment or disappointment. His brilliant plan is to protect and provide for us; it is a plan so simple that most people never even grasp it.

A Bond of Love and Trust

You should give your mate your very best, not put her or him at the bottom of your list. Your body is a savings account to give to your mate as a wedding present, not to be spent on anything else.

♡ ♡ ♡

As a Christian, I feel I am going to love the man I marry more than anyone else in the world. If that isn't the case, I shouldn't marry him. Because of this, abstaining from sex before marriage is one way to show my future mate how much I love him. Abstinence shows that my marriage is so important to me I am willing to practice faithfulness to my mate even before we meet. A romantic view? Perhaps. But I want my marriage to be romantic.

♡ ♡ ♡

I want to save myself and my virginity for my wedding night. I believe it is a wedding present and a sign of love for my spouse.

♡ ♡ ♡

Being patient about sex gives you the added security that your partner loves you and has based his decision to marry you on your character and qualities, not on heated passion.

♡ ♡ ♡

There is one more reason a person should wait for marriage to engage in sex. Last July, God gave me the most wonderful man in the world to be my husband. I had asked for Prince Charming, and the Lord gave me *much more* than that. He gave me someone I can share my deepest feelings with, someone I can talk to God with, someone I know will always love me and be faithful to me, someone I am glad I waited for.

On our wedding night, I experienced sex for the first time, and it was with my husband. I wouldn't have wanted to share my first time with *anyone* else. I had no riches or jewels to offer my husband, but he asked for none. All he wanted was me, and that is just what I had to give him — all of me, untouched, his alone. That meant a great deal, and we both knew it. This was a good enough reason for me to wait.

———————— ♥ ————————

As the writers above have shown, God has provided us with a powerful way for us to show love to our marriage partners. When we wait until the wedding night to have sex, we establish a bond of trust and love that has no equal.

When we try to create that bond without marriage, we fall flat. It is a self-defeating process. If we want to show love, we will strive for what is to the greatest benefit of the other person. We will seek to see his (or her) social life stimulated, his intellect challenged, his emotions and spiritual life strengthened, his health protected. None of that is possible in a sexual relationship outside marriage, so any attempt (or supposed attempt) to show love by premarital sex is defeated from the start.

God's command is to limit sex to marriage, a command that protects us from hurting each other and provides a setting in which we *can* express love through sex.

PART 4

HOW TO COPE WITH THE PRESSURE

INTRODUCTION

If we are ever to help our young people say no to sexual pressures, we must be certain we understand what it's like out there in the real world in which most teens live. Earlier we talked about living in a two-culture world. As parents and youth workers most of us live almost entirely in a Judeo-Christian culture. Our teens do not. With the possible exception of their church and their homes, they live in a world that has totally rejected Christian standards and values — especially in the area of sexuality.

What is it really like out there, in a world where young people are more sexually active than at any other time in the history of civilization? If we're over thirty we probably have no idea, no idea at all.

Do we older Christians understand how tough it is to live by biblical sexual standards? Those young people who want to preserve their virginity until marriage are in the minority. Do we realize how powerful the sexual pressures are? Can anyone actually be expected to be celibate in an "oversexed" world?

It is one thing to develop biblical convictions based on 1 Thessalonians 4:3-8, but it is quite a different thing to live these convictions out in our lives and relationships.

We have discussed the media's daily bombardment of young people with messages about sex. Radios, television sets, theater screens, record and cassette players, books, magazines, newspapers — all of them scream out at teens that "sex is normal, available and certainly not restricted to adults, much less to married couples."

Another problem is that our culture offers few, if any, good role models for lovers. The lovers featured in the media know all about lust, but little about true love. Whereas in the Bible true love is fulfilled in bed, in the media "love" begins in bed. And because of the breakdown of the American family, good role models are rapidly disappearing from the home.

Further, there is the incredible pressure of social consensus: "Everyone's doing it!" I'm sure it seems that way to many of our young people, even though everyone is not doing it. Some young people are saying no to premarital sex. Why? Because it's the smart thing to do. It's the right thing to do. If we are believers in Christ, we have the assurance that He came into our lives to set us free from these kinds of social pressure. As Christians we are free to live our lives on the basis of biblical convictions, not social consensus.

One's desire for sex is far greater than one's need for sex. For that reason teens need all the help they can get to cope with the sexual pressure facing them in today's "sex-saturated society." The more help we give them, the more capable they will be of making right choices.

This section is designed to give an extensive array of support systems or helps for teens to say no and then act out their decisions in responsible, loving relationships.

However, please don't read only this section without reading the context of teenage sexuality in the entire book. Only to the extent that you genuinely understand what and why young people are feeling, thinking and doing, can you help them say no!

Two letters to Ann Landers describe how the handling of premarital sexual pressure effects relationships and lives. Those letters contained poems, written by a man and a woman, printed October 24, 1985. The woman's poem reads as follows:

I met him; I liked him.
I liked him; I loved him.
I loved him; I let him.
I let him; I lost him.

The second is written by a man:

I saw her.
I liked her.
I loved her.
I wanted her.
I asked her.
She said no.
I married her.
After sixty years, I still have her — Ft. Worth, Texas. 291/E2

How can we help more teens and young singles say no? Here are some principles developed with the help of Christian young people. They have been tested in the "trenches" where teens and singles are fighting daily for their personal morality.

16

NEW RELATIONSHIPS

1. You Are Not Alone

In their own words:

I feel so alone — as if no one cares about what I'm going through. I wish there were someone I could talk to and confide in, someone who's been where I am and could help me through this. I'm so tired of fighting with myself, fighting back my sexual desires, fighting against the sexual desires of my dates. Sometimes I just want to stop fighting. I'm tempted to give up the battle and give in. During those times when I feel so weary I wish I had someone else to encourage me and keep me going, someone to fight my battle for me, someone to be strong when I am weak.

———————— ♥ ————————

For any teen who has ever felt like that — as if he were completely alone in his battle for sexual purity — I have some good news. *You are not alone.*

The Bible tells us that "The LORD himself goes before you and will be with you, he will never leave you nor forsake you" (Deuteronomy 31:8, NIV). Though we sometimes tell ourselves otherwise, the truth is that God is present with us, each and every moment of our lives. This includes our moments of greatest temptation and even defeat, as well as our times of triumph and victory.

Sometimes our problem lies in translating the "head knowledge" of God's constant presence with us into "heart knowledge." We need to act on what we know to be true. One teen advises his friends, "Talk to the Lord just like you would to any close friend. He's a friend who will stick closer than a brother." Another gives this advice:

> It is hard to withstand the constant peer pressure to have sex, but it is not impossible. With God nothing is impossible. Teens should realize that God is always right by their side — when they are walking down the hall, when they are in the classroom — and He holds their hand as they take a stand for Christ.

God can be with us. If we have received Jesus as Saviour, *He lives within us.* It is Jesus, alive in us, who enables us to say no to sexual involvement when our hormones want to say yes. One young person, recognizing the Source of his strength, says:

> God's Spirit, the essence of purity, empowered me to be free from the relentless drive to give in to sensuality. It was the Holy Spirit, not the skillful rationalizing of my intellect, who gave my sexuality its correct perspective and my life its purposeful discipline.

When we feel as if the Lord cannot understand our struggle, we need to remember that "we do not have a high priest who cannot sympathize with our weaknesses, but one who has been tempted in all things as we are, yet without sin" (Hebrews 4:15, NASB). When we feel that we are fighting a losing battle, let us open our hearts and minds to the Lord, asking Him to give us strength. Let us claim victoriously the words of Paul, "I can do all things through Christ who strengtheneth me." (Philippians 4:13, KJV).

2. God's Perspective on Sex

In their own words:

> We are not to feel guilty about sexual desires. We are all sexual creatures. God made us this way, and it's nothing to be ashamed of, yet it must be controlled. God is not against sex. He made it to be pleasurable and fun within the commitment of marriage. It is something for us to enjoy and feel good about, not guilty about. But when we take this gift and twist it and pervert it to satisfy our own selfish desires, we are disobeying God and must suffer the consequences.

♡ ♡ ♡

"Rejoice with the wife of thy youth. Let her be as the loving hind and pleasant roe; let her breasts satisfy thee at all times; and be thou ravished always with her love" (Proverbs 5:18,19, KJV). The Hebrew word used in this text for *ravished* means "totally absorbed." It is a command to love your mate always.

♡ ♡ ♡

Keep sex in the right perspective. God intended sex to be a beautiful expression of love between a husband and wife, shared privately. "Drink water from your own cistern, and running water from your own well . . . Let your fountain [wife] be blessed, and rejoice with the wife of your youth" (Proverbs 5:15-18).

♡ ♡ ♡

God created sex for reproduction and unity, and also for enjoyment. God is not "down on sex." The Song of Solomon is not only a beautiful love story, but also a wholesome sex manual. Paul not only encourages sex between marriage partners but also encourages it on a regular basis.

───────────── ♥ ─────────────

It is healthy for young people to study the Scriptures and gain a thorough understanding of God's perspective about sex. "The Bible is not a manual on the techniques of sex. It is a guide to the values of sex and the proper perspective of sex in God's plan for man and woman." 96 Such an understanding is essential for anyone who wants to say no to premarital sex.

God designed and created sex. It is a carefully planned aspect of our humanness, intended for our benefit and His glory. Anyone who questions whether sex is good is actually questioning God's goodness.

In the Beginning Was Sex

To put sex into God's perspective we need to go back to the beginning.

"And the LORD God formed man of the dust of the ground, and breathed into his nostrils the breath of life; and man became a living soul" (Genesis 2:7, KJV). Adam was the culmination of God's creative plan. "God saw every thing that He had made, and, behold, it was very good" (Genesis 1:31, KJV).

Yet, after the creation of man, God observed that something was not good. "And the LORD God said, It is not good that the man should be alone" (Genesis 2:18, KJV). God's creation, although good, was incomplete. God had "created man in His own image" (Genesis 1:27, KJV). This made man a social being, because God

Himself is a social being. Anyone created in "God's image" has the God-given ability to relate to others — to God and to creatures like himself. Good as God's creation was, it was not good that Adam was alone.

It is interesting to note that God didn't solve Adam's loneliness problem by creating more men. Instead, He created woman. "Eve was like Adam, yet unlike him. Same humanity, different gender. Man and woman were equal but not the same. Their oneness was not a uniformity stemming from sameness but a unity transcending differentness." 62/176 With the debut of the second sex, God's creation was now complete.

It is important for young people to feel good about being male and female and to accept their sexuality as a gift from God. The psalmist says, "I praise you because I am fearfully and wonderfully made." 138 The creation of the human body, with its sex drives and organs is something to thank Him for. There are no reasons to be ashamed. From the beginning, human sexuality is seen as a reflection of the character of God and its existence is described as "very good."

As you study God's perspective on sex, three things become apparent:

1. God is pro-sex. He created sex, and He wants us to enjoy it to the fullest. If anyone has any doubts, read the Song of Solomon.

2. Sexual intercourse is intended for oneness. There is no expression of unity between a man and a woman that is more intimate than this. Oneness, along with reproduction, is one of the primary purposes of sex.

3. God designed sex for marriage — it is meant to take place between a husband and wife. Since oneness is the primary purpose for sexual intercourse, it is evident why God has restricted it to the context of marriage.

Sex Is Designed to Be Enjoyable and Fulfilling

God intended for sex to be enjoyable for a husband and wife. Sex is designed to be a fulfilling and enjoyable experience within the context of marriage. However, enjoyable sex is not selfish sex.

> Sex is fulfilled not with a selfish attitude, but with a giving one. Paul states in 1 Corinthians 7:3-5 that fulfillment in the sexual relationship of husband and wife is found as their mutual needs are met. It is not, What can you do for me? but, What can I do for you? 96

Sex Is Oneness

Eve not only provided companionship for Adam, but her arrival made possible a special kind of male-female unity or oneness — physically, psychologically and spiritually. "For this reason a man will leave his father and mother and be united to his wife, and they will become one flesh" (Genesis 2:24, NIV).

> This means not just the blending of bodies, but also the merging of minds, the assimilation of souls. Genesis 2, the last account of a world without sin, ends gloriously with two sexual beings, unclothed and unashamed, free to enjoy sex. God looks on their nakedness and their sexual union with the smile of complete approval. 62/177

Marriage, in God's plan, is the permanent bonding of two people. Paul uses the analogy of Christ and the Church to provide a deeper understanding of that union (Ephesians 5:31,32).

> Based on that relationship, divorce is not an option for two believers. To a culture that lives for the moment and marries for the moment, the Christians' concept of lifelong commitment to one person stands out in sharp contrast. 109/8

God's Specific Plan

> Know that there is a God in heaven who cares for you very much. He has designed you and your sexuality for a specific plan in your life — to take place in the context of marriage.

———————— ♥ ————————

It helps young people say no if they realize that God has a special purpose for their lives and a specific plan for their sexuality, within the context of marriage.

There are three basic reasons for sex in marriage: procreation, identification, and recreation.

Procreation: for the purpose of having children and creating a family.

Identification: for the purpose of developing "oneness" between a husband and a wife in three important dimensions — the physical, psychological and spiritual.

Recreation: for the purpose of pleasure and enjoyment.

The pleasure that sex provides — the very reason it is so appealing even outside of marriage — is God's creation. When, according to God's plan, sex is experienced within the context of marriage, the pleasure is maximized. In the commitment of marriage — without guilt and without any sense of "lustful taking" — the act of intercourse becomes indescribably enjoyable and beautiful.

Think of the beautiful compositions of Mozart or Beethoven — it is incredible the number of rules these composers strictly adhered to regarding intervals, rhythms, chord progressions and so on. Yet their music is far more lovely, harmonious and free than the discord that results when no rules are followed. Rules, and especially God's rules, are good discipline that yield greater peace and joy in our lives than we could ever imagine!

If You've "Gone Too Far"

If you are already involved in sexual immorality, it isn't too late. God will forgive you and help you begin a relationship that is pleasing in His sight. No matter what you've done, no matter how many times you've done it, Jesus Christ has the capacity to heal, to cleanse, and to purify.

--------------------♥--------------------

Young people who are sexually active today need a new beginning. Most college students, even those from Christian homes, are not innocent in the area of sex. Increasingly that is becoming true for high school students. Many young people have already "gone further" than they may want to admit.

The problem is that sexual sin can cause a person to lose all hope of ever again living a chaste lifestyle. These young people have resigned themselves to a life of promiscuity, sometimes just because of one bad experience. "After what I've done, what difference does it make? It doesn't matter any more." If one has yielded to sexual pressures, it is all too easy to adopt the attitude of the escaped convict who is fleeing a death sentence for murder: "I've got nothing to lose!"

Without knowing the reality of God's forgiveness and restoration, many young people assume that because of their past the future is already lost. We need to understand that one crime does not doom a person to the life of a criminal. It's never too late to begin saying no.

Therefore we must begin with forgiveness. Forgiveness is not a license for sexual permissiveness, but rather an opportunity to make a fresh start. With God we can have a new beginning. We don't have to feel trapped into continuing down a particular wrong-way path. Through forgiveness, God can make possible the choice of a new path in which we can walk according to His principles.

One teen's remarks about forgiveness were especially encouraging:

You may be feeling very guilty now. That's because real guilt is caused by real sin and needs to have real forgiveness. You may feel that God doesn't love you or won't forgive what you've done because He feels so strongly against it. But I can tell you that there is nothing you could ever do to keep God from loving you or to make Him stop. His love is unconditional and no matter what you do, God is always standing there with open arms, ready to receive you when you turn back to Him. He wants to take your sins and throw them into the depths of the seas . . . and as Corrie Ten Boom said, put up a "No Fishing" sign.

Remember the story of Jesus and the woman taken in adultery? Jesus said, "He who is without sin, cast the first stone." Because He extended forgiveness and acceptance, I'm sure that woman never forgot His request to "go and sin no more."

I keep a little sign on my desk which says, "Remember, *today* is the first day of the rest of your life." There's always a new beginning.

A young newlywed says:

> My fiancé and I knew we had to get out of our sexual immorality. With God's help we did not engage in sex during the nine months until our wedding . . . The first time we made love after our wedding, tears of joy streamed down my face. I experienced the true beauty of the sexual relationship as God intended it . . . Choose to enjoy that special sexual relationship that God has designed to be exhilarating and refreshing within marriage. Choose to wait.

When we understand God's perspective on sex, we realize why sex should be experienced only within the sanctity and security of a total commitment of marriage. We can understand why it is important to say no to premarital sexual involvement.

We must recognize and respect God-designed limits. Maximum enjoyment of sex comes when God's guidelines are followed, His protective commandments are obeyed, and His sexual boundaries are observed.

For more information on God's specific plan regarding being forgiven — and forgiving others — see the section entitled "Forgiveness," beginning on page 416.

3. Intimacy With Jesus

Establishing a Relationship

Perhaps one of the greatest reasons for teenage sexual activity is found in the teen's need for intimacy. Our need for intimate, fulfilling relationships is a valid one. Psychologists tell us that the greatest human need is to love and be loved. We long to share ourselves totally with another person. That's what *true intimacy* is: sharing every part of our life with someone else. We all desire someone who will love and accept us for who we are, someone whom we can trust and open up to without fear of rejection. We desire love and intimacy, but we don't know how to find it.

Because we don't know where to find *true* intimacy, we often pursue the illusion of "instant intimacy." Of course, the quickest, easiest, most convenient way to become seemingly intimate with someone is through sex. But the problem with instant intimacy is that it creates an illusion of love that is no more than skin deep, which ultimately leads to frustration.

Sexual intimacy alone can never fulfill our deepest needs. There is, however, a source of lasting love, acceptance and intimacy that will meet our every need. The source of this intimacy is a personal relationship with Jesus Christ. He is the only one who is able to love us constantly and consistently with a flawless, unconditional love. If you are a parent, a youth worker, or a teen, and have never experienced this kind of personal relationship with Jesus, I'd like to share four points with you that can change your life.

1. Not only does God love you perfectly but He also desires to give you the best in all areas of your life, including your relationships — and, in its proper context, your sex life.

2. We all have a basic attitude problem of rebelliousness and self-centeredness that leads us to "push" the limits of God's commands (not only in regard to sex but in other areas also). The Bible calls this attitude *sin* and says that there are penalties for sin: separation from God and inability to experience all He wants to give us. The Bible also says that there is no way we can bridge this separation on our own.

3. God has solved the problem of separation by sending His Son, Jesus, to die for us, thereby paying the penalty for our sin. Then Jesus was raised from the dead to give us a new life, opening up the way to God so that we can experience His intimate love for us.

4. We each individually have a choice to make. We can choose to accept or reject the provision that already has been made for us. If we reject it, we can continue searching unsuccessfully for true intimacy on our own. If we accept it, God will fulfill our needs for love and intimacy as we experience His perfect love and plan for our lives.

What I'm talking about here is *not a religion but a relationship,* a relationship with the person of Jesus Christ. If you'd like to enter into this intimate relationship with God through His Son, Jesus, I'd like to invite you to pray the following prayer, keeping in mind that it is not the words you say that are important but the attitude of your heart.

> Dear Jesus, I need You. Thank You for dying on the cross to pay the penalty for my sins. I desire at this moment to begin a close relationship with You. Please come into my life as my Savior and fill my heart with Your love. Thank you for forgiving my sins and giving me eternal life. Help me to live for You from now on, and make me the kind of person You want me to be.

Once we begin a relationship with Jesus, we need to build that relationship continually. Whether a person is a brand-new believer or has had a relationship with Christ for many years, in order to be able to say no to sex, he needs to develop and maintain a close, intimate walk with God.

In the words of our teens:

> We are only human. We need to be loved and to have the feeling of being accepted. The love needs to be given to us at home, but if it is not given to you there, go to your church and get it. Do not let the empty space in your heart leave you vulnerable and open to sin. Fill your heart with the Lord. He gives us love overflowing forever and ever. We will never need to depend on anyone else so long as we keep Him near. If our peers do not accept us, who cares? We know what we want out of life and we do not compromise it. There is someplace else to turn besides just to our friends. Turn to God.

♡ ♡ ♡

> Even sex at its height cannot erase the loneliness of the innermost heart. There exists only one source to fill that need. Jesus Christ is the only one who can satisfy those deepest longings of your heart.

♡ ♡ ♡

> It's important to stay in a close relationship with Jesus. My boyfriend and I have discovered that if we start drifting away from Jesus, we are more vulnerable to our sexual feelings. If your relationship with God is not right, then no other relationship can be right either. If both of you are right with God, it is so much easier to go to Him when you need assistance.

———————————— ♥ ————————————

Developing an intimate walk with Christ will do at least three important things for you:

1. Your need for intimacy will begin to be fulfilled; your relationship with God is comparable to the growing process of a love affair. Your loneliness will be eased, so there will no longer be a need to fill that void in your life through sexual activity.

2. As you develop a closer relationship with God, there will come a natural desire to please Him. Out of love for Him you will want to do what He commands and will desire to abstain from sexual involvement before marriage.

3. You will have available to you the power of God to resist temptation.

As 1 Corinthians 10:13 reassures us, "No temptation has overtaken you but such as is common to man; and God is faithful, who will not allow you to be tempted beyond what you are able, but with the temptation will provide the way of escape also, that you may be able to endure it" (NASB).

The section, "Doing What Comes Supernaturally," in Part 5 (pages 404-409), will give you an in-depth look at how to tap into the availability of the power of God through being filled with the Holy Spirit. We also recommend the *Handbook for Christian Maturity* by Bill Bright, which will give you a thorough study of the ten basic steps that can lead you to spiritual maturity in all of your personal life.

Weakness in Handling Temptation

We like to pretend we are able to handle anything. It takes humility to admit we have a problem with something. Yet, when we pretend we can handle any kind of sexual temptation, we are just setting ourselves up for failure. As one young woman points out:

> No one is immune from the possibility of falling into sexual immorality. Scripture says that pride comes before a fall. In the same way our pride in thinking "I don't have any problem controlling my sexual desires" is often the warning sign that we are getting ready to tumble.

Another teen comments:

> Young people often find themselves in situations they can't say no to. So many times we say, "Oh, I can handle it if I'm ever in that situation." We don't decide before going in. Instead we try to stop in the middle. It's like reading a good book; once you've started, it's hard to put it down. Sex is the same way. Once you've begun, it's hard to stop.

So, don't venture to the edge of your sexual control — you'll probably find you're not as strong as you thought. If you insist on placing yourself in compromising situations, sooner or later you're going to find yourself yielding. The first step in avoiding immorality is to admit to yourself and to God that you are weak and vulnerable. When you acknowledge your weakness, you give yourself motivation for consciously avoiding tempting situations and relying on God's strength through the Holy Spirit, rather than on your own strength.

Finally, keep your focus on the Lord, realizing that where you are weak He is strong and His strength will never fail as we saw in 1 Corinthians 10. As one teen said:

> Temptation will surely come. Jesus himself was tempted. The only thing we should fear is that we might think ourselves so great and independent that we take our eyes off of Jesus. How quickly we give in to wrong. But Jesus never designed us to live this life apart from Him, and He has promised to bring us victory.

Meditating on His Word

> Psalm 119:9 says, "How can a young man stay pure? By reading your word and following its rules" (TLB). It is easier to turn away from sin when you are concentrating on God's Word.

♡ ♡ ♡

> Another precaution I have taken is to immerse myself in God's Word. I have made it an absolute *must* to spend time reading the Bible every night before I go to bed. That has been a protective shield for me.

———————————— ♥ ————————————

We live in a world that is constantly exposing us to a variety of images and sounds. If they are negative, they detract from the principles that God has for us. If they are positive, they reinforce His principles. Therefore it is important to meditate on God's principles as a means of avoiding and controlling sexual temptation.

One of the Proverbs says, "As a person thinks, so he is." Basically, what we set our minds on, we will do. World class athletes are a good example of this. When the time comes to perform, they visualize their goal in their minds before going for it. Whether pole vaulting or high jumping, the champion athlete visualizes an ideal vault or jump and then tries to do what has been visualized. If the visualization is faulty, so is the performance. A poor mental image will usually be followed by failure.

When Dick Fosberry was doing the high jump in the 1968 Olympic Games, before he took off for his jump he would rock back and forth for almost a full minute. As co-author Dick Day watched, he could sense that the athlete's mind was not focusing on where he had missed before, nor on what his competition had done. No, he was visualizing the ideal form necessary for going over the bar at the present height. Then he did what he visualized.

Temptation begins with a visual or aural stimulus. The stimulus produces a thought. The mind meditates on that thought. That meditation, in turn, brings about the determination to do what the mind has been thinking about.

STIMULUS + THOUGHT + MEDITATION +
DETERMINATION = **ACTION**

The way to break this cycle when it's going the wrong direction is to discipline one's mind. Now, with the tremendous sexual orientation of our culture, we can't always avoid exposure to sexual stimuli. Remember that sexual thoughts or feelings are not sinful, but they can lead to temptation. What counts is what we do with those thoughts and feelings. We have to make a choice and deal with them immediately.

One obvious thing that can be done to discipline the mind is to choose what goes into it. For example, it's much easier to squelch sexual temptation when one is reading the Bible than when one is looking at *Playboy*.

Now, I am not the disciplined type at all, but I read the Bible every night — no matter how tired I am or how late it is. Sometimes I'll read for an hour, sometimes for just ten minutes. I also make sure that I spend time in prayer at my bedside before getting in. You know, after having made this decision in my life — and it's been close to a year now — I am absolutely amazed at how God's wonderful grace has protected me.

———————— ♥ ————————

Let this mind be in you, which was also in Christ Jesus. 186

It is difficult, if not impossible, to entertain a negative, lustful, or impure thought if one's mind is focused on Jesus. One reason is that Jesus was never lustful or impure. So if a teen wants to say no, he can saturate his mind with God's Word and focus his attention on Jesus Christ.

My son, keep my words,
And treasure my commandments within you.
Keep my commandments and live,
And my teaching as the apple of your eye.
Bind them on your fingers;

Write them on the tablet of your heart.
Say to wisdom, "You are my sister,"
And call understanding your intimate friend;
That they may keep you from an adulteress,
From the foreigner who flatters with her words.

Proverbs 7:1-5, NASB

Other helpful verses include: 1 Corinthians 10:13; Philippians 4:8; Colossians 3:2.

Pleasing Him

Scripture also tells us that we cannot serve two masters (Matthew 6:24). This is especially true in the sexual area of our life. We cannot follow both the desires of our bodies and the desires of God's Spirit who calls us to sexual purity. Our sexual desires tell us to please ourselves, to do what feels good at the moment. God's Spirit calls us to please Him, to deny the cravings of our body when those cravings cannot be satisfied in a manner pleasing to Him. In this battle between flesh and Spirit we must consciously choose to please the Lord rather than ourselves.

As one young teen emphasizes, "When you are in your teen years, your only concern should be pleasing the Lord, not your peers. Your friends could, and probably will, turn on you, get mad at you, or even hate you, but the Lord will never leave you or forsake you."

Another teen, with strong motivations for saying no to premarital sex, explains,

> For the sake of love (love for God, love for your future mate, love for yourself), WAIT! If you love that person you are dating, if you love the person you are going to marry, if you love God, you will wait because . . . "love is patient, love is never selfish . . . it does not demand its own way" (1 Corinthians 13:4,5). Why wait until marriage to engage in sex? For the sake of love. That's why.

Practicing self-denial to please God builds strong Christian character in your life.

> Character is a word used for the quality of moral excellence that distinguishes your life. Character is not inherited from your parents. You have to form your character as you grow. Christian character gives evidence of the lordship of Jesus Christ in the life of the believer. 36/6-8

As we meditate on God's Word, and seek to please Him, we will develop important Christ-like qualities of character: love, joy, peace, patience, kindness, goodness, faithfulness, gentleness, self-control.

4. A Set of Convictions

In their own words:

It is difficult to wait, to be self-controlled, and not give in when "everybody else is doing it," but convictions and strong character are great benefits for any of us to possess.

♡ ♡ ♡

How are young persons to answer the unchecked invitations to be sexually indulgent? If an individual does not already possess the inner convictions to delay such "gratification" until after marriage, where will he draw his strength?

♡ ♡ ♡

You need to have a good set of moral values and know what Jesus would want you to do.

♡ ♡ ♡

Living on a college campus, I am free to live my life as I want — even my mother offered to buy me birth control pills. I have to live by my own personal convictions.

♡ ♡ ♡

The decision to have or not have sex before marriage has to be a personal decision, made in one's own heart. If you wait until the pressure is on, chances are . . . you'll be left with a broken heart because of your own failure to make a firm decision.

♡ ♡ ♡

Thinking right about God determines right thinking. Right thinking determines right actions.

♡ ♡ ♡

We must state our firm convictions against immorality and declare our identity in God, for "I have been crucified with Christ; and it is no longer I who live, but Christ lives in me" [Galatians 2:20, NASB].

———————— ♥ ————————

People with strong convictions are willing to risk nonconformity with their peers because of their convictions about themselves — "That's not the kind of person I want to be" — and their convictions about values — "I don't think that's right, and I'm not going to do it!"

Developing positive convictions can help a young person face negative peer pressure without giving in. A person without convictions will generally follow the lead of whatever group of people he or she happens to be with. However, someone who can stand up and say "Hey, I've got my reasons" will usually have the strength to act independently of other people.

The Word of God is our only basis for strong convictions. Scriptures are clear about sexual activities to be avoided for our own good, such as premarital sex (fornication) and extramarital sex (adultery).

"Flee fornication. Every sin that a man doeth is without the body; but he that committeth fornication sinneth against his own body. What? know ye not that your body is the temple of the Holy Ghost which is in you, which ye have of God, and ye are not your own? For ye are bought with a price: therefore glorify God in your body, and in your spirit, which are God's" (1 Corinthians 6:18-20, KJV).

That means that we no longer own the rights to our bodies! God has paid for us with the very high price of the blood of His only Son, Jesus Christ. Not only that, but the Spirit of God dwells within us! Are those not two very good reasons to yield to God's commandments for our bodies?

---- ♥ ----

For this is the will of God, your sanctification; that is, that you abstain from sexual immorality; that each of you know how to possess his own vessel in sanctification and honor, not in lustful passion, like the Gentiles who do not know God (1 Thessalonians 4:3-5, NASB).

Don't you realize that your bodies are actually parts and members of Christ? So should I take part of Christ and join him to a prostitute? Never! And don't you know that if a man joins himself to a prostitute she becomes a part of him and he becomes a part of her? For God tells us in the Scripture that in His sight the two become one person. But if you give yourself to the Lord, you and Christ are joined together as one person. That is why I say to run from sex sin. No other sin affects the body as this one does. When you sin this sin it is against your own body. Haven't you yet learned that your body is the home of the Holy Spirit God gave you? . . . Your own body does not belong to you. For God has bought you with a great price. So use every part of your body to give glory back to God, because He owns it (1 Corinthians 6:15-20, TLB).

Certainly scriptural passages like those above are clear about the quality of sexual behavior expected of Christians. The Bible teaches us to refrain from sex outside marriage and later to enjoy sex within marriage.

But it is not enough to know only passages dealing specifically with sexual behavior. It is insufficient to know only God's
moral standards and principles. Young persons also need to have
a basis for answering such questions as Who am I? Why am I
here? Where am I going? Who is God? How does He see me?
What is unconditional love? They need a total Christian world
view. What is a Christian world view?

We each have a world view. We may not be able to articulate
it or explain it, but we all have one. It is not some vague philosophical concept, but rather a personal perspective on the totality
of life, a controlling force in each of our lives. Our world view
is the sum total of everything recorded within our mind. Rooted
deep down in our psyche, our world view affects all aspects of
behavior, including one's sexual relationships and moral behavior.

Most young people today have world views not based entirely
on God's truth (if at all). They have been programmed with views
about sexuality that are contrary to God's views.

The Need for De-programming

During the Korean War a number of captured American
servicemen were subjected by the enemy to experiences that were
intended to "program" their minds and thus control or change
their behavior. Such a mind-altering process has come to be
known as "brainwashing."

Interestingly, the apostle Paul was concerned about a related
process when he wrote his epistle to the Romans: "Don't let the
world around you squeeze you into its own mold . . . " Almost
2,000 years later, American prisoners-of-war in Communist prisons
were "squeezed" by the "world" around them "into its own mold."

Most young people today have also in one sense been
brainwashed. The media has had an impact on teens and singles
and so have their experiences with parents and peers. Their
world has squeezed them into its mold.

In contemporary psychological terminology, young people
have been "scripted" by their education and the media, and also
by their life experiences, particularly with their families. This
scripting, which can be either negative or positive, has a significant
effect on their personal identity, self-worth and sense of well-being.
As a result, they may be seriously handicapped in their ability
to develop the foundational convictions needed to say no to
premarital sexual pressures.

The Family — A Common Source of Negative Scripting

A person's convictions about love and sexuality really begin with the role modeling of his (or her) parents. Convictions are built as children watch the actions of their parents and hear explanations about why they act as they do. That's why God gave us the family — to be the environment in which children learn and develop their own convictions about love, sex and marriage. Regrettably, as has been discussed earlier, that critical learning process often is malfunctioning.

For one thing, many of the parents of today's teens have little or no convictions themselves about sexual values or morals. It is difficult for a child who grows up with people who have no strong convictions to develop any personal convictions of his or her own, particularly in such an area as tempting as the sexual. This situation shows us that a process of remolding is necessary for both the teens *and* their parents.

> Let God re-mold your minds from within, so that you may prove in practice that the plan of God for you is good, meets all His demands, and moves toward the goal of true maturity (Romans 12:2, Phillips).

The remolding process involves three essential factors: God's truth, God's Spirit and God's people. First, we need to teach the key biblical principles (truth) that relate to sexual morality. Second, we need the Holy Spirit to be the facilitator of the remolding process. Third, God's people — parents and church leaders — need to be models of the convictions we want our youth to develop.

If we are going to help provide young people with the convictional basis for controlling their sex lives, we need to help them find an environment in which that remolding or reprogramming of their minds can begin. That is the only way our young people can erase or overcome the results of having the world's sexual stimuli, poor parental modeling and hurting relationships squeeze them into its mold.

When we work with children from homes where the family has failed, the body of Christ must try to provide an environment in which God can remold their minds. We must become a "parafamily" to them. As Christian brothers and sisters, or even "paraparents," we must become the role models these young people never had. It is not enough to communicate data, no matter how doctrinally correct our words may be. Only in the context of loving relationships can truth be internalized and made a living part of one's life.

Learning the Whole of God's Truth

As we mentioned earlier, young people need to know the whole truth, not merely the truth about sexual behavior. They need to know that:

they are created in God's image, with the ability to have relationships with God and with other human beings;

they have value and worth because of the price that the Father paid for them: the death of His Son;

God loves them with unconditional love and desires a relationship with them;

God's love and acceptance are the basis for their own security;

the way to express their love to God is to serve others;

through serving others they can gain a sense of significance and identity.

An understanding of these truths, learned not by rote but in the context of loving relationships, is the Christian's basis for all behavior and all relationships, including the sexual.

Without this basis, sex is reduced to a matter of hormones and ultimately becomes nothing more than *lust*. But when sexual relationships are seen from the perspective of a Christian world view, sex is elevated to its proper place alongside marriage and love. A person with these convictions will have a much easier time controlling his or her hormones because true love will be the motivating force rather than lust. Remember: Lust can't wait to get, whereas love can't wait to give.

Owning One's Own Convictions

A young person's convictions must ultimately come from his (or her) own experiences and study of God's Word, not from another person. They must not merely be "head knowledge." They must be internalized deep within the psyche. The young person must "own" his convictions. Only then will those convictions be respected by others. One teen realizes this:

A simple "I believe sex belongs only in marriage" will be respected, but you have to be decided and firm in your conviction or you will not convince anyone else about your sincerity.

As we mentioned, the role of the Holy Spirit is a key factor in remolding our minds. We cannot live out our convictions apart from the indwelling power of the Holy Spirit. One aspect of the fruit of the Spirit is self-control. Other aspects are gentleness, kindness, and desiring the well-being of the other person.

Relationships Build Convictions

How do we help young people develop strong convictions? We don't do it by superimposing our views on them. We can't force people to accept our convictions with a "believe this — or else!"

Let's look at the model of Jesus. When Jesus called His disciples He didn't say, "First of all, you have to subscribe to my ethical convictions, my doctrines." He simply said, "Follow me." Then in the context of a loving relationship, in which Jesus accepted them and encouraged them, those men became willing to be accountable to their Lord. They grew in their understanding of the doctrines and truths of the faith, and they developed convictions that enabled many of them to face a martyr's death. It began, not with subscribing only to the doctrinal convictions of Jesus, but with making a commitment to a loving, accepting person.

A young man recognizes the importance of preparing for this commitment:

When I realize a sexual opportunity . . . I will react either according to the environmental stimuli, or according to a predetermined strategy. If I have no convictions, I will surely find myself in a compromising situation and will be overcome by passion. As a Christian, it was and is enough for me that God has said in the Bible that Christians should not have sex outside marriage. Anyone who claims to believe in the Bible and knows what it commands about this issue can have no other view. God has our ultimate good in mind when He gives us principles to live by . . . It is ironic that the very thing sought by sexually active singles eludes their grasp because of the action they take.

Another young person says:

Convictions are the things that make people rise to the top. It wasn't by chance that the climber found himself at the top of Mt. Everest one day. It took great conviction, careful planning, and knowing what to avoid. I would like a set of convictions that will cause us to be different; to rise to the top; to be a light to the world around us. A set of convictions that we could and would die for. At the top of that list should be the conviction of where our dating and sex life are going to go; and how far we're going to go. If we were to allow ourselves simply to drift in this area of our lives, we would be no different from the rest of our sick and dying world out there. Now, I don't know about you, but I don't want to be numbered with them. They're going nowhere fast.

A seventeen-year-old guy sums up well how one must

question sexual involvement based upon personal convictions:

> When it comes to this, I have learned that I must constantly use my mind to evaluate my situation realistically, and with that I have to ask myself the risk questions: Am I willing to risk destroying the respect that we have for each other? Am I willing to risk creating long-term feelings of guilt because of a decision made in two seconds? Am I willing to risk destroying a good relationship? Am I willing to give up everything that I have always valued as a Christian? After asking myself these questions, I realize that we, she as well as I, are too important to allow momentary urges to change the shape of the Christian life we have been living and have left to live.

Standing up for convictions will result in conflict, not conformity. Teens must be aware that they are going to run into conflict with their friends as they develop and act on their convictions. Yet by developing convictions they will be rewarded with self-respect and maturity.

A young woman expresses it this way:

> Both fathers — heavenly and earthly — instilled some deep, yet healthy fears in me that have been valuable in my dating life. I am so limited in my "touching relationships" with the men I date (only committed Christian guys — or none at all) because I know that I want it all in marriage. I'm not going to be giving my virginity away in bits and pieces — a kiss here, a fondle there. No way. My wedding night is going to be something else!

5. A Christian Conscience

In their own words:

> A conscience is a collective of attitudes and beliefs that we monitor our behavior with.

♡ ♡ ♡

> If you let your sense of right and wrong be your guide, you'll be giving yourself the gift of self-respect.

♡ ♡ ♡

> If my girlfriend and I did not feel bothered by our consciences, perhaps it was because we hadn't fully developed a Christian conscience.

♡ ♡ ♡

> My sweeping passions would doubtlessly have led me into the grief of lost virginity, but for God's presence in my conscience . . .

———————— ♥ ————————

God has equipped each of us with a kind of moral compass, or prompter, which we call the conscience. C. S. Lewis illustrates the working of the conscience this way: If we see a man who can't swim fall into a river, we will have two conflicting thoughts. One advises us to jump in and save him, and a second advises us not to try, because we might get hurt or even drown. But there is also a third voice that says, "Whether you succeed in doing it or not, you ought to try to save him." This third voice is the conscience.

Our conscience monitors our behavior and reminds us to do the "right thing." We may argue with it, disagree with it, or even try to silence it, but it continues to nag us about any behavior that conflicts with our world view — how we see the world. If we see the world according to God's principles, our conscience will reflect that viewpoint. If we see our world from a nonbiblical viewpoint, our conscience will be effectively disabled in the area of moral guidance.

The conscience is created in such a way that we can determine how and how much it works. It can be sensitized or desensitized by the response we make to it. The kinds of people we admire and spend time with, the ideas we entertain, the media we see and hear, all have a part in shaping our conscience. Squelching its promptings can silence it. One teen says:

> A conscience can be a manmade thing. When something is done repeatedly, any doubts about it seem to wither. Compromise after compromise inevitably desensitizes us to the reality of what we were doing.

A young woman in college wrote:

> I was raised in a good Christian home. I was always taught that sex before marriage was wrong. When my boyfriend and I began to get involved sexually, I felt guilty at first. Before long, I couldn't understand why I ever felt bad at all.

God has given us the freedom to participate in the shaping of our conscience. It can be shrunk or enlarged, dulled or sensitized, depending on how we respond to it. If I, as a Christian, listen to my conscience, I can become more sensitive to the Holy Spirit's voice as He seeks to guide my behavior through it.

How sensitive is your teen's conscience? Has it been weakened by a post-Christian or nonbiblical world view? Has it been disabled by ignoring it? Here are some questions for teens to ask themselves as they evaluate the condition of their conscience in the area of sexuality.

Are you doing things now that you once said you would never do?

Was there ever a time when you looked down on others for doing what you are now doing?

Are you doing things now, without feeling guilt, that once bothered you?

Have you allowed a boyfriend or girlfriend to dull your conscience by going further and further sexually?

If any of the answers is *yes,* the teen is in the process of desensitizing his (or her) conscience. Unless it is restored to normal functioning, his conscience soon will be useless to protect him against sexual pressure.

How can one's conscience be restored? First, stop ignoring it and begin listening to it.

Remember what a person puts into his mind directly affects his conscience. "Whatever is true . . . whatever is pure . . . whatever is lovely . . . think about these things."

A friend of mine told me how shocked he had been the first time he saw sexual intercourse portrayed on the screen of a movie theater. He admitted he isn't bothered at all by those scenes today. Repeated exposure to certain kinds of movies, television programming, books, records and magazines can dull our consciences.

How can we develop a Christian conscience? By developing a Christian world view outlook. Again, this is done through God's truth, with the empowering of His Spirit and with the help of His people. Remember that Paul said to Timothy, "The goal of our instruction is love from a pure heart and a good conscience and a sincere faith" (1 Timothy 1:5, NASB).

Here are some simple suggestions you can use to help a person develop a working Christian conscience:

Ask the Holy Spirit's help to cleanse and restore your conscience.

Flood your mind with God's principles about life, love and values.

Limit your relationships to mature Christians who already have developed a Christian conscience.

17

PREVENTIVE MEASURES

1. Set Standards Beforehand

In their own words:

Sexual desires are practically impossible to harness once let loose. It is important to stop the process before it begins.

♡ ♡ ♡

Set your standards. Write down what you will and will not do on a date.

♡ ♡ ♡

You must determine where you want to end . . . before you begin.

♡ ♡ ♡

Set your standards NOW, not when you're deep into a relationship. Set them according to what is right in the eyes of God.

♡ ♡ ♡

I have to live by my own convictions, and for me this has meant setting strict standards in the area of purity.

♡ ♡ ♡

Back when our relationship began, we made a mutual agreement that we would not have sex until after we were married. Because we had set our standards from the very beginning, we knew deep down that it would be morally wrong to become physically involved.

♡ ♡ ♡

Draw a line that you will not cross over. Define those areas you think are restricted to marriage. Consider these areas off limits.

♡ ♡ ♡

We put time limits on our kissing . . .

♡ ♡ ♡

There are many strong temptations. But there are ways to avoid potentially dangerous situations. This is something that you need to decide beforehand or it will be almost impossible to control.

♡ ♡ ♡

Don't test your limits. Don't play games with sexuality. Don't experiment to find out how far you can go without sinning. Set limits and stick to them.

♡ ♡ ♡

Don't put yourself in a position to be tempted.

——————————— ♥ ———————————

Remember, the time to look for a fire escape is before the building catches on fire.

Daniel found this to be true. When faced with overwhelming odds to compromise his moral convictions, this teen already had decided: "But Daniel made up his mind that he would not defile himself with the king's choice food or with the wine which he drank; so he sought permission from the commander of the officials that he might not defile himself" (Daniel 1:8, NASB).

Young people need to be encouraged to set limits for sexual activity before they go out on a date, even before any relationship begins. As someone has said, "It is much easier to break no standard than it is to break some standard. Don't just slide; decide!" If a person waits to set his or her standards until their hormones are aroused they'll probably "blow it."

If they haven't done so, I suggest that a young person sit down and set standards about how far he or she intends to go on a date. It is best if this process is completed long before the teen comes close to involvement in any compromising situations.

What are some guidelines for setting sexual standards? For

Christians, the answer is clear: Begin with God's principles as presented in His Word.

How do Christian young people "draw the line"? Here are some examples:

> I have made a commitment not to have any kind of physical relationship with a man before I'm married. Not even kissing. It seems odd to people in this day and age, because sex is taken so lightly and kissing is just for fun. But how can I think thoughts that are "pure and honorable and lovely" (Philippians 4:8) when I am pressed close to someone's chest? How can I possibly set my mind on "things above" (Colossians 3:2) when someone's mouth feels so warm on mine?

♡ ♡ ♡

> Abstinence is the best preventative. You cannot finish something you never start. Refraining from even nominal physical contact until permanent commitment has been made may be the best for you.

This is the standard I adopted before I married: I will treat a woman on a date the same way I want some other man to treat the woman I will someday marry. In other words, I decided ahead of time to act on dates in such a way that I would never be afraid of my wife meeting any of my former dates.

We also recommend that young people share their standards with their dates. It's amazing how it clears the air for a couple to talk over their dating standards as they begin a relationship. Doing so also minimizes the frustration and anger caused by false expectations. For example, if a young woman doesn't let her date know her standards early on, she had better be prepared for a furious response when the guy who tries to violate her standards gets stopped. It's so much better for each person concerned to share his or her standards openly from the beginning. It also develops a kind of accountability. When the other person knows what the standards are, it's not quite so easy for the first one to forget them either.

Once they've set their standards, young people should be encouraged to stick to them, even when they think they've met "Mr." or "Ms. Right."

_____

> We were going to get married. For the first time, going beyond the usual hugs and kisses seemed justifiable. The absolutes I had held on to before disappeared into thin air and were no longer absolutes to me. I firmly believe now that this agony would not have been half so bad if I had not let go of my absolutes. Not

only was this the loss of a dear and loved friend, it was the loss of one who had been part of me. However, as I look back now, the loss of the man was minor. The real heartbreak lay in the confusion and depression that engulfed me.

♡ ♡ ♡

Perhaps you can't change society now. But be courageous enough to go against the flow. Maintain your integrity. Don't give in. Don't compromise. Allow God to bestow on you His rewards by obeying Him. You'll never regret it!

———————— ♥ ————————

Setting standards ahead of time and sticking to them may not be easy, but it's worth it.

2. Be Accountable

In their own words:

On paper write down exactly what your moral standards are (for example, "no prolonged kissing") and then find a reliable person to keep you accountable. A parent is an excellent person to help you. They love you and you can be certain that once you share your struggle they will be watching over you.

———————— ♥ ————————

I strongly recommend that teens make themselves accountable to other people regarding their dating behavior. Making yourself accountable to another person is a valuable way to strengthen self-discipline and control sexual desires.

The word *accountable* means "able to answer for one's conduct." To make yourself accountable to someone means to share honestly with that person, on a regular basis, areas of your life with which you are struggling. For example, a teenage boy might go to someone and share his struggles with sexual desire for his girlfriend. He might ask that person, "Would you hold me accountable in the area of sexual temptation with my girlfriend?" He might share specific things that he does or does not want to see happen in their relationship and request that he be asked periodically (perhaps after each date) to report on how he's doing.

Someone once wisely said,

If you don't have enough willpower to submit to someone else, you'll never have enough willpower to submit to yourself.

All of us seem to be far more disciplined in activities when we have a commitment to other people. Dick finds this, for example, in his running. He's far more apt to be disciplined when he has a commitment to get up in the morning and go running with someone else.

We need to be accountable to other people. But accountability needs to be built on acceptance and appreciation. Acceptance gives us security. Appreciation gives us a sense of significance. Accountability then helps us with self-control.

If we've grown up with demanding, autocratic parents who weren't all that accepting and appreciative, we may not want to be accountable to anyone. However, we all need accountability in our lives — not autocratic accountability, but loving, caring accountability. The ideal persons to be accountable to are one's parents, provided they are accepting and appreciative. The standard-setting process offers an excellent time to establish this principle. As the parents use this tremendous opportunity to guide and encourage the teen, he will find it easier to work out his own standards for sexual behavior on dates. If parents are autocratic, though, a teen will have to look elsewhere — perhaps to a loving relative such as a grandparent, an aunt, or an uncle, or to someone from church, perhaps a teacher, the youth pastor, or his wife.

One teen gives the following advice about accountability to parents:

1. Ask permission from your girlfriend's parents to take her out.

2. Take steps to build a good relationship with your girlfriend's father and mother to gain their trust.

3. Make sure you both get home before each other's curfew expires.

4. Tell your parents where you are going *every time* and when you plan to be back.

A teenage girl advises, "If you have continued problems *make yourself accountable.* Share *your* problem with an older woman and ask your boyfriend to talk to an older man. Knowing that you'll have to answer to someone is a powerful deterrent."

3. Let One's Lifestyle Show

In their own words:

The bottom line is that we are all judged on the basis of our words and our actions, and by this representation, others will seek what they want. Because I have been outspoken about my beliefs, those who would be inclined to have premarital sex avoid me and I them.

———————— ♥ ————————

My reputation in the locker room is that I'm a prude. I don't ask why because I know. I'm not "loose" with the guys I go out with. I would rather stand strong and gain their respect, because it's pretty well known that I'm a Christian and I stand for what I believe in. I have found that I still get asked out by some guys — the guys who respect me for who I am are the ones who ask me out. 185/29-30

Conversation, body language and clothes are ways of saying no to sexual permissiveness. Simply through our lifestyle we can communicate, "Hey, I'm not available for that."

In all our years of counseling and ministry, Dick and I have hardly ever been propositioned by a Christian who knew who we were. The reason is that we're always sharing our values and talking about the tremendous joy we have with our wives and families. By so doing, we are saying clearly, "Hey, I'm not available."

Young people should be encouraged to take it as a compliment if someone says, "She (or he) doesn't put out!"

The secret is to be secure in your self-identity, to know yourself and be your own person. If you know who you are, you can stand beside your peers, without taking a "holier than thou" attitude, and tell them that premarital sex is not for you. If you're confident of your identity, you will be free to be yourself and to accept others as they are, without conforming to their expectations or condoning their behavior.

The person who accepts others, just as they are, is usually accepted and well liked even if he or she observes a different lifestyle. It's amazing how often that kind of person will become a leader (and even a role model) for his peers, Christian or otherwise.

By the way, are you aware that sexual pressures no longer come exclusively from males? Traditionally we have viewed the male as the aggressor, out to prove his manhood by seducing vulnerable females. But today the female is often the aggressor, encouraging and enticing a young man to join her in having sex.

That's why it meant so much to this young man to know a girl who was different:

I dated a girl for seven months who never played on my emotions and told me things to lead me on. She knew that by just saying certain things, she might arouse me physically. It's far better not to lead each other on physically and play a big game with one another. She knew what it meant to be truthful and honest in our relationship.

Whether male or female, how can you act out your convictions about premarital sex? It comes back to your sense of identity. How do you see yourself? Are you a person whose actions are determined by your personal set of values? Or do you act the way you do to gain the acceptance and approval of others? Who's "calling the shots?" You or your friends?

If you have Christian convictions about sex, stand up for them. Be in charge.

Keeping the Mind Pure

Scripture tells us to take every thought captive to the obedience of Christ; we are to be in control of our thought life. Now we may not have much control over thoughts that just seem to pop into our minds whether we want them to or not, but we can control whether we let our minds dwell and linger on those thoughts.

What we feed into our minds determines what we think about, so it is important to be selective. As Larry Tomczak asserts, "Let's steer clear of all phony stimulants like magazines, videos, programs or films that can engrave impure impressions on our minds' sensitive photographic plates." 69/7

Proverbs 23:7 warns that "as a man thinks within himself, so he is" (NASB). In other words, what is hidden on the inside will be seen on the outside. Many Christian teens recognize this truth.

In their own words:

It's important to realize that lust and sexual desires are products of the mind first. If you nurture and cultivate sinful thoughts, they'll continue to flourish, eventually overpowering you. With God's help you will learn not to entertain lustful thoughts, but meditate on things that are lovely, pure and holy.

♡ ♡ ♡

The sin nature loves to warp and twist things that God meant to be holy and good. It feeds off warped and twisted things. It loves to distort the true purpose of sex, so it will grow stronger when you expose yourself to those kinds of views. For example, many young men look at magazines like *Playboy* and *Penthouse,* which present a distorted version of sex. The mind feeds off things like this, producing an unnatural view of sex while fanning the sex drive. Many young men then wonder why they can't control themselves on a date.

♡ ♡ ♡

If we are constantly feeding our minds with pornography, tasteless jokes, or even Harlequin romances, our actions will demonstrate this.

♡ ♡ ♡

Wrong action starts with wrong thought. Have you ever noticed how often the Bible refers to keeping our minds pure? Jesus tells us that if a man looks at a woman with lust, he has already committed adultery with her in his heart. In other words, dwelling on the thought is bad. Therefore, any activity that leads you to lust after another person is wrong. When you lust after someone you begin to view them as an object rather than as a person and this viewpoint will eventually be evidenced in your actions.

———————— ♥ ————————

How do we succeed at taking our thoughts captive to the obedience of Christ? First, we need a correct knowledge of the character of God. We need to understand that God is righteous, with high standards of morality. He is truthful. He will not deceive us.

God's character is just and loving. As we understand His character we will want to respond to Him by wanting to please Him and do His will.

The second step is to discover the will of God. Knowledge of it comes from a study of the Scriptures and from listening to godly people in the body of Christ. God's Word, for example, speaks in several places about the importance of maintaining purity of thought.

The third step is to place ourselves in an environment of encouragement and accountability. This means that we will share our struggle to control impure thinking with mature Christians, asking them to pray for us, to help us plan a specific strategy to overcome the problem and to check up on us to see how we are doing in this area. Accountability will eventually lead to self-discipline and in time we will be able to self-monitor our areas of weakness.

Other strategies include asking the Lord to set a shield around our minds so that each time an impure thought enters we immediately surrender that thought to the Lord, asking Him to cleanse our mind and help us deliberately think about something else. Avoid conversation and written or visual material that would stimulate wrong thoughts.

Another effective tool is Scripture memorization. Psalm 119:11 says, "I have hidden your word in my heart that I might not sin against you" (NIV).

Finally, remember that God always gives us the strength and ability to do what He commands. In Philippians 4:8 Paul says, "Whatever is true, whatever is honorable, whatever is right, whatever is pure, whatever is lovely, whatever is of good repute, if there is any excellence and if anything worthy of praise, let your mind dwell on these things" (NASB).

Avoiding Sexually Oriented Media

What is the best source of information about sex on the market these days? Afternoon soap operas on the television screen? No. Dirty jokes and stories? Not on your life. Behind-the-counter sex magazines? No. If you answered, "The Bible," you are right. The Bible is the best resource available because it tells the whole truth about sex. It shows that sex can be both delightful and dangerous. The Bible, when taken as a whole, contains great truths for the teenager who is trying to understand sex. 97/1

In the words of our teenagers:

Stay away from pornography, magazines, movies, TV, or anything else that stimulates you sexually. Don't buy into the Hollywood line that life is a constant romance seeking sexual satisfaction. Reject the concept that the other person is there to fulfill your expectations. People are not to be manipulated, either for sexual satisfaction or for security in marriage. Learn to trust God for both. The bottom-line is: Don't let anybody or anything, including yourself, convince you that sex is the best or only highway to happiness and fulfillment in life.

♡ ♡ ♡

Stay away from the dirt on television, or at the theater. Avoid books that emphasize premarital sex. Most of all, don't be misled by what the majority of the world thinks. Instead look to God for direction. And remember Proverbs 4:25, "Let your eyes look directly ahead and let your gaze be fixed straight in front of you" (NASB).

♡ ♡ ♡

I'm learning that with the Holy Spirit within me, I *can* resist temptation. However, I find that if I've been filling my mind with ungodly things (e.g., certain movies, books, magazines, etc.), then my defense is weak and I fall so easily to temptation.

———————— ♥ ————————

Remember that the standards portrayed in most media today are falsely alluring. God's standard is based on reality and protection. I'm not saying don't ever go to the movies, watch TV, or read books. Scripture does not teach that movies or TV, in and

of themselves, are sinful. We must distinguish between the form
of the medium and the content of the medium. There is nothing
wrong with writing, or with movie and TV production, but the
message or content can be harmful. After all, they didn't have
the mass media as we know it 2,000 years ago. However, as
Stacy and Paula Rinehart point out,

> What does emerge from Scripture are relationship principles
> that are clear, transcultural and timeless. For instance, the
> Bible teaches, "Abstain from sinful desires, which war against
> your soul" (1 Peter 2:11, NIV). In Corinth many centuries
> ago, the application of that verse might have been "Stay
> away from the temple prostitutes." In our culture today it
> might mean "Check the rating on a movie before you decide
> to see it." 109/3

Be discerning about what you watch, read, or listen to.
Remember that once an image is imprinted on your mind, it's
there to stay. It becomes a part of you. It becomes a part of what
Paul called "conformity to this world" or what the contemporary
computer programmer calls GIGO (garbage in, garbage out). One
part of our mind is like a computer, in that it stores information.
But unlike the computer, much of what the mind remembers is
accompanied by great emotion. So, be selective. The more we
have conformed, the more challenging is the process of transform-
ing our mind into the thoughts, ideas and values of God.

Dressing to Reflect Convictions

> The trend is to wear tight pants and revealing sweaters,
> but trends don't mold my lifestyle . . . God does! If I dress
> sexy or tease a boy and lead him on, he will make more
> out of it than it actually is. 185/29.

In 1 Timothy 2:9, Paul says, "I want women to adorn
themselves with proper clothing, modestly and discreetly"
(NASB). In blatant contrast, the dress of many girls and women
screams of sensuality. From Barbie Doll fashions to the covers of
trendy magazines, a lot of women's clothing is seductively attention-getting. Influenced by this, most teenage girls, including
Christians, think nothing of wearing the latest provocative fashions. A young girl usually does not realize that a guy does not
look on her dress in the same way she does. She may be quite
confused and angered when her parents and other adults react
to her "showiness." In her eyes, she has done nothing wrong.
This is an area where parents, especially mothers, need to educate
their daughters to understand the effect their dress can have on
men.

Modesty in dress is important because guys are turned on by what they see. Since girls are stimulated more by touch than by sight, many of them don't realize this difference. Author Clayton Bauman makes a good comparison in the following example. "I once said to a girl, 'What would happen if you were on the beach, and every guy who walked by touched you with a nice warm stroke?' 'I'd go bonkers in about an hour,' she replied. That feeling is somewhat comparable for guys when they just see a girl." 84

> Girls need to be aware that certain types of dress really cause guys problems. Tight blouses, tight slacks, halters, no bras and skimpy bathing suits are all immodest. Any kind of dress that accents the sexual aspect of a woman is immodest. Often a girl will dress to emphasize her body when she feels that her personality will not attract guys. There is something wrong when a girl thinks that the only way she can attract guys is with her body. 117/95

Of course, modesty is not the same thing as frumpiness. Christian men and women should have the most beautifully kept bodies, faces, hair and clothing of all people. They are not called to deny or destroy their masculinity or femininity but to use it in a manner that is glorifying to God and will not cause others to stumble.

How does one find the balance between being provocative and frumpy? One teenage girl gives this excellent advice, "On a date, (really, all the time) wear clothes that you would want to meet Jesus in. It can be cute and stylish but not designed to turn a guy on." If a girl uses just a little common sense, she can dress modestly. Realize that what looks good on fashion models doesn't always look good on you. As you choose your clothes, ask God to give you concern for the spiritual welfare of the guys you're around. Yes, you are free in Christ to dress as you like, but true freedom limits itself in consideration of others.

Glorifying the Lord With the Body

In their own words:

The Lord wants us to glorify Him not only with our hearts and voices but also with our bodies. "Now the body is not for fornication, but for the Lord; and the Lord for the body." (1 Corinthians 6:13, KJV).

♡ ♡ ♡

"I urge you, brothers, in view of God's mercy, to offer your bodies as living sacrifices, holy and pleasing to God . . ." (Romans

12:1, NIV) That verse has had a tremendous impact on how physically close I could ever get to Dan. My body belongs to Christ and I desire to live a transformed life, not conforming to the lustful patterns of this world.

♡ ♡ ♡

For me to have sex before I'm married would disappoint my very best friend and hurt my relationship with Him terribly. Because I love Jesus so much, I don't ever want to care more about a human person who will never be able to love me as much as He does . . . Keeping my body a living sacrifice for Jesus is one clear way I can show Him I love Him and care for Him.

───────────── ♥ ─────────────

The above paragraphs are examples of convictions based on total commitment to a Christian world view. In order for such convictions to have an impact on one's behavior, they must be internalized or "owned" by each person.

A teenage girl who found herself on the verge of having sex to please her boyfriend says:

I'd always been taught that premarital sex was wrong. So when everything but premarital sex happened, I realized it was time to think of my motives and decide why I was really doing this.

I'd never gone so far with a guy before. Almost all of my friends had lost their virginity. I was so unlike them, and so proud. Yet, I wanted to be loved so much. God gave me the love I needed until I stepped out of His band of love and decided I could handle things myself.

Then, approaching the world in a way I never had before, I was constantly faced with the question of "Should I wait?" I wanted love again and my boyfriend seemed the only one to give it truly in the way I wanted it. The only thing holding me back time and time again was a feeling deep down inside saying, "It's wrong. Don't give in."

In searching the Bible, I came across 1 Corinthians 6:18-20 which says, "Flee from sexual immorality. All other sins a man commits are outside his body, but he who sins sexually, sins against his own body. Do you not know that your body is a temple of the Holy Spirit, who is in you, whom you have received from God? You are not your own; you were bought at a price. Therefore honor God with your body" (NIV).

The question arose inside me, "How can you honor God with your body when you feel guilty about having premarital sex?" Examining my reasons, I realized I was treating my body as if it were my own, not God's. Thinking further, I also realized that you can't go into the bedroom and leave God outside. He's with you no matter where you go, what your do, what sin you commit.

I found my answer written out and made clear. Premarital sex is wrong. Now, I'm back on my feet again, proclaiming from the highest hill that I'm a virgin and proud of it!

As Christians we are called to glorify God by serving others. When one's purpose in life is to serve others, premarital celibacy becomes a freely offered gift, rather than a grudging sacrifice — a gift to God and to one's future mate.

4. Choose Companions Carefully

Hanging Around People With the Same Values

"Approval is one of the greatest slave drivers of all time. It will take a person and never let him go until he feels as though he is finally a success in the eyes of others," writes Jacob Aranza. 50/37

Psychologists call it "perfectionistic thinking," a syndrome that affects about one person in three. It has been documented that "the more perfectionistic people are, the more unhappy they are in both their personal lives and careers. Furthermore, there is no proof that a perfectionistic approach makes people more successful." Perfectionism's effects can include procrastination, low self-esteem, psychosomatic symptoms that can lead to anorexia and bulimia, problem-filled relationships, stress, anxiety, depression and may ultimately lead even to suicide. 270/D4

Many teens today are searching for approval. If they don't receive approval from their parents, they will seek it from their peers. Regrettably, peer approval for most teens revolves around conformity to the values of the group. In their search for approval, teens may go along with the standard of their peer group even though it violates their own personal moral standard. For example, a 1982 survey by Planned Parenthood reveals that 30 to 35 percent of all teens who have had sex felt that peers pressured them into it. 108/84

The apostle Paul recognized the tremendous problem of peer pressure. In 1 Corinthians 5:9 he says, "I wrote you in my letter not to associate with immoral people" (NASB). When you hang around and associate with immoral people you become immoral yourself. In confirmation of Paul's words, one teenage girl says:

> If everyone is having premarital sex and talking about it, your conscience becomes salved and you no longer feel the conviction against it. In fact, your friends encourage it. You begin to feel the pressure after so long. The girls make you feel that you aren't very attractive and aren't worth much and the guys make you feel like a wimp because you're not experienced like others. After so much of that from the crowd that you are with, you say, what the heck, and do it! Even so, you know it was wrong, but peer pressure

overruled. At that point, you laid down your morals and turned your back on God's commandments.

Another young man has this to say about peer pressure:

When dealing with peer pressure, sometimes people get confused with what the real issue is. They think it is whether or not conforming to something is going to give them friends and make them happy. I look at it in a different way. In the Bible, Daniel said, when he was dealing with peer pressure, that he made up his mind not to conform, but the issue wasn't whether or not he would have friends; it was whether or not he would please God. It is the same for us. If we strive to please God rather than men, God will reward those who love and obey Him.

Of course, peer pressure doesn't always have to be negative. If the morals of the group involve doing what is right, a peer group can be a great source of support for the teen who wants to live a righteous life. As one teen says, "I know that my friends have a great influence on who I am and also on what my values are. Godly friends can be a real source of encouragement when struggling with sexual desires."

The issue for teens comes down to one of carefully choosing friends. The early part of Proverbs contains great instruction on the wisdom of being with like-minded people and the danger of being caught in the wrong crowd. All of us are subject to peer pressure to one degree or another.

Teens who are struggling with low self-esteem are particularly vulnerable. In choosing their companions, teens should do two things.

1. "Deliberately avoid repeated *intimate* contact with people who don't share your basic ideas about how to live, regardless of how attractive they are." 87/89

2. Recognize the importance of selecting the right people to be with. Choose to develop friendships with those who share your values and convictions.

Whether we like it or not, we tend to become like the people we hang around with. Jesus stressed the importance of role-modeling in Luke 6:40 when he says that *a student shall be like his teacher.* To a great extent our friends are like teachers to us, so it is important to choose them carefully.

Getting Involved in Support Groups

It is important that Christian teenagers be involved in some kind of support group. Hebrews 10:25 tells us not to give up the habit of *meeting together* with other believers. Galatians 6:2 admonishes us to help *carry one another's burdens.* Meeting regularly with like-minded people is helpful and encouraging. A supportive group such as a church youth group or Bible study at school will reinforce a teen's commitment to a godly lifestyle. In a world where it seems as if everyone is saying yes to premarital sexual involvement, it is strategic to bond together with others who say no. Reinforcement of convictions from peers really can help a teen face sexual pressure.

One of the key things teens can do as a group is to write out their goals and desires for dating relationships. These goals should be shared with a group. In this way, teens can provide positive role models for one another and can establish a degree of accountability to each other.

One young woman who learned the value of group support says this:

> I have never engaged in premarital sex in my relationships. It is largely due to my Christian upbringing. Throughout my adolescence and college years I had a strong network of friends and fellow church members who provided the support and caring needed through those unsure times. The care and intimacy derived from those special people have given me enough security and love to save the act of sexual intercourse for the person I choose to become one with in marriage.

Don't Be in a Hurry to Go Steady

Avoid the "steady" relationship until the time is right. Familiarity often leads to lower moral standards.

♡ ♡ ♡

If I said "no" would he say "goodbye"? Am I being drawn closer to or further from the Lord? Am I a stumbling block not only to myself, but to him and others around me?

♡ ♡ ♡

When you date before you are ready, sometimes you let your emotions get in the way and you cannot control them.

——————— ♥ ———————

Going steady too early can cause problems. In most cases it is best to avoid going steady at all until a person is mature enough to consider marriage.

All too often teens go steady because it is convenient and comfortable — it's nice to know that you have someone to be with at every event and at all the times in between.

However, as a couple goes steady, they slowly begin to

lower their guard. They start frequenting the same places, doing the same things. They begin taking each other for granted and it becomes almost impossible to resist physical intimacy. In fact, recent research indicates that teens who go steady for more than six months almost always become sexually intimate. The power of sexual attraction is such that any two mutually attracted people who spend large amounts of time alone are tempted to express their feelings through intercourse.

The problem is aggravated when the going steady begins at a relatively early age.

> One way to guard against this is to avoid forming exclusive, long-term relationships. If such a relationship does develop, then wise parents will help teenagers plan their time so that they do not have extended periods of time alone together. 99/93

We recommend that teens spend most of their dating time on double or group dates and avoid exclusive one-on-one relationships until they are older and seriously contemplating finding a person to marry.

Developing Close Relationships With Family and Friends

We all have a need for love and for the physical affection that is an expression of that love. Research tells us that there is an actual *need* for physical touch. In a study of babies in an orphanage, babies who were given proper nutrition without physical affection had a tendency to die. In contrast, babies who not only were nourished but also were held and given loving attention tended to thrive.

The primary context where physical touch is learned is in the family. Children can learn the affectionate use of touch by seeing their parents express love to each other and to their kids. If we're able to experience intimacy through hugging and affectionate touching in a family, it is much easier to control ourselves in a dating situation. We won't need to strive for acceptance or intimacy, because we already have it within our family structure.

In addition to the family, close non-dating friendships can also fill the need for intimacy. One young woman gives the following advice for meeting intimacy and affection needs:

> *Cultivate close intimate friendships* with the same or opposite sex. Being able to share honestly and openly is one of our greatest needs and to ignore it because we feel it can come only through a dating relationship is to give up one of life's most important experiences, that of intimate friendship.
> *Give and receive physical affection from your friends.* It is possible

to alleviate this by hugs, pats on the back, handshakes, or whatever form of affection you feel comfortable with. Don't get caught up in the myth that all affection is sexual or the lie that sexual activity is the only way to quench the need for physical affection.

Pour your energy into a worthy cause. Whether it be a lonely elderly person, a rowdy group of seventh graders, or a young child, invest yourself in someone else. This not only will take your mind off yourself, but will bring great satisfaction.

In an article emphasizing not to go to strangers, Robert and Leota Tucker encourage young people,

> Before making love, try making friends. Friendship is the one common ingredient among couples who seem to have it all together. Friends are the people you miss most when you're lonely — the ones who warm your life, comfort, applaud, support and forgive you. Friends work out problems, accept differences, have patience and grow together. 87/89

Having and being friends can give greater freedom and enjoyment to your dating life. As one teen says:

> I go out with guys and I have a tremendously fun time with them — as good friends. I let them know as soon as I can how I feel about sex, and oftentimes, it is a great relief to them. There is a much more relaxed atmosphere as we get to know each other as friends. And *I do believe that it is possible to have intimacy with a person without having sex.* There are times when I have been able to share with a guy about my hopes and dreams or how I feel about God, and have him share with me also — and that, to me, is intimacy.

5. Seek Others' Wisdom

Role Models

In their own words:

> The parents are much to be blamed. So many parents are divorced or committing adultery that they have no right to tell their children not to go to bed with someone, because they are doing the same things.

♡ ♡ ♡

> Maybe, just maybe, if some teenager was a better example, Jane could have a brighter future.

———————— ♥ ————————

As mentioned earlier, a person develops his or her world view, or perspective about life that determines our behavior, largely as the result of the modeling influence of parents and peers.

Children growing up have a great need for role models who demonstrate what Christian love, marriage and sexual love are all about. They need those models on a continuing basis during their teen years, as they finish school and then begin their careers.

Recently at The Julian Center Dick was talking to a group of adults, from college to middle age, about personality development from a biblical perspective, and about the critical role of the family in that development. He asked how many of them still felt the need for a parent-figure in their lives. Ninety percent of them raised their hands. Whatever our ages, we need parent-figures.

But we don't have enough positive models. Why?

One reason is that many parents do not understand God's perspective on love, acceptance and encouragement. Without the personal "remolding" of their minds that Paul speaks of in Romans 12, they can never be positive role models to their children.

Another reason for the shortage of good role models for young people is the age segregation spoken of earlier. As a result of this age segregation, young people rarely experience the influence of role models other than their parents and peers. Dr. Urie Bronfenbrenner of Cornell University sees this as the number-one reason why we are not transmitting our traditional values — which historically have been Judeo-Christian — to our young people. He sees age segregation as a major problem today in the personality development of children. 188/120-121

Then, too, there is a need for young people themselves to be role models to their peers. It's very difficult; it isn't popular or easy to go against the tidal waves of peer pressure. But it can be done.

I was impressed by a young man in Anaheim, California, who took a stand for Jesus Christ and became a role model to his peers. He had been a student leader in his high school and after "going public" with his faith his popularity plummeted to "ground zero." He told me, "I have never been more lonely in my entire life . . . but I have never felt closer to God."

After about four months one student after another started coming to him and saying, "Hey, I can't understand all this stuff about Jesus, but I see something in your life that's different." One at a time he began to lead his classmates to Christ.

When this young man completed high school he was chosen to give the graduation speech. He described what Jesus Christ had done in his life and that he believed it was impossible to be personally successful, in any area of life, from marriage to business, without knowing Jesus. When he finished, his classmates gave him a standing ovation.

It's not the popular thing for a young person to control his or her sex life and become a positive role model for their peers. But those who do so will definitely help someone else say no.

Wise Advice

Scripture teaches us that "there is much wisdom in much counsel or advice." Sometimes, confused by our emotional involvement in a situation, we need someone else to help us see things from a more objective point of view. Sometimes we have blind spots in our ways of thinking and acting. Sometimes we just need someone to act as a sounding board for us: to let us discuss our ideas and feelings, give us feedback and advise us about possible courses of action.

In seeking advice you need to go to someone you respect and someone who you know loves and cares for you, who is concerned for your best interests. Youth ministers, pastors, older church friends (and even some parents) can be sources for good advice. One thing to keep in mind is that there is a difference between seeking advice and seeking confirmation. To seek confirmation means to go to someone who will agree with you about what you have already decided. To seek advice means to go to someone you respect because of his or her walk with the Lord and ask that person for guidance.

Of course, when we seek advice it doesn't necessarily mean we have to follow the advice given. Ultimate responsibility for decision-making belongs to the individual who seeks counsel.

Seeking advice about premarital sexual activity can help a young person form and uphold his convictions as the counselor assists him in thinking through what God's Word has to say about the subject. Seeking godly advice also can be of great value to a person who has been involved in premarital sex, has confessed and received forgiveness for that sin, and yet continues to feel guilt because of it. As the Rineharts say,

> If you feel that Satan still plagues you with feelings of guilt you are unable to shake, then it would be helpful for you to open up your life to an older person who is more mature in the faith and able to accept and counsel you. This step is based on the scriptural principle in James 5:16 — "Therefore confess your sins to each other and pray for each other so that you may be healed" [NIV]. Although transparency always involves risk, God sometimes uses another person to mirror His love and acceptance for us and to give us the guidance we need. 109/113

6. Ask God to Help

In their own words:

I asked God to help me control my passions and to show me how to have a relationship without sex. He helped me to avoid situations that were conducive to sexual response.

♡ ♡ ♡

We both knew we couldn't do it on our own, but that we had to rely on the self-control of Christ . . . We finally took it to the Lord in prayer and got down on our knees each time we met, because . . . we had tried everything else!

♡ ♡ ♡

Although it may seem that your sexual impulses cannot be controlled, there is one certain way to help you restrain — give your life completely to Jesus Christ. Ask Him to come into your heart and be the Lord of every corner of your life, including being the Lord of your sexual nature and desires.

♡ ♡ ♡

Admit to God that you need His help in conquering your sexual desires. Prayer is one of the biggest helps there is.

—————————— ♥ ——————————

Most young people who have successfully coped with sexual pressures acknowledge the importance of asking God for help. None of the strategies for saying no suggested in this book will be effective without recognition of one's need for His help. It is not necessary to try to "go it alone" in this difficult area when we realize that God wants to help.

Obviously, the idea of asking God for help presumes a life-changing relationship with Him through Jesus Christ. Although the solution of youth sexual problems requires more than evangelism — evangelism must be central in any "Why Wait?" strategy. I have found that when young people realize their need for help in dealing with their sexuality, they are also very open to Christ's invitation to personal relationship.

———————————————————

Jesus Christ died 2,000 years ago in order to set you free from your bondage to sin, including bondage to sexual sins. He paid the price with His life long ago so that you wouldn't be required to pay with your own life. He understands every emotion and every temptation in your life at this very moment. Jesus Christ knows that you can't handle your situation alone and He's waiting for you to turn everything over to Him. God created you and your sexual nature and called it GOOD. But, only through an intimate relationship with your Creator can your sexual impulses be controlled. If you pray and ask God for the strength to deal with your temptation, together with Him you will overcome it.

------------------- ♥ -------------------

Young people need to know that without God's help they have a strong likelihood of failure in the area of sex. But with His help they can be "more than conquerors." I've often said to teens that "God is more concerned about your sex life than you are." You see, God didn't just give us difficult-to-follow sexual rules and regulations and then abandon us. Of course not. He also has promised His help and power, because He wants us to succeed. Being a morally responsible person requires effort, but God provides the strength needed.

We must encourage our young people to use prayer as the first step to a sexual lifestyle that is honoring to God. They must admit their frailty and depend on His supernatural power to reserve their active sexuality for marriage.

After you've turned everything over to Him, take steps to fill your life with His desires for you. Read His Word daily and spend time in prayer. Remember Galatians 5:16, "Walk by the Spirit, and you will not carry out the desire of the flesh" (NASB).

------------------- ♥ -------------------

We must also encourage young people to go beyond merely a "please-help-me" relationship with God. No one should be satisfied with just asking His help to avoid sexual involvement Ultimately one's goal should be to learn and follow His will in all things, including potential sexual relationships. The deeper and closer one's relationship to the heavenly Father becomes, the more help one will receive for living a moral Christian lifestyle.

Sex is performed as an expression of love. "Be exhilarated always with her love" (Proverbs 5:19, NASB). It seems only right then that, in order to understand sex, one must understand love. To fully understand love, one must understand God. ("God is love.") To understand God, one must know Him personally.

------------------- ♥ -------------------

To know God personally one must learn His principles.

A basic principle for Christians is that we are committed to love God with our whole hearts and to love our neighbors as ourselves (Matthew 22:37-39). Growing out of this basic principle are other principles about the dignity of human life, the sacredness of sex and the importance of truthfulness.

———————— ♥ ————————

These Christian principles are quite meaningless to someone who is unrelated to the Father and His Son. However, the better acquainted we are with God the Father through Jesus Christ, the better we understand the reasons behind His loving commandments — and the more we are motivated to obey them. Ask God for help in the area of sexuality. He wants to give it!

18

CONTROLLED DATES

1. Set Dating Goals

In their own words:

Establish God-honoring goals. Don't be self-centered.

♡ ♡ ♡

When a system of priorities is defined, it becomes easier to resist the pressures of becoming sexually active.

———————— ♥ ————————

A girl wrote to her boyfriend:

What do you say we make a list — together I mean — of the things we would really like to see accomplished in our lives? I think we could be great accountability partners for each other, don't you? Let's help each other be all that God created us to be.

♡ ♡ ♡

If you have something to look forward to, then you're going to be responsible about your sexuality.

♡ ♡ ♡

To know He has purposes and plans for me — among the other

billions on this earth — excites me.

——————— ♥ ———————

It is important for young people to have objectives and goals for their lives and for their dating relationships. Researchers have discovered that a serious commitment to "religion," with the sense of purpose it gives, makes a noticeable difference in the sexual activity of teens.

A good relationship with Mom and Dad makes a difference, too. For those who have that kind of relationship, I encourage them to interact in establishing dating goals. Obviously, parents should not dictate these goals for their children, but their counsel and assistance can be invaluable. Once the goals have been decided, Mom and Dad can play a key part as members of a young person's accountability team. For example, if a teen decides on an 11 P.M. date curfew, then he can say to his parents "Mom and Dad, I want you to hold me accountable for getting home on time."

Here are some suggested dating goals for young people:

1. Be accepting of the other person by honoring his or her God-given dignity. (This gives a person a sense of security.)

2. Build up the other person by showing appreciation for that person's uniqueness, gifts and abilities. (This gives a person a sense of significance.)

3. Encourage the fulfillment of the other person's goals. (Part of that encouragement would be to hold the other person accountable in the fulfillment of those goals.)

4. Be accountable to the other person for fulfilling your own goals according to God's principles. (This develops your self-discipline.)

5. In every situation, try to reflect Jesus Christ in your attitudes and actions.

Some suggested desires might be:

1. that the other person might become a better person as the result of knowing you and of your spending time together;

2. that as the result of your relationship the other person might develop a closer relationship with Jesus Christ.

In whatever you're doing — whether sharing activities and feelings or expressing legitimate affection — the real purpose in a dating relationship should be to build up the other person, to minister to the other person. One's primary desire should be that the other person will respond positively to these efforts and as a result will walk more closely with the Lord.

2. Make Definite Plans

In their own words:

Before going out on a date you should have it well planned. Plan so that there will be little space where you can get into trouble sexually.

♡ ♡ ♡

Don't spend long periods of time together without anything to occupy your time.

♡ ♡ ♡

To avoid the possibility of premarital sex, make sure you have something planned to fill the whole evening. Don't get yourself in a situation where you have nothing to do.

♡ ♡ ♡

We found we needed to do things with other unmarried couples. It was so nice to spend a quiet evening at home, but all too often when the lights and music got soft it was easy to get carried away.

♡ ♡ ♡

We need to plan dates. Be creative. Do something fun and silly. Use your imagination to really have fun and stay chaste.

♡ ♡ ♡

Be creative in your activities. Go bowling, play chess, swim, play golf, roller-skate, take walks, host parties, conduct a youth Bible study, or give your pastor and his wife a night out by babysitting their children.

♡ ♡ ♡

Don't stray from the original plan of what you will do, or where you will go on a date. Impulsive changes of plans usually spell trouble.

———————— ♥ ————————

This is how to implement the standards one has set: Plan carefully. It's not only smart to be creative in planning dates, but it's also a lot of fun. Before young people go out on a date, they should know where they're going to go and what they're going to do. It is easiest to stay out of trouble on dates when you make them creative, make them fun, and stay out of situations that can lead to problems. Plan your dating life carefully.

Wayne Wright has wisely said, "The best companion against

immorality is geography." This is not to suggest that you
should move to the next state, but that if you plan ahead
to avoid compromising situations and run from the ones you
didn't plan ahead for, you won't be caught repeating the
words of Bert and Ginny: "We just never thought that this
would happen to us." 109/109

When planning a date, one should keep in mind the goals
which have already been set. Such planning should be seen not
only as a way to avoid sexual involvement, but also as a means
of bringing about growth in the other person and in oneself.

Thoughtful advance planning is a basic prerequisite to saying
no to premarital sex. Young people themselves have come up
with many helpful suggestions and cautions:

> Be very careful of the things you do on a date. Stay away from
> listening to suggestive music. Be careful of what movies you see
> on a date. You may not think it makes much difference but it
> really does. It's just that much easier to go ahead with what you've
> already seen (or heard).

♡ ♡ ♡

> Remember, we men get turned on more easily than women, so
> avoid places where the "switches" are more likely to get "bumped"!
> Don't take dates to parents' homes when nobody's there. Avoid
> parties where booze and drugs are available, and think twice about
> taking a girl to a drive-in movie.

♡ ♡ ♡

> There are many ways of expressing your affection toward the
> person you love without excessive physical contact. Many of these
> alternatives can be more creative, exciting and romantic. They
> demonstrate true love and concern for the other person's best
> interest. The recognition that you love someone enough not to
> want to compromise their standards, or put their spiritual walk in
> jeopardy, demonstrates more love than anything else I can think of.

3. Date Only Those Who Have the Same Convictions

It's not a pretty picture. It's not a TV soap opera, either. The
reality of pregnancy outside marriage is scary and lonely. At twenty-
four, I'm single and eight months pregnant. To have premarital
sex was my choice one hot June night, forcing many decisions I
thought I would never have to make. Those decisions have radically
changed my life.

Perhaps the biggest surprise is that I am a born-again Christian
who loves the Lord. How did this happen? *It all started when I
made a choice to date a non-Christian.* "There's nothing wrong
with just dating," I reasoned.

I was honest with my boyfriend in sharing the importance of my relationship with Jesus. He knew I was a Christian and he knew that I believed sex was for marriage. Rick thought I was outdated and couldn't believe I had never spent the night with a guy. However, he knew where I stood and didn't push me.

Twice in the eight months before I got pregnant I told him I thought we should break our relationship off. The Holy Spirit was convicting me like crazy. I knew 2 Corinthians 6:14: "Do not be yoked together with unbelievers . . ." But Rick would say, "Just because I don't have the same beliefs doesn't mean we don't get along and have a great time together."

To me Christianity wasn't just a belief; it was a way of life, yet what he said seemed to be true enough. Once when I said I would never marry a non-Christian, he said he didn't want to get married, but he did want to date me.

Without ever intending to, I was slowly falling in love. Almost every evening he worked out at the health club where I was employed. This made it convenient to see him every day, and we spent extra time together on weekends. We enjoyed many of the same activities and we talked honestly and openly with each other on most issues. I felt the freedom to be myself when I was around him. Having previously dated a Christian who expected nothing less than perfection, this was a refreshing relationship.

During that time I was slowly becoming more and more comfortable with Rick. Without wanting to admit it, it was also the beginning of compromise. From all outward appearances, there was no indication that I was pushing God aside. I was still active in our church and remained in fellowship. The longer we dated, and the more attracted to him I became, the easier it was to let my guard down. A good-night kiss that put me on cloud nine during our first month of dating turned into hours of passionate kissing in front of his fireplace. I started to justify staying at his house on occasion, due to the half-hour drive home.

I was slipping, making small allowances for further advance in our relationship. Oh, I knew it wasn't right, and I knew it wasn't the relationship that God would want for me, yet I wasn't strong enough to end it. I felt apathetic toward God, and I didn't feel like saying no to Rick. Compromise had weakened me. By the time we had intercourse, it was so easy to let down the final defense.

Romans 12:1 says we are to offer our bodies as living sacrifices, holy and pleasing to God. In verse two, Paul continues by telling us not to conform to the world. I always knew what was right. I knew that my dating Rick was not God's will — that's clear from Scripture. I initially justified it because the relationship wasn't that important to me. Then, when I could not use that justification any longer, I simply decided not to care. At that point I wasn't afraid of sinning. My reason for not committing fornication was I was afraid I would get pregnant. And that's exactly what I got — pregnant.

I was horrified and resentful. "Why me, God? It's not as though

I'm some tramp who sleeps around and deserves this." My reaction was the opposite of many of my married friends. I didn't want anyone to find out. There would be no congratulations or celebrations, no birth announcements or baby showers, only fear. I became angry and spiteful toward God. I thought, *Now I can have sex without the worry. I'll show you, God. Since I'm already pregnant, what have I got to lose?* With that fear gone, I saw no reason to be accountable to God. Faced with the alternatives though, of an unwanted pregnancy, I knew that I, not God, had jumped the gun.

Many tough decisions needed to be made. Most important I needed to get right with God again. I needed not only the forgiveness that God grants when we ask for it, but also I needed to become steadfast in the Word, and to trust in God again. I decided to leave my great job, wonderful church and network of friends, to move to another state and live with friends who have become like family to me and who also love the Lord. I also came to realize that an unwanted pregnancy on my part did not equal an unwanted child. I opted for adoption.

"Why me, God?" Because I knew better, but was disobedient anyway. "Why wait until marriage?" I believe it's a simple answer and there need be no other reason: because God tells us to wait. He tells us that, not to be a party pooper, but because He loves us and ultimately knows what is best for us. My feelings got in the way. However, whether we like it or not, we are to be obedient to God. Feelings can color the way we see things. They, rather than the Word of God, become the benchmark.

Over the past several months I have been dealing with the consequences of this particular sin. I have also seen, as never before, the goodness of God. Ephesians 1:7 has become a reality through many tough days and decisions: "In him we have redemption through his blood, the forgiveness of sins, in accordance with the riches of God's grace that he lavished on us with all wisdom and understanding" (NIV). I purpose to choose God's way.

———————— ♥ ————————

I have chosen to share this young woman's story with you in its entirety because it poignantly illustrates what I would like to communicate. It is crucial to date only those who have convictions similar to your own. In the above story the young woman made the mistake of justifying dating a non-Christian, and then began compromising to his level of morality. The Scripture that talks about "be not unequally yoked" was disobeyed and she ultimately had to deal with the consequences of her decision.

That Scripture applies not only to dating non-Christians, but also to dating Christians who do not share the same convictions. If you really want to control the sexual area of your life, then be careful not only about your own lifestyle but also about the lifestyle of those you date. If you date others who are like-minded there will be a commitment to encourage and be accountable to each other. However, if the person you date has lower moral standards than yours, you may easily find yourself compromising to their level rather than upholding your own convictions.

4. Communicate Openly About Sex

Have you ever wished that someone else could read your mind? That they could know your thoughts, feelings and opinions about something without your having to make the effort to tell them? Often we are afraid of self-disclosure, afraid that the other person may not accept us if we tell him or her how we really feel about something.

When we expect others to read our minds, to discover our convictions about sexual involvement, we may get ourselves in trouble. A lot of confusion and misunderstanding can be avoided by learning to tell our dates how we feel about sexual involvement.

In their own words:

We shouldn't wait till the time of temptation to set our limits. Discuss your values with the one you date. Maybe he doesn't want to have premarital sex either and is just as afraid of what you would think.

♡ ♡ ♡

The most important thing for a couple to do is talk about their views on premarital sex. It may seem a little embarrassing, but it is essential to know how each person feels. If one person doesn't think that having sex before marriage is wrong at all, then their whole relationship should be reevaluated. Chances are, if both are Christians and want to please the Lord, they will agree that premarital sex is wrong.

———————————— ♥ ————————————

One teen brings up the point that "couples need to discuss their limits and values when they are not 'in the mood' in order to avoid later problems." In the midst of arousal it's easy to rationalize away the standards we have set when in a calmer frame of mind. Discussion of standards needs to be done at a time and place where both people can be objective in evaluating their limits. Then, once standards are set, they need to be followed totally. There must be a commitment to the standards. As another teen comments, "Unless we both were committed to God's principles and to His will before we got into the tempting situation, we were almost sure to fail."

Sometimes, despite our best intentions we do make mistakes and cross over the limits we set for ourselves. What do you do when you've overstepped your limit (this doesn't necessarily mean you've gone "all the way") and want to start over again? One teen who had been fighting sexual pressure from her boyfriend recommended this approach:

> Try to describe your feelings in as many ways as possible and keep talking to him (perhaps on several different occasions) until you are sure he understands what you are saying. Use "I" statements and appeal to his desires. Here are some examples that may help you:
> (a) I don't like the spiritual side effects that erode my relationship with God and make me irritable with you.
> (b) I feel I'm beginning to lose respect and admiration for you and I need those things if we're going to have a quality relationship.
> (c) I feel like I'm being conditioned to reach a certain level of sexual excitement at which point I have to "turn myself off" and I'm afraid that will keep me from giving myself to my husband fully when I'm married.
> (d) I feel I'm learning to associate sex with shame and secrecy rather than with love, trust and openness.

Another teen advised,

> You need to agree that you have been involved in sin and that it must stop now — not next week, not tomorrow night, but today. You need to be able to discuss this problem openly and decide what can and will be done to conquer it. You will probably need to reevaluate your relationship as well and try to rediscover the reasons you are dating.

There is, however, one word of caution in talking about your feelings toward sexual involvement. Whenever we share anything with another person our purpose should be to edify (help to build up) the other person. It is not necessarily helpful to share your feelings of weakness. In fact, sharing vulnerability about sexual weaknesses can be dangerous. It can be used against you. For example, a guy tells his girlfriend that he gets very "turned on" and has a hard time controlling himself when she nibbles on his earlobes. He has just given her ammunition to use against him in a moment of weakness.

Let's reverse the situation and look at two possible approaches a girl could take to communicate to her boyfriend that she doesn't want to have her breasts caressed.

(1) "Tom, I don't feel comfortable when you touch me there. Please don't do that anymore!"

Or —

(2) "Tom, I just love it when you caress me there. But it feels so good that I get really turned on and it makes me want to have sex with you right away. I'm afraid that if you keep on getting me hot and bothered like that, one of these times I may not be able to control myself and we could end up going all the way. So please don't!"

While the two approaches may communicate the same information, the second approach points out an area of weakness. Tom may pick up on this weakness and later on use it to gain sexual control. The same principle could apply to sharing about past sexual experience, tempting situations, or any other area of sexual vulnerability. Actually, for some couples this kind of communication is as unwise on a date as a dieter discussing "sweets" in a bakery.

The key to sharing your feelings is to be positive. Don't share negative feelings such as "I feel lonely," "I want to be loved," "I wish it was OK to have sex outside marriage," or "I'm afraid I can't control myself." The goal in communicating feelings about sexual involvement is not to confess weak areas but to share positive desires, desires to be obedient to God and desires to protect each other and the relationship.

With that warning in mind, strive to talk openly with each other. As one teen sums up, "Make your boundaries known to each other. Be honest when you see a problem coming. Remember, the ball is *always* in your court. *You* bring up the subject. *You* start being honest and your partner will begin to feel comfortable sharing as well."

Remember, "If you love me, you'll help me wait till marriage."

5. Include Prayer

Before the Date

One teenager's prayer:

Dear Lord,
Trusting you for strength, I promise to keep myself pure for the person I am to marry, by abstaining from sex and from any other physical expressions that do not honor you.

Such a prayer, prayed before each date, could certainly help to keep a person's dating life on the right track. The attitude conveyed here is one of recognizing that there will be temptation and that the strength to resist temptation must come from the Lord. This teen is ready to take God up on His promise: "Commit thy way unto the LORD; trust also in Him; and He shall bring it to pass" (Psalm 37:5, KJV).

Another teen who recognizes the importance of giving his date life to the Lord says:

> To stay out of a "sex trap" one must first commit all his dating relationships to the Lord. He is to be Christlike, and act like Jesus would if He was on a date. He should also look at his girlfriend or date as the Lord does — at her inward character, not her outward appearance. If he really loves his girlfriend, he should not have to "prove" it to her through sex, but it should be evident in the way he treats her daily through kindness, patience, unselfishness, and forgiveness. If your motive in relationships is to please and bring glory to God, and you practice it, I am sure that God will greatly bless you.

A student from UCLA described the power of committing a date to Christ through prayer. He went to Biola University to pick up his date. He let her in the car and went around and got in on his side. He looked over and her head was bowed. He said to her, "What are you doing?" She replied, "Praying."

He said, "Josh, she ruined everything I had planned for that evening."

On the Date

As one teen points out, "Reading the Bible and praying together is one way to spend time alone without having to worry about sexual temptation. The benefits are obvious: a spiritual bond is created; the couple grows closer to God; and more biblical knowledge is gained."

May I suggest that you begin and end your dates with a brief time of prayer. Starting off the date with prayer will give you the opportunity to commit your date to the Lord together and ask His guidance on it. Knowing that you will be ending the date in prayer will give greater motivation to keep your words and actions such that you won't need to be ashamed before God.

Incorporating prayer into your date life can add a new dimension of depth and security to your relationship. An eighteen-year-old girl describes her experience:

> I am familiar with the temptations that can arise in a dating relationship. I'm just as exposed to the sin around me in high school as anyone else. However, because I am in fellowship with Jesus Christ, my standards of living and conduct are different, and I do not participate in events that may cause a separation between God and myself. As a spiritual leader, my boyfriend Todd begins our moments alone with a time for God and for sharing with each other what the Lord is doing in our lives. *It's exciting!* After a good time of fellowship and prayer, we enjoy holding hands and spending silent moments together with a peace, knowing that we

are not entering into the boundaries of impurity.

Another young woman described one way she keeps herself prepared to resist temptation when on a date. She says:

> I pray for my future husband every night, even though I have no idea who he is. I pray that he will grow strong in the Lord, strive to do His will, have a strong desire to obey Him in every situation and will always love the Lord more than he loves me.
>
> The more I pray for him, the more special he becomes. And the more special he becomes to me, the more I want to save myself for him. It really helps in tempting situations.

Although I want to encourage teens to pray together, I also need to warn them to be cautious. Prayer can be extremely intimate. In fact, nothing in this world is more intimate than going to our heavenly Father in prayer. When this kind of intimacy begins to be expressed in a male-female relationship, under proper control, it can be edifying, but it carries a definite risk. If there is a vulnerability to the sexual, it is easy to move from the spiritual intimacy of prayer to physical intimacy. I've known enough young people who have said they originally became so close through prayer that the next thing they knew they were becoming physically intimate. Be careful. It's a very fine line.

Some keys to using prayer effectively in a relationship are:

1. Be brief. Commit your goals and desires for your time together to the Lord, but remember that spending extended amounts of time alone together in prayer may create a degree of intimacy that you are not able to handle.

2. Be positive. Express your love for the Lord and your desire to please Him in all you do. Thank the Lord for positive Christlike qualities that you appreciate in each other and for the things that He is teaching you through your relationship.

3. Pray for the needs of others. Couples sometimes have a tendency to make their prayer life so introspective that they forget there are other people with needs also. Praying for others will help to create a healthy outward focus for your relationship.

4. Be careful of your physical contact when praying. Remembering that prayer will naturally create a sense of intimacy between you, it is wise to avoid a lot of physical contact during prayer. You may wish simply to hold hands or not to touch each other at all.

5. Don't pray about your negative feelings or your sexual struggles (i.e., "I feel lonely. I want to be loved. I want to be held." Or, "I really want to make love to my girlfriend even

though I know it's wrong." "I so desire my boyfriend but not until it's the way the Bible says it must be"). You need to be honest with the Lord about your negative feelings and struggles with sexual desire, but that kind of honesty needs to take place in the privacy of your time alone with Him.

Keeping guidelines like these in mind, allow God to build prayer into your dating life as a natural expression of your commitment to Him individually and as a couple.

6. Avoid Being Alone

Imagine that a teenage girl's parents are out of town for the weekend and have given her permission to entertain her boyfriend in their home. After a candlelight dinner for two has soothed their hunger pangs, the couple finds their way to a comfy sofa in front of a blazing fire. Feelings of romance run high and soon they find themselves saying, "Let's do it. It seems so right."

Proverbs 6:27 tells us in effect that if you play with fire you're going to get burned. The same principle applies to controlling dating situations. A lot of time alone together is more than most teens can handle. Research shows that the first act of sex doesn't happen most often in a car, but at the home of one of the couple when parents are away (usually between 3 and 5 P.M.). The way to handle that kind of temptation is not to put yourself in it in the first place. Don't place yourself and your date in potentially compromising situations. For example, parking in a car, watching sexually oriented films or videos, being at a date's house while parents are away or asleep are all compromising situations. One teenager warns, "Being in the dark and/or being someplace with no fear of interruption for a long period of time are plainly things to avoid."

Another teen advises:

Avoid seductive situations. Avoid extended periods of aloneness. Always have something planned ahead of time when going out on a date. Avoid skimpy dress, lying-down situations — and especially avoid alcohol. Avoid petting; keep your clothes on. Watch your sexual excitement level.

Think through goals ahead of time and determine what kinds of activities you want to do. One adult looks back and says:

"Do nothing in private that you wouldn't do in public." That advice once seemed a bit stiff to me, unrealistic, even prudish and unreasonable. It even seemed to suggest that what you did when alone depended on how brazen you were prepared to be in public.

Looking back now on my experience and that of other Christian friends, such advice seems much more sensible than I then thought.

Parents can help their teens minimize compromising situations. When your son or daughter asks to have a date at the house when you aren't home, you have the right to say no. Ironically, we're afraid to give the kids the keys to the car, but we leave the front door wide open.

Don't be afraid to ask teens where they're going, what their plans are, and when they'll be back. Set reasonable curfews and let your teens know what you expect from them in their dating. By holding them accountable you also provide them with clear answers to pressures from their dating partners. When pressured they can simply give a reply such as "I can't have you come over after school today. My parents don't allow me to have friends over when they're not home," or "I'm sorry, but my parents are expected home in a few minutes." Parents can give kids an *out* by setting boundaries.

Teens shouldn't assume they are strong enough to handle compromising situations. The temptations of being completely alone can be too much for even the strongest Christians. Below is the story of one college student who learned this lesson the hard way.

During my freshman year, I began dating Brad, one of the leaders in a Christian movement on campus. Because both of us were involved in the group's music ministry we spent a great deal of time together planning music for our weekly meetings and other special events. One thing led to another and soon we were an "item."

At our high-pressure university, most of our time was spent studying. Because I had a single room in a house full of other girls from this Christian group, it seemed like the perfect place for Brad and me to study. *It wasn't.* "Study breaks," as any college student knows, are a required part of a good study time. For Brad and me, study breaks went from running down to the kitchen for a Coke to talking and hand-holding in my room to kissing and so on. I don't really remember how we justified everything that happened in that room, but I remember that we tried to.

I remember standing in front of 100 college students on a Friday night and leading singing, with Brad right behind me playing the guitar, and I was pretending that I was right with God. I remember leading a Bible study on holiness with my disciples, while I was writhing inside with shame. I remember sharing the gospel with many students who were probably purer in the realm of the physical than I was. I remember how the power of the Holy Spirit began to ebb from my life. And I remember I hated myself.

I took a one-year leave of absence from college and moved 3,000 miles away from school and my hypocrisy and my sin. During that time, just like a baby, I learned to walk with God again. I learned that He could forgive me for my selfishness and my sin. *And I learned that His commandments are meant for our good.*

7. Set Aside the Physical and Focus on Building the Relationship

Once a couple becomes sexually involved, their priorities often shift away from the spiritual, emotional and social sides of the relationship and focus on the physical. Couples who desire godly relationships need to set aside the sexual part and focus on building the other aspects of their relationship.

As one teen says:

When you begin to develop a relationship, try to start out on a friendship level. Generally, you would never consider taking advantage of a friend. Moreover, you would tend to relate to the person in a spiritual or emotional way. This is important. A couple needs to know each other spiritually and emotionally so that later problems can be properly resolved.

If you sense that the physical has become too great a part of your date life, you may need to evaluate your relationship honestly. One young woman advises asking these questions:

Are you really seeking ways to strengthen your relationship? Are you seeking to help your boyfriend grow spiritually and emotionally? Is your sexual relationship drawing the two of you closer together or pulling you apart? Do you think that your relationship is stronger now than it was before you were sexually involved?

Another young woman points out that stopping sexual involvement can bring about several positive benefits:

1. It will put a new spark in the fire! Withholding yourselves sexually from each other will give you something to look forward to in the future.
2. A commitment not to engage in premarital sex will please the Lord, and thus will begin to eliminate much of the guilt you may be feeling.
3. It will help build a foundation of commitment because you will have made a commitment to continue seeing each other even though your sexual relations have changed.
4. It will motivate you to discover new areas in each other's personality you have not yet explored.

Focusing away from the sexual aspects will definitely alter a relationship. If the relationship is based on nothing more than sexual chemistry, the couple probably will break up. But if there is a good foundation of love and respect, the relationship will become stronger as the couple gets to know each other's *person* rather than each other's body.

Though our society tells us otherwise, it *is* possible to have a fulfilling date life without sex. In fact, over the long run, it is easier. As one young woman who takes a strong stand on this issue says:

> I am nineteen years old and have dated several different guys during high school. At present I have been dating a fantastic Christian guy for the past two years. We have only held hands and I have never kissed anyone, let alone engaged in any kind of sexual relationship. Most people today feel that this kind of lifestyle is crazy and just plain stupid. Don't misunderstand me. This kind of dating relationship is not easy, but it's by far the best. I don't know any girl who has had more fun in her teenage dating life than I have. I have dated the neatest Christian guys who respected me and took me out for the sole purpose of having fun and getting to know me better.

So, is the waiting worthwhile? One now-married person sums it up this way:

> I learned a lot about self-control from waiting. This knowledge has helped me in many areas of my life. I learned that true love requires self-sacrifice, and putting the best interests of both persons above temporary pleasure. Finally, I was reminded that virtue is its own reward, and that there are intangible benefits in doing what you know is right.

19

ESCAPE ROUTES

1. Make a Commitment to God

In a teenage girl's own words:

Now was the time to take that first step. I knew what I had to do. I had to give Ken back to the Lord and put Jesus first, where He should have been all along. I knew I had to do this, but I was so afraid. For over a year I had been holding on to Ken and putting all of my faith in him only. I had a dream that I would one day become more to Ken emotionally than I was physically. Yet how could I become more to Ken, when I had let myself become so much less?

––––––––––––– ♥ –––––––––––––

This girl recognized that as a Christian she had to give Jesus his rightful first place in her life. As teens become involved in close relationships they are tempted to make their boyfriend or girlfriend the center of their lives. When that happens, activities, thoughts and decisions all begin to revolve around that "one special person." This is especially dangerous if that special person begins to pressure his or her date for sex. If the teen's desire to please his partner has taken precedence over the desire to please God, he will often give in to the pressure, perhaps out of fear of losing his partner's love.

Yet no matter how much we love another person — even in marriage — Jesus Christ must always be our first love and the highest priority of our lives. When He is the center of our lives, everything else will fall into its proper place. For example, teenagers can evaluate their dating life and relationships with the opposite sex by asking, "Would this be pleasing to God?" If God has first place in their lives, they will not engage in any activity that would displease Him.

If God is no longer first in our lives we need to recommit our lives to Him, trusting Him to work out what is best for us. If we have been sexually involved outside marriage, we need to give that over to the Lord, make a commitment before Him to end our sexual activity and depend on Him for the power and ability to carry out that commitment.

As one young man advises his peers:

I challenge you to give God a chance to work in your relationship. Make a commitment to Him to stop being sexually involved and to wait for the right time with the right person. If you and your girlfriend really are in love, then your love for each other will only grow stronger and deeper as you build your relationship on the Lord and save sex for its proper context. If your relationship doesn't survive without the physical part, then it obviously wasn't right and wasn't God's best for you. And why settle for anything less than the best?

2. Break Off the Relationship

Pat first had sex when she was sixteen. She became a Christian the next year and although she eventually learned that sex outside marriage was wrong, she was often frustrated by her inability to break an established habit pattern of exchanging sex for love. Finally, Pat decided to stop dating for a couple of years so she could get her thoughts together. It was a time of incredible spiritual growth and it seemed that God gave her victory in an area that had been a thorn in the flesh for so long.

———————— ♥ ————————

Pat's story illustrates the fact that sometimes, when teens find themselves unable to break an established habit involving sexual activity, the best thing they can do for themselves is to stop dating for a while. This is more than just "fleeing" the immediate situation. It involves breaking off any ungodly relationship altogether and not dating until the teen develops strong godly convictions and gains the spiritual and emotional maturity needed to put those convictions into practice.

There is a kind of "catch 22" in this area. The person who most needs to back away from a dating relationship is the teen who is most insecure and immature. Yet an immature person will have a hard time recognizing and acknowledging his (or her) immaturity, while more mature people will be able to admit their weaknesses. This is where good advice can be valuable — advice from a respected older person who can discern maturity levels in various areas of a teen's life. If a person is too immature to make wise decisions, and cannot resist peer pressure, then the best thing that person can do is to back away from a dating relationship until he or she can develop the needed maturity.

Another part of the "catch 22" is that backing away from ungodly dating relationships and ungodly friendships is very difficult for an immature person. Insecurity is one reason a person becomes hooked in a dating relationship. This often causes one to hang on even when being hurt. It's like the battered wife who hangs in there with her husband. Despite the negative environment, there is still some sense of security because she doesn't know what will happen if she leaves that environment.

In a parenting situation, tough love may be needed. For the teen's own good, parents may need to prohibit their son or daughter from dating for a time. Tough love has two aspects which must balance each other, love and authority. Tough love exercises authority, but tough love also demonstrates acceptance and appreciation. Parents shouldn't be "tough" until they have first demonstrated love.

A teen who has been sexually active may be filled with confusion and guilt and will need to allow God to work a healing process in his life. This non-dating time can be a rich experience of developing intimacy with the Lord, experiencing His love and forgiveness, and cultivating convictions about His standards. One girl gives this advice to her friends:

> If you have already had sex, don't despair. Don't feel that the Lord is through with you and there is no hope now since this has happened. If you've sinned you need to ask the Lord's forgiveness, but you also need to forgive yourself. Although you can't change the past, if the Lord has forgiven you, there's nothing to do but forget it and go forward. By forward I mean, break off your sinful relationship. That would be the first step toward true repentance — turning away from your sin. Don't feel tied to your boyfriend just because you've already given yourself to him. Don't feel that you're bound to him, and no one else is going to want you now. I don't know what the Lord has planned for you, but if you seek His will for your life, He promises to show it to you. You'll just have to trust God that whatever man He may bring into your life later will be as forgiving and understanding as He

is concerning your past.

Romans 8:28 promises that all things work together for good to them who love God and are called according to His purpose. That's a pretty reliable promise, coming from God. Don't let the devil continue to trip you up with sin. After all that's just what he wants to do: mess up your life. Ephesians 3:20 says God is able to do *exceedingly abundantly* above all that we ask or think, according to the power that works in us. Give Him that chance.

3. Look for the Way of Escape

The Bible is clear that "the wrong desires that come into your life aren't anything new and different. Many others have faced exactly the same problems before you. And no temptation is irresistible. You can trust God to keep the temptation from becoming so strong that you can't stand up against it. He will show you how to *escape*" (1 Corinthians 10:13, TLB). In other words, no temptation or trial will come to us that is beyond human experience, or beyond what we can bear.

As one teen put it, "God has not left us on our own to try to control our sexual desires, but promises the strength to resist temptation and keep sex under control." There is always a way of escape from temptation. We may feel that we are trapped in tempting situations, but the truth is we are trapped by disobedient choices.

Listen to this teen share what he has learned:

Jerry Bridges, in his book *Pursuit of Holiness*, states that an individual is not defeated by an area of sin in his or her life, but rather the individual is willingly choosing to disobey God. In the same sense, individuals choose to have sex, regardless of what God says in the Bible. For the Christian, we can claim that "with the temptation He will always provide the way out — the means of escape to a landing place — that we may be capable and strong and powerfully patient to bear up under it" (see 1 Corinthians 10:13). The individual must realize in that split second of decision as to whether or not to go to the apartment, the empty house, the back seat of a car or wherever the place, the power to say NO and WAIT is provided by God.

God will always give us strength equal to the temptation. But the best way out is to escape before the compromising situation develops. The most effective way of escape, of course, is simply to learn to say no when faced with temptation. Obedience is difficult, but the rewards far outweigh the temporary pleasure of disobedience.

4. Make a Fast, Strategic Exit

Controlling our sexual desires in volatile situations often means doing one of two things: escaping from the situation or breaking off the relationship. Since teens don't like having to break off relationships, let's look at the option of escape — making a strategic exit.

First, when you get into a situation that you cannot control, *be honest with yourself about your weakness.* If you can't handle it, get out of there. Run as fast as you can! An excellent biblical example of this is the story of Joseph. As one teen retells the story and the lesson learned from it:

> When you try to point out that the Bible says premarital sex is wrong, the common reaction is, "They didn't have the same kinds of temptations we do today." That reaction is a cop-out. In Genesis 39:7-12 we are told the story of Joseph's being tempted by Potiphar's wife. Potiphar's wife was absolutely infatuated with Joseph. She tried her best to seduce him. "Lie with me," she said. Now, Joseph was left in charge of the entire household while Potiphar was away on business. There was no one there to catch them, and Potiphar's wife was very beautiful. But Joseph was smart, and in verse 10 it says, "Joseph day by day harkened not unto her, to lie by her, or to be with her." I suppose Joseph thought that if he wasn't around her, he wouldn't be tempted.
>
> We can escape from temptation the same way Joseph did. It may be true that there are more temptations today, but we haven't changed. Human beings are the same, and our desires are the same. Most important, however, God has not changed; He is still on our side. As it says in 1 Corinthians, God will not allow you to be tempted beyond what you can handle. He has provided ways of escape. On the other hand, His ways of escape are mostly before you enter the temptation.

Here are thoughts from other teens on this subject:

> We must flee from temptation. In James 4:7 the Bible tells us to "resist the devil and he will flee from you." However, in 1 Corinthians 6:18 we are told to "flee sexual immorality"; in 2 Timothy 2:22 God warns us to "flee youthful lusts." God doesn't want us to stand around trying to "overcome" sexually immoral situations but to run from them and not look back!

♡ ♡ ♡

> Stand clear of tempting circumstances. Never place confidence in the flesh. In other words, never deceive yourself by assuming that you have control over the degree of your involvement with your dates. Since fire burns, wise men avoid it.
>
> It's like two men who applied for the same job. The interviewer asked both of the men, "Why do you feel you're most qualified

to drive my trucks?" The first man gave elaborate details of his driving experience and bragged about how he could drive on the edge of a cliff without losing control. The second individual got the job, not because of his experience, but because of his wisdom. He admitted to the interviewer that he had little road experience but promised to stay as far from the edge of the cliff as possible. Similarly, we need to stay as far away as possible from tempting situations.

What happens when you find you are caught in a cycle of compromising situations and frequently give in to temptation?

As R. C. Sproul points out,

If your personal integrity and your obedience to Christ are at stake; if you cannot control your emotions and your behavior, then you have only one option. And that is to break up. Otherwise, you commit treason to Christ. Christ says, "If you love me, keep my commandments." There comes a moment in many Christians' lives when they have to make a choice: Christ or their boyfriend or girlfriend. Obedience or disobedience. And when it comes to that, then I have to say that your obedience to Jesus Christ is more important than your romantic relationship with a human being, and you'd better break up. 59

As has been said, though it will hurt to do so, the best thing you can do for yourself and for your boyfriend or girlfriend is to break off the relationship. The deeper you go into a sinful relationship, the more hurt there will be for you — and the more hurt for other people as well. When you are in a sinful relationship, the faster you "flee," or leave it, the better.

PART 5

ADDITIONAL HELP

THE POWER OF POSITIVE PARENTING

The following letter from a seventeen-year-old boy to his parents expresses what many young people would like to say to their parents, but never do:

Mom and Dad: There have been times when you say you understand me. But you really don't. There have been times when I tell you about my problems in hope of your advice or support. But quite often you just shrug me off saying, "That's nothing . . . you should have our problems."

It was your responsibility to tell me about sex before I discovered it the wrong way. You may not know it, but I learned sex from the street. Believe me, that is not a very good place to learn it.

Often parents abdicate their God-given responsibility to help their children with sexual development. As one teen wrote:

If only all parents could understand that we teens want to learn about sex from our parents, not from school or from the streets. Unfortunately, many parents shy away from the subject of sex.

Research shows that adolescents desire to have their parents talk to them about sex and be their primary information source.

A survey of 1,400 parents found that less than 15 percent of mothers and 8 percent of fathers had ever talked to their children about premarital sex or sexual intercourse. 193/29

Can we expect our young people to say no to sex if their own parents have never suggested this to them? Because of the lack of parent-teen discussion in this area, the battle is lost without a fight.

Parents are the child's earliest models of sexuality. Some teenagers like the one who wrote this, feel confused because their parents are ambivalent or indefinite in expressing their own convictions about sex:

Despite the fact that I grew up in the Bible belt, no one ever told me premarital sex was wrong, *not even my mother*. She didn't want to bias me with her opinion, so she never told me one way or the other. I believe this is one major reason that people of my age participate in premarital sex.

Why are many parents reluctant to participate in their children's sexual development? *Family Life and Sexual Learning of Children* suggests,

> Most parents did not learn about sexuality from *their* parents and thus lack role models to help them in approaching their own children; they often perceive themselves to be uninformed about sexuality and may be confused about the sexual values they wish to communicate to their children. 193/172

There is an obvious principle here. *You cannot lead — if you don't know the way.* Parents can never provide leadership to their children if they are uncertain what they themselves believe about sex, or if they feel uncomfortable about their own sexuality. And, as has been suggested, one reason for this uncertainty is that some parents themselves never learned about sex from their parents.

It would be helpful at this point to consider *God's plan for love, sex and marriage training.*

God's Plan for Sexual Training

Recently we have heard a lot of talk about the need for schools and churches to become involved in sex education and training. Have you ever wondered how children received this training before modern educational concepts were developed? Let's go back to the creation of man and examine how God Himself planned for children to learn of sexuality.

In God's plan the *place* of learning was the *family.* The *teachers* were the *parents.* The teaching *method* was *role modeling.* Let's consider how God's training process was intended to work.

According to God's design, the process would begin with loving and caring parents who were neither autocratic nor demanding. They would provide a nurturing environment in which their children would each be *accepted* as unique persons and *appreciated* for their individual accomplishments.

In that environment of acceptance and appreciation, children would gain a sense of *security* and *significance.* Secure in their parents' love, they would learn moral rules and guidelines from them. They would follow those guidelines willingly — not because they had to but *because they wanted to* — led by loving *example* (role modeling).

Mom and Dad, created in the image of God as male and female, were to model God's unlimited love and truth. Of course, neither the parent, nor any other person, can provide the ultimate security that can be found only in God's infinite unconditional love. The idea was that parents would bring their children close to them by love in order to bring the children to the ultimate one who is love, God. Parents were to guide those whom God had given them stewardship over, that is their children.

In the process, children would learn *self-control* and *self-discipline* by exercising their wills in an environment in which rules or *limits* were balanced by love. They would understand that those limits expressed their parents' love and concern, and were for their benefit and protection. The children would respond willingly to love rather than react to force or fear.

Then, according to God's plan, the young generation would grow up to repeat the cycle. As mature, loving, accepting parents they in turn would provide for their children a nurturing family environment and become the role models God intended for the communication of His truth about love, sex and marriage. In that way God's blessings would be passed from generation to generation.

Role modeling in the context of a loving family is God's plan for the sexual training of young people. Because of the breakdown of the home, however, most families are not functioning according to God's plan. Youngsters are left unprepared to face today's sexual pressures.

Even worse, *negative* parental role modeling is often responsible for teen involvement in premarital sex. One young person wrote:

> In order for a child, teenager or young adult to receive instruction, they must first see their parents "practicing what they preach." So many parents are divorced or committing adultery that they have no right or desire to tell their children not to go to bed with someone, because they are doing the same things. We cannot expect the young adults to have strong principles or to be moral persons if parents have no principles or standards.

Young people are more likely to follow what their parents do, than what they say. According to God's plan, children are to be led by loving *example* rather than pushed by dictatorial demands.

The Ecology of the Family

In God's economy there is an "ecology" or balance of the family that is just as sensitive as environmental ecology. When things get out of balance in the world of nature, plants and animals suffer. When the ecology of the family gets out of balance, people suffer — particularly children.

Most parents sincerely want to be good models for their

children. But often it's one thing to want something and quite another thing actually to do it. One of the tragedies of our time is that we have a generation of young people now at the marrying age who have grown up largely without good adult examples. Although many of these young people say they want the traditional marriage commitment, they are seriously handicapped by their lack of parental role models. The White House Conference on the Family described the plight of families as early as 1970 in the opening paragraph of a report prepared by the Forum on Parents and Children. It stated:

> America's families, and their children, are in trouble, trouble so deep and pervasive as to threaten the future of our nation. The source of trouble is nothing less than a national neglect of children by those primarily engaged in their care — America's parents. 276/252

Urie Bronfenbrenner of Cornell University says, "In summary, whether in comparison to other contemporary cultures, or to itself over time, American society emerges as one that gives decreasing prominence to the family as a socializing agent." 188/103

The Power of a Close Family

Family closeness fortifies children with inner resistance to the "toxins" of life. One adolescent-parent study shows that

> adolescents in a close family unit are the ones most likely to say no to drug use, premarital sexual activity, and other antisocial and alienating behaviors. They are also the ones most likely to adopt high moral standards, develop the ability to make and keep friends, embrace a religious faith, and involve themselves in helping activities. All of these characteristics pertaining to adolescents from close families are significant — which means that the evidence cannot be attributed to mere chance. 107/72

After extensive research, the Strommens observed that

> a strong incentive to moral living, and a powerful inhibitor of living for the instant gratification of one's desires, is found in the expectations of an adolescent's parents. Where love and respect are the common bond, the opinions and wishes of the parent carry considerable force. One young man, reminiscing on past behavior says, "What helped me decide against doing something I knew was wrong were the expectations of my folks. I respect and care for them and did not want to do something I knew would hurt them." 107/127

What Kind of Role Model Are You?

As parents and as adult leaders we must examine our own lives. What kind of examples are we? Have we assumed our rightful places as God's role models for our young people? Adults may be ineffective in this area because their parents were poor models for them. What kind of role models were your parents? We must each do our part to restore the God-intended role-modeling cycle.

If you model love and acceptance, your young people are more likely to act out that kind of relationship to their peers, including their dates. The more *unconditional* your love for your children (following our Lord's example), the less likely they are to give in to sexual pressure. The "if you love me you'll let me" approach is the sexual expression of someone who has not experienced enough acceptance and appreciation to be able to develop a sense of security and significance.

We adults may be poor role models because we have never experienced the truth of God's love and acceptance for ourselves. Have we allowed the Holy Spirit to illuminate our lives with that truth? Have we begun to see ourselves as God sees us, as unique persons created in His image, with infinite worth and value? Perhaps we have not had the opportunity to be loved and accepted by a company of God's people who see us as He sees us.

No one can lead anyone else to where they have never been. If parents themselves have never experienced God's love through acceptance and appreciation, it is difficult for them to help their children gain a sense of security and significance.

Parents Must Reexamine Their Values

If a parent is not a good role model, perhaps his or her world view is wrong. (For an in-depth discussion of world view and its relevance to sexuality, see chapter 16, the section subheaded "A Set of Convictions," beginning on page 324.) Remember, your world view is that sum total of experience and training that determines your behavior. In the times in which we live it is crucial that every parent have a biblical world view. Sexual behavior is directly related to one's holistic perception of the world. Since our daily experiences impact and sometimes alter our world views, they should be reexamined periodically.

As parents we need to review our specific sexual attitudes and values. Are we clear about what we believe and why we believe it? Do we need a refresher course? Have our convictions been weakened by the influences of the world in which we live?

We discussed earlier the tremendous impact that today's

media has on our young people. Are we as parents immune from those influences? Were you outraged the first time you watched an explicit media portrayal of sex? I'm sure you were. I know I was. But what about today when we have sexual acts portrayed regularly on television? Do we continue to be outraged? Probably not. Why? Because constant exposure to the media's lies about sex has subtly invaded our minds and, without our knowing it, has *influenced our thinking!*

Remember the warning of Paul, "Don't let the world around you squeeze you into its own mold" (Romans 12:2, Phillips).

We strongly urge pastors and church leaders to review the biblical principles of sexuality with the adults in their congregations. We need to reawaken our consciences in these areas. We need to regain our sense of outrage — without fear of being considered prudish or Victorian.

If being a prude means that I practice and uphold biblical sexual values, then I pray that by God's grace I will always be a prude. And I want my children to know where I stand.

Parental Sexual Influence Must Be Positive

However, I don't want to communicate primarily negative attitudes about sex to my children. They need to know that, although I totally disapprove of the media's jaded and warped depictions of sex, I wholeheartedly approve of sex within God's context of marriage . . . and *I enjoy it to the fullest.* When Mom and Dad are not happy in the relationship, or when either parent is absent because of death or divorce, such parental expression is not possible. A friend whose wife died several years ago expressed the difficulty he had of communicating the joy of sex to his children because he had no mate to show affection to, no one to be a role model with — but instead only good memories to share verbally with his children.

I want my children to know I love their mom and she loves me — not just platonically, but sexually. They know their mother and I sometimes "steal away and have our little honeymoons." Charlotte had been speaking back in Chicago, and Dick was due to pick her up at the airport. He asked his boys, Jonathan, 13, and Timmy, 12, if they would mind if he picked their mom up and spent the night in San Diego in a motel and relaxed the next day with her. Timmy with a gleam in his eye said, "Go for it, Dad." Both boys understood the joy of sex their mom and dad express to each other.

Often young people grow up without an awareness that their parents are sexually attracted to each other. A survey among college students revealed that many of them couldn't imagine their parents having sex. How tragic! Parents should let their kids know that they love each other and enjoy their "honey-moons." The more kids see their parents treat sex in a wholesome, normal way — as God intended — the more likely they will do the same.

Are You Comfortable With Your Own Sexuality?

As parents we should be the primary guides for our children's sexual development and education. Why is it often so difficult? If we are embarrassed or uncomfortable talking to our children about sex, it may be that we aren't comfortable with our own sexuality.

Surgeon General C. Everett Koop believes that "the best thing we could do to help parents is to make them feel comfortable about their own sexuality." 208

How many of you husbands and wives communicate with each other about your sexual needs or problems? Do you talk openly about which aspects of sex give you the greatest pleasure? If a husband and wife aren't free to talk to each other about their sexuality, how can they ever feel free to talk about the subject with their children?

Often the problem is that we are embarrassed with our sexuality. Either because of our backgrounds or our experiences we may have a serious misunderstanding of this special gift that God has given to us. Our confusion may go back to the role modeling provided us by our own parents.

In order to offset that ineffective role modeling, we recommend a thoughtful reading of *Love Life for Every Married Couple* by Ed Wheat and *The Act of Marriage* by Tim LaHaye.

The Need for Parental Openness

Parents should be intimate and open (transparent, showing loving concern, caring) with their children. Unless parents and children have genuine intimacy in the totality of their relationship, sex is likely to be the last area in which they will be open.

Psychologist Catherine Chillman says, "If communication has been open with parents and if the parents themselves believe that sex should be connected with love, then teens are less likely to be affected by what peers are doing." 172/D6

It is crucial to build an open relationship with our children, one in which it is easy and natural to communicate about *every-thing,* not just sex. Such open communication includes the sharing not only of facts and information but also of feelings. Teens need parents who are willing to share with them their hopes, dreams and hurts. When parents have this kind of relationship with their children it becomes natural and easy to talk about sex.

Dr. Koop, speaking about the AIDS epidemic, emphasizes that

> if we could get this generation of kids to come into young adulthood having been taught about sex and life [by their parents], it [sexual promiscuity] wouldn't be a problem in the next generation because they would be able to express themselves and understand their own sexuality. The way we face the problems of educating our young people will really determine whether or not our young people even survive. 208

A Matter of Time

Parents can't influence the sexual development of children if they don't spend time with them. A recent study of church parents and their children found that the majority of teens spend less than thirty minutes a day with their fathers. Forty-four percent spend less than thirty minutes a day with their mothers.

> Even more alarming, one-fourth of the ninth-graders in this study spend less than five minutes (on an average day) alone with father to talk, play, or just be together. No doubt this neglect is one reason why 46 percent of the fathers in the study admit they worry ("quite a bit" or "very much") about how their child feels about them. 107/79

Remember, young people don't need sexual facts and information from their parents as much as they need a loving, intimate, caring relationship.

No parent-teen relationships are possible without the investment of more time than most spend daily in watching TV or reading the newspaper. Without a relationship it is impossible to be a positive influence on a young person's sexuality.

Again, please take note that *rules without relationships lead to active or passive rebellion.* Teens respond to relationships. That's why their peers carry such weight with them.

People Are More Important Than Things

Someone has wisely stated that "people are more important than things." Yet we can, by our example, make our children feel less important than our possessions.

Today children rarely have any idea what their parents do at work. All they know is that from early morning to late in the day their parents are away "working." Then, if lucky, they may get five to thirty minutes of time with their parents, little of which is exclusive. No wonder kids feel insignificant and insecure. No wonder many of them, after the age of puberty, are vulnerable to the "sexual advances" of their peers.

Most adults today spend the majority of their time in the accumulation of material possessions. Forty-five percent of all mothers with children less than a year old work outside the home, and the percentage is expected to increase. 277/A15 More than three-fifths of all married couples in the United States have become two-income families. According to George Sternlieb and James W. Hugh, in *American Demographic Magazine,* "The good life in America increasingly requires a household economic team of two workers." 278/A1 Is it any wonder that children learn to follow their parents' example and look to *things* for security? Why do we have two-income families? In many cases it is to pay for more and more *things.*

Why have we taken this materialistic plunge? Because of our own insecurities. When people lack security in relationships they look to "things" for security. I see this illustrated in marriage counseling over and over again. A couple that has a secure relationship can weather the problems of financial difficulty. There will be moments of tension, perhaps even harsh words, but a committed couple's relationship will grow as a result of this difficulty. But what happens when a couple with an insecure relationship suffers financial reversal? That's right. Divorce.

As Christian parents we need to examine our priorities. We need to arrest this "materialistic plunge." Are we investing more time in things than in our children? What is the source of *your* security? The love and acceptance of God the Father? Or your automobiles, wardrobe, home and furnishings, possessions? Even our children can be looked upon as part of one's possessions if we don't recognize and appreciate their own uniqueness.

Many parents give their children things as a substitute for love. The greatest gift parents can give their children to help them in their sexual development is the gift of themselves — not a book, not a tape, not a condom or the pill — but *themselves.*

The Bible says, "The love of money is the root of all evil." 209 But consider the flip side: The love of people is the root of all good.

Parents, love your children.

* * * * * *

OPEN MOUTH, CLOSED EARS?

(Communicating With Your Teen)

By Josh McDowell
with Dave and Neta Jackson

"Do you know what I am?" a teenager once asked. "I'm a comma."

"What do you mean?" the listener replied.

"Well, whenever I talk to my dad, he stops talking and makes a 'comma.' But when I'm finished, he starts right up again as if I hadn't said a thing. I'm just a comma in the middle of his speeches."

Many of our young people are crying out for a real conversation with a parent — one that involves not only the exchange of thoughts, but also of feelings. A conversation that throughout includes both a listener and a talker.

Teens are very sensitive to rejection or ridicule. If they feel ignored, or experience being "put down" when they speak up, or get an argument every time, they will hesitate to share their real feelings or opinions. Who wants to feel ridiculed or rejected? And though they may try, what teen can hope to win an argument with an adult?

Surgeon General Everett Koop was asked that if he had one thing to say to parents, what would it be? His answer: "Make yourself available for dialogue with your children, because they desperately want to know how you feel about them." 208

Some parents think that communication consists of stating the rules loud and clear; what those parents don't realize is that *rules without relationships lead to rebellion.* If you don't have a good relationship with your children, the rules will elicit rebellion instead of response. Teens respond to relationships. The relationship necessary for good communication with your teens is built on mutual respect. If you respect your children, they will respect you.

Where does respect begin? With *listening.* If you feel that someone is listening to you, you feel respected. So does your teen.

Listening: The Foundation for Good Communication

The biggest problem with listening is we usually just don't want to take the time. But when we are too busy to listen to our children, we are *too busy.* Jesus was not too busy. Dr. Bruce Narramore illustrates the importance Jesus placed on children:

> Jesus was conducting some important business in Judea. Hundreds were following Him and He was healing many. As He was engaged in a vital discussion with the Pharisees, some children came to visit. Jesus' disciples brushed them off. They said, "Can't you see He's busy? He has important things to do." But Jesus rebuked His mistaken disciples. He said, "'Suffer little children, and forbid them not, to come unto me: for of such is the kingdom of heaven.' And he laid His hands on them, and departed thence" (Matthew 19:14, 15, KJV). Jesus put the little children first! 230/88-90

Hear What Your Teen Is Really Saying

Even when we do listen, we often can get hung up on the *words* we hear, and miss the *message.*

Teenager, slamming the door after school: "I hate Katie McDaniel, and I'm never going to speak to her again!"

The real message may well be: "I feel really rejected because Katie went off with Tanya and didn't bother to tell me."

It takes practice, but parents need to listen for the feelings behind the words. This is possible if we're not too quick to jump in and respond, but give time for the real feelings to emerge.

We can pick up some clues to the teen's feelings if we remember that part of good communication is listening with our eyes as well as our ears. Look for physical and nonverbal communication: the way your teen uses his eyes, the gestures he makes, the body posture. Is your teen anxious? excited? indifferent? depressed? If you watch for these nonverbal signs, you'll catch a great deal more of the communication.

Eleven Principles for Good Communication

"Communication is essential to showing love," writes Dr. Bruce Narramore. "It is a prerequisite to gaining knowledge. To help our children grow to maturity, we must improve our communication skills."

We found that communication with our teens is essential also in helping them determine their approach to their own sexuality. Some research suggests that "increased communication between parents and children may reduce irresponsible sexual behavior." 225/649

A number of studies indicate that "parental communication about sex may postpone a child's sexual activity and increase the likelihood that they will not engage in premarital intercourse." 226/74

We also find that some parents are quite ready to listen, but their teenage children won't talk. All they get is a grunt on the way through the kitchen to the telephone. Or the parents are thoroughly bewildered when the teens do talk because the parents don't understand the world the teens refer to or the language they use.

How can you encourage your kids to open up? How can you become a better communicator with your teenagers?

The following eleven principles have helped Dick and me a good deal over the years as we have worked at becoming better communicators with our wives. And I've discovered that what works for adult-adult communication works with adult-teen communication as well. Learning to apply the following principles will greatly reduce the complaint, "You never listen to me!"

1. Work at It

Doing what comes naturally may be the motto for many in our culture, but becoming a good communicator does not just happen naturally. All of us are twisted by self-centeredness, so we need to make a lot of effort to communicate better with our teens.

Some parents plan for occasional meals out (just Dad and daughter, for instance) to help create an opportunity for communication. Sometimes the talk is low-key; other times deeper issues are raised or feelings surface that might not otherwise come up in the everyday world at home. One father and his teenage son go away for a hunting weekend each fall. Besides doing something together that they enjoy, the long ride in the car and the evenings camping out help them get to know each other better.

Other suggestions include:
- swimming together, jogging, cooking, attending an evening class or a concert, etc.;
- planning topics for discussion at dinner or during rides to and from school or church;
- inviting your teen into your bedroom to talk, or asking to come into theirs from time to time;
- asking their opinions, and respecting those opinions.

2. Seek to Understand

A little placard I've frequently seen posted on office walls reads: "I know you believe you understand what you think I said, but I am not sure you realize that what you heard is not what I meant." One of the keys to communication and developing intimacy is to convey to the other person that you are not only trying to understand, but you truly care. That kind of empathy will cause both individuals to be more open in the relationship.

On the other hand, if a teen senses that a parent doesn't want to listen, or is not trying to understand him, it affects his self-esteem. He soon begins to withdraw because he feels that what he has to say is not viewed as being important.

"Acceptance," according to Dr. H. Norman Wright, "does not mean that you agree with the content of what is said. Rather, it means you understand that what your [teen] is saying is something he/she feels." He adds that "sensitive listening is reaching out to the other person; actively caring about what he says and what he wants to say." 228/90

Parents need to enter their teen's world enough so that they are speaking the same language. You need to get your child's perspective. I'm forty-six years old, and it's hard for me to think back to junior high and recall exactly what I was going through. Still, I'm constantly trying to see my children's viewpoints. I want to know their world, and I *must* know it if I am going to communicate with them. I need to listen to their music, read what they read, know their friends, laugh at their jokes.

I also need to consider how what I say will affect them. They may not take things the same way an adult would, so I need to look at my statements to them from their perspective. If a light-hearted statement (by me) gets a big negative reaction (from the teen), that's a clue that I need to develop more understanding of his perspective. When I do that, it expresses my love more clearly to that teen.

3. Give a Response to Show You're Listening

Concentrating on what your teen is saying can be difficult sometimes. For every one hundred words spoken, our minds could have received and understood five hundred, so it's easy for the mind to wander. A parent may seem to be listening, but mentally may be making out the grocery list. We move the conversation along with a few well-spaced Uh-huh's and I see's. But it helps to ask yourself, "Can I repeat back to my child what he or she is saying?" Taking the time to hear, between the words, the feelings that are being communicated helps me concentrate.

If there is one thing that always encourages sharing, it is giving either verbal or body-language feedback. Here are some helpful suggestions to show that you are absorbing what your teen is saying:

React physically. Turn toward your teen. Lean forward. Nod your head in response. Keep looking at your son or daughter's eyes. Nothing shows greater interest than eye contact.

Request more information. Ask a question that seeks clarification or additional details: "What did you mean by that?" Or "Why is that important to you?" In asking questions you are saying, "Tell me more — I'm interested."

Reflect on what has been said with a leading statement: "You seem quite excited by meeting him." Or "That must have been rough on you." Reflective listening pays off in more intimate sharing.

Repeat or rephrase statements with feeling. "Your history class might go to Washington, D.C.? That *is* exciting." Echoing the meaning or feeling of a statement both clarifies that statement and encourages further communication.

Remain silent when your teen is telling a story. Don't interrupt, and don't finish sentences for him. This is a hard one for me. I have to keep telling myself, "Don't interrupt, don't interrupt." Also, don't rush to fill a pause in the conversation simply to avoid the silence — you may cut off something important your teen was preparing to share.

Refrain from concentrating on your answer while your teen is still talking; it makes you impatient to speak. When you are constantly constructing a rebuttal or a way to justify something you've said, you are merely building up a defense mechanism. As a result, you are not truly listening.

Express your encouragement and appreciation for what your teen has been sharing. Both of these enhance healthy communication. Solomon in his wisdom knew that "kind words are like honey — enjoyable and healthful" (Proverbs 16:24, TLB). Say, "I really appreciate your sharing that with me, Honey. I didn't know you felt that way." Or "What you've said makes a lot of sense. I want to give it some thought."

These techniques are just a few ways to respond actively when your teen is trying to talk to you. Remember that your open ear can open the door to your teen's heart.

4. Affirm Your Teen's Worth, Dignity, and Value

Every person has a deep need to be heard, to be *listened to.* The very act of listening communicates a sense of value, esteem, love and dignity. It makes your teen feel important.

A teenager with low or unhealthy self-esteem will fear transparency because of possible rejection. I can't stress strongly enough how important the parent's role is in helping the teen develop a healthy self-esteem. A parent who belittles his son or daughter's opinions ("That's stupid! You don't know what you're talking about."), teases about physical characteristics the teen is sensitive about (weight, pimples, height), expresses contempt for choices the teen makes about clothes or friends, or fails to express confidence in the teen ("You're so lazy; you'll never amount to anything."), will soon discover a thick wall around the teen that blocks out all real communication.

On the other hand, a parent who makes a point of expressing unconditional love, affirms the importance of the teen making his or her own choices in certain areas, respects a child's feelings, refuses to embarrass the teen in front of others, allows room for the teen to make mistakes and in other ways affirms the *personhood* of his son or daughter, will find a foundation being built not only for a good relationship, but also for communication. And don't assume your kids know you love them; tell them, every day!

5. Be Positive and Encouraging

Being positive is a real plus factor in communication. It promotes openness with your children, whereas criticism tends to hinder healthy communication.

During a three-day lecture series at the University of Tennessee, I was in a meeting with some Campus Crusade staff people and several key students. One of the students walked in and said, "I'm not going to hand out any more fliers. Everybody's negative about the meetings. All I've heard is negative reports this morning."

I immediately asked, "How many people have given you a hard time? Twenty-five?"

"No."

"Ten?"

"No."

"Five?" I asked.

"No."

We discovered that only two people had reacted negatively to the two- or three-hundred fliers she had handed out. Everyone in the room, including her, realized that she had accentuated the negative.

In our communication, we tend to notice and remember only the negative statements about ourselves. Ten positive statements and one negative one may be made, but we remember the negative one. Thus the ratio of praise to criticism in a conversation with your teen needs to be 90/10 — 90-percent praise for every 10-percent criticism.

Touching and hugging is another key to reaching children in a positive way, even after they become teenagers. Hug them when they hurt; hug them when they're joyful; hug them just for the fun of it.

6. Keep Their Secrets

Recently two mothers were commiserating about childrearing. Later that day, however, one called the other and apologized for having revealed something of a very private nature about her child. She said, "If she knew I had told anyone, she would be extremely embarrassed." She was right; there was no reason for the other parent to have to know. Respect for the child's confidence was the real issue. We need to talk about our children with the same kind of respect we do other human beings, and not embarrass them unnecessarily.

When your teen knows that you are able to keep things to yourself he automatically feels a greater willingness to be open with you. In speaking, I regularly use personal illustrations to amplify my points, but I must be very careful of what I say about my relationship with my kids. If I were to speak too openly about their struggles, they would become cautious and defensive.

Many kids hate to be talked about in front of others. One mother thought her pre-teen's remark was clever; but when she mentioned it to a friend over the phone in the child's hearing, the child was very upset. Another emerging adolescent was totally embarrassed whenever her parents referred to her bedtime in front of her peers. Parents need to learn to be sensitive to the level of trust and confidence that each child expects. If you blow it, apologize — but remember next time.

7. Wait for the Right Time

In Proverbs we read: "How wonderful it is to be able to say the right thing at the right time" (15:32, TLB). In any relationship, dialogue will be enhanced if the timing is right. Love must be your guide as to when and where you share bad news or discuss a difficult subject with your teen.

One of the hardest places to apply "gracious speech" is with your own children. One parent described the following incident:

One morning recently my oldest got off to a bad start. As he was grabbing his books and his lunch, I noticed that his bed wasn't made, the dog wasn't fed and his laundry hadn't been put away.

"Don't plan on doing anything with your friends when you get home from school today," I fumed at him as he went out the door. "We've got to get a few things straight around here. You can count on some adverse consequences!" He threw me a frustrated look and ran belatedly for the bus.

The moment the door closed, I wanted to bite my tongue. What a way to send a kid off to school. He was already late and frustrated. He might miss the bus and get marked tardy. Yes, we did need to get a few things straight about his morning preparation. But was when he was going out the door the right time to stick it to him?

The timing of a correction or criticism can make it a building experience or one that tears a child down. There are three especially crucial times when parents should choose their words carefully: (1) when your child is going out the door (What words do I send him off with?), (2) when your child first comes home from school (What words is she greeted with at the end of the day?), and (3) when your child is ready to go to bed (What words do I leave my child to sleep on?).

8. Share Your Feelings

Learn to say *how you feel* in conversation with your teens, as well as *what you think.* If they experience your willingness to be vulnerable too, your teens may be more willing to be open about what they are feeling. Do they know that you sometimes feel lonely? afraid? unsure of yourself? That can be a real revelation to a teenager!

Sometimes parents suppress their feelings to avoid conflict, but holding in your gripes diminishes real communication with your teen and usually creates pressures that will cause the feelings to come out in other ways. Rather than stating clearly, "I'm feeling very angry right now," a parent may stuff down feelings which come out in an explosion a few hours or days later over some minor provocation.

Some parents misuse their feelings as a way to manipulate their children. "You don't care how I feel!" Or "Yes, I'm depressed, and it's all your fault!" Or "You make me so mad!" That kind of venting of feelings will indeed make children feel guilty, but it usually also makes them withdraw.

Psychologists and family counselors encourage us to use *"I messages"* when we express our feelings to another person. "I am feeling angry" — not "You make me so angry!"; "I feel ignored" — not "You never listen to me!" Adopting a first-person style is hard (especially when we feel that our teens really *do* "make us mad"). But, though our teens need to be responsible for their actions, we cannot make them responsible for our feelings.

9. Don't Make Assumptions

Warning: Don't take it for granted that your teen understands your gestures, tone of voice, or body language. It becomes very frustrating in a relationship when each person assumes that the other knows what he or she is thinking and feeling and wants to do. Mind-reading never works. You can't hold your teen responsible for knowing that loud music gives you a headache, that you want wet towels hung up, that you like home-made cards on your birthday, or that you're tired and need extra help with supper. Speak up.

One mother was frustrated by her son's habit of watching TV before supper, just when she could use extra help. "You never offer to help!" she fumed.

He said sincerely, "All you need to do is ask."

Teens can seem really dense. They aren't; actually they can be very sensitive. But what they consider important at any one moment, and what you consider important at that same moment, may be as far apart as night and day. They are worried about whether they will have a date for homecoming; you wish they wouldn't run up the phone bill. Expectations need to be communicated clearly; rules need to be specific: "Come in at 11" — not "Don't be too late." When they are thoughtless and hurt your feelings, you need to say so. Don't just assume or hope that your teen will figure it out and come to you first. Every relationship would become more harmonious and more intimate if we would just stop assuming and start communicating our feelings.

10. Learn to Compromise

A healthy relationship with your growing teen children is a give-and-take situation. While it may have been appropriate to "lay down the rules" when they were younger, teens want more say in the things that affect their lives. They are becoming their own persons, and family life needs to adjust to give them more responsibility for decisions (freedom to try their wings and make mistakes) and to take their needs into account in the family schedule.

If your teen decides you are inflexible, he or she simply will give up and not talk to you about rules and expectations that are causing tension between you. They will be frustrated, sullen, or angry, or they will devise ways around the rules behind your back. But if you are willing to discuss issues, negotiate, or compromise, your teen will be much more willing to talk.

This doesn't mean a parent has to be wishy-washy about rules or expectations. But as one family counselor cautions, "You need to choose your battles." In other words, not every issue is of equal importance. You may decide that family rules about curfew and use of drugs or alcohol are nonnegotiable; but expectations for use of the car, chores, dress, and how many meals the family eats together may be open for discussion and mutual agreement.

If teenagers are behaving responsibly, it may be necessary and appropriate to renegotiate and increase their privileges more often, possibly even every four to six months. At certain stages of their development, they actually may mature at that rate. It's sometimes hard for us to keep up with how fast we're "losing little Johnny," but it is important to avoid engendering resentment over rules more suited to someone younger.

11. Be Honest

The apostle Paul saw the issue clearly when he admonished us to be "speaking the truth in love" (Ephesians 4:15, NASB). To speak the truth in love means to take into consideration the other person's feelings. A truly skillful and loving communicator is sensitive to the consequences of his words and actions.

The barriers to being honest are numerous. When we feel we need to be honest in something that could hurt another, we not only need to review the style in which we deliver the message, but we also need to examine our motives. Many cruel things have been said by parents to teens in the name of honesty. Is our motive to accuse? or tear down? Or is it to reconcile? to build up?

Another barrier is that honesty can become nit-picky. No teenager is going to reveal weaknesses and imperfections, if he or she suspects that a complete record is on file of every personal flaw. Honest communication, spoken in love and heard in love, does not "keep score." If you need to speak honestly with your teen about a problem, don't drag out any other sins or failures, past or present.

Speaking the truth in love requires care not to exaggerate. *Always* and *never* are loaded words. Keep your communication simple, direct and on the subject.

Part of being honest is your willingness to ask your kids for forgiveness when you blow it. Some parents think they shouldn't say "I'm sorry" to their children; they might lose their children's respect. The opposite is actually true. Our kids already know we make mistakes. They know when we've acted in haste or been unfair. If we're unwilling to admit it, their trust in us erodes. But if we can admit our mistakes, the damage can be mended; trust is reestablished and confidence in us grows stronger.

Finally, speaking the truth in love means verbalizing your love for your teen — putting it into *words:*

"I'm proud of you."

"I enjoy having you around."

"You are special to me."

"I love you so much."

The best commentary I've heard on Jesus' commandment to "love your neighbor as yourself" (Matthew 22:39) is by David Augsburger. "To love you as I love myself is to seek to hear you as I want to be heard and understand you as I long to be understood." 229/74 It takes work to stand in another person's shoes in order to understand that person; it takes even more work when that person is your teen! But it will make a world of difference in your communication with him or her.

Begin Today

As in acquiring a foreign language, learning to communicate skillfully with your teenagers takes time, dedication, focus and practice. Some families may be better at it than others, so patience with ourselves — and with our teens — is necessary.

Look back over the eleven principles above. Are there one or two that you especially need to work on? Being an effective communicator doesn't happen overnight, but you can start today. Every effort goes a long way toward telling your kids that they are important. As the jingle says, "Reach out and touch someone" — reach out . . . and touch your teen. Good communication will help build the foundation for a lifelong family relationship and eventually will help your child to cope with sexual pressure.

* * * * * *

HOW FAR IS TOO FAR?

After having established with teens that sex before marriage is forbidden by God and that it's not "smart" for them to be involved sexually, we need to be prepared to answer a difficult question: How far *can* I go? Or even better, How far *should* I go?

At first glance it may seem that the Bible isn't very helpful in answering that question. It's true there is no list of specific "do's" and "don'ts." You won't find a passage that states "It's all right to hold hands, but not all right to kiss for longer than one minute." The Bible does not give specific black-and-white answers in every area of sexual behavior. Yet the Bible does give some clear guidelines for avoiding sexual immorality, guidelines that can be used to set personal limits to "necking" and "petting."

The lack of explicit direction, however, has given rise to a number of misconceptions, and we want to look at them here.

"Everything But — "

One common misconception is what I call the "Everything but — " philosophy. According to this view, since the Bible offers no express prohibition against anything except actual intercourse, a person can meet biblical standards for chastity as long as they stop short of actual penetration. But does this "technical virginity" really meet God's standards for sexual purity?

In actuality, such an outlook is a kind of reverse legalism. We're all familiar with the kind of legalism that sets up an artificial list of rules and regulations for Christian behavior based on human standards. Yet there is a reverse legalism that sets up a specific list of "don'ts" and then proclaims that all unspecified actions are acceptable behavior. R. C. Sproul calls this "legal loophole-ism." 59 This kind of legalism searches for loopholes to get around the laws of God. Somehow one manages to keep the *letter* of the law, but he totally disregards the *spirit* underlying the law.

True godliness results not only in obedience to the letter of the law, but also in obedience to its spirit. Doing everything but — certainly disregards the spirit of God's commandment to "flee fornication." If we sincerely want to please God, we cannot base our sexual behavioral limits on "everything but — "!

Sexual Brinkmanship

"Sexual brinkmanship" is also an unacceptable approach to the question, How far can I go? It is human nature to test the limits, to go as close to the brink of disaster as we can without getting hurt. While we don't want to go too far, we do want to go as far as possible — because we're afraid of cheating ourselves out of anything that might be pleasurable or exciting. So we go right up to the edge. We push ourselves to the limits of our sexual control. It's like driving a car along a steep cliff and asking, How close can I get to the edge?

The problem is that if we lose control and go further than intended — and the odds are that anyone playing "sexual brinkmanship" will — we end up hurting ourselves and other people. You see, most people who play sexual brinkmanship end up disobeying not only the spirit of the law but also its letter.

Many young couples don't understand that sex is a progressive activity that culminates in intercourse. They think they can just start downhill and then slam on the brakes when they reach the brink of intercourse. However, this is a misunderstanding of how we were created. Once arousal begins it is unnatural to stop short of full expression.

Sexual stimulation was designed by God to prepare marriage partners for intercourse, not as a pleasant activity that can be easily interrupted. Stimulation, or foreplay, is intended for one thing only: precipitating a married couple into a complete expression of their sexuality.

Not only is the interruption of sexual foreplay almost impossible, but it is also highly frustrating. When sexually frustrated, our bodies don't care about Christian convictions. "Instead of trying to figure out how to derail a fifty-ton locomotive traveling at high speed, wisdom suggests we would do better to stay off the train and avoid the crisis in the first place." 62/221

Lust has an insatiable appetite. The more we feed it the hungrier it gets. With each progressive step of sexual intimacy we take, desire is increased, never decreased. That's why allowing ourselves "minor" compromises of ever increasing sexual intimacy ultimately violates the spirit of the law and leads us to commit sexual sin.

One of the worst preparations for marriage is to become passionate before it takes place. Many women today complain that their husbands don't know how to express intimacy and affection outside the bedroom.

Practical Guidelines

At this point you may be asking what guidelines Scripture offers that will help us obey *both* the spirit and the letter of the law.

First, here is one insight that will help you answer the question, How far should I go? The apostle Paul, to show believers how to live a God-pleasing life, wrote: "For this is the will of God, your sanctification; that is, that you abstain from sexual immorality; that each of you know how to possess his own body in sanctification and honor, not in lustful passion, like the Gentiles who do not know God; and that no man transgress and defraud his brother" (1 Thessalonians 4:3-6a, NASB).

The word *transgress* means "to sin by going beyond a limit or boundary." The word *defraud* means "to take advantage of." In this passage, transgress and defraud can mean: "to arouse sexually outside the bounds of God's limits." What are God's limits for sex? Marriage, and marriage only.

You have transgressed and defrauded a brother (or sister) when you've gone beyond the limits and aroused him (or her) to the point where that arousal cannot be fulfilled in a way that would be pleasing to God. Within the boundaries of a loving marriage, arousal is not defrauding, because our sexual fulfillment is pleasing to God. However, in a dating relationship arousal *is* defrauding, because there is no way to fulfill that arousal without displeasing God.

Now, the exact point of defrauding may vary for different individuals. Not everyone has the same "turn-on point." Some get turned on by just holding hands. Others are able to go further without being aroused:

> Of course, some arousal is normal and should not be worried about too much. But if it becomes so strong that it rules your actions, then it is sin. When your hormones instead of your better judgment start controlling your actions, then you have gone too far. 61

If your actions cause your partner to want to go all the way, even though you may not have reached that point, you have gone too far.

Some teens do not actually understand what "turns on" members of the opposite sex. Arousal can be the result of your words, actions, activities in which you participate, what you read and look at, and even the way you dress. A good rule of thumb to remember: Guys are primarily stimulated by sight; girls are stimulated by touch. Also, there are erogenous zones, primary areas of sexual sensitivity in the body. Obviously, it is wise to "stay far away" from these sensitive areas before marriage.

To avoid defrauding a brother (or sister) each person must first determine that precise point at which one loses control to his or her hormones. Then that point must become an absolute personal limit, never to be crossed. We recommend that young people in premarriage relationships avoid reaching those limits.

In setting limits, teens need to consider their backgrounds and their emotional and spiritual maturity. Your parents and youth director can be two of your best resources when setting your limits. The decision needs to be made both individually and as couples. Remember that your dating partner's limit may be different from yours. You must agree to accept whichever limit would be reached first. Keep in mind that it is defrauding to arouse a brother or sister to the point where that arousal cannot be fulfilled in a God-pleasing way.

Is Your Freedom Limited?

You can know you've gone too far when your "heart is pounding like a jackhammer and your hormones are flowing like water through a firehose." 62/221 When you get sexually aroused, your body doesn't know if you are married or not. *You've gone too far* when you are no longer able to make intelligent, responsible decisions and act them out immediately. Once your hormones have been aroused you begin to limit your freedom, i.e., your ability to make right choices.

Many situations rob a teen of his or her freedom to say no.

1. Sensually stimulating activities and situations, such as certain types of music, dances, parties and so on, appeal to physical passions and arouse sexual desires.

2. Necking and petting — "making out" — are "turn ons" which prepare the body for sexual intercourse. When one is sexually aroused it becomes extremely difficult to make right decisions. The pleasurable sensations which come from the caressing of sensual areas of your body, whether inside or outside clothes, can cause your feelings to overpower your mind. "You've lost your freedom," writes Colleen Kelly Mast of Sex Respect, "when your drive for pleasure takes over your decision-making ability." 255

3. Drugs or alcohol. Drinking or taking drugs affects the mind. They give a false sense of security and wellbeing, weakening the brain's decision-making ability. This euphoria permits your feelings to make irrational decisions.

Just remember, regardless of how the decision is made, you, your date, and often others, will have to live with the consequences.

The Holy Spirit Guides Us

The Holy Spirit can help us know when we are going too far. Scott Kirby points out,

> As believers we have the Holy Spirit living within us. One of the ministries of the Holy Spirit is to convict us of sin through our conscience. We need to be very sensitive to this conviction and obey it instantly. If you feel that something is wrong and you violate your conscience and do it anyway, then the Bible teaches that to you it is sin (Romans 14:14, 22,23). Unfortunately, a person's conscience can become hardened.
>
> Do you remember when you were a kid and went barefoot during the summer? At the beginning of the summer your feet were very tender and it hurt to walk some places. But by the end of summer your feet had become hardened and you could even walk over gravel without feeling it. Our

hearts are this way. The longer we ignore the conviction of the Holy Spirit in our lives, the more hardened our hearts become to him (Titus 1:15). 117/77

Other Practical Suggestions

It is important for young people to be concerned about the *other person.* The Scriptures are explicit about not violating the conscience of another person. Don't light the fires of sexual passion in another person outside marriage. Remember that sexual involvement is progressive. Even extended kissing begins that arousal process. That's why it makes good sense to draw the line somewhere in the early stages of that progression.

An important guideline — particularly for young men — *Don't light a fire that you can't put out!* Never overestimate your or your partner's ability to resist sexual temptation.

At times a *quick exit* is the smart thing to do.

> You can imagine what would have happened if Joseph, in the Old Testament, had said to Potiphar's wife, "Let's sit down on the couch over here and rationally talk this over." 117/94

If you have any reason to believe that a specific situation could end up "out-of-control," *don't be afraid to make a strategic retreat.*

Of course the best way to keep from going too far is never to start. Instead of asking how far I can go without suffering the consequences, it is best to avoid precarious situations altogether. How do young people set their limits? Here are a couple of examples given by teens:

> My suggestions: no extended periods of kissing, not lying down while kissing, no wandering hands, no revealing clothing. I would also recommend spending time in groups. Plan activities where there won't be much free time to get into trouble.

♡ ♡ ♡

> Do not lie down together anywhere . . . Undressing can also lead to problems . . . Being scantily clad, like in your bathing suit or other summer clothes, can have the potential for problems if you aren't careful of where you are and who you are with.

Remember that teens often face strong sexual desires with neither the experience or the know-how to control what they may have set in motion. Paul said to young Timothy, "Flee youthful lusts." 211 We must help our teens to be aware of their vulnerability.

Dawson McAllister suggests that, as teens set their own limits, they ask themselves these kinds of diagnostic questions:

How far would I go if Christ were sitting right next to us (since, in fact He is)?

Think of someone who really respects you. What would that person think of what you are doing?

If we break up, will we still be able to look each other straight in the eyes?

Are we getting so turned on that we'd have to plunge further into sin to satisfy our desires?

Am I misleading him/her by sexual activity? (That is, does that person interpret my romantic feelings as being stronger than they actually are because of the intensity of our sexual actions?)

Finally, when young people are considering where to set their limits, questions like these are helpful: *What is my motivation? Do I really want to honor and serve the Lord?*

When you ask the question, How far can we go? you are coming at the whole dating issue from the wrong perspective. Instead you should ask, What can I do to help my dating partner and myself grow closer to Christ?

An ideal verse to use as a motto for one's date life is this: "Whatever you do, do it all for the glory of God" (1 Corinthians 10:31).

As one person puts it: "If the time together leaves you enriched, encouraged, relaxed; if it brings glory to the Lord, then you know it is time well spent." 109/38

* * * * * *

DOING WHAT COMES SUPERNATURALLY

by Chuck Klein

Has anyone ever told you that you need more self-control when it comes to your sex life? I'll bet you tried. Any luck?

The reason a lot of God's kids today (and a whole lot of adults) have trouble in the sexual area is that living a good clean sex life, the kind that God asks us to live, is just plain tough. In fact, to a lot of folks it seems hopeless. The pressures and desires are just too great. A friend of mine once said, "A good Christian sex life isn't hard to live — it's impossible!"

One of the most important things in learning to say no to premarital sex is learning to say yes to the Holy Spirit's leadership in our lives. Only one person has ever lived a perfect Christian life and that is Jesus Christ. Now, by His Spirit, He wants to live that life through us.

God's design for sex is an A-1, award-winning, top-of-the-line blueprint. What's best, He designed it for our protection and pleasure. But let's be honest. His plan is *beyond* our power. We can't make it alone by tightening our belt buckle or gritting our teeth.

However, if there is one thing we soon learn about God, it is this: God never asks something of us without giving us the resources to do it.

That's what knowing God is all about. Christianity is not a self-improvement program; rather, it is letting God improve us — or should I say *change us?* — His way, with His power. How does God do this?

The definition of the word *Christian* gives us the answer. A Christian is someone who has Christ in him. That is the phenomenon that makes Christians unique people. We can tackle big issues like sex because Jesus Christ, by His Spirit, God's Spirit (Romans 8:9), actually lives inside us.

In the Bible, 1 Corinthians 3:16 asks us, "Don't you know that you yourselves are God's temple and that God's Spirit lives in you?" (NIV). If you have received Christ, God's Spirit (the Holy Spirit) lives in you right now. What a mind-staggering thought!

But the Holy Spirit doesn't just live within you. If you allow Him, He will give you more power than you could ever dream of or imagine. Here's the kind of power we are talking about: "And if the *Spirit* of Him who *raised Jesus from the dead* is *living in you,* He who raised Christ from the dead will also *give life* to your mortal bodies through His Spirit, who lives in you" (Romans 8:11, NIV, italics mine). Awesome, death-defying power! The Holy Spirit makes us new people in Christ. Then He offers us the resources to live a new kind of life. He gives us the tools to deal with serious pressures and problems, like *the big issue of sex!*

How does the Holy Spirit do all this? He does it with a lot of cooperation on our part. You see, the Holy Spirit is a person the same as God our Father is a person, and because of that the Holy Spirit is very personal and sensitive with each one of us.

He knows us intimately and loves us unconditionally, but He also gives us a lot of "space."

As God's kids, however, we want to make sure we aren't taking advantage of that space to express all the desires of our sinful nature — those desires that can produce some gross behavior, especially in the area of sex. Instead, God wants us to exercise our free will by *responding* to His Spirit, letting Him give us His power to tackle our sexual problems.

In Galatians 5:22,23 the apostle Paul tells us that one of the qualities God's Spirit wants to develop in us is self-control (not a bad quality to have when it comes to sex). In addition, He wants to develop love, patience and kindness, qualities that produce great relationships with the opposite sex, the kind of relationships that fill our lives with satisfaction, not with the empty feelings and stains of premarital sex.

Where the Holy Spirit is producing His qualities in us, we have freedom to experience God's kind of relationships. There is power to say no and to wait. How can we give the Holy Spirit the green light in our lives?

Confess Sin

The Holy Spirit cannot fill us with His power if we choose to live independent of God. We can't do things our own way and expect the Holy Spirit to produce His qualities in our lives at the same time. So we need to begin with *confession*. As has been said, confession means to "agree with" God concerning what He already knows about our sin, attitudes and behavior.

God has a perfect verse of Scripture to help us: "If we confess our sins, He is faithful and just and will forgive us our sins and purify us from all unrighteousness" (1 John 1:9, NIV). Confession clears the air with God and restores our intimacy with Him. You see, He hasn't withdrawn from us, but we have withdrawn from Him.

What are some symptoms that tell us we need to confess? Here are a few: bad relationships . . . a lot of jealousy . . . diminishing faith . . . critical attitudes . . . apathy . . . misuse of sex.

If your desire is to make things right with God, take time right now, privately, and list the things you know you should confess. Agree with God about those things, through prayer. Then thank God for His forgiveness, which he has already given you.

Once you have confessed your sins, God expects you to *forget them* — not to dwell on them or to feel guilty. Agree with Him on what you have done: You have sinned. Agree with Him on what He has done: He has forgiven you. If you don't accept what He has done for you, you are denying the sufficiency of His grace — and that, I suspect, brings greater grief to Him than your original act of sin did.

Recognize God's Will

What lies ahead? God wants you to be filled (led and empowered) by His Spirit. Ephesians 5:18 says, "Don't drink too much wine, for many evils lie along that path; be filled instead with the Holy Spirit, and controlled by Him" (TLB).

That verse of Scripture tells us not to rely on the synthetic influence of things like alcohol, drugs, or anything else we might be using to find satisfaction. Rather, we are to allow the Holy Spirit to fill us and let Him begin to "grow" his qualities in us. That's real living, and it is God's *will* and *command.*

If God's will is for us to be Spirit-filled, what should we do next? First John 5:14,15 tells us, "This is the assurance we have in approaching God: that if we ask anything according to his will, he hears us. And if we know that he hears us — whatever we ask — we know that we have what we asked of him" (NIV).

Talk about promises from God! That verse of Scripture is one of the clearest and most exciting in all the Bible. When we ask God for something that He intends for us to have, He is going to give it to us. Does God want us to be filled with His Spirit? Does He want to "grow" His fruitful qualities in our lives? Does He want to give us power in our sexual lives? You can count on it. Does God stick to His promises? You can lay your life on His faithfulness.

Ask for His Filling

God wants us to come to Him humbly and sincerely and ask Him, by faith, to fill us with His Spirit; to begin to produce His love in place of our fear and jealousy; to give us His patience in place of our anger; to fill us with His self-control in place of our being controlled by our sexual desires.

Let's face it, when it comes to our sexual lives, we can't afford not to be under the loving influence of God's Spirit. This is what living the Christian life is all about.

If that is your desire, then ask God's Spirit to take over right now. If you didn't do it earlier, take some time first to confess (agree with God concerning areas of your life that have been under your own control). Remember God's command (Ephesians 5:18) and His promise (1 John 5:14,15). Trust Him to fill your life with His Spirit.

You may or may not feel different when God's Spirit takes

control. Feelings are not consistent and we should never use them as indicators of God's work in our lives. Remember, *God works in our lives because we put our faith in the facts of His Word.*

Follow His Leading

Being filled and led by God's Spirit is both an event and a process. In other words, there are specific times in our Christian lives when we realize that God is not in charge, and we give the controls to Him. Those are important events. But the other side of the Holy Spirit's work in our lives is a process.

Fruit on a tree is not produced instantly. It takes an entire season for it to grow from a green bud to a ripe piece of fruit. The Spirit's fruitful qualities in our lives are like that. Self-control, for example, may not be overwhelming when we first learn how to allow God's Spirit to fill us. But as we grow in our faith and spend day after day trusting His Spirit to lead us, that fruit of self-control will grow and mature. The lustful desires of our flesh never go away, but the strength of God's self-control becomes a greater and greater force in our lives.

You Decide

But, beware. You must always be cooperating with God's Spirit. *You* have to make the decision to give the Holy Spirit leadership in your life. He won't control someone who chooses to control his or her own circumstances. There will be times when you again will need to confess particular sins and ask God again to fill you with His Spirit. When you stumble, let God pick you up.

There will be other times when you just need to *turn and run* from something that is tempting you, whether it is a magazine, movie, television, or you are alone with someone in the back seat of a car. That is why Paul told Timothy: "Flee the evil desires of youth . . . " But he didn't leave Timothy hanging with nothing to turn to: "and pursue righteousness, faith, love and peace . . . call on the Lord" (2 Timothy 2:22, NIV).

We have to make choices and turn from the things that damage our sexual lives, our personalities, our relationship with Christ. If we are willing to turn, God's Spirit bursts through with His power and helps us make those critical choices. Let Him fill you. Learn to walk with Him today.

Let's review. To be filled and led by the Holy Spirit you need to:

● *Confess* your sin.

● *Remember God's will* for you: to be filled with the Holy Spirit.

● *Ask God,* by faith, to fill you — He promises to answer.

● Keep *cooperating* with the Holy Spirit. Learn to *make right choices* and God will keep producing His powerful qualities in your life.

Where the Spirit is in control, we find power and liberty.

* * * * * *

"Dad — I'm Pregnant"
How Should a Father Respond?

Anonymous

It seemed only yesterday that I was holding little Amy on my lap reading her bedtime stories. Now, with college classes and extracurricular activities, she had little time for Dad. But this morning was different. She wanted to talk and I figured it must be about school, her job, or needing a loan.

She toyed with her food as my wife and I gave her time to gather her thoughts. Finally, she took a deep breath and said two words I thought I would never hear my unmarried teenage daughter say: "I'm pregnant."

It was as though an instant in time stood still. I was numb. Kay, my wife, picked up the conversation. "Are you sure?" Other such questions were asked, but I couldn't get my thoughts together to discuss it further. I've always had a subconscious fear that my children might engage in premarital sex. My fear had become a reality. What was I to say? How should I respond and counsel my daughter?

Perhaps every parent struggles with that fear. Oh, there are those who court the idea that "My kids are above average. I've taught them better and they're not really involved." They resist the thought that it may happen to them. But, down deep, most parents are concerned that their children will become sexually active. It's tragic, but the fact is that your own son or daughter, your grandchild, your friend's child, or some of the kids at your church *are* sexually active. If one of them becomes pregnant, what will be your attitude? What will you say? What action will you take?

I would like to share here the help I received — from books, friends and God's Word — which guided my wife and me through this difficult period of our lives. My hope is that it can help youth directors, pastors, anyone with a friend in this situation and especially you parents who find yourselves struggling through the ordeal of an unmarried child's pregnancy.

Becoming pregnant is perhaps the most traumatic experience an unmarried girl will ever endure. If she is a Christian, she will probably feel she has lost everything she holds dear. She will be tempted to give in to such feelings as:

I've lost my past. I've lost my morals and I am strapped with the social stigma of being an unmarried pregnant teenager. I'll be looked on as loose, immoral and impure.

I've lost my freedom. Now that I'm pregnant, there will be some things I won't be able to do physically. I may not feel comfortable going to school, work, church, or even shopping.

I've lost my future. If I decide to keep the baby, the next eighteen to twenty years of my life are planned. I will be making a commitment to my child, and my future will feel out of hand or pushed aside. As I feel less in control, I may feel pressured to marry.

I've lost my positive self-image. As my body changes physically, it will be a constant reminder of what I've sacrificed. I'll have a tendency to blame myself, think degrading things about myself, to punish myself emotionally for it.

I've lost my relationships. How will my family and friends feel about me? Boys may shy away from going out with me when they know I have a child. Family members and other adults who respected me before may not respect me now.

Such thoughts and emotions pouring down on her could cause some of these responses:

Grief. When a girl contemplates these losses, she will undoubtedly experience pain and suffering. She may grieve over losing control of the life she had planned out.

Depression. If she doesn't obtain relief from her grief and suffering, she will go into depression and if depression is allowed to take over, she'll face despair and feel there is no hope — no light at the end of the tunnel.

Shame. Except for the grace of God, feelings of shame will affect her attitude toward herself, her friends, her closest loved ones and even the baby. Accepting feelings of shame is a devastating blow to her self-image and outlook on life. Shame can cloud every aspect of her life: work, school, caring for her child, working in the church, counseling and helping others, etc.

If there is any time a girl needs the love, support and wise counsel of her parents, it is during an unplanned pregnancy. But because parents also are experiencing tremendous emotional turmoil, they run the danger of reacting negatively rather than responding lovingly.

The next few days after learning of my daughter's pregnancy were some of the most emotional and confusing of my life. Rarely do I shed tears, but that week I wept bitterly every day. I found myself reacting negatively to the entire situation. If it hadn't been for dedicated counselors at a Crisis Pregnancy Center urging me to follow two very crucial principles, I would have probably driven my daughter to despair. Those principles are what I'd like to share with you. Simply stated they are: (1) The power of forgiveness can untangle the emotions and clarify the thinking; and (2) committing the future to God can provide a sense of direction.

My Need to Forgive

I sat in the counselor's office pouring out the hurt raging inside me. The counselor asked, "Why do you think you are hurting so?" "Well," I responded, "This whole ordeal is so painful. My little girl is hurting so much now and it's going to get a lot worse before it gets better. She'll suffer shame; may have to drop out of school; will bear a child she can't provide for; and may face other consequences I haven't even thought of." The counselor nodded slowly. I went on, "Amy has all these tough decisions to make. She'll have to decide whether to carry the baby to full term or abort the child (and, thank God, Amy doesn't even consider abortion an appropriate option). What about marrying Mark, who fathered the child? Should she keep the baby or should the child be put up for adoption? Then there's her schooling. Should she go away to live with another family until the baby is born? There are so many variables within those questions that it boggles the mind, let alone the emotions. No matter what is done, everyone involved will feel the pain."

The wise counselor allowed me to wind down. After I finished, she leaned forward and said softly, "You say you have accepted Amy and aren't angry with her, but is the pain you feel all for your daughter?"

I wasn't sure what she was driving at. "What do you mean?" I questioned.

She continued, "I really encourage you to examine the reason for your personal hurt. Do you feel you have lost some of the things you wanted to share with your daughter?"

Yes, I had. Down deep I, too, suffered a loss. I wanted to give my lovely daughter as a virgin to a Christian young man. But now I had lost that possibility. I wanted to experience the joy of my daughter's first child, but I couldn't have that either. I wanted to be a part of my first grandchild's life, but it appeared I had lost that opportunity too. My tears weren't just for Amy, they were for me as well. I would also feel the shame and pain of her mistake.

I prayed for a spirit of forgiveness. Now more than ever, Amy needed my support, love and acceptance. As I confessed my resentment and selfishness to God, He filled me with a supportive love for my daughter that I never thought possible. God's power of forgiveness took away the resentment. But there was more. My emotional confusion began to fade. The act of forgiving put the choices that would have to be made into perspective.

You see, the consequences of a few fleeting moments of uncontrolled passion seem endless. No matter which alternatives are considered — premature marriage, single parenting or adoption — they are all painful and appear unacceptable. Confusion becomes the order of the day. Yet when I found the power to forgive, I gained not only a supernatural supportive love for Amy, but a clarity of heart and mind to understand the alternatives. As my emotions untangled, I sat down and wrote her a long letter. Here are some excerpts from that letter:

> Dear Amy,
> I know that during this past week you have suffered pain as never before; the burden that you bear is perhaps the heaviest you've ever carried. Yet through it all God assures us: "My grace is sufficient for you, for my power is perfected in weakness" (2 Corinthians 12:9).
> And one thing I've come to realize is that God has not declared that life is over because of an unplanned pregnancy. God has great plans for your future. You have not been disqualified from the race. In fact, He plans to draw you closer to Him and teach you to know Him better than you have ever known Him before. Once we realize that our main purpose in life is to know God and glorify Him, life comes into proper perspective. And I believe, Amy, the more you and I know Him and see life from His perspective, the more life and all its struggles and problems begin to be resolved.
> God has an answer for this situation. He has a solution. One without pain and suffering? Probably not. Yet, He has plenty of grace, that when appropriated to our lives, will be for our good and His glory. But, I've learned I can't appropriate His grace while responding to life in an un-Christlike manner. So, I strive to "stay

always within the boundaries where God's love can reach and bless [me] you" (Jude 1:21, TLB). Once we begin to respond according to God's Word, we are then able to move on and clearly *understand the choices we have to make.*

I know you are struggling, even more than Mom and I are, with a flood of emotions; it's difficult to think straight. I sense that this pregnancy represents the loss of everything you were holding dear. And while it may appear to be that way on the surface, you have not lost everything when you have God as your Savior and Friend. In fact, by properly responding to God and His Word, you will gain far more than you ever imagined.

Remember, Amy, you have sought God's forgiveness and that means your slate is clean — as far as God is concerned, you've committed no sin, ever! Mom and I too have forgiven you. We can walk down the street with our daughter as proud as we've ever been. What makes us proud, and God too, is the fact that you've acknowledged your error, sought God's forgiveness and committed your life to Him.

But what about the rest of your life? You have many difficult decisions to make. You have your life and the life of your baby to consider. There are no "perfect" answers. One of the things that makes this so difficult is that there are so many alternatives, and none of them is pleasant. But as you align your responses to the instructions of God's Word, the clouds will clear and He will make His will known.

I can't tell you what to do. You have engaged in an adult act and you have an adult decision to make. However, I want to point you to the context in which to make your decision. When you consider your options, do so with one central purpose in mind: What will bring the most honor to God?

Right choices become clear as you:

1. Maintain right attitudes (align yourself with God's Word during trying times, love those who mistreat you, and accept your humbling position with grace);
2. Continue to consider only those options that would bring honor to God; and
3. Obtain wise counsel from mature Christians to confirm the leading you have.

If you decide to keep the baby, you can rest assured we will do all in our power to be the best grandparents possible. We will fill our responsibility in being a godly influence as best we can under God.

If you decide to make a placement plan for the baby, you can rest assured we will be there to support you, love you, weep with you and heal together with you.

I love you dearly, Amy, more than you can know. You will always be my little girl. There are brighter and more beautiful days ahead for all of us. God will use this as a stepping stone in all our lives. We will learn much together. We can more effectively

minister to others because of how we allow God to use this in
our lives.

Through this we can all become even closer as a family than
before. Mom and I felt honored and want to thank you for sharing
this with us on the very day you found out. We thank you for
the opportunity to be a part of the decisions that affect the life of
our first grandchild. No matter what, this will always be a special
child to both of us; we have lots of love to share with you and
your first child — in whatever way God chooses to let us be a part.

The road may seem dark and lonely at times, but remember
we're always here and want to help. And, more important, Christ
is with you always, your dearest friend, your closest companion,
the one who knows you most and loves you best. Mom and I
pray for you daily. I love you; I love you; I love you.

Your Dad

My Need to Commit the Future to God

Amy had more than seven months to make the biggest
decision of her life. She was confident that marrying Mark would
further complicate matters. We agreed. But was she to raise her
child as a single parent? Or were we to assume the responsibility
of raising our first grandchild? Or did God have a Christian
couple prepared to raise our daughter's baby? Weeks turned into
months and still no clear direction. We prayed daily that God
would provide clear direction to Amy.

One afternoon while discussing the options with her, she
became frustrated. "Dad," she said in tears, "I've got to know
what's right to do. Why won't you tell me what I should do?"

My eyes blurred as I tried to explain, "Amy, you know that
I love you. And I want what is best for you and the baby." My
voice choked with emotion. "I *could* tell you what was right if I
could only see some twenty years into the future, but I can't.
Honey, I don't know exactly what to do either, but I do know
how you can find out." She sobbed quietly as I went on. "Commit
your future into God's hands; He *does* know the future. Give
Him your baby, relinquish that life within you into His care.
Once you're so committed, ask *Him* what *He* wants to do with
His little unborn child. Tell God you are gladly willing to raise
your baby if He so desires, and you are equally willing for Him
to hand your child to some other family to raise."

As weeks went by, God gave Amy the ability to relinquish
her child and her own future into God's hands. Slowly pieces of
the puzzle came together. One confirmation after another made
it clear to her, and eventually to all of us, what she was to do.
I hesitate to share her decision simply because I would not want
it to be considered a determining factor for anyone else. Each

family situation is unique and must be considered separately before God. However, I believe the principle is applicable to all: Commit your future and the life of the baby to God and He will direct you.

As I look back over the year, I see that actually I offered very little advice to my daughter, but did give lots of love and support. And it was that love and support from both Kay and me that allowed what little counsel we did offer to be of help.

If you find yourself in a similar situation, I urge you to seek God's grace early along with the support of wise biblical counselors. Transparently confess the pain and hurt you feel. Allow God to fill you with the power of His forgiveness and then commit the future of your daughter and her baby into His hands. I'm confident that God makes His will known to those who honestly and unselfishly seek His leadership.

The bitter consequences of an unplanned pregnancy in the life of an unmarried girl and her family is beyond my ability to describe here. God certainly knew what was best when He commanded against premarital sex. Our entire ordeal causes us to praise God for His specific moral commands of love. They are commands designed for the protection and provision of young people.

But, perhaps even more than that, we praise God for being the gracious forgiver and loving friend who lifts the fallen and restores a broken life. He was there through every moment of every day, drawing my daughter to His soothing breast. In the lonely night-hours of pain and regret, He was there; during the time of indecision and confusion, He was there; and He'll be there for you, too, if you find yourself in a similar situation. His "grace is sufficient for you, for power is perfected in weakness" (2 Corinthians 12:9, NASB).

* * * * * *

FORGIVENESS

I had sex with my boyfriend thinking I owed it to him . . . Later when I learned I was pregnant he blew up and said I should get an abortion — that it was all my fault. So, to save my parents heartache and to keep Matt, I had an abortion. Now Matt has left me . . . How can God love me after all I have done? I'm just so confused. Can God really love and forgive me?

———————♥———————

We live in a day of so-called sexual liberation, when society tells our young people that morality doesn't matter. "If it feels good, it's OK to do it." Despite being told there's no reason to feel guilty, sexual guilt among young people is increasing.

I meet so many young people who want to be forgiven.

- Ten years ago 22 percent wished they hadn't engaged in premarital sex. Today 44 percent have regrets.
- In 1974 only 10 percent said they found it difficult to forgive themselves for sexual sin. Today 27 percent have that difficulty.

How do we help those who say "I've blown it. I've been involved sexually" or "I've lost my virginity, so what's the use?" or "After all I've done, how can God love or forgive me?" What do we say? What do we do? Do we simply quote Bible verses about God's forgiveness and send them on their way? Or what?

I think we need to recognize that people with sexual guilt may have serious difficulties with the concept of forgiveness. For example, some have problems believing that God can, or will, forgive them. Others are either unable or unwilling to accept His forgiveness. And few can forgive themselves. As a result there are many young Christian people who have asked for God's forgiveness — and are forgiven — yet who go through life without experiencing the benefits of that forgiveness.

I believe that whatever help we provide must be in the context of loving relationships. Whether we are pastors or parents it is not enough to talk about forgiveness. We must live it.

First We Must Be Forgiving

We must begin by accepting and forgiving those persons who are seeking God's forgiveness. This should be our first step. We can never help anyone we cannot accept. To tell someone about God's forgiveness is meaningless unless we ourselves show acceptance. Especially for parents, acceptance begins with forgiveness.

Do you have a son or daughter who is struggling with the guilt of sexual misconduct? What about young persons in your youth group or congregation? Do you want to help them experience the power of God's forgiveness and cleansing? Then, first of all, be forgiving yourself.

Here are three helpful principles:

1. Take the Initiative

Have you ever thought, *Why should I forgive her? She hasn't even said she's sorry!* God's love compels us to take the initiative.

"Herein is love, not that we loved God, but that He loved us, and sent His Son to be the propitiation [the atoning sacrifice] for our sins" (1 John 4:10, KJV). If God had waited for us to repent and ask His forgiveness before reaching out to us, we would still be lost. But "while we were yet sinners, Christ died for us" (Romans 5:8, KJV). He took the first step — paying the death penalty for our sins — and then offering us His pardon.

As human parents we must follow our heavenly Father's example and take the initiative. God wants parents to reach out to their hurting sons and daughters. Forgiveness takes the initiative.

2. Try to Restore Relationships

Remember, the goal of forgiveness is reconciliation. So often when young people become involved sexually the relationship with their parents is either strained or broken. God wants parents to assume responsibility for their part in the collapse of their relationship and initiate reconciliation.

Did you know that God doesn't want you to worship if you have a broken relationship with your children which you haven't tried to make right? Jesus said, "If therefore you are presenting your offering at the altar, and there remember that your brother [son, daughter] has something against you, leave your offering there before the altar, and go your way; first be reconciled to your brother [son, daughter], and then come and present your offering" (Matthew 5:23,24, NASB).

How many parents would show up for church next Sunday if they followed Jesus' instructions?

Regardless of who's "at fault," it is so important to restore your relationship. If parents wait for their child to ask forgiveness first, reconciliation may never happen. Forgiveness seeks reconciliation.

3. Be Genuinely Forgiving

Forgiveness means to release from a debt. It's not the same as saying "Oh, that's all right," when someone says he's sorry. Forgiveness recognizes that a wrong has been done, but is willing to accept and forget anyway.

So many parents say they have forgiven, but they continue to hold the past over the heads of their children. "I forgive you . . . but I won't forget." Forgiveness means not keeping a score card: "There you go again." God has said He puts all our sins behind Him. He'll bury them in the deepest ocean and, as Corrie Ten Boom liked to say, He will put up a "No Fishing" sign. This is what God does when He forgives us. We as parents must do the same when we forgive our children. Be genuinely forgiving.

By giving our own acceptance and forgiveness to young

people who are desperately seeking God's forgiveness, we provide them with a credible basis for understanding God's forgiveness. This truth is effective to the extent that we demonstrate it.

A Young Woman Named Tracy

Young people generally see God through parents and church leaders. They project their image of us onto God. This is particularly true of parents. If we are forgiving, it is relatively easy for our children to conceive of God as forgiving. If we are stern and unforgiving, it may be impossible for our children to imagine a God who loves and forgives.

The actions and attitudes of parents can be barriers standing in the way of their children ever receiving and accepting God's forgiveness. For example, a young woman who recently attended The Julian Center was severely handicapped in her ability to experience forgiveness because of her relationships with her parents, particularly her father.

> My mother was an alcoholic and was never really there for me. I was the youngest of five children and, in a way, my sister Donna, who was two and a half years older, kind of became my mother.
>
> My father was never there for me either except for discipline — strict discipline. You know, "belt-on-the-table" type stuff. I had no relationship with him. I've got pictures where I have my arm around him, trying to show him affection, and he is just sitting there. I was scared to death of my father, but I still wanted his attention.

Tracy's autocratic father, with his lack of caring and affection, would have a serious effect on her future relationships with others, especially men.

> As I grew up I was always getting sick or hurt, trying to get attention. My sister Donna was like that, too. I remember a day when we both bashed her arm with a stick. She hit it for awhile and then made me do it, too. We kept at it until her arm was actually broken. But my father looked at it and said, "No. It's not broken. It's fine. Sure, you got a big old welt and bruise, but it's fine."
>
> Most of the time my sister Donna could get away with anything. She was always the "black sheep" type, getting busted for drugs and stuff. But my folks believed everything she said. When it was me, they always thought I was a liar. I hated it. All my life I hated it, but I could tell them anything. They never knew I was on drugs. They never had a clue. I don't know if Donna told them I was a liar or what, but they always said to me, "Tracy, you're lying to us." I wasn't a liar; that's what was real weird.

Tracy became involved in drugs at the age of ten, when

she began to smoke marijuana. By the age of twelve she was popping "uppers" and "downers" regularly. At fourteen she had her first sexual experience with a childhood boyfriend. She was not sexually involved again until she was sixteen when, after a single act of intercourse with another boy, she became pregnant.

Her mother, who had recently accepted Christ, and her unbelieving father insisted she have an abortion. Tracy was devastated. Following the abortion, she spent the next three months crying almost constantly, hating her parents, grieving for her baby and suffering severe depression.

Several months later, after her father's conversion to Christ and after watching the spiritual growth of her mother, Tracy realized her own spiritual need and invited Christ into her life. For the next two years she concentrated on growing as a Christian. She generally avoided men and seldom dated.

Then Tracy enrolled in a Christian college and became active in the anti-abortion "Pro-Life" movement. As she shared her testimony publicly she felt other Christians judging her. This had a negative effect on her Christian walk.

Tracy began dating a Christian student, who asked her to marry him. Although a wedding date had not been set, the couple was given a book on Christian marriage. After reading it, Tracy's boyfriend began pressuring her for sex. Finally one night he forced himself on her physically. That virtual rape was a traumatic experience for her. She lost the limited self-esteem she had built up since becoming a Christian.

Over the next three years Tracy had unsatisfying relationships with seven different men. In most cases sexual intimacy terminated the relationship.

> I would start a relationship. The guy would start trying things and I would try to stop it. But I would end up sleeping with him and then walk away. I wanted affection. I wanted to feel accepted. But whenever I became physically involved I wouldn't feel accepted at all . . . I'd feel dirty.
>
> It was like originally the guy's opinion would be, "Oh, you're so wonderful. You walk with God. You're so on fire. You minister here and there." And then he would find out my background, which is no secret. In front of large Pro-Life audiences I told my background. But once a guy knew about me he would begin pushing me to have sex, and that made me feel I wasn't OK . . . that I wasn't a new creature . . . that I was just fooling myself into thinking I was a good girl.
>
> I began to think, *Well, these are Christian guys, who have a relationship with God, and they obviously don't respect me . . . or they wouldn't try things. They think I'm nothing . . . that I have no worth or value. Maybe this is all I'm worth.*

We all want to be accepted. Acceptance is a God-given need

which must be met before we can ever feel a sense of security. The problem for most of us is that we look to the wrong things for our acceptance. Like Tracy, we often look to other people or to sexual involvement for our acceptance. It never works.

I decided I might as well go back to being what I used to be. I intended to go back to drugs and everything. But first I went and slept with this guy who wasn't a Christian. I was torn to pieces inside. In that encounter I realized that wasn't me. That wasn't my nature any longer. I knew it was wrong. It wasn't something I really wanted to do, but somehow I just hadn't found the answer yet.

I was still reading the Bible. I was active in the church. Everybody who didn't know my background respected me and thought I was a really wonderful person.

Actually it was having Christians judging me that pulled me away. As that kept getting worse, I pulled back from the church. There was this really neat guy whose parents found out about my abortion and who ordered him to stop going out with me. Here was a twenty-two-year-old man and his parents were telling him, "You can't see this girl." Out of obedience to them we broke off the relationship.

How important it is for those of us who are parents and church leaders to show acceptance and forgiveness to young people. Tragically, well meaning but unforgiving Christian people have pushed more than one young person "over the edge."

Next I was deeply hurt by a guy with blond hair and blue eyes. He'd been talking marriage until he found out about my background. One night he sat me down and told me he couldn't accept my background or me. He said, "I want to . . . but I can't." I kept asking him to forgive me. But he said "No. There's nothing to forgive." And he just walked away from me. I was devastated.

I was so hurt and angry I decided I would find a young man with blond hair and blue eyes who looked like this guy, sleep with him and become pregnant. And then people would blame it on the guy who had hurt me so much. I would never say that it was his child, but it would look like him. And so I did exactly that and became pregnant — but I miscarried.

Tracy spent the next two years in and out of depression. She was ready to give up on God completely, when she met Dave. Dave was also a Christian. After a month of dating they were engaged. Then, when they became physically involved, Tracy fell apart. Unable to handle it any more, she broke off the relationship.

It was at that point I became suicidal. But the day I was preparing to kill myself I thought of my nieces and nephews. A picture went through my mind of my brothers and sister telling them that Aunt Tracy had killed herself. I began to think I mustn't do this, because my nieces and nephews would grow up thinking, *Christianity doesn't work. Look at Aunt Tracy!*

At that moment the phone rang. It was my older brother who had left home when I was only eight years old. He knew nothing of what was going on in my life, but he said, "Tracy, you're suicidal, right? You're thinking you have no hope." I couldn't believe it. This was my older brother whom I'd never really known.

I said, "Wait a minute; are you serious?" He told me he and his wife had been praying just moments before and God had shown them exactly what I was going through.

Then I knew that Christianity did work, and I knew that God was real and God was capable of changing me. I had begged Him to do it for years, but I still was missing something and I didn't understand what that was.

What Tracy was missing was a true understanding of God's forgiveness and acceptance. She found *that* at The Julian Center, where she spent several months.

I had gone through counseling before, but it was mostly self-help kinds of stuff. You know, we'll make you feel better about yourself. But feeling better about myself didn't change anything, because my concept of God was so wrong.

Like so many of us, Tracy's concept of God was very much affected by her relationship with her father. Whenever she pictured God, she saw Him in her father's image. To her, God was autocratic, unforgiving and distant. Clearly, without a change in her concept of God she would never be free to understand and accept His forgiveness.

At the Center I listened to Dick Day talking about repentance — and about changing my attitude about God. I began to have an understanding of who God is; that He loved me and wanted me; and why He paid for my sins. I had heard those things before, but at the Center I finally understood them. It was almost as if the veil was lifted.

I learned about God's character. He is righteous and holy. And righteousness cannot fellowship with or relate to unrighteousness. When God sent His Son to die for us He did this to satisfy His character, because the "wages of sin is death." But I also realized that because of Jesus' death, God's character was satisfied where I was concerned. It was so fresh to understand that God loved me unconditionally and gave His Son so I could be forgiven and cleansed.

I used to hear people talk about being hidden, or covered, by Jesus. People would hold a little "Jesus thing" and say that God sees Jesus but he doesn't see them. But that kind of thinking didn't help me to stop my sin. It seemed I was back there behind Jesus,

still being as ugly and gross as I had always been . . . with no
power to stop.

Slowly I began to understand that because of Jesus' death, I
wasn't just "covered" . . . I was forgiven.

For Tracy it was the turning point. As her concept of God
began to change, so did her understanding of His forgiveness.

I began to see my infinite worth and value to God. He created
me — who I am and how I am. God didn't need me but because
of His love He wanted me. And because He wanted me He
provided a way for me to repent — to confess not only my sin,
but also to confess that it is forgiven. And that was incredible.

I have had a hard time praying and believing — for myself. I
could always pray that God would move mountains for somebody
else, and believed He could do anything. But for me, I couldn't
see it. I couldn't see that He could do anything for me. So, I
would pray for myself, totally doubting that anything would ever
happen for me.

But when I realized that God wanted me, not just to cover my
sin, not just to make me "look" OK, but to cleanse everything
and love me — it gave me a whole new concept. From then on I
had a new concept about prayer, about God and about myself.

When Tracy first came to The Julian Center she was anxious,
depressed, inhibited, subjective, passive and hostile. Three
months later she was calm, lighthearted, socially expressive,
objective and tolerant of herself and others. As a result of Tracy's
new understanding of God's acceptance and forgiveness, she has
a new self-image. She sees herself as God sees her, a person
created in His image with infinite worth and value. Because she
now sees herself differently, Tracy is also beginning to see other
people differently. She is even beginning to see her father differently.

Over the years, since my father became a Christian he has been
changing. But I didn't see it. I had this picture of my father, like
I once had of God, that I had projected on him for so long, because
of the past. So, when he was changing I couldn't see it.

Seeing herself as God sees her has also given Tracy a new
concept of sex, making possible a different kind of relationship
with men. Sex is no longer needed as the basis for relating.
Forgiven and cleansed, Tracy has become free to begin a new
relationship with Dave. For both of them this is a new beginning.

Before this we didn't really have a relationship. Although we
loved each other we didn't really know each other as people. We
just had this physical desire and affection for one another. We
knew each other somewhat, but the physical had just taken over.

After understanding God's character and after repenting, we came back together. But it's totally different. Now Dave and I have the freedom to talk . . . to communicate . . . to understand who each of us is really. While I was at the Center we became re-engaged.

This time I am free to make the kind of commitment I was never able to make before. Until now, I couldn't trust God and I couldn't trust Dave. Those other times I'd been engaged, I couldn't really make that commitment of my whole self. I could just commit my body.

Tracy no longer needs sex as a basis for love and acceptance. She is free to love and be loved as a total person. This young woman, who has lived through years of sexual guilt, has finally experienced the liberating power of God's forgiveness and cleansing grace. The beautiful thing about developing a healthy self-image — that is, seeing yourself as God sees you, and therefore being able to forgive yourself as God forgives you — is that you will then be able to be a channel of God's love and forgiveness to others.

After experiencing tremendous difficulties in relating to men, Tracy is now free to commit herself completely to a marriage relationship. She and Dave were recently married, and I believe that this relationship is going to work. It is based on a proper understanding of who God is and what love and forgiveness are all about.

What helped Tracy most in her forgiveness/growth process? The love and acceptance given her by The Julian Center staff. They don't just lecture about God's love, acceptance and forgiveness. They live it.

Biblical Insights for Those Who Seek Forgiveness

What hope can we offer to someone who feels like "damaged goods"? Can lost virginity ever be restored? Can that person ever find deliverance from the emotional pain that keeps her (or him) in bondage? Is the abundant life that Jesus promises really for her?

Now that you know how important it is to accept and forgive those who seek God's forgiveness, here are some biblical insights you might share.

First, let's consider one important figure in the Old Testament, David. If anyone's ever "blown it," he did. He had everything going for him. He was the king. God's hand of blessing was on him. He was a "five-point student on a four-point system." And then he saw Bathsheba.

Now David didn't just look at this beautiful woman. He stared. And the moment you begin to stare, you're hooked. David got himself hooked.

After learning that her husband, Uriah, was fighting the Ammonites with the Israeli army, David sent for Bathsheba. If that wasn't bad enough, the Bible says, "he lay with her" (2 Samuel 11:4). And she became pregnant.

David knew he was in trouble, so he devised a "cover-up." He sent for Uriah, hoping that while he was home the soldier would sleep with his wife.

But David's plan didn't work. Uriah spent his first night back in Jerusalem sleeping in the palace servant quarters. How frustrated David must have been. He even tried to talk Uriah into going home to his wife and "enjoying himself." But Uriah replied, "The armies and the general and his officers are camping out in open fields, and should I go home to wine and dine and sleep with my wife?" (2 Samuel 11:11, TLB) In desperation David tried to get Uriah drunk (2 Samuel 11:13), hoping he would then go home and make love to his wife.

When none of that worked, David ordered Uriah sent to the front lines, where he was killed. What began with a stare led not only to adultery, not only to an unwanted pregnancy, but also to murder. David really blew it.

But consider what happened next. David admitted his sin and asked God for forgiveness:

> Mine iniquities [sins] have taken hold upon me, so that I am not able to look up; they are more than the hairs of mine head: Therefore my heart faileth me (Psalm 40:12, KJV).
>
> Be gracious to me, O God, according to Thy lovingkindness; . . . Wash me thoroughly from my iniquity, and cleanse me from my sin. For I know my transgressions, and my sin is ever before me. Against Thee, Thee only I have sinned . . .Wash me, and I shall be whiter than snow. Make me to hear joy and gladness . . . and blot out all my iniquities. Create in me a clean heart, O God . . . Restore to me the joy of Thy salvation, and sustain me with a willing spirit. Then I will teach transgressors Thy ways, and sinners will be converted to Thee (Psalm 51:1-13, NASB).

Here was a man, who had killed someone, believing that if he allowed God to forgive and cleanse him, he would once again be used to bring sinners to the Lord.

Are there some sins too terrible even for God to forgive? Can He forgive? Can He cleanse? Can He restore? If you don't think He can, please read all of Psalm 51.

Steps to Forgiveness

If you have "blown it," here are several important steps to take.

1. Admit Your Sin

It is so easy to blame other people, or our circumstances, for our sins. That's as old as Adam and Eve. So many people say, "God, I've sinned, but I loved her! but I was vulnerable! but I had needs!" God can't work in your life if you insist on saying "I have sinned, but . . ." "If we confess our sins . . ." (1 John 1:9). To confess means to agree with God about your sin.

The first step on the way to forgiveness is admit your sin to God. "God, I've sinned, period."

True repentance means more than just feeling sorry for what we've done or regretting that we are going to suffer the bad effects of the sin. Repentance gives the sense of feeling so sick about what we've done that we don't ever want to do it again. True repentance acknowledges that we sinned against our Creator.

Acknowledge your sin.

2. Accept God's Forgiveness

Read 1 John 1:9: "If we confess our sins, He is faithful and righteous to forgive us our sins and to cleanse us from all" — *all* means everything, including sexual immorality — "from all unrighteousness" (NASB).

Also read Hebrews 10:11,12: "One sacrifice for sins for all time" (NASB). And read Colossians 2:12-14 where you will see "He has forgiven us all our transgressions."

If you were the only person alive, Christ still would have died for you. You may have heard that before, but do you believe it? If you were the only person alive, you would stand in the place of Adam. You would sin, just as Adam did. And God would provide a redeemer for you, just as He did for Adam (Genesis 3:15).

In living the Christian life, we fail every day. Yet every day God is waiting to forgive us. Accepting the fact that we are sinners, that we sin, doesn't mean we should wallow in unworthiness. God wants to lift us up and set us free.

Some people, however, are sure that God could never forgive them because they have sinned too much or for too long. A seventeen-year-old high school girl asked after her abortion, "How can God really love and forgive me?" She didn't yet realize the significance of Christ's death on the cross and how it related to her. If only she could grasp the good news of forgiveness. The good news, the gospel, is that Jesus didn't come to save righteous people. He came to save sinners. He isn't interested in your proving to Him how good you are. His message is forgiveness!

The record is wiped clean.

Right after moving to Julian, California, I bought a Volkswagen Rabbit. It turned out to be a dud on those mountain roads, so I had a turbo charger put on — and convinced my wife it made the car safer. That same day I had to go down to Ramona, and on the way there's a long straightaway. A motorcyclist was ahead of me, not going too fast, so I decided to pass and pulled out. Well, he figured he wasn't going to let some Rabbit pass him and he stepped on the gas. There I was, with a new turbo, and I thought I might as well test it. I floored it and it worked. I passed the motorcycle and was doing 85 as the straightaway ended and I hit my brakes for the curve.

Two curves later, the biggest red lights I've ever seen flashed in my rear view mirror. A cop pulled me and the cyclist over and ticketed both of us.

When I went down to Ramona to pay the ticket the clerk said, "You don't need to pay this if you take a three-hour driver's safety class." So I did, and went back to Ramona with the little slip signed by the driving instructor. I gave it to the clerk, who said as she took it, "Your record is wiped clean."

After I was back in the car it hit me. My record is wiped clean. It was a powerful reminder of what Jesus Christ did on the cross with my sins. He wiped my slate clean. He canceled my debt and made it possible for me to be reconciled to God.

Acknowledge God's forgiveness.

3. Show Fruits of Repentance

Matthew 3:8 says, "Bring forth fruits in keeping with repentance" (NASB). Repentance means turning around, changing one's mind. At this point you need to look at your life and your relationship. Ask God what fruits of repentance you need to show. It might be breaking off a relationship. It might be making major lifestyle changes. It might be not frequenting certain types of places again or not watching certain kinds of movies or TV programs. It also might be limiting your dates to double-dating situations. It could be any one of a number of other things, anything you know is wrong for you.

Experience the fruits of repentance.

4. Forgive Yourself

Early in my Christian life I would confess my sins to God, acknowledge His forgiveness — but then get down on myself. *McDowell, how could you have done that? What makes you think God can use you after what you did? Sure, God forgives you, but . . .* Such thoughts would set me off on a major guilt trip.

My problem was that, although I knew God could forgive me, I didn't always forgive myself. Somehow I thought I had to earn the right to forgive myself. I had to prove I was worthy. I couldn't make mistakes and then minister in His name. Isn't it interesting that we can be harder on ourselves than God is?

However, refusing to forgive ourselves can be a form of pride. We think we should be beyond sin. We refuse to accept ourselves as we really are — fallible human beings who are capable of blowing it, not just once, but again and again.

In not forgiving ourselves we are implying that Jesus Christ's death on the cross is not sufficient for all our sins. We are saying, "God, I'm a better judge of what can be forgiven than You are." What an insult to Almighty God.

The real issue in forgiving ourselves is not how many times or how badly we blow it. The real issue is how you and I respond when we do sin.

For example, one day in a restaurant I hurt a brother in Christ deeply by saying something I should never have said. On the way home I realized the impact of my uncalled for, "off-the-wall" remark. Immediately I confessed my sin to God. I also realized I needed to return to the restaurant and confess my sin to the one I had hurt.

So I turned around, found this brother and said, "What I said was wrong and I know I hurt you. I've confessed it to God and I've come back to ask your forgiveness. Will you forgive me?"

To my amazement he said, "No. I won't forgive you. Someone in your position shouldn't have said that."

I went home frustrated and confused. Soon I was off on another of my guilt trips, asking myself, "How could you have said that? How can anyone in Christian work hurt a brother like that? How can God use you now?" My self-chastisement almost sounded like a new hymn about the misery of personal guilt. "Oh, Woe Is Me."

Do you see what I was doing? I was making forgiveness from a brother the prerequisite for being able to forgive myself. I was letting someone else's response control my life and relationship with God.

Then the Holy Spirit started working on me. "Just a minute, Josh. You're not handling this right. You can make one of two responses: You can wallow around in guilt, focus on your failings — or you can realize that Jesus died for this situation, confess it to God and the one you hurt [which I had done], and get on with your life, having learned something."

After wrestling awhile with the alternatives, I confessed the whole thing to God one more time, and then I added, "And Father, I forgive me too." I determined to do all I could from then on to heal the relationship with my wounded brother, but not to allow his response to impair my assurance of God's forgiveness for me.

As time went on I repeatedly went out of my way to express love to the person I had hurt. One day about a year later I said to my wife, "You know, I think the relationship is healed. The hurt seems to be gone, and from all appearances I think he has forgiven me. In fact, the relationship seems better than ever before."

One of the things that hurts God the most is for someone to reject or "cheapen" His grace. God's grace comes out of His loving heart: "For God so loved the world that He gave His only Son." Although we don't deserve it, because of the Father's love Jesus Christ came down to earth and died on the cross for us. When we refuse to forgive ourselves, we are actually throwing God's loving grace right back in His face.

No matter who you are, if God's grace can't cover that sin in your life, it can't cover any sin. Confession is agreeing with God not only about the wrong done, but also about what He has done in forgiving. I suspect that to reject forgiveness is more grieving to God than the original act; it is a denial of God's grace for which He paid so dearly.

Forgive yourself.

5. Don't Let Satan Deceive You

Satan will try to make you feel condemned. But if you know Jesus Christ personally as Savior and Lord, you can never be condemned. Romans 8:1 says, "There is therefore now no condemnation for those who are in Christ Jesus" (NASB).

Be sure, however, to discern the difference between condemnation and conviction. When sin enters your life, the Holy Spirit doesn't work to condemn you, but He does work to convict you. When you respond to God's conviction in your life through the Holy Spirit, you are drawn to Christ and the result is joy. Condemnation, on the other hand, pulls you away from Christ and leads to despair. Discern the difference between condemnation and conviction.

So, if you've "blown it" — even in terms of sexual sin — this is what you need to do to experience forgiveness and cleansing: Admit your sin to God; repent, which means change; acknowledge God's forgiveness; forgive yourself; and don't let Satan prevent you from experiencing the full benefits of God's forgiveness.

Can Virginity Be Restored?

No one can regain his or her physical virginity. That's lost forever. But I really believe that one's spiritual and emotional virginity can be regained.

"Don't let the world around you squeeze you into its own mould, but let God re-make you so that your . . . mind is changed" (Romans 8:2, Phillips). The negative experiences of our lives have squeezed us into their mold. The only way to be cleansed to the point of emotional virginity is to let God re-mold our mind from within. To do that, God has provided three resources:

● His truth — to understand who He is and who we are.

- His Holy Spirit — to illuminate His truth and to bring it to fruition in our lives.
- His People — to express His love and forgiveness in relationships.

Remember Tracy. She learned God's truth (who He is and who she is) in relationship with His people (at The Julian Center). When the Holy Spirit illuminated God's truth for her, Tracy experienced restoration of her emotional and spiritual virginity. This has given Tracy a fresh start.

BIBLIOGRAPHY

1. Levin, Steve. "Survey shows mostly upbeat views of life." *Dallas Morning News,* September 7, 1986, pp. A1, A6, A7.

2. Strommen, Merton P., and Strommen, A. Irene. "How To Talk and Listen to Your Kids." *Ladies Home Journal,* March 1985, pp. 31, 33.

3. Jameson, Michael. "Update on News." *CWNC Newsletter,* January 1986, p. 11.

4. "Issues and Insights." *The Evangelist,* December 1940, p. 40.

5. Jacob, Bonnie. "Teens Need to Bond With Buddies." *USA Today,* January 8, 1986, p. D5

6. "HTLV-III/LAV Antibody and Immune Status of Household Contacts and Sexual Partners of Persons with Hemophilia." *Journal of the Medical Association,* January 10, 1986, p. 67.

7. Bright, Dr. William R. "Love: The Major Emphasis, or Dialogue Between a Single Staff Member and God's Word." A message to the staff of Campus Crusade for Christ.

8. Langway, Lynn, with Gelman, Eric. "The Joy of Not Having Sex." *Newsweek,* September 15, 1980, p. 67.

9. "Newline — The Graduate School Divorce Itch." *Psychology Today,* October 1980, p. 20.

10. "A Time to Embrace." Author unknown.

11. Leo, John. "The New Scarlet Letter." *Time,* August 2, 1982, pp. 62-66.

12. Kesler, Jay, gen. ed., with Beers, Ronald A. *Parents and Teenagers.* Wheaton, IL: Victor Books, 1984.

13. St. Clair, Barry. "The Power of Peer Pressure." *Parents and Teenagers.* Jay Kesler, gen. ed., with Ronald A. Beers. Wheaton, IL: Victor Books, 1984, pp. 628-32.

14. Meer, Jeff. "Teens: A Sexual Sampler." *Psychology Today,* August 1985, p. 78.

15. Eicher, Diane. "Self-Esteem Puts Sex in Perspective." *Denver Post,* June 25, 1985, Section C.

16. Gerler, Edwin R., Jr. "Skills for Adolescence: A New Program for Young Teenagers." *Phi Delta Kappan,* February 1986, pp. 436-39.

17. Linthicum, Leslie. "Lifestyle Education: Key to Preventing Teen Pregnancy?" *Houston Post,* October 27, 1985, p. G18.

18. Brozan, Nadine. "New Look at Fears of Children." *New York Times,* May 2, 1983, p. B5.

19. Interview with Dick Day. October 22, 1981.

20. Seligmann, Jean. "A Nasty New Epidemic." *Newsweek,* February 4, 1985, pp. 72-73.

21. Sheehy, Gail. "Introducing the Postponing Generation . . . The Truth About Today's Young Men." *Esquire,* October 1979, pp. 25-31.

22. Gelman, David, "The Games Teenagers Play." *Newsweek,* September 1, 1980, pp. 48-53.

23. Zorn, Eric. "Is Virginity Finding an Unwanted Ally?" *Denver Post,* 1981, pp. 27-28.

24. Kotulak, Ronald. "A Healthy Sex Life Is, Well, Good, and Healthy." *Chicago Tribune,* September 13, 1981, Section I, p. 18.

25. Kotulak, Ronald. "Sex: The Continuing Revolution." *Chicago Tribune,* September 13, 1981, pp. 1, 18.

26. Martin, Yvonne M. "Lack of Parental Closeness Seen as Teen Sex Cause." *Orange County Register,* May 6, 7, 1981, pp. 1, 2.

27. Johnson, Ellis B. *Youth Views Sexuality.* Nashville, TN: Graded Press Methodist Publishing House Readingbook, 1968.

28. Smedes, Lewis B. *Sex for Christians — The Limits and Liberties of Sexual Living.* Grand Rapids, MI: William B. Eerdmans Publishing Company, 1976.

29. Hefley, James C. *Sex, Sense and Nonsense.* Elgin, IL: David C. Cook Publishing Company, 1971, p. 7.

30. Diegmueller, Karen. "Breaking the Ties that Bind." *Insight,* October 13, 1986, p. 8.

31. Lunceford, Cynthia. "Child Welfare Interest Area — Project Proposal." Prepared for Junior League of Baton Rouge, 1986/87, 2219 Myrtledale, Baton Rouge, LA 70808.

32. "Teen Pregnancy in the U.S. — A Fact Sheet." U.S. House of Representatives, 1986.

33. Lord, Lewis J. "Sex, With Care." *U.S. News and World Report,* June 2, 1986, pp. 53-57.

34. Brothers, Dr. Joyce. "Should Couples Live Together First?" *Parade,* October 20, 1985, pp. 4-7.

35. Wallis, Claudia. "Children Having Children." *Time,* December 9, 1985, p. 78.

36. "Session One: Morality." *Christian Life-Style for Youth.* Christian Life Commission of the Southern Baptist Convention, Nashville, TN, 1984, pp. 6-8.

37. Smith, Susan. "Teenagers and Sex: Attitudes Are Surprising." *Dallas Times Herald,* January 27, 1980, p. F1.

38. Fury, Kathleen. "Sex and the American Teenager." *Ladies Home Journal,* March 1986, pp. 58-60, 155-60.

39. Seligmann, Jean. "Memory." *Newsweek,* September 29, 1986, pp. 49-50.

40. "The Hass Report: Are Teens Sexually Experienced? No." *People,* May 5, 1980, pp. 107-10.

41. "The Problems of Sexual Freedom: An interview with Theodore I. Rubin, M.D." *Harpers Bazaar,* March 1977, pp. 94-95.

42. Mark, Alexandra, and Mark, Vernon H. *The Pied Pipers of Sex.* Plainfield, NJ: Haven Books, a division of Logos International, 1981.

43. Fletcher, Sheila. "Experts Seek Answers About Teen Pregnancy." *Oklahoman,* February 2, 1984.

44. Barber, Sandra. "Don't Miss Opportunity to Teach Kids About Sex." *Lifestyle,* June 15, 1984.

45. Coles, Robert, and Stokes, Geoffrey. *Sex and the American Teenager.* New York: Harper Colophon Books, Harper and Row Publishers, 1985.

46. Bibby, Reginald W., and Posterski, Donald C. *The Emerging Generation — An Inside Look at Canada's Teenagers.* Toronto: Irwin Publishing, 1985.

47. Lasswell, Marcia, and Lobsenz, Norman. "Why Some Marriages Can Survive an Affair and Others Can't." *McCall's,* November 1977, pp. 50-54.

48. Goldsmith, Marsha F. "Sexually Transmitted Diseases May Reverse the 'Revolution.' " *Medical News and Perspectives,* 255 (April 4, 1986):13:1665-72.

49. Stanton, Greta W. "Parental Divorce and Remarriage Seen as Leading Cause of Problems for Today's Teens." *Children and Teens Today,* 6 (July 1986):11:1-2.

50. Aranza, Jacob. *A Reasonable Reason to Wait.* Shreveport, LA: Huntington House, 1984.

51. "Most Teens' Outlook Is Positive, Survey Finds — The Teen Survey." *Dallas Morning News,* September 8, 1986, p. C7.

52. Wicker, Christine. "Parents, Peers, Relationship." *Dallas Morning News,* September 8, 1986, p. C1.

53. Pryzant, Connie. "Drugs and Alcohol." *Dallas Morning News,* September 10, 1986, pp. C1, C5.

54. Levin, Steve. "Pressures, Values, Self-Worth." *Dallas Morning News,* September 10, 1986, pp. C1, C5.

55. Lasswell, Marcia and Lobsenz, Norman. "The Varieties of Intimacy." *McCall's,* June 1976, pp. 50-55.

56. Newcomb, Paul R. "Cohabitation in America: An Assessment of Consequences." *Journal of Marriage and Family,* August 1979, pp. 597-603.

57. Russell, Diann. "Startling New Study Shows One in Six Women Incestuously Abused before Age 18." *Children and Teens Today,* 6 (July 1986):11:1-2.

58. McKinney, Mark. "Feedback: Minister Responds to CERTS Guidelines." *Children and Teens Today,* 6 (July 1986):11:6-7.

59. Sproul, R. C. "How Far Is Too Far?" Notes from conference talk.

60. Wharton, Ann. "Children Having Children." *Fundamentalist Journal,* October 1986, pp. 22-24.

61. Popenoe, Paul. "Do Your Children Know You Love Them?" *Parents and Better Homemaking,* 40 (December 1965):43-45.

62. Alcorn, Randy C. *Christians in the Wake of the Sexual Revolution.* Portland, OR: Multnomah Press, 1985.

63. Toth, Ronald S. "Teen Pregnancy." *The Plain Truth,* September 1986.

64. Fritze, David. "Polling the Class of '86 . . . They Mix Great Expectations, Quiet Fears." *Dallas Times Herald,* June 1, 1986, p. A1.

65. *New Bible Dictionary.*

66. Miles, Joan. *Sex and Sexuality: A Christian Understanding/Student's Book.* Nashville, TN: Graded Press, United Methodist Publishing House, 1982.

67. Gaylin, Jody. "What Girls Really Look for in Boys." *Seventeen,* March 1978, pp. 107-13.

68. Rothenstein, Richard. "A Boy's Dating Secrets." *Seventeen,* August 1978, pp. 124-25.

69. Tomczak, Larry. "How to Win Over Sexual Sin and Live Victoriously." *People of Destiny,* March/April 1986, pp. 5-7.

70. Watkins, James. *The World's Worst Date.* Marion, IN: Creative Communications, 1985.

71. Peterson, Noram. "Why the Heat of Passion Cools Off." *USA Today,* April 18, 1985, p. D4.

72. "Twentieth Century Sex." *Buzz,* October 1985, pp. 30-35.

73. Smith, Gill. "Why Do My Relationships Last?" *Buzz,* December 1985, pp. 41-42.

74. Cummings, Tony. "Sex Needs a Driver." *Buzz,* November 1985, pp. 4-42.

75. Banning, Margaret Culkin. "The Case for Chastity." A position paper, n.d.

76. White, Joe. "Answers to Your Most Urgent Questions — What About Sexual Purity?" *Prime Time,* 1:36-37.

77. Gordon, Sol, and Everly, Kathleen. "Increasing Self-esteem in Vulnerable Students . . . A Tool for Reducing Pregnancy Among Teenagers." Reprinted from *Impact '85,* 2:Article 41:9-17. Publication of Institute for Family Research and Education, 760 Ostrom Avenue, Syracuse, NY 13210-2999.

78. Troncale, Dr. Joseph. "Venereal Disease, Herpes, AIDS, Will it Ever Stop?" *New Wine,* March 1986, pp. 25-27.

79. "Sixty Minutes." Transcript, 28:30, CBS-TV Network, April 6, 1986.

80. Bronfenbrenner, Urie. "Alienation and the Four Worlds of Childhood." *Phi Delta Kappan,* February 1986, pp. 430-436.

81. Mahoney, C. J. "God Is *For* Sex." *People of Destiny,* March/April 1986, p. 8.

82. Houston, John P. *Fundamentals of Learning.* New York: Academic Press, 1976.

83. Huggins, Kevin. Associate Pastor for Youth, The Chapel, Akron, Ohio.

84. Bauman, Clayton. "Masturbation." *Parents and Teenagers.* Jay Kesler, gen.ed., with Ronald A. Beers. Wheaton, IL: Victor Books, 1984, p. 641.

85. Grady, Emory. *Postponing Sexual Involvement.* Teen Service Program, Atlanta, 1985.

86. Carlinskym, Dan. "Lines That Boys Use on Girls — and the Comebacks That Girls Should Use." *Seventeen,* February 1978, pp. 116-117, 159.

87. Tucker, Robert C., and Tucker, Leota M. "Lovers and Other Friends." *Essence,* October 1980, pp. 88-89, 118.

88. Marks, Judi. "Teen Report on . . . Teens and Sexuality." *Teen,* November 1980, pp. 28, 33.

89. Van Buren, Abigail. "What Every Teenager Ought to Know." Phillips — Van Buren, Inc., 1979.

90. Brenna, Susan. "U.S. Surveys Sexual Habits of Single Women." *Dallas Times Herald,* June 1, 1986, pp. A1, A16.

91. Van Buren, Abigail. "Dear Abby." *Dallas Times Herald,* June 1, 1986.

92. Phillips, Michael E. "Family Devotions in the Space Age." *Leadership,* Winter 1986, pp. 72-74.

93. "Keys to a Family-Friendly Church." An interview with James Dobson. *Leadership,* Winter 1986, pp. 12-21.

94. Procaccini, Joseph. "Parent Burnout: Latest Sign of Today's Stresses." *U.S. News and World Report,* March 7, 1983, pp. 76-77.

95. Helgesen, Sally. "Your Right to Say No." *Seventeen,* August 1981, pp. 284-285, 337.

96. Word Action Series, Senior High Leader's Guide, Sunday School Youth Curriculum. Kansas City, MO: Nazarene Publishing House, 1986.

97. "Sex." *Christian Life-Style for Youth.* Christian Life Commission of Southern Baptist Convention, Nashville, TN, 1984.

98. "Summary of Findings: Young Adolescents and Their Parents." Search Institute, Minneapolis, MN, February 1984.

99. Williams, Dorothy L. *There Is A Season . . . Studies in Human Sexuality for Youth of Christian Churches and Their Parents.* Dubuque, IA: William C. Brown Publishers, Religious Education Division, 1985.

100. *Live Planning Education: A Youth Development Program.* By the Center for Population Options, Washington, D.C., 1985.

101. "Young Love: How to Talk to Your Kids About You-Know-What." Minnesota Institute of Public Health, Anoka, MN, n.d.

102. Jenkins, Carri P. "Making Moral Choices." *BYU Today,* April 1985, pp. 38-39, 42, 44.

103. *Teenage Pregnancy: The Problem That Hasn't Gone Away.* New York: Guttmacher Institute, 1981.

104. Bell, Ruth, et. al. *Changing Bodies, Changing Lives: A Book for Teens on Sex and Relationships.* New York: Random House, 1980.

105. Center for Population Options. *Facts,* September 1985.

106. Meer, Jeff. "A Sound Memory." *Psychology Today,* November 1986, p. 76.

107. Strommen, Merton P., and Strommen, A. Irene. *Five Cries of Parents.* San Francisco: Harper & Row, 1985.

108. Nonkin, Leslie Jane. *I Wish My Parents Understood.* New York: Penguin Books, 1982.

109. Rinehart, Stacy, and Rinehart, Paula. *Choices.* Colorado Springs: Navpress, 1982.

110. Harris, Myron, and Norman, Jane. *The Private Life of the American Teenager.* New York: Rawson, Wade Publishers, Inc., 1981.

111. Remsburg, Charles, and Remsburg, Bonnie. "The Case Against Living Together." A Question and Answer Interview with Dr. Clatworthy. *Seventeen,* November 1977, pp. 132-33, 162-63.

112. Curry, Jack. "Free love gives way to responsibility." *USA Today,* April 23, 1987, pp. D1, D2.

113. Collins, Robert J., M.D. "A Physician's View of College Sex." *Journal of the American Medical Association,* April 28, 1975, p. 392.

114. Strommen, Merton P. *Five Cries of Youth.* New York: Harper & Row Publishers, 1979.

115. Bustanoby, Andre. *Just Talk To Me.* Grand Rapids, MI: Zondervan Publishing House, 1981.

116. Gallup, George, Jr. *Religion in America.* The Gallup Report No. 222, March 1984.

117. Kirby, Scott. *Dating.* Grand Rapids, MI: Baker Book House, 1979.

118. Powell, Stewart. "What Entertainers Are Doing to Our Kids." *U.S. News and World Report,* October 28, 1985, pp. 46-49.

119. Kotulak, Ronald. "Teens, Sex Can Be Unhealthy Mix." *Orlando Sentinel,* January 31, 1987, p. E4.

120. Stone, Michael. "Trying to Raise Children In the City." *New York,* February 2, 1987, pp. 26-33.

121. Safran, Claire. "Troubles That Pull Couples Apart." *Redbook,* 1979, p. 83.

122. Schultz, Terri. "Does Marriage Give Today's Women What They Really Want?" *Ladies Home Journal,* June 1980, pp. 90, 150.

123. *Arkansas Democrat.* January 2, 1986, p. H1.

124. Gelman, David. "AIDS." *Newsweek,* August 12, 1985, pp. 20-29.

125. Zillman, Dolf. "Effects of Prolonged Consumption of Pornography." A paper prepared for the Surgeon General's Workshop on Pornography and Public Health. Arlington, VA, June 1986.

126. Wallis, Claudia. "AIDS: A Growing Threat." *Time,* August 12, 1985, pp. 40-47.

127. Findlay, Steven. "Infections put moms-to-be at high risk." *USA Today,* October 10, 1986, p. D1.

128. Zillman, Dolf, and Bryant, Jennings. "Effects of Pornography Consumption on Family Values." 1986, p. 7.

129. *USA Today,* June 23, 1986, p. D5.

130. *Journal of the American Medical Association.* April 4, 1986, pp. 1672-1673.

131. *USA Today,* October 24, 1986, p. D1.

132. McMillen, S. I. *None of These Diseases.* Old Tappan, NJ: Fleming H. Revell Company, 1984.

133. Lauer, Jeannete, and Lauer, Robert. "Marriages Made to Last." *Psychology Today,* June 1985.

134. Baldwin, Wendy. *Adolescent Pregnancy and Childbearing — Rates, Trends, and Research Findings from the CPR-NICHD.* Bethesda, MD: Demographic and Behavioral Science Branch, NICHD, 1985.

135. Day, Dick. *Where Youth Are.* San Marcos High School, Jim Sanderson, *Los Angeles Times.*

136. Mark, Allandra, and Mark, Vernon H. *Medical World News,* April 8, 1985, p. 156.

137. Hass, Aaron. *Teenage Sexuality — A Survey of Teenage Sexual Behavior.* New York: Macmillan Publishing Company, 1981.

138. Psalm 139:14.

139. Genesis 1:27.

140. Vobejda, Barbara. "Koop and Bennett Issue Joint Advice on AIDS." *Washington Post,* January 31, 1987, p. A3.

141. Mosbacker, Barrett. "Teen Pregnancy and School-Based Health Clinics." *Vision,* October/November 1986, pp. 3-10.

142. Fox, Greer L. "The Family's Role in Adolescent Sexual Behavior." *Teenage Pregnancy in a Family Context.* Theodora Ooms, ed. Philadelphia: Temple University Press, 1981.

143. From an Associated Press release, February 25, 1984.

144. Kasun, Jacqueline R. "The Economics of Sex Education." A position paper, Department of Economics, Humboldt State University, CA, 1986.

145. Falwell, Jerry. "Keep contraceptives away from teenagers." *USA Today,* May 20, 1985, p. 8.

146. Ellis, Tottie. "Most 'advice' on sex promotes promiscuity." *USA Today,* March 20, 1985, p. A8.

147. Kasun, Jacqueline R. "Turning Your Children Into Sex Experts." A position paper, Department of Economics, Humboldt State University, CA, October 1979.

148. Maddock, James W. "Sex in Adolescence: Its Meaning and Its Future." Reprinted from the pamphlet, *Adolescence,* and distributed by Planned Parenthood.

149. Kosterlitz, Julie. "Split Over Pregnancy." *National Journal,* June 21, 1986, p. 1538.

150. Report of the House Select Committee on Children, Youth and Families, "Teen Pregnancy: What Is Being Done? A State-by-State Look." December 1985.

151. Fossedal, Gregory A. "Dartmouth's 'safe sex kit' is far from morally neutral." *Orange County Register,* February 10, 1987, p. B7.

152. Chairman of the House Select Committee on Children, Youth and Families as quoted in *St. Paul Pioneer Press Dispatch,* February 10, 1986, p. 1.

153. Beyette, Beverly. "Teen Sex-Education Campaign Launched." *Los Angeles Times,* October 17, 1986. pp. V1, V22-23.

154. "A Teen-Pregnancy Epidemic." *Newsweek,* March 25, 1985, p. 90.

155. Kasun, Jacqueline R. "Teenage Pregnancy: What Comparisons Among States And Countries Show." A position paper, Department of Economics, Humboldt State University, CA, 1986.

156. Kasun, Jacqueline R. "Rates for American states computed from data on unmarried births from National Center of Vital Statistics and data on abortions from U.S. Centers for Disease Control; rates for foreign countries from Elise F. Jones, et. al." *Teenage Pregnancy in Developed Countries: Determinants and Policy Implications* (Family Planning Perspectives) 17 (March/April 1985):2:53-63.

157. Scott, David, ed. *Proceedings of the Symposium on Media Violence and Pornography.* Toronto: Media Action Group, February 1984, p. 105.

158. Thomas, Cal. "What Did Teen Sex Study Prove?" *Inside Washington,* March 30, 1985, p. 4.

159. *Family Planning Perspectives.* 12 (September/October):5:229.

160. "Muskegon Heights School-Based Clinic — A Survey." Muskegon Heights Area Planned Parenthood, September 1984 — June 1985, p. 2.

161. Kirby, J. Report issued by the Support Center for School-Based Clinics, pp. 8-9.

162. Weatherly, Richard, et al. "Comprehensive Programs for Pregnant Teenagers and Teenage Parents: How Successful Have They Been?" *Family Planning Perspectives,* 18 (March/April 1986):2:77.

163. Dawson, Deborah Anne. "The Effects of Sex Education on Adolescent Behavior." Quoted in *Family Planning Perspectives,* July/August, 1986, pp. 162-170.

164. McManus, Michael J., ed. *Final Report of the Attorney General's Commission on Pornography.* Rutledge Hill Press, 1986, p. 264.

165. United Families of America, Press Release, March 8, 1983. Based on data from the Utah Department of Health.

166. Minnery, Tom, ed. *Pornography, A Human Tragedy.* Wheaton, IL: Tyndale House Publishers, 1986, p. 139.

167. "Fewer Girls Under 16 Have Abortions." *Daily Telegraph,* London, September 27, 1985.

168. Davis, Kingsley. "The American Family, Relation to Demographic Change." *Research Reports,* U.S. Commission on Population Growth and the American Future, Volume 1. *Demographic and Social Aspects of Population Growth.* Robert Parker, Jr. and Charles F. Westoff, eds. Washington D.C.: U.S. Government Printing Office, 1972, p. 253.

169. Howard, John A. "AIDS Grew in a Hothouse of Permissiveness." *Orange County Register,* February 10, 1987, p. B7.

170. These books are excellent resources: *I Wonder, I Wonder* (ages 5 to 8), *Wonderfully Made* (for preteens), *Life Can Be Sexual* (ages 15 and above), *Parents' Guide to Christian Conversation About Sex,* Concordia Sex Education Series, Concordia; Clyde M. Narramore, *How To Tell Your Children About Sex,* Zondervan; James Dobson, *Preparing for Adolescence;* Ken Taylor, *Twelve,* Tyndale House Publishers.

171. Fischer, Irene, and Barrett, Katherine. "The Babies Who Never Came Home." pp. 58-61.

172. Stapen, Candyce. "Speaking frankly isn't being permissive." *USA Today,* September 3, 1986, p. D6.

173. Cryderman, Lyn. "The Flipside of Sex Education." *Light and Life,* May 1986, p. 42.

174. Strommen, Merton P., and Brekke, Milo L., et al. *A Study of Generations.* Minneapolis: Augsburg Publishing, 1972.

175. Bennett, William J., United States Secretary of Education. "Sex and the Education of Our Children." Address to the National School Board of Education, January 22, 1987.

176. "Men, Women, Sex and AIDS." The NBC Television Network, New York, January 13, 1987, 10:00 P.M.

177. "When a Boyfriend Becomes No Friend." *Insight,* April 20, 1987, p. 58.

178. Zelnik, Melvin, and Kantner, John F. "Sexual Activity, Contraceptive Use, and Pregnancy Among Metro-Area Teens." *Family Planning*

Perspectives, 12 (September/October 1980):5.

179. Findlay, Steven, Elias, Marilyn, and Woller, Barbara. "Experimental Drug Could Be the Next Pill." *USA Today,* January 22, 1987, p. D5.

180. 1 Thessalonians 4:3-5, NASB.

181. Romans 12:2, Phillips.

182. Philippians 4:8.

183. 1 Timothy 1:5, NASB.

184. See 1 Thessalonians 4:3-5; Ephesians 5:3.

185. *Prime Time.* Volume 3. Published by Joe White, Branson, MO, 1986.

186. Philippians 2:5.

187. Proverbs 7:1-5.

188. Bronfenbrenner, Urie. *Two Worlds of Childhood: U.S. and U.S.S.R.* New York: Pocket Books, 1970.

189. "Premarital Experience No Help in Sexual Adjustment After Marriage." *Family Life,* May 1972, pp. 1-2.

190. Simon, Roger. "Muffled Scream of Ruined Dream." *Chicago Tribune,* February 9, 1986, p. 5.

191. Check, James. "The Effect of Violent and Nonviolent Pornography." Ottawa: Department of Justice for Canada, Department of Supply and Services contract 05SV.19200-3-0899, June 1984, p. 1.

192. Goldfarb, J. L. "An Attempt to Detect 'Pregnancy Susceptibility' in Indigent Adolescent Girls." *Journal of Youth and Adolescence.* 6 (1977):127-44.

193. Roberts, E. S., Kline, D., and Gagon, J. *Family Life and Sexual Learning of Children* Volume 1. Cambridge, MA: Population Education, Inc., 1981.

194. Block, D. "Sex Education Practices of Mothers." *Journal of Sex Education and Therapy.* 4 (1978):1:7-12.

195. *Washington Post.* February 3, 1982.

196. Hamilton, Eleanor. *Your Engagement.* Plano, TX: Workman Publishing Co., Inc., 1970.

197. Blamires, Harry. *The Christian Mind.* New York: Seaburg Press, 1963.

198. Benant, Mary. "The Lonely Life of a Teenage Girl." *USA Today,* November 5, 1986, p. D1.

199. Crabb, Lawrence J. *The Marriage Builder.* Grand Rapids, MI: Zondervan Publishing House, 1982.

200. Greene, Bob. "AIDS — New American Tragedy." *Dallas Morning News,* July 17, 1985.

201. Echenique, Jeannie. "Early Dating May Lead to Early Sex." *USA Today,* November 12, 1986, p. D1.

202. "Crisis in the Schools." *U.S. News and World Report,* September 1, 1975, pp. 42-43.

203. Bell, Robert R. *Premarital Sex in a Changing Society.* Englewood Cliffs, NJ: Prentice-Hall, Inc., 1966.

204. Schaeffer, Frances A. "The Chief End of Man." *Hymns for the Family of God.* Nashville, TN: Paragon Associates, Inc., 1976, #364.

205. Gordon, Sol. *The Sexual Adolescent: Communicating With Teenagers About Sex.* North Scituate, MA: Druxbury Press, 1979.

206. "27.5 % of Coeds . . ." *Arizona Republic,* April 23, 1987, p. A6.

207. Leonard, George. *The End of Sex.* Los Angeles, CA: J. P. Tarcher, 1983.

208. Koop, Everett J. Personal interview. February 2, 1987.

209. 1 Timothy 6:10.

210. Romans 14:14,22,23.

211. 2 Timothy 2:22, NASB.

212. McDowell, Josh. *Givers, Takers and Other Kinds of Lovers.* Wheaton, IL: Tyndale, 1981.

213. McDowell, Josh. *The Secret of Loving.* San Bernardino, CA: Here's Life Publishers, 1985.

214. *Doctor,* May 29, 1986, pp. 6-10.

215. Dobson, James. *Emotions — Can You Trust Them?* Ventura, CA: Regal Books, 1980.

216. Unwin, J., and Unwin, D. *Sex and Culture.* London: Oxford University Press, 1934.

217. Bendroth, Norman B. Quoted in "Abortion and the Third Way of the Kingdom." *The High Cost of Indifference.* Edited by Richard Cizik. Ventura, CA: Regal Books, 1984.

218. "Abortion — The Ultimate Form of Child Abuse." *Christian School Comment.* 16:8, n.d.

219. Calderone, Mary, and Johnson, Eric W. *The Family Book About Sexuality.* New York: Harper & Row, 1979.

220. Blood, Robert O., Jr. *Marriage.* New York: Free Press, 1969.

221. Fromm, Erich. *The Sane Society.* Greenwich, CT: Fawcett Publications, Inc., 1955.

222. 1 Thessalonians 4:3-5; Ephesians 5:3.

223. *Dallas Times-Herald.* March 13, 1980, p. B1.

224. Dryfoos, Joy, and Lincoln, Richard. "A New Report Finds Disturbing Increase in Teenage Pregnancies — and Tragic Problems Born With Them." *People,* May 4, 1981, pp. 56-60.

225. *Involving Parents in Sexuality Education Programs: The Role of Agencies Serving Youth.* n.pub., 1984, p. 649.

226. Spanier, G. B. "Sources of Sex Information and Parental Sexual Behavior." *Journal of Sex Research.* 13 (1977):2:73-88.

227. Wright, Norman. "Finding Time to Listen." *Parents and Teenagers.* Jay Kesler, gen. ed., with Ronald Beers, Wheaton, IL: Victor Books, 1984.

228. Wright, H. Norman. *More Communication Keys for Your Marriage.* Ventura, CA: Regal Books, 1983.

229. Augsburger, David. *Caring Enough to Hear and Be Heard.* Ventura, CA: Regal Books, 1982.

230. Narramore, Bruce. *Help I'm A Parent.* Grand Rapids, MI: Zondervan Publishing House, 1972.

231. "Teen-age Sex: Letting the Pendulum Swing." *Time,* August 21, 1972, pp. 34-40.

232. Peterson, Karen S. "Kids may be troubled by mom's live-in lover." *USA Today,* October 24, 1986, p. D1.

233. Duvall, Evelyn. "Mature Enough to Marry." *The Marriage Affair.* Wheaton, IL: Tyndale House Publishers, 1971.

234. Ard, Ben A., Jr., and Ard, Constance C. *Handbook of Marriage Counseling.* Palo Alto, CA: Science and Behavior Books, Inc. 1976.

235. Strauss, Dr. Richard. *Marriage Is for Love.* Wheaton, IL: Tyndale House Publishers, 1979.

236. Wright, H. Norman, and Inmon, Marvin. *A Guidebook To Dating, Waiting, and Choosing a Mate.* Eugene, OR: Harvest House Publishers, 1978.

237. Duvall, Evelyn, and Hill, Reuben. *Before You Marry.* New York: Association Press, 1981.

238. Van Biema, David. "What's Gone Wrong With Teen Sex?" *People,* April 13, 1987, pp. 110-121.

239. Trobisch, Walter. *I Loved A Girl.* New York: Harper & Row, 1963.

239. Taylor, Robert B. "Behind The Surge In Broken Marriages." *U.S.News & World Report,* January 22, 1979, p. 53.

240. Swindoll, Charles R. *Commitment: The Key To Marriage.* Portland, OR: Multnomah Press, 1981, p. 18.

241. Gelman, David. "How Marriage Can Last." *Newsweek,* July 13, 1981, pp. 73-76.

242. Klein, Chuck. (Director of Student Venture High School Ministry.) *So You Want Solutions.* Wheaton, IL: Tyndale House Publishers, 1979. And *So You Want To Get Into the Race.* Wheaton, IL: Tyndale House Publishers, 1980.

243. Barlow, Daniel L. "Help Your Child Develop Self-Esteem." *Fundamentalist Journal,* June 1983, pp. 29-31.

244. Mast, Coleen Kelly. *Sex Respect: An Option of True Sexual Freedom.* A Public Health workbook for students. Bradley, IL: Respect, Inc., 1986.

245. Augsberger, David. *Caring Enough To Confront.* Scottsdale, PA: Herald Press, 1981.

246. "How to say 'No.' " A pamphlet by Womanity, 2141 Youngs Valley Road, Walnut Creek, CA 94596.

247. Rodriguez, Theresa. "A Teen Mother's Message . . ." *San Diego Union,* February 8, 1987, p. C3.

248. Davis, Frances, M.D. "Troubled by Planned Parenthood Stand." *Los Angeles Times,* November 16, 1986, p. IV20.

249. "Problems born of teen-age sex." *Orlando Sentinel,* January 31, 1987, p. E4.

250. Arrington, Carl. "Animal Magnetism." *People,* December 19, 1983, p. 113.

251. Stewart, Sally Ann. "Divorce Clouds Outlook For Teens." *USA Today,* October 14, 1984, p. D1.

252. Painter, Kim. "What Women Want Most: Intimacy." *USA Today,* October 14, 1986, p. D1.

253. "The Teen Environment." Based on *A Study of Growth Strategies for Junior Achievement.* The Robert Johnston Company, Inc., 1980, p. 4.

254. Liebert, Sprafkin, and Davidson. "The Early Window: Effects of Television on Children and Youth." 1982, p. 171.

255. Sanderson, Jim. "The Importance of Thanking Dad." *Los Angeles Times,* June 4, 1986, p. V3.

256. Towarnicky, Carol. "Positive images needed to combat teenage pregnancy." *Houston Chronicle,* January 12, 1986, pp. 7, 17, 18.

257. Simon, Roger. "Casual Sex on TV Part of the Problem." *Los Angeles Times,* January 4, 1987. p. 6-8.

258. "Teenagers Cresting New Values For the Future." Based on a Gallup/AP youth survey. *Emerging Trends.* Princeton Religious Research Center, October 1985.

259. Klucoff, Carol. "Teens: Speaking Their Minds." *Washington Post,* February 3, 1982, p. B5.

260. Slater, Wayne. "TV's Kathy Anderson survives life in Hollywood's Death Zone." *Phoenix Gazette,* August 20, 1983, p. 8.

261. "Teen Pregnancy: 16.6 Billion." *Chicago Tribune,* February 19, 1986, Section 1, p. 3.

262. Wallis, Claudia. "Stress: Can We Cope?" *Time,* June 6, 1983, pp. 48-54.

263. Rothchild, Barbara S. "Kick the Curse of Modern Romans." *USA Today,* February 6, 1986, p. D5.

264. "After the Sexual Revolution." Transcript of ABC-TV Special, Summer, 1986.

265. Curry, Jack. "A Life Lost in Confusion and Crisis." *USA Today,* April 6, 1984, pp. D1-2.

266. Rivenburg, Roy. "Sexually Transmitted Diseases, the New Epidemic." *Focus on the Family,* September 1985, pp. 2-4.

267. Marin, Peter. "A Revolution's Broken Promises." *Psychology Today,* July 1983, pp. 50-57.

268. *Ad Age,* May 14, 1984, pp. 62-63.

269. Greenberg, Bradley S.; Abelman, Robert; and Neuendorf, Kimberly. "Sex on the Soap Operas: Afternoon Delight." *Journal of Communication,* Summer 1981.

270. "Self-defeating perfectionism." *USA Today,* April 10, 1985, p. D4.

271. 1 Corinthians 10:13, TLB.

272. 1 Thessalonians 4:4.

273. 1 Corinthians 6:19.

274. Galatians 5:23.

275. Ainship, Beth. "Making Decisions About Sex." *Highwire,* Summer 1983.

276. "Report to the President: White House Conference on Children." Washington, D.C.: U.S. Government Printing Office, 1971.

277. "House Panel urges child care incentives." *San Diego Union,* October 5, 1984, p. A15.

278. "62% of married couples are two-income families." *San Diego Union,* April 1, 1984, p. A1.

279. Macklin, Eleanor D., Ph.D. "Nonmarital Heterosexual Cohabitation." *Marriage & Family Review* 1 (March/April 1978):2:4.

280. Rubin, Z. "Dating Project Research Report." Unpublished manuscript. Harvard University Department of Psychology and Social Relations, April 1975. Noted by Eleanor D. Macklin, Ph.D. in "Nonmarital Heterosexual Cohabitation." *Marriage & Family Review* 1 (March/April 1978):2:4.

281. Brothers, Joyce. "When Unmarried Couples Live Together." *Readers Digest* 128 (April 1986):41.

282. Clatworthy, N. M. and Scheid, L. "A Comparison of Married Cohabitants with Non-premarital Cohabitants." Unpublished manuscript. Ohio State University, 1977. Noted by Eleanor D. Macklin, Ph.D. in "Nonmarital Heterosexual Cohabitation." *Marriage & Family Review* 1 (March/April 1978):2:8.

283. Demaris, Alfred, and Leslie, Gerald R. "Cohabitation With the Future Spouse: Its Influence Upon Marital Satisfaction and Communication." *Journal of Marriage and the Family,* February 1984, p. 83.

284. Pattison, E. Mansell, M.D. "Living Together: A Poor Substitute for Marriage." *Medical Aspects of Human Sexuality* 16 (November 1982):11:79.

285. Leerhsen, Charles, with Greenberg, Nikki Finke, Malone, Maggie, and Michael, Renee. "Aging Playboy." *Newsweek,* August 4, 1986, p. 51.

286. Renshaw, Domeena C. "Intimacy and Intercourse." *Medical Aspects of Human Sexuality* 18 (February 1984):2:73.

287. Lasswell, Marcia. "Marrying Too Early." *Medical Aspects of Human Sexuality* 17 (July 1983):7:24-25.

288. Elster, Arthur B., M.D. "Teenage Fathers." *Medical Aspects of Human Sexuality* 18 (November 1984):11:71.

289. Personal correspondence with Dr. John Raney, February 1987.

290. Weis, David L., Ph.D. "Reactions of College Women to Their First Coitus." *Medical Aspects of Human Sexuality* 17 (February 1983):2:60HH-60LL.

291. Landers, Ann. "The Name of the Game: It's Never Solved." *Phoenix Gazette,* October 24, 1985, p. E2.

292. "The New Tyranny of Sexual Liberation." *Life,* November 6, 1970, p. 4.

293. Begley, Sharon. "Nature's Baby Killers." *Newsweek,* September 6, 1982, pp. 78-79.

294. Morris, Desmond. *Man Watching: A Field Guide to Human Behavior.* Mexico: publisher unknown, 1977. (Also published in USA — New York: Abrams, 1979.)

295. Phillips, Debora. *Sexual Confidence.* Boston, MA: Houghton Mifflin, 1980.

296. Speckhard, Anne Catherine. "The Psycho-Social Aspects of Stress Following Abortion." A thesis submitted to the Faculty of the Graduate School of the University of Minnesota, May 1985.

297. Wright, Norman, and Johnson, Rex. *Communication: Key to Your Teens.* Eugene, OR: Harvest House, 1978.

298. Levin, Robert J. "The Redbook Report on Premarital and Extramarital Sex: The End of the Double Standard?" *Redbook,* October 1975, p. 40.

299. Duvall, Evelyn Millis, Ph.D. *Why Wait Till Marriage?* New York: Association Press, 1970.

300. Small, Dwight Harvey. *Design For Christian Marriage.* Old Tappan, NJ: Flemming H. Revell Company, 1972.

301. Blood, Robert O. *Marriage.* 2nd Edition. New York: Free Press, 1969. Quoted in "The Fraudulent New Morality." *Family Life,* October 1972, p. 2.

302. Lowen, Alexander, M.D. *Love and Orgasm.* New York: Macmillan Publishing Company, 1975, pp. 317-318.

303. "Reaching Out for Inner-Awareness — An Interview With Dr. Rollo May."(Author of *Love and Will.*) *Nutshell,* 1973-74 school year edition.

304. Byrd. Robert. "Rise of other sex viruses lost in the AIDS shuffle." *Chattanooga Times,* April 6, 1987, pp. A1, A8.

305. Koss, Mary. "The Scope of Rape Incidence and Prevalence of Sexual Aggression and Victimization in a National Sample of Higher Education Students." *Journal of Consulting and Clinical Psychology,* April 1987, pp. 162-170.

306. Painter, Virginia. "Kids' drug pressure: crack, wine coolers." *USA Today,* April 24-26, 1987, p. D1.

Josh McDowell

For more than 20 years Josh McDowell has equipped Christians with overwhelming evidence to defend their faith in Christ and the Bible. In that same apologetic tradition, Josh is now equipping parents, pastors and youth workers with "evidence that demands a verdict" against premarital sex.

Josh McDowell is a traveling representative for Campus Crusade for Christ and a graduate of Wheaton College and magna cum laude graduate of Talbot Theological Seminary. He is the author of several bestselling books including *Evidence That Demands a Verdict*, *His Image . . . My Image*, *The Secret of Loving* and *Teens Speak Out: "What I Wish My Parents Knew About My Sexuality."* Josh and his wife, Dottie, have four children.

Dick Day

A licensed Marriage, Family and Child Counselor, Dick Day is co-founder and director of The Julian Center, an in-resident center offering a 12-week program to help Christian laypeople and leaders clarify their personal and cultural world view. Teaching a biblical view of individual and family development, Dick lectures both internationally and at The Julian Center in Julian, California. He has appeared in several films with Josh McDowell including *The Sexual Puzzle*, *His Image . . . My Image*, and *Maximum Dating*.

Dick has two graduate degrees, one in theology from Talbot Theological Seminary and the other in psychology from Asuza Pacific University. He and his wife, Charlotte, have six children.

LET'S STAY -IN- TOUCH!

If you have grown personally as a result of this material, we should stay in touch. You will want to continue in your Christian growth, and to help your faith become even stronger, our team is constantly developing new materials.

We are now publishing a monthly newsletter called 5 Minutes with Josh which will

1) tell you about those new materials as they become available
2) answer your tough questions
3) give creative tips on being an effective parent
4) let you know our ministry needs
5) keep you up to date on my speaking schedule (so you can pray).

If you would like to receive this publication, simply fill out the coupon below and send it in. By special arrangement 5 Minutes with Josh will come to you regularly — no charge.

Let's keep in touch!

Josh

☐ **Yes!** I want to receive the free subscription to **5 Minutes with JOSH**

_____
NAME

_____
ADDRESS

_____
CITY, STATE/ZIP

SLC-2024

Mail To:
Josh McDowell
c/o 5 Minutes with Josh
Campus Crusade for Christ
Arrowhead Springs
San Bernardino, CA 92414

Josh McDowell and Dick Day have ministered together for more than twenty-five years. In 1979 they co-founded The Julian Center, a Christian learning center, designed to impart a personal Christian world view and a cultural Christian world view. Both men are resident teachers at The Center.

The Center's 12-week resident programs focus first on helping students personally to integrate the physical, social, psychological and spiritual aspects of their lives according to scriptural principles. The additional emphasis on understanding God's design for society as well as the philosophy currently shaping our society further equips students for a lifetime of ministry.

Participants have come from many countries and include businessmen, housewives, seminary and graduate students, Christian workers, missionaries, and young believers.

For additional information, contact:
The Julian Center
P.O. Box 400
Julian, CA 92036
    Telephone: (619) 765-1266